WORLD MISSION

WORLD MISSION

Theology, Strategy, and Current Issues

EDITED BY SCOTT N. CALLAHAM AND WILL BROOKS

LEXHAM PRESS

World Mission: Theology, Strategy, and Current Issues

Print ISBN 9781683593034
Digital ISBN 9781683593041

Lexham Editorial: Todd Hains, Claire Brubaker, Sarah Awa
Cover Design: Kristen Cork
Typesetting: Scribe

CONTENTS

Dedication vii

Abbreviations ix

An Invitation to World Mission xi

I: Theology and World Mission 1

   1. Old Testament Theology and World Mission. 3
      Scott N. Callaham

   2. New Testament Theology and World Mission 33
      Wendel Sun

   3. Biblical Theology and World Mission 67
      Wendel Sun

II: World Mission Strategy 103

   4. Discipleship as Integral Component
     of World Mission Strategy 105
      Stephen I. Wright

   5. Focus on "All Nations" as Integral Component of
     World Mission Strategy 131
      Jarvis J. Williams and Trey Moss

   6. Baptism as Integral Component of
     World Mission Strategy 149
      John Massey and Scott N. Callaham

7. Theological Education as Integral Component of World Mission Strategy 177
Sunny Tan and Will Brooks

III: Current Issues in World Mission 205

8. Language and World Mission 207
Scott N. Callaham

9. Grammatical-Historical Exegesis and World Mission 239
Will Brooks

10. Biblical Theology for Oral Cultures in World Mission 269
Jackson W.

11. Paul as Model for the Practice of World Mission 291
Will Brooks

Afterword 319
Bibliography 321
About the Authors 355
Subject Index 357
Scripture Index 367

DEDICATION

In chapters 11–12 of his letter, the author of Hebrews reminds us that we are surrounded by a "great cloud of witnesses." These mighty men and women of faith have finished their race and are now standing along the sidelines encouraging those of us who are still running. The author mentions many of these heroes by name in Hebrews 11, but throughout church history untold numbers of others have served faithfully, built up the local church, and passed into eternity with hardly anyone even knowing their names. Those of us presently serving in local churches and on the mission fields of the world should soberly reflect that we stand on the shoulders of these servants "of whom the world was not worthy" (Heb 11:38).

For many of the contributors to this book, two of those "unnamed" heroes are Bill and Marsha Lawson. The Lawsons spent more than thirty years on the mission field teaching and training church leaders. Through decades of service, Bill taught a seemingly countless number of students how to interpret the word of God. In fact, in his most popular work, *Ears to Hear*, he explains that the purpose of that book—and in some sense his entire ministry—is "providing some sound methodologies for biblical interpretation."[1] These methods seek to understand the meaning of the biblical author, apply that meaning to the contemporary context, and then communicate the Bible's contextualized message to others. Bill considers biblical interpretation so crucial to the task of the local church that he published several other volumes demonstrating his method of interpretation in both Old and New Testament Scripture.[2]

---

1. William H. Lawson, *Ears to Hear: A Guide for the Interpretation of the Bible* (Penang, Malaysia: Institute for Biblical Interpretation, 1994), 22.

2. See for example William H. Lawson, *The Lion Roars from Zion: A Guide for the Interpretation of the Book of Amos*, rev. ed. (Penang, Malaysia: Institute for Biblical Interpretation,

In their zeal to reach the world for Christ, missionaries and missiologists may unfortunately cast concern for sound biblical interpretation and theology aside. Likewise, without a healthy focus on application, some discussions in biblical studies can easily scale the ivory tower of practical irrelevance. Such is the outworking of the sinful human nature. Many seem to forget that billions of people now living have yet even to hear the name of Jesus. The Lawsons did not forget. We note well that another aspect of Bill Lawson's enduring legacy was his ability to bring together the twin disciplines of biblical studies and missiology. By teaching biblical studies on the mission field for so many years, Bill Lawson's dedicated service testified that the urgent task of world mission calls for biblically faithful theology, and in turn biblical theology leads directly to obeying the Great Commission.

Marsha, too, gave the majority of her time to teaching at the seminary level. She founded the biblical counseling program at Malaysia Baptist Theological Seminary. Not only did she teach counseling to a large number of students, but she also personally counseled them through marital problems, depression, church conflicts, family pressures, and many other weighty life issues. She loved the people God called her to serve, and years later her former students still speak about the compassion with which she taught from the word.

Those who worked alongside Bill and Marsha and know them well would add that it is their humility and selflessness that have left the deepest and most lasting impression on us. Through all his years of ministry, Bill was never concerned with making a name for himself or moving up to some supposedly more prestigious place of ministry. He simply labored year after year, teaching the word and building up the local church in a place of spiritual darkness. And in that region of the world, wherever you find a church leader who is faithfully preaching and teaching God's word, it is likely due to Bill's and Marsha's personal investment in him. It is for this reason that we dedicate this book to Bill and Marsha Lawson, in thankfulness for their legacy.

2003); Lawson, *Obedient unto Death: A Guide for the Interpretation of Paul's Epistle to the Philippians*, rev. ed. (Penang, Malaysia: Institute for Biblical Interpretation, 2003).

ABBREVIATIONS

BBR	*Bulletin for Biblical Research*
BDAG	Danker, Frederick W., Walter Bauer, William F. Arndt, and F. Wilbur Gingrich. *Greek-English Lexicon of the New Testament and Other Early Christian Literature.* 3rd ed. Chicago: University of Chicago Press, 2000.
BECNT	Baker Exegetical Commentary on the New Testament
CBR	*Currents in Biblical Research*
DCH	*Dictionary of Classical Hebrew.* Edited by David J. A. Clines. 9 vols. Sheffield: Sheffield Phoenix Press, 1993-2014.
EMQ	*Evangelical Missions Quarterly*
EMS	Evangelical Missiological Society Series
ESV	English Standard Version
HALOT	Ludwig Koehler, Walter Baumgartner, and Johann J. Stamm. *The Hebrew and Aramaic Lexicon of the Old Testament.* Translated and edited under the supervision of Mervyn E. J. Richardson. 5 vols. Leiden: Brill, 1994-2000.
HHE	*Hebrew Higher Education*
IBMR	*International Bulletin of Missionary Research*
JAM	*Journal of Asian Mission*
JBL	*Journal of Biblical Literature*
JETS	*Journal of the Evangelical Theological Society*
JSOT	*Journal for the Study of the Old Testament*
JSOTSup	Journal for the Study of the Old Testament Supplement Series
LXX	Septuagint

Missiology	*Missiology: An International Review*
MT	Masoretic Text
NAC	New American Commentary
NASB	New American Standard Bible
NIB	*The New Interpreter's Bible*
NICNT	New International Commentary on the New Testament
NICOT	New International Commentary on the Old Testament
NIDNTT	*New International Dictionary of New Testament Theology*. Edited by Colin Brown. 4 vols. Grand Rapids: Zondervan, 1975–1978.
NIDNTTE	*New International Dictionary of New Testament Theology and Exegesis*. Edited by Moisés Silva. 4 vols. Grand Rapids: Zondervan, 2014.
NIGTC	New International Greek Testament Commentary
NIV	New International Version
NRSV	New Revised Standard Version
NSBT	New Studies in Biblical Theology
NTS	*New Testament Studies*
Pillar	Pillar New Testament Commentary
SBJT	*Southern Baptist Journal of Theology*
TE	*Theological Education*
TESOL Quarterly	*Teachers of English to Speakers of Other Languages Quarterly*
TynBul	*Tyndale Bulletin*
WBC	Word Biblical Commentary
WTJ	*Westminster Theological Journal*
WUNT	Wissenschaftliche Untersuchen zum Neuen Testament
ZECNT	Zondervan Exegetical Commentary on the New Testament

AN INVITATION TO WORLD MISSION

Sanctify them in the truth; your word is truth.

John 17:17

Core convictions matter. What one *really* believes structures one's entire worldview and translates into action. In contrast, what one only *claims* to believe are those principles that often readily slough off in the face of arduous testing in the "real world." We editors and contributors to this book certainly bring our various national and ethnic backgrounds, diverse academic specialties, and distinct personalities to bear as we write on pressing issues in world mission today. Yet we share a core conviction on the authority and sufficiency of Scripture. We hold that what the Bible says about world mission matters, and moreover that it matters intensely.

More specifically, we assert that the significance of biblical teaching on world mission extends far beyond the limits we see implicitly advocated in much missiological literature. Thus contributors to this book are not content merely to describe the biblical "foundation" or "basis" for world mission. Instead, this book calls the church to return to a thoroughly biblical ethos for world mission, placing every aspect of the missional task under the authority—and thus the corrective critique—of biblical teaching.

This book issues its reforming call to the church in three stages. First we examine the biblical theology of world mission. Old and New Testament theology indeed establish a secure foundation for missional practice. However, the theology of both Testaments should stand in the foreground rather than recede to the background in all aspects of mission

work. Having anchored our discussion of world mission on biblical theology, next we focus specifically on the Great Commission in Matthew
28:18–20. The individual chapters of the second section of this book thus
address selected aspects of Jesus' command in sequence, demonstrating
that each is an integral and essential component of world mission strategy. Finally in the third section of this volume we treat current issues in
world mission practice, always from the perspective of the authority and
sufficiency of Scripture.

We ask that you, our reader, approach this study with a critical eye.
We urge you to follow the example of the Bereans in Acts 17:11, who regularly checked human-transmitted teaching against the word of God.
Thus if the claims we advance in this book exceed what the teaching
of Scripture can support, then of course biblical teaching must remain
preeminent. However, we have written this book precisely because we
believe that the contemporary practice of world mission has not adequately heeded the voice of the Holy Spirit through Scripture. Thus we
pray that all of us may hear his voice more clearly and in turn respond
wholeheartedly in faith.

Indeed, God withholds no good thing from those who walk uprightly
(Ps 84:11), and the wonders of his word lay open for his people (Ps 119:18).
Therefore in the following pages we warmly invite you to journey with us
into the theology, strategy, and practice of world mission, keeping Scripture constantly before us as our guide.

I

THEOLOGY AND WORLD MISSION

Theology doesn't just think. Theology walks. Theology weeps.
Theology bleeds.

Russell D. Moore,
"Theology Bleeds: Why Theological Vision Matters
for the Great Commission, and Vice Versa"

A familiar trope in contemporary evangelical Christianity posits two kinds of knowledge: the kind that resides in the "head," on one hand, and the kind found in the "heart," on the other. According to this line of thinking, one can dispassionately acknowledge the truth of certain facts but fail to allow those facts to ignite one's passions. Thus one conjures up an impersonal culprit to blame for lethargic lack of ardor toward Great Commission obedience: head knowledge.

This line of thinking is foreign to the Bible. Furthermore, splitting knowledge into categories in order to assuage guilty feelings is obviously rather self-serving and therefore inherently questionable. Even worse, though, the faulty head-heart distinction draws attention away from the real problem. God's people rarely have a *knowledge* problem. Instead, lack of action testifies to our *obedience* problem.

If God's people are to overcome the inertia of the sinful human nature and obey the Great Commission, they need to know theology. Most importantly, they need to know biblical theology, the theological thinking that arises directly from the interpretation of Scripture. Grasping biblical theology enables God's people to recognize the drama of redemption in the Bible as their own story and begin participating in it themselves.

1

In this first major section of our book we first consider Old Testament theology and world mission. The near-absence of Old Testament preaching and teaching from many contemporary churches underscores the urgency of recovering the theology of the Old Testament, for this foundational stage of special revelation carries significant implications for world mission. Indeed, this first chapter closes with discussion of specific ways that the practice of world mission should change to align with the teaching of Old Testament Scripture.

The second chapter asserts that the New Testament is a collection of missional texts produced by a church on mission. Thus the New Testament is also saturated with significance for the practice of mission in the contemporary church. Jesus' mission of rescue and restoration calls for the church's participation in union with him. The natural result is the spread of the church across all worldly boundaries for the glorification of God.

The third chapter treats God's display of his glory among all nations as it draws together the grand narrative of Old and New Testament Scripture. Yet this chapter on biblical theology is not a mere recapitulation of the themes developed in the first two chapters. Rather, here the reader experiences the unfolding of God's purposes through his covenants with humanity. The finale of the book's section on theology and world mission thus casts the vision of a renewed humanity in covenant relationship with God, worshiping him throughout all eternity in the new creation.

1

OLD TESTAMENT THEOLOGY
AND WORLD MISSION

Scott N. Callaham

INTRODUCTION

"What does Old Testament theology have to do with world mission?" Anyone who considers Old Testament theology and world mission to be worthwhile enterprises should be prepared to answer this question. That said, one could possibly cast world mission in solely New Testament terms, treating Old Testament Scripture as irrelevant to mission-related theological reflection. One could also theoretically study Old Testament theology at great breadth and depth without once contemplating the issue of world mission. Both of these stances are flawed, and neither because they lack some elusive sense of balance nor simply because they fail to connect the two fields. After all, if Old Testament theology and world mission truly have little to do with each other, coercing them into contact through brute force or novel flights of ingenuity would hold meager value.

Against the backdrop of weighty issues such as this, the present study takes the first steps in shouldering the burden of this book: to call the church to return to a thoroughly biblical ethos for all aspects of world mission. This biblical ethos stems from biblical theology, such that the content, themes, and story line of the Bible determine everything else. Therefore, after setting its foundation on biblical authority, this chapter specifically asserts that if the first three-quarters of the Christian canon has something to say about world mission, then the church must listen and respond.

WORLD MISSION WITHOUT OLD TESTAMENT THEOLOGY: A CHALLENGE TO BIBLICAL AUTHORITY

World mission is a derivative idea, which is to say that it should derive from theological reflection on the Bible and take place in obedience to scriptural teaching. World mission shares this derivative nature with systematic theology, which also theoretically springs from but is not identical to Scripture.[1] While established systems of doctrine have matured through the centuries within venerable complexes of theological thought, in the end even the most deeply rooted theological convictions must defer to Scripture at any point of dissonance. A necessary overarching implication of the concept of biblical authority is that Scripture as the word of God holds priority over all theological systems and philosophical worldviews.[2] Similarly, all programs of world mission are subordinate to biblical teaching in every respect.

While a thoroughgoing presuppositional commitment to biblical authority might lead to ready acceptance of the concepts sketched out above, at the risk of repetition it is necessary to draw out at least three more specific implications of a robust view of biblical authority for world mission. For the purposes of the present study, the first implication of biblical authority is that the context-laden meaning of Scripture must exercise a controlling influence over theology. Therefore, at least in theory, present-day theologians reject the prooftexting practices of the past in favor of contextual biblical interpretation.[3] "Rightly handling the word of truth" (2 Tim 2:15) unleashes the voice of the Bible to speak afresh into

---

1. Bernard Lonergan writes, "Now it is true that theology is neither a source of divine revelation nor an addition to inspired scripture nor an authority that promulgates church doctrines"—this despite a career as a theologian in the Roman Catholic Church. See Bernard J. F. Lonergan, *Method in Theology* (London: Darton, Longman & Todd, 1971), 331–32.

2. Reserving the highest level of authority for the Bible is a core Reformation conviction. Sharply contrasting is this Catholic perspective on Scripture: "Scripture is *not* revelation, but, rather, attests to it, albeit in a privileged (inspired) manner." See Ignacio Carbajosa, *Faith, the Fount of Exegesis: The Interpretation of Scripture in Light of the History of Research on the Old Testament*, trans. Paul Stevenson (San Francisco: Ignatius, 2013), 152.

3. John H. Hayes and Frederick C. Prussner, *Old Testament Theology: Its History and Development* (Atlanta: John Knox, 1985), 17–19. For a second-century argument against prooftexting see Irenaeus, *Adversus haereses* 1.8.1. For perspective on how broad an interpretive gap nonetheless remains between systematic and biblical theologians, see Arthur J. Keefer,

the theology and practice of the church. Thus in the specific case of world mission, assuming a certain theory or shape for world mission and then seeking scriptural teaching to shore it up is fundamentally at odds with the concept of biblical authority.[4] Sound biblical teaching must instead give birth to theology of mission.

A second implication of biblical authority is that God and his word stand at the center of the Christian life. Now if God and his word occupy the center, there is no room for anything else there. In fact, this center overflows into the whole of life. Faithfully following Jesus through the empowerment of the Holy Spirit in obedience to the teachings of God's word—for his glory alone—is the hallmark of being a Christian. Discrete elements of this full-orbed image of discipleship do not by themselves embody the whole; or to restate in another way, one's degree of involvement in certain Christian activities is not a measure of faithfulness.[5] Thus, for example, personal participation in missions is neither the purpose nor the essence of being a Christian. Additionally, in terms of preparation for Christian ministry, mission can never be the integrating center of theological education.[6] On the broader scale of the Christian community, vibrant mission efforts do not necessarily imply healthy churches. Despite noble intentions, proposals such as these are critically imbalanced, for they unduly maximize the missional aspect of following Jesus

---

"The Use of the Book of Proverbs in Systematic Theology," *Biblical Theology Bulletin* 46 (2016): 35–44.

4. Assuming a certain model of mission practice and then reverse-engineering theological justification for it is the explicitly stated approach of V. David Garrison, *Church Planting Movements: How God Is Redeeming a Lost World* (Bangalore: WIGTake Resources, 2004), 11–12. See the context-free employment of Hab 1:5 on page 15 as an example of thematic prooftexting, and pages 199–219 for serial prooftexting to justify a missional paradigm following its creation.

5. This is not to suggest that there are actually any valid measures of faithfulness in a statistical, analytical sense.

6. Jeffrey P. Greenman, "Mission as the Integrating Center of Theological Education," in *The Bible in World Christian Perspective: Studies in Honor of Carl Edwin Armerding*, ed. David W. Baker and W. Ward Gasque (Vancouver: Regent College Press, 2009), 193–210. The helpful insights of Greenman's chapter in the end do not support his thesis that mission itself should become the center of theological education, which after all would entail theological education morphing into missiological education. A similarly mission-sensitive but more Scripture-centered approach to the place of mission in theological education is Millard C. Lind, "Refocusing Theological Education to Mission: The Old Testament and Contextualization," *Missiology* 10 (1982): 141–60.

at the expense of others. Instead the proper focal point of a Christian's whole-life devotion must be God himself; otherwise one risks stealing the glory that belongs to God alone.

A third implication of biblical authority is acceptance of the entire canon of Scripture as authoritative. While rehearsing the critical questions surrounding the definition of the Christian canon is well beyond the scope of this chapter, it is necessary to raise the issue of canon in order to underscore that the canonicity of the Old Testament is a settled matter.[7] If the Old Testament is inspired Scripture, then it cannot be Scripture in any kind of honorary sense, perhaps tolerated as a rather bulky historical prelude to "Christian Scripture": in this case meaning the New Testament. Furthermore, if the Old Testament is inspired Scripture then there can also be no question of pitting the New Testament (or even portions of the New Testament) against it in an unreflective manner, as if the way of Jesus constitutes a repudiation of all that came before.[8] Instead, merely observing the New Testament's host of direct quotations of, allusions to, and verbal parallels with the Old Testament should refute crudely supersessionist thinking about God's interactions with humanity leading up to the time of Jesus.[9] Yet the Old Testament not only serves New Testament authors as an authoritative literary reference but also preemptively lays out the guiding principles of New Testament faith and thus is nothing less than, as C. H. Dodd puts it, "the substructure of all Christian theology."[10] Indeed, recognition of the Old Testament as canon requires that the entirety of the Old Testament be relevant to theological thinking. There

---

7. In this book the term "Old Testament" refers to the Hebrew Bible and not to the wider collection of writings attested in the Septuagint.

8. See Lynne Hybels, "Lynne Hybels Answers, 'What Is an Evangelical?,' " *Sojourners*, October 7, 2011, https://sojo.net/articles/what-evangelical/lynne-hybels-answers-what -evangelical. Hybels endorses a friend's advice: "For a while, forget everything you've ever thought about Christianity; forget the Old Testament; forget Paul and the epistles—and just read Jesus."

9. Barbara Aland et al., eds., *The Greek New Testament*, 4th rev. ed. (Stuttgart: Deutsche Bibelgesellschaft, 1983), 887–901. Wide-ranging studies of biblical intertextuality appear in D. A. Carson and H. G. M. Williamson, eds., *It Is Written: Scripture Citing Scripture—Essays in Honour of Barnabas Linsars, SSF* (New York: Cambridge University Press, 1988).

10. C. H. Dodd, *According to the Scriptures: The Sub-Structure of New Testament Theology* (London: Nisbet, 1952), 127.

can be no separating out of some parts as more authoritative than others.[11] In the words of Bruce Waltke, "Every sentence of the Bible is fraught with theology, worthy of reflection."[12]

To review, submission to biblical authority requires first listening to the voice of God through Scripture and then forming theology. In the process of constructing theology, interpreters must resist the urge to seize on and maximize certain theological themes (such as world mission) in a way that Scripture itself does not. Finally, respect for biblical authority requires that the Old Testament feature prominently in discussion of issues across the theological spectrum, including world mission. Taken together, these principles require a different approach to world mission from the panoply of alternatives commonly seen in contemporary missions practice. Simply put, it is time to return the word of God—including the Old Testament—to its rightful place at the center.

WORLD MISSION WITHIN OLD TESTAMENT THEOLOGY

In order to commence this recentering project, the present study turns its attention primarily toward Old Testament theologies. Therefore works specifically written to advance biblical foundations for mission or a missional understanding of the grand narrative of the Bible only appear in a minor, supporting role rather than a leading role. One expects these specialized works to discourse on missional undertones within broader theological themes in the Old Testament and thus exemplify a bottom-up approach to an Old Testament theology of mission. The bottom-up method is valuable for its concentration on mission, though in the background must always loom the potentially unfair suspicion of imbalanced issue advocacy.

---

11. Gerhard von Rad, "Typologische Auslegung des Alten Testaments," *Evangelische Theologie* 12 (1952–1953): 17–33. On page 31 von Rad singles out for criticism the idea that the interpreter should search the Old Testament for "high religion" and reject "priestly, cultic religion" as somehow less representative of God's interaction with people. See also John Goldingay, *Approaches to Old Testament Interpretation*, 2nd ed. (Leicester, UK: Apollos, 1990), 33, who frames such thinking as attempting to distinguish what in the Old Testament is truly God's word and what is not.

12. Bruce K. Waltke and Charles Yu, *An Old Testament Theology: An Exegetical, Canonical, and Thematic Approach* (Grand Rapids: Zondervan, 2007), 21.

In marked contrast, the Old Testament theology field as a whole is virtu-ally invulnerable to the charge that it maintains an outsized interest in world mission. Accordingly, at first one might not expect a top-down approach, starting with Old Testament theologies, to deliver substantive theological reflection to missiologists. After all, mining the entire Old Testament in order to refine its theology requires treatment of a vast array of themes. Yet the following sections demonstrate the potential enrichment of mis-sional theory and practice that await those who are willing to allow this first and largest part of the Christian Bible to shape their theology.

In order to provide a brief orientation to Old Testament theologies as a literary genre, the present study first raises awareness of the diver-sity manifested among such works. Then the following section reviews themes that spring from Old Testament theologies' varying yet quite complementary treatments of the fate of gentile nations before Israel's God. Last, a concluding section offers specific suggestions on how the contemporary practice of world mission should change in light of these elements of Old Testament theology.

DIVERSITY AMONG OLD TESTAMENT THEOLOGIES

Old Testament theology is a distinct field of study; therefore it is rea-sonable to open a book spanning the theology of the Old Testament with certain preconceived notions regarding what should appear within. However, alongside this expectation of fundamental commonality should stand concomitant awareness of broad diversity among these works.

Old Testament theologies differ widely from one another for a host of interrelated reasons. For example, confessional commitments cannot help but manifest themselves in an author's writings. Thus in theory one might expect adherence to Christianity (whether Catholicism, Ortho-doxy, or Protestantism), Judaism, some other religion, or perhaps no religion in particular to influence the development of an author's Old Tes-tament theology. However, in reality Protestant theological thinking has birthed, defined, and dominated the field, thus making Old Testament theology more or less a subcategory of Protestant theology.[13] Accordingly,

---

13. Walter Brueggemann, *Theology of the Old Testament: Testimony, Dispute, Advocacy* (Minneapolis: Fortress, 1997), 1-4. Eight Catholic-authored Old Testament theologies appeared in the twentieth century, by Hetzenauer (1908), Heinisch (1940), Van Imschoot

the diversity of Old Testament theology is at least partly due to its relative freedom from ecclesiastical control. Thus individual authors' own intellectual landscapes largely channel their streams of theological reflection.

Old Testament theologies can express widely disparate viewpoints on certain subjects, for example on the fate of gentile nations: a key component of any conceptualization of world mission. On one hand, in the first Old Testament theology ever written, Georg Bauer expresses confidence that unaided human reason eventually leads to recognition of "a single, most perfect primeval being, the Creator and Conserver of the Universe."[14] On the other hand, Bauer asserts that according to Jewish belief, such nascent leanings toward monotheism would cast no light on "pagan nations." The nations would instead "be condemned by the Jews on a solemn day of judgment, and be cast down to the lake of fire of Gehenna for everlasting punishment."[15] Consistent with this nationalistically charged depiction of Jewish eschatology, there was no place for a theology of mission in Bauer's representation of ancient Judaism. Incidentally, limiting the task of Old Testament theology to tracing the historical development of ancient Jewish religion—like Bauer and many who have followed him—is a decision that carries significant ideological consequences. One such outcome is that assertions of contemporary theological significance for the Old Testament seem rather out of place, an alien imposition on a historical survey.[16] Even the assumed connection

---

(1954–1956), Cordero (1970), McKenzie (1974), Mattioli (1981), Schreiner (1995), and Nobile (1998). Regrettably, they have left little impression on biblical studies generally and the field of Old Testament theology specifically. A helpful introduction to Jewish perspectives on biblical theology appears in Benjamin D. Sommer, "Dialogical Biblical Theology: A Jewish Approach to Reading Scripture Theologically," in *Biblical Theology: Introducing the Conversation*, ed. Leo G. Perdue, Robert Morgan, and Benjamin D. Sommer, Library of Biblical Theology (Nashville: Abingdon, 2009), 1–53.

14. Georg Lorenz Bauer, *Theologie des alten Testaments: Oder Abriß der religiösen Begriffer der alten Hebräer; von den ältesten Zeiten bis auf den Anfang der christlichen Epoche* (Leipzig: Weygand, 1796), 19. Bauer evokes "eines einzigen allervollkommensten Urwesens, des Schöpfers und Erhalters des Universums." English translations of non-English quotations appear in the main text for ease of reading. Incidentally, Bauer was aware that his was the first-ever biblical theology of the ᴏᴛ. See page iv.

15. Bauer, *Theologie des alten Testaments*, 366: "hingegen werden an einem feyerlichen Gerichtstage von den Juden verdammt, und zu immerwahrenden Strafen in den Feuerpfuhl Gehenna hinabgestoßen werden."

16. The classic assertion of the incompatibility of the fields of the history of Israelite religion and Old Testament theology is Otto Eißfeldt, "Israelitisch-jüdische Religionsgeschichte

between Old and New Testament studies weakens if one views the Old Testament as a desiccated historical artifact rather than something yet "living" and "active" (see Heb 4:12) clothed in writing.[17]

There is perhaps no starker contrast with Bauer than Robin Routledge's treatment of the destiny of gentiles: "[God] will bring all nations to share in the relationship and blessings at first enjoyed by Israel. As we have seen, this was God's intention from the start, and is to be achieved through the witness of a restored and renewed Israel."[18] In view of the extremes of Bauer on one hand and Routledge on the other, a reader of Old Testament theologies may well wonder how can one rely on a field so densely sown with disagreement on theoretical approach, format, and results to articulate a cohesive theology of mission. After all, the concept that gentiles could indeed share in the blessings of God and even become part of the people of God struck the early church as lacking theological precedent.[19] However, it is precisely the existence of such rich diversity

---

und alttestamentliche Theologie," *Zeitschrift für die alttestamentliche Wissenschaft* 44 (1926): 1–12. A standard survey of the problem of history and Old Testament theology appears in Gerhard F. Hasel, *Old Testament Theology: Basic Issues in the Current Debate*, 4th ed. (Grand Rapids: Eerdmans, 1991), 115–38. Brevard Childs expresses a likely reason for the present uneasy consensus that Old Testament theologies must somehow engage with the problem of history as he writes: "All genuine theology is closely tied to the events of world history." See Brevard S. Childs, "Old Testament Theology," in *Old Testament Interpretation Past, Present, and Future: Essays in Honour of Gene M. Tucker*, ed. James Luther Mays, David L. Petersen, and Kent Harold Richards (Edinburgh: T&T Clark, 1995), 293–300, esp. 300.

17. This portion of Heb 4:12 is Ζῶν γὰρ ὁ λόγος τοῦ θεοῦ καὶ ἐνεργὴς. Placement of the participle ζῶν ("living") before rather than after its modified noun, λόγος, signals heightened syntactical prominence. See Daniel B. Wallace, *Greek Grammar beyond the Basics: An Exegetical Syntax of the New Testament* (Grand Rapids: Zondervan, 1996), 307. On the discourse level, use of the conjunction γάρ indicates that "the word of God is 'living' " strengthens a preceding proposition. See Stephanie L. Black, *Sentence Conjunctions in the Gospel of Matthew: καί, δέ, τότε, γάρ, οὖν and Asyndeton in Narrative Discourse*, The Library of New Testament Studies 216 (Sheffield, UK: Sheffield Academic, 2002), 280. As for significance within Hebrews as a whole, Cockerill views 4:12–13 as the climax of the entire first section of the book. See Gareth Lee Cockerill, *The Epistle to the Hebrews*, NICNT (Grand Rapids: Eerdmans, 2012), 214. All this is to say: on every level of textual analysis, the scriptural assertion in Hebrews that the word of God is "living" is no small matter.

18. Robin Routledge, *Old Testament Theology: A Thematic Approach* (Downers Grove, IL: InterVarsity Press, 2008), 326. As noted in Routledge's title, he chooses a thematic rather than historical or historical-critical approach to Old Testament theology, which is not to say that all thematic approaches necessarily lead to such a strong assertion about the intentions of God toward the nations as revealed in the OT.

19. G. B. Caird, *New Testament Theology*, ed. L. D. Hurst (Oxford: Clarendon, 1994), 394. One resolution to this theological problem is to conceive of the possibility of a gentile church as an OT-portended "mystery" that awaited actualization in New Testament times.

that makes any emergent consistency in thought all the more compelling. That is to say, if writers from many different backgrounds strike similar chords when discussing the Old Testament's perspective on the nations, the resulting resonances are all the more sonorous and arresting. Discerning the underlying harmony of Old Testament theologies' outlook on the nations is the promise of the following section.

THE NATIONS IN OLD TESTAMENT THEOLOGIES

Many Old Testament theologies explicitly address the fate of gentiles. From time to time sojourners live in the Israelites' midst, and individual gentiles such as Rahab and Ruth enter into the covenant people, but neither the Old Testament itself nor its many written theologies imply that their example of assimilation was normative for all foreign peoples.[20] By definition gentiles are not the people of Israel, thus prompting the question of how the God of Israel deals with them.

Interestingly, a cohesive pattern emerges as one considers how Old Testament theologies in aggregate treat this "gentile question." Old Testament theologies commonly examine the fate of the nations in light of God's work in *creation, election, judgment,* and *new creation.* Thus the present study now surveys treatment of these concepts among Old Testament theologies.

Creation

Theological thinking about the gentiles begins with *creation.* Of course, this must be true in a logical sense, in that creation has to do with the origin of all created things and thus serves as a plausible starting point for all theology.[21] Furthermore, the creation of human beings came before the commissioning of Israel as a special people of God; thus creation naturally carries significance beyond Israel. Literally from "the beginning," Yahweh could not be a mere patron god of a single ethnic group, utterly

---

See G. K. Beale, *A New Testament Biblical Theology: The Unfolding of the Old Testament in the New* (Grand Rapids: Baker Academic, 2011), 654.

20. See comments on Rahab and Ruth as faithful gentiles in Waltke and Yu, *Old Testament Theology,* 515–16, 864–65.

21. It is possible to think theologically about God as he was before his acts of creation, but those who are carrying out that theological thinking are all created beings embedded within God's created universe.

unconcerned with (and likewise of no concern to) all others. As Paul later argued, "Is God the God of Jews only? Is he not the God of Gentiles also? Yes, of Gentiles also" (Rom 3:29).

Yet the significance of the creation narrative for gentiles extends beyond the single fact of creation itself, but also to the specific teaching about the creation of humanity in God's image. It far exceeds the scope of this chapter to plumb the depths of the theological significance of creation in God's image by tracing the reverberations of this teaching throughout Scripture.[22] However, two complementary implications of creation in God's image stand above others in significance for defining what it means to be human and thus grasping the place of gentiles in Old Testament theology. One can phrase the first implication as a denial: creation in God's image means that ethnicity is *not* a fundamental element of human identity. After all, it is humans whom God creates in his image, not Israel. Thus all teaching of the Old Testament on the gentiles after the creation narrative rests on the idea that humans—including gentiles—uniquely reflect God as his image bearers. All humans inherently bear glory and honor and also exercise power under God's authority. One's ethnicity neither adds to nor subtracts from the overriding significance of creation in God's image. Thus while Jonah may have held completely understandable grievances against Assyrians in general or even Ninevites in particular, refusal of God's command to preach to them constituted lack of compassion for people who bore the same divine image as he. The final verse of the book of Jonah dramatizes God's concern and extends it even to animals under the Ninevites' care: "And should not I pity Nineveh, that great city, in which there are more than 120,000 persons who do not know their right hand from their left, and also much cattle?" (Jonah 4:11).

While creation in God's image *denies* ethnicity pride of place as a definitive marker of humanness, the second implication of creation in God's image is contrastingly an *affirmation*. Genesis 1:27 reads: "So God created man in his own image, in the image of God he created him; male and female he created them." The only explicit terms Scripture uses to

---

22. Paul van Imschoot, *Théologie de l'Ancien Testament* (Tournai: Desclée, 1954-1956), 2:7-11; Otto Kaiser, *Der Gott des Alten Testaments: Theologie des Alten Testaments* (Göttingen: Vandenhoeck and Ruprecht, 1993-2003), 2:307-12.

explain creation in the image of God are "male" and "female." The author of Genesis clearly understands that the concepts of maleness and female-ness specifically and sexual reproduction generally came into creation before humans did, for this is how animals will "be fruitful and multi-ply" (Gen 1:22). Thus humans will "be fruitful and multiply" by sexual reproduction as well. However, though animals are indeed living beings (נֶפֶשׁ חַיָּה), they lack God's image: a concept explained in the concrete cat-egories of male and female. Thus a defining attribute of human identity, intertwined in the most intimate way with God's own identity, is to be male or female. Creation in God's image is a central cross-cultural truth claim of Old Testament theology.

Alongside all of its universal application to all cultures in all times in history, Old Testament creation theology presents itself fully garbed in specificity. That is to say that it was specifically the God of Israel who crafted the universe and all life within it.[23] The content and structure of the creation story he supplied to his one special people seem to rebut any speculation that it simply recapitulates those of neighboring ancient peo-ples or even stakes out a similar underlying agenda.[24] Thus the meaning of creation for all peoples could only come into focus through the lens of Hebrew Scripture, and reciprocally, the Hebrews could only grasp their place before God in light of his creation of all humanity. Since Gerhard von Rad believed that in the nations God realized one of the purposes of his creation, he wrote that the "main question" Genesis 1–11 raises for the reader is "that of the further relationship of God to the nations."[25]

Von Rad's statement is in fact stronger than it may appear if read by itself, in that von Rad's earlier scholarship asserts that creation played a role in Old Testament theology subordinate to that of God's saving acts. It is possible to interpret von Rad's primary sources in Psalms and Isaiah differently than he and on that basis alone assert a more prominent role for creation in Old Testament theology. However, von Rad's own discern-ment of the Hebrew writers' theological agenda is nonetheless striking.

---

23. Elmer A. Martens, *God's Design: A Focus on Old Testament Theology*, 2nd ed. (Grand Rapids: Baker Books, 1994), 266.

24. Paul Heinisch, *Theologie des Alten Testamentes* (Bonn: Peter Hanstein, 1940), 120–23.

25. Gerhard von Rad, *Old Testament Theology*, trans. D. M. G. Stalker (New York: Harper, 1962–1965), 1:162–63.

Von Rad posits that the typical function of creation theology in the Old Testament was to elicit a faith response.[26] To focus on a specific example, the creation theology of Psalm 136:5-9 leads intentionally—rather than abruptly transitions, as von Rad suggests—into the recital of God's iconic acts of deliverance of Israel. Then when ancient liturgy recounted God's triumph over specific gentile peoples (Egyptians in 136:15, Amorites in 136:19, and inhabitants of Bashan in 136:20), Hebrew worshipers meditated on God's "steadfast love" in special covenant relationship with Israel and simultaneously pondered his mysterious purposes in creating those opposing nations.

Election

Consideration of the special covenant relationship highlights a second crucial theological theme: *election*. According to Horst Dietrich Preuß, election supplies the "fundamental structure of Old Testament faith." The election of Israel was God's means of communing with his creation through his people's obedient response to him.[27] As central as the theme of election may be to Old Testament theology, at first glance God's election of Israel may seem the least likely doctrine to point toward the redemption of nonelected nations.[28] A decontextualized reading of parts of Malachi 1:2-3 appears to confirm this intuition and ring harshly in modern ears: "I have loved Jacob but Esau I have hated."

Perhaps the first step in coming to grips with the significance of the election of Israel should actually be a conceptual step backward

26. Gerhard von Rad, "Das theologische Problem des alttestamentlichen Schöpfungsglaubens," in *Werden und Wesen des Alten Testaments*, ed. Paul Volz, Friedrich Stummer, and Johannes Hempel, Beihefte zur Zeitschrift für die alttestamentliche Wissenschaft 66 (Berlin: Töpelmann, 1936), 138–47, esp. 140, 146.

27. Horst Dietrich Preuß, *Old Testament Theology*, trans. Leo G. Perdue (Louisville: Westminster, 1995–1996), 1:25.

28. Moberly sensitively discusses the particularity of election and the consequences of God choosing some people and not others in R. W. L. Moberly, *Old Testament Theology: Reading the Hebrew Bible as Christian Scripture* (Grand Rapids: Baker Academic, 2013), 41–74. Kautzsch sees the particularism inherent in God's election of Israel as something that the postexilic prophets would overcome. See Emil Kautzsch, *Biblische Theologie des Alten Testaments* (Tübingen: J. C. B. Mohr, 1911), 317. Similarly, see Donald Senior and Carroll Stuhlmueller, *The Biblical Foundations for Mission* (Maryknoll, NY: Orbis, 1983), 83–89. Piepenbring emphasizes that the prophets envisioned salvation for the gentiles only in the context of their subordination to Israel. See C. Piepenbring, *Théologie de l'Ancien Testament* (Paris: Librairie Fischbacher, 1886), 193–94.

to reevaluate why the concept of election *of anyone* is offensive to modern readers of Scripture. In other words, one may question the fairness of God's election of Israel but not another people specifically, or even merely God's election of some but not others generally. The pivotal consideration is thus fairness. As Barton Payne notes, however, fairness constitutes an altogether inappropriate frame for discussion of election.[29] That is to say, critiquing God's fairness in election implies that God owes election to all, because God has no reason to deny anyone access to him.

The presumption of moral standing to criticize God's fairness in election is breathtaking and supplies further evidence that sin numbs the conscience of the sinner. Despite any minor protestations to the contrary, in practice humans seldom grasp the gravity of sin. Possessing a sinful nature is not an abstract problem lacking real-world consequence; a sinful nature means that one naturally commits sin. Sin constitutes offense against God regardless of any knowledge of God on the part of the sinner. Thus Amos' announcement of judgment against Israel's neighbors in Amos 1:3–2:5—far from the ears of Israel's neighbors—was not merely a rhetorical device to draw a crowd before Amos lowered the boom of judgment on Israel. Lacking any explicit relationship with Israel's God, even the nations' crimes against each other made them worthy of judgment (e.g., see Amos 2:1).

Following the necessary step backward to rethink human sinfulness above, now it is possible to step forward with the realization that absolutely no one deserves election. Election is purely an act of grace, of receiving a standing with God that can only come by sheer mercy. Thus Old Testament theologies highlight the entirely gratuitous nature of Abraham's election. Old Testament theologies also typically note that God's blessing on Abraham will result in further blessing for "all the families of the earth."[30] Word choice and literary context suggest that these

---

29. J. Barton Payne, *The Theology of the Older Testament* (Grand Rapids: Zondervan, 1962), 194.

30. Brevard S. Childs, *Old Testament Theology in a Canonical Context* (Philadelphia: Fortress, 1985), 103–7, esp. 103–4. See also van Imschoot, *Théologie de l'Ancien Testament*, 1:269–70. The way that Gen 12:3 depicts blessing reaching the "families of the earth" via Abraham depends partly on the semantics of the *Niphal weqatal* form of the blessing verb ברך in the verse's final clause. For a recent study of this issue see Chee-Chiew Lee, "Once Again: The

"families" or "clans" are those listed in the Table of Nations of Genesis 10, underscoring a revolution in the prevailing state of relations between humanity and God before Abraham's election.[31] Though previously God's election of a single person (Noah) limited God's blessing to him and his family alone, now God's election of a single person (Abraham) will become a means of blessing extended to all people.[32]

Edmond Jacob asserts a specifically missional implication of Abrahamic blessing: "The election of Israel was to lead of necessity to a missionary duty." Jacob's treatment of Israel's missionary responsibility depicts transformative engagement with gentile peoples, particularly those who conquered and enslaved them. He goes as far as to state that "Moses was a missionary to the Egyptians by demonstrating to them the weakness of their gods." Once a people comes to understand that their gods stand under Yahweh's judgment, their gods' power over them dissipates, and people of that society "will be ready for the worship of Yahweh."[33] One of Jacob's passing comments on the mission of God's elect people seems uncharacteristically pointed for academic writing and even jarringly prophetic, as if sealed in a time capsule to await recovery in the contemporary postmodern era: "Tolerance never leads to mission."[34] While some gentile religions could easily accommodate the notion of one supreme god among many others, a loosely defined polytheism with an ever-expanding pantheon of gods was utterly incompatible with Isaiah's

---

Niphal and the Hithpael of ברך in the Abrahamic Blessing for the Nations," *JSOT* 36 (2012): 279–96.

31. Von Rad wrote of the "scandal" of Abraham's election: "Thus that difficult question about God's relationship to the nations is answered, and precisely where one least expects it." See Gerhard von Rad, *Genesis: A Commentary*, trans. John H. Marks, Old Testament Library (Philadelphia: Westminster, 1961), 150.

32. Sellin saw in this blessing an "indirect announcement" that the nations will one day turn to Abraham's God. See Ernst Sellin, *Theologie des Alten Testaments*, 2nd ed. (Leipzig: Quelle and Meyer, 1936), 125.

33. Edmond Jacob, *Theology of the Old Testament*, trans. Arthur W. Heathcote and Philip J. Allcock (London: Hodder and Stoughton, 1958), 217–20.

34. Jacob, *Theology of the Old Testament*, 219n2. Monotheism logically requires denial of competing religious systems and their alternative truth claims. See Josef Schreiner, *Theologie des Alten Testaments*, Neuen Echter Bibel—Altes Testament 1 (Würzburg: Echter, 1995), 335. The more recent opinion of Gerstenberger stands worlds apart: "In the light of our claim, grounded in the Old Testament, to confess the one God, we cannot in principle exclude any other religion." Erhard S. Gerstenberger, *Theologies in the Old Testament*, trans. John Bowden (New York: T&T Clark, 2002), 298.

and Micah's vision of the nations streaming to Zion to worship Yahweh alongside Israel.

While treating the concept of election, Old Testament theologians emphasize the role of elected Israel as mediator.[35] The elected people's mediation prepares for God's eschatological reign over a restored cosmos that includes both Israel and gentiles.[36] Mediation of course implies a middle position, in that Israel would stand before God in covenant relationship, and Israel would also in turn represent God to the nations.[37] Israel's position as mediator is never in doubt in the Old Testament, which is to say that it would only be possible to speak of salvation for the nations as an extension of the salvation God works for Israel. It is clear that Israel "is YHWH's witness to the world," but the outworking of that witness remains somewhat undeveloped in the Old Testament. Due to biblical anticipation of severe judgment of the nations, on one hand, and intimations of salvation for them, on the other, Preuß finds it impossible to place the destiny of the nations under any single rubric, stating that "The Old Testament continues to be of two minds in its expressions, hopes, and expectations" for the gentiles.[38]

Judgment

The theme of *judgment* awaiting the nations is indeed significant in the Old Testament and is prominent enough to merit mention as the third major theme among Old Testament theologies regarding the fate of gentiles. As with the doctrine of the election of Israel, the juxtaposition of judgment and missional theology might at first glance seem nothing less

---

35. Gustav Friedrich Oehler, *Theologie des Alten Testaments*, 3rd ed. (Stuttgart: J. F. Steinkopf, 1891), 828.

36. Theodorus C. Vriezen, *An Outline of Old Testament Theology*, trans. S. Neuijen (Newton, MA: Charles T. Branford, 1958), 229–30.

37. Davidson acknowledges the prophets' interpretation of God's election of Israel as an expression of love and grace but speculates that the Israelites possessed a natural "genius for religion" that rendered them especially apt mediators for God. See Andrew Bruce Davidson, *The Theology of the Old Testament*, ed. S. D. F. Salmond (New York: Charles Scribner's Sons, 1914), 249.

38. Preuß, *Old Testament Theology*, 2:301–3. Preuß's insight about the interplay of judgment and salvation for the nations is valuable, and as Goldingay notes, the same tension prevails in the NT. See John Goldingay, *Old Testament Theology* (Downers Grove, IL: InterVarsity Press, 2003–2009), 2:733.

than a forced union of thesis and antithesis. Indeed, one may wonder how the judgment of the nations could somehow lead to their redemption in the purposes of God.

Egypt is a paradigmatic example of a nation that experiences God's judgment. Yet depiction of Egypt prior to the exodus event is relatively benign. Joseph's slavery there is not due to any systematic program of oppression against Israelites. Furthermore, the Old Testament harbors no particular animus against the pharaoh of Joseph's era and in fact portrays him as facilitating refuge for Jacob and his family.

However, as John McKenzie notes, Exodus departs sharply from the prior neutral or even relatively affirming characterization of Egypt. The Israelites' adopted home transforms from haven into hell. Receiving the command to release his Israelite slave force for the first time, Pharaoh questions not the existence of Israel's God, but why he should concern himself with this God at all: "Who is the LORD, that I should obey his voice and let Israel go? I do not know the LORD" (Exod 5:2). From that moment forward, the great crime of Egypt for which they will face judgment is refusal to acknowledge and obey God.[39]

Intriguingly, in Exodus 7:4–5 God announces the aftermath of coming "great acts of judgment": "The Egyptians shall know that I am the LORD," as if directly to address Pharaoh's claim of no such knowledge. Another explanation of judgment follows in Exodus 9:14: "so that [Pharaoh] may know that there is none like me in all the earth." Pharaoh's rule itself realizes a similar divine goal, as narrated in Exodus 9:16: "But for this purpose I have raised you up, to show you my power, so that my name may be proclaimed in all the earth." Discerning the common thread of these stated reasons for judgment requires no refined skills of literary interpretation; they all have to do with communicating knowledge of God to Egyptians. Centuries later, when Israel experiences its second exodus and return from Assyrian and Babylonian captivity, Isaiah asserts that the national mission of Israel is to proclaim a similar programmatic message to the nations: Yahweh alone is God.[40]

---

39. John L. McKenzie, *A Theology of the Old Testament* (Garden City, NY: Doubleday, 1974), 166.

40. McKenzie, *Theology of the Old Testament*, 295.

Most prophetic books prominently feature an entire literary sub-genre dedicated to judgment: the "oracles against the nations."[41] Occasionally in commentaries one encounters a more graphic title for this literary form: "hymn of hate."[42] Yet once again the Old Testament presents a more nuanced picture than its popular caricature suggests. Through most of the oracles flows an undercurrent of pathos and perhaps even sympathy toward nations that stand under God's judgment.[43] For example, the verbs and infinitives absolute within Isaiah 19:22 specify that God's action of "striking" Egypt will simultaneously heal them such that they would turn to him.[44] Scandalously, Isaiah then prophesies a day of blessing for Israel shared with its archetypal oppressors: "In that day Israel will be the third with Egypt and Assyria, a blessing in the midst of the earth, whom the LORD of hosts has blessed, saying, 'Blessed be Egypt my people, and Assyria the work of my hands, and Israel my inheritance'" (Isa 19:24–25). Given a conclusion such as this, it is possible to question whether Isaiah 19 is ultimately an oracle "against" Egypt at all.[45]

One might at first assume that Egypt and other gentile nations comprise the primary audience of the prophetic oracles directed toward them. Yet among all of the prophets only Jonah actually carries a message

---

41. Pancratius C. Beentjes, "Oracles against the Nations: A Central Issue in the 'Latter Prophets,'" *Bijdragen: Tijdschrift voor filosofie en theologie* 50 (1989): 203–9, esp. 203. Beentjes notes that oracles against the nations occupy a central position in the prophetic programs of Isaiah, Jeremiah, and Ezekiel, nestled between oracles against Israel and oracles of salvation for Israel. As Beentjes indicates, this schema holds true with the Septuagintal but not the Masoretic ordering of chapters for Jeremiah.

42. Kenneth L. Barker and Waylon Bailey, *Micah, Nahum, Habakkuk, Zephaniah*, NAC 20 (Nashville: Broadman & Holman, 1998), 183.

43. McKenzie, *Theology of the Old Testament*, 171–72. Sympathy could derive from understanding that Israel stands under God's judgment as well, as in Amos 1:2–2:16. See Routledge, *Old Testament Theology*, 317.

44. Christo H. J. van der Merwe, Jacobus A. Naudé, and Jan H. Kroeze, *A Biblical Hebrew Reference Grammar*, 2nd ed. (New York: Bloomsbury, 2017), 182. Van der Merwe et al. schematize this "simultaneous action" adverbial use of independent infinitives absolute as "Main verb x + infinitive absolute x + infinitive absolute y." Simultaneous "striking" and "healing" is certainly unexpected, as a similar expression in 1 Kgs 20:37 shows.

45. Egypt arguably receives even more favorable treatment in Ezekiel. Vogels asserts that Ezekiel's depiction of a future restoration of Egypt employs the same vocabulary, formulas, and theology that the prophet uses in laying out the implications of God's new covenant with Israel. See Walter Vogels, "Restauration de l'Égypte et universalisme en Ez 29,13–16," *Biblica* 53 (1972): 473–94, esp. 491.

of judgment to gentiles. Jeremiah is perhaps the most internationally minded of the prophets due to his situation in life and his commission as "prophet to the nations" (Jer 1:5), and in fact Yahweh commands him to send a message through intermediaries to foreign kings in Jeremiah 27:2–11.[46] With notable but rare exceptions such as these, literary context suggests that only Hebrew ears heard biblical oracles of judgment, signaling that the oracles against the nations are actually somewhat indirect speech acts directed toward the Hebrews, reminding them to trust in Yahweh rather than form alliances with doomed foreign nations.[47] Of course, these *indirect* speech acts appear within the context of *direct* speech acts, and the message of the direct speech acts is God's judgment on the nations.

New Creation

A final theme rises to the fore in the aftermath of judgment: *new creation*. Perhaps the most dramatic depiction of new creation in all of Scripture begins with Isaiah 65:17: "For behold, I create new heavens and a new earth, and the former things shall not be remembered or come into mind." Here Isaiah evokes Genesis 1:1 and God's creation of everything in a somewhat startling way, for there is actually no "I" in Isaiah 65:17. A literalistic translation would be more like, "For behold, creating new heavens and new earth!"[48]

The prophets proclaim that the new creation will exhibit Eden-like conditions bursting with life, as explicitly stated in Ezekiel 36:35 and implied elsewhere (Isa 35:1–10; Amos 9:13–15). Strikingly, on that day "the LORD will be king over all the earth" and "the LORD will be one and his name one" (Zech 14:9), and a river of "living waters" will flow out from Jerusalem to both the east and west (see also Ps 46:4), much as Eden served as the source of rivers. According to Ezekiel this life-giving river

---

46. Georg Fischer, *Theologien des Alten Testaments*, Neuer Stuttgarter Kommentar—Altes Testament 31 (Stuttgart: Katholisches Bibelwerk, 2012), 94–96; Jerry Hwang, "The *Missio Dei* as an Integrative Motif in the Book of Jeremiah," *BBR* 23 (2013): 481–508.

47. Paul R. Raabe, "Look to the Holy One of Israel, All You Nations: The Oracles about the Nations Still Speak Today," *Concordia Journal* 30 (2004): 336–49, esp. 341–42.

48. The following verse later specifies what the reader already knows with the subject pronoun "I"; of course God is the only possible agent of creation and the only one who can create everything anew as he sees fit.

issues from the temple, and on its banks grow trees whose "fruit will be for food, and their leaves for healing" (Ezek 47:1-12, esp. 47:12). Later, Revelation specifies that these leaves are for the healing of "the nations" (Rev 22:2).[49]

Re-creation of the heavens and the earth inherently affects all peoples and demonstrates God's absolute sovereignty over them as part of his creation.[50] In the course of Yahweh's re-creating acts, the nations observe him acting to redeem Israel.[51] One facet of eschatological redemption will be the inauguration of a new covenant.[52] Jeremiah 31:31-34 is the classic statement of this new covenant: a phrase that appears only there in the Old Testament. Jeremiah states that the LORD will inscribe his Torah—his teaching—directly on the heart, which will enable everyone to know God directly in a way not possible before. Ezekiel elaborates that God's work of re-creation in the new covenant will include granting his people a new heart (specifically a "heart of flesh" as opposed to stone, Ezek 36:26) and a new spirit (specifically God's own Spirit, Ezek 36:27). God will provide a "fountain" to cleanse the people from sin, such that their idols and false prophets will be no more (Zech 13:1-2).[53] Accompanying these dramatic developments in the history of God's redemption of humanity will be "many peoples" and "strong nations" streaming to Jerusalem to seek the LORD—apparently with a sense of urgency and desperation—for "In those days ten men from the nations of every tongue shall take hold of the robe of a Jew, saying, 'Let us go with you, for we have heard that God is with you'" (Zech 8:22-23).

---

49. Huang Yi Zhang, *Jiu yue shen xue: Cong chuang zao dao xin chuang zao* (Hong Kong: Tien Dao, 2003), 393-412.

50. Claus Westermann, *Elements of Old Testament Theology*, trans. Douglas W. Scott (Atlanta: John Knox, 1982), 101-2.

51. John Kessler, *Old Testament Theology: Divine Call and Human Response* (Waco, TX: Baylor University Press, 2013), 163. By the time of the new creation, the nations already will have witnessed Israel's interactions with God through history, including God's judgment on, as well as his restoration of, his chosen people. See Christopher J. H. Wright, *The Mission of God: Unlocking the Bible's Grand Narrative* (Downers Grove, IL: IVP Academic, 2006), 467-74.

52. Walther Eichrodt, *Theology of the Old Testament*, trans. J. A. Baker (Philadelphia: Westminster, 1961-1967), 1:482; Van Imschoot, *Théologie de l'Ancien Testament*, 1:255-59.

53. Van Imschoot writes that the regeneration of God's people represents the very pinnacle of Old Testament theology. See Paul van Imschoot, "Heilige Geest," in *Bijbelsch Woordenboek*, ed. Adrianus van den Born et al. (Turnhout: Brepols, 1941), cols. 474-85, esp. 477.

Israel's obedient response to God's acts of redemption will serve as a witness to the nations, at once attracting gentiles to Israel centripetally, as seen above, and dispatching Israel out to gentile lands centrifugally.[54] Thus in some Old Testament theologies there is a very personal dimension to Israel's role in the redemption of the nations, for some Israelites will apparently carry God's revelation to them in some way.[55] Even so, Old Testament theologies manifest differences of opinion on the identity of the primary agent who will undertake the task of reaching the gentiles such that they submit to God. To enumerate a few examples, the "missionary" whom Preuß sees in the Old Testament is God himself, sometimes finding his own people (such as Jonah) to be an obstacle in the way of actualizing his agenda to reach out to the nations.[56] Stephen Dempster and John Kessler emphasize the servant prophesied in Isaiah as the one who will bring history to a close with a remnant of the gentiles subsumed under God's universal kingdom.[57] Otto Baab writes that Israel as a set-apart community will transmit God's "word of redemption" to the gentiles.[58]

Yet it may not be entirely necessary to identify a single missionary agent to the exclusion of others, for, as Routledge points out, Isaiah points to the servant as the agent of renewal. Ezekiel highlights the Spirit, and Jeremiah the Messiah.[59] God works both directly and through others to draw the nations to himself at the climax of history. To state in summary that the actions of the servant, the Spirit, the Messiah, Israel as a

---

54. Routledge, *Old Testament Theology*, 326–28.

55. Although present-day Judaism is not a convert-seeking religion, sufficient historical evidence exists to argue that the Judaism of the Second Temple period was more open to the proselytization of gentiles. See Michael F. Bird, *Crossing Over Sea and Land: Jewish Missionary Activity in the Second Temple Period* (Peabody, MA: Hendrickson, 2010).

56. Preuß, *Old Testament Theology*, 2:302–3. Preuß asserts the direct agency of God so strongly that he denies "mission work" by the servant and Israel.

57. Stephen G. Dempster, *Dominion and Dynasty: A Theology of the Hebrew Bible*, NSBT 15 (Downers Grove, IL: InterVarsity Press, 2006), 179–81; Kessler, *Old Testament Theology*, 164–65. Stade and Heinisch straightforwardly identify God's rule at the culmination of history as the kingdom of the Messiah. See Bernhard Stade, *Biblische theologie des Alten Testaments* (Tübingen: J. C. B. Mohr, 1905–1911), 309–11; Heinisch, *Theologie des Alten Testamentes*, 288, 309–11.

58. Otto J. Baab, *The Theology of the Old Testament: The Faith behind the Facts of Hebrew Life and Writings* (New York: Abingdon, 1949), 100.

59. Routledge, *Old Testament Theology*, 325.

community, or individual Israelites all evidence the work of one redeeming God is not to advance a claim that is so generalized that it evaporates into meaninglessness. Instead it accounts for the fact that God orchestrates every aspect of his new creation to act together for his purposes, for example by introducing the servant in Isaiah 42:1–4 and placing his Spirit on him so that he will "bring forth justice to the nations."[60]

WORLD MISSION THROUGH OLD TESTAMENT THEOLOGY

Following the all-too-brief survey of *creation, election, judgment,* and *new creation* in Old Testament theologies above, now it is time to consider the implications of these doctrines for the practice of world mission. Just as a fuller treatment of themes touching on the nations in Old Testament theologies must await a lengthier study, so also these proposals must remain somewhat suggestive and serve to stimulate further reflection.

CREATION

Creation theology is essential for understanding the place of humanity before God. One God—*the* God—created all that is, and in his eyes it was "good" (Gen 1:4, 10, 12, 18, 21, 25). Finally, after the creation of humans it became "very good" (Gen 1:31). Creation by one God means that all other assertions of divinity are illusory. That single God's creation of all humans means that God has rightful claim to lordship over all peoples. That creation theology unfolds an origin story for the universe different from every other means that conflicting accounts are untrue, which only underscores that the gods associated with them are false. Therefore missionaries should be exceedingly circumspect about affirming aspects of world religions such as their scriptures, which from "the beginning" onward contest the Bible's sacred narrative.

Theological thinking about creation is indeed preferable to sifting through the ideologies of other religious systems in the hope of unearthing something of apologetic value. However, contemporary approaches to evangelism typically overlook creation theology altogether and instead

---

60. Walther Zimmerli, *Old Testament Theology in Outline,* trans. David E. Green (Edinburgh: T&T Clark, 1978), 222.

employ the idea of creation for other purposes such as setting up the "sin problem" that Jesus will solve. This is the creation-fall-redemption plot line, which carries the advantage of forming a self-contained story that is sufficiently brief for a missionary to relate in a single encounter.

Yet one should think critically about storytelling logic and brevity; these advantages alone should not decide missionary practice. As for logic, the creation-fall-redemption pattern makes good sense. That said, its logic is not the Bible's own; its rhetorical leap from Genesis 3 to the New Testament leaves out the majority of Scripture.[61] Similarly, the brevity of typical creation-fall-redemption stories all the more aptly demonstrates that this three-step progression is woefully insufficient to convey the message of Scripture. Indeed, creation is not only the necessary first act of a drama that leads to redemption. Instead, the significance of creation reverberates throughout biblical theology.

Creation theology should indeed exert more influence on the mission field, specifically regarding the doctrine of creation of humans in the image of God. As mentioned above, the word of God teaches that ethnicity is not a primary identity marker of what it means to be human. Thus church planters should resist the natural, pragmatic, and unbiblical tendency to group believers into churches by ethnicity. Instead, missionaries should train national leaders in common-language, multiethnic areas to plant churches that tear down ethnic barriers between believers.[62] Furthermore, from the very beginning of church-planting efforts, missionaries should teach that creation in the image of God means creation as male and female, and that these are theologically significant terms. Indeed, the qualifications of church leaders in the Pastoral Epistles are gender specific, and 1 Timothy 2:13–14 explicitly links these qualifications to creation theology. Admittedly, the applications of the doctrine of creation in

---

61. Theological disregard of the Old Testament is not only a missiological problem. Decrying theological interpretation guided by systematic theology, Goldingay writes, "The Rule of Faith has no room and no hermeneutic for any episodes in the scriptural story between Genesis 3 and Matthew 1." See John Goldingay, *Do We Need the New Testament? Letting the Old Testament Speak for Itself* (Downers Grove, IL: IVP Academic, 2015), 173.

62. Creation theology thus stands opposed to theories of missiology for which ethnicity plays an outsized role, which is a tendency in "people movements" thinking. See for example Donald A. McGavran, *The Bridges of God: A Study in the Strategy of Missions* (New York: Friendship Press, 1955), 10.

God's image in this paragraph are extremely offensive to the sensibilities of many cultures, particularly the Western culture of many missionaries. Yet starkly countercultural implications of biblical teaching such as these should serve as a reminder that theology matters, including the often-ignored theology of the Old Testament.

In light of creation theology, at least one use of creation in apologetics merits rethinking: the framing of creation as primarily an issue of science rather than of theology. At least some of the impetus toward scientism understandably derives from reaction to the inexorable advance of materialistic evolutionary philosophy. Yet the truth claims of creation theology do not rest on scientific theories, and missionaries—especially those untrained in science—should not portray creation as if it were a scientific hypothesis.[63] Neither scientifically expressed principles nor their degree of verification through experimentation constitutes the missionary message. Instead, missionaries should relate the Bible's message within the theological context the Bible itself provides. Perhaps the most common and glaring omission in popular missional presentations of creation has to do with the specificity of creation theology, which is to say that the Creator God is at once the Creator and rightful king of all peoples and also the God of Israel.[64]

ELECTION

The Creator-King is God of Israel because of his election of them, and there would be no mission to the scattered peoples of the world without a preexisting covenant relationship with the Hebrews.[65] God's choice of one

---

63. When missionaries who are untrained in science attempt to use science for apologetic purposes, their communication strategy is untenable and self-defeating. Yet lack of training in science hardly constitutes a debilitating weakness in mission work. In contrast, commissioning missionaries who are untrained in theology is an open invitation to disaster.

64. The popular Creation to Christ presentation never once mentions the Hebrew people. See Creation to Christ, http://t4tonline.org/wp-content/uploads/2011/05/creation-to-christ-oral-version-english.pdf. This would be less of a liability but for expansive claims commonly advanced for the Creation to Christ presentation such as this one found on the same website: "It's simply the whole Bible story in 10–20 minutes." See Stephen R. Smith, "Gospel Presentations Used in T4T Packages," http://t4tonline.org/wp-content/uploads/2011/02/3d-Gospel-Presentations-Used-in-T4T-Packages.pdf (accessed January 4, 2018).

65. It is possible to advance a strong biblical-theological argument that the story of God's dealings with Israel constitutes the "single idea that is pervasive enough to establish unity

people eventually leading to the salvation of all—a seeming paradox—calls for fresh rethinking in order to provide proper context for missional theology.

First it is necessary to acknowledge that election roots mission deeply in the soil of particularism. Deuteronomy explains that God's choice of Israel is not due to the Hebrews being a particularly prominent people, and in fact they were not a large ethnic group. God's reason for election then appears in Deuteronomy 7:8: "but it is because the LORD loves you and is keeping the oath that he swore to your fathers." Straightforwardly, it is love and being true to his promise that motivate God's election of Israel. Thus Israel's election was due to God's initiative rather than their own, and the fact of Israel's election incurred responsibility: obedient response to God's commands (see, e.g., Deut 27:18).

Regarding obedient response to God, the Old Testament idea that the election of Israel is an integral part of God's plan to redeem all of humanity disallows too rapid a leap into generalization. To elaborate, Old Testament theology supports the premise that humans are sinners and therefore will never be fully obedient. Yet the concept of human sinfulness is only "merely" true, a generalization that is not necessarily the point of most Old Testament theology. Instead, in the Old Testament the specific people of God are accountable to specific obligations within a specific covenant relationship. It is for specific and intentional violations of that covenant—not for possessing a sinful nature or falling short of an amorphous ideal of perfection—that God exiles his people (see, e.g., Deut 28:15).

At least four immediate applications to mission theology derive from taking proper stock of the particularism of God's election of Israel and thus keeping Israel in God's story where it belongs. The first application is to agree with Jesus that "salvation is from the Jews" (John 4:22). That is to say, it was completely necessary within God's plans to elect Israel and then to raise up his own Son from among the disobedient people to be contrastingly obedient and fulfill the scriptural roles of servant, prophet, priest, king, and messianic deliverer, each of which would fade into abstraction without the meaning that the Old Testament invests in them. Minimizing

---

within the Bible." See C. Marvin Pate et al., *The Story of Israel: A Biblical Theology* (Downers Grove, IL: IVP Academic, 2004), 278.

or eliminating mention of Israel in telling God's story radically decontextualizes Jesus and the gospel message.

The second application of the election of Israel also directly derives from its inherent particularism. That is to say, in Old Testament times God set apart the people of Israel for himself, drawing a definitional line circumscribing his covenant community. There was no doubt regarding the identity of the elect people. The staggering numbers of converts some missionaries and mission organizations regularly report should be cause for rejoicing that an ever-increasing multitude from every nation surrounds the throne of God in worship (Rev 7:9-12). Understandably, verifiable information on mass movements (such as names of baptized Christians) can be difficult to obtain. Yet it should become a matter of concern whenever observable evidence of conversion among a supposedly evangelized population remains elusive over time. It should not be difficult to differentiate the elect community—the church—from surrounding society.

The third application of the election of Israel to contemporary mission practice is that the Old Testament theology of election should correct popular misconceptions about election in general. A common misunderstanding is that emphasizing God's election of some people for adoption into his covenant people (and not others) "before the foundation of the world" must necessarily lead to a loss of urgency toward engaging in world mission (see esp. Eph 1:4-5). According to this line of thinking, God's sovereign choice logically relieves Christians of the responsibility to engage in mission, for God shall save whom he chooses to save no matter what his people do. Opposing this viewpoint, Old Testament theology not only endorses God's absolute and thoroughgoing sovereignty, but also leaves no room for abdication of responsibility among the elect people to obey him. In other words, if a person, a church, a denomination, or a religious movement refuses to obey the clear command Christ handed down to his followers in the Great Commission, that noncompliance is by no means testimony to firm belief in the doctrine of election. In fact, refusal to obey—spurning the elect people's role of mediating God to the world—is evidence of disbelief. Furthermore, intentional disobedience to Christ's specific command is an incitement to judgment. Questions logically follow: "Why would the supposedly elect people of God choose to disobey him so insistently and shamefully?" More ominously, "Are such people among the elect themselves?"

The fourth application is to agree with Paul that God has by no means rejected his people (Rom 11:1). As surely as "salvation is from the Jews," God's message of salvation must return to them. Otherwise Paul would not feel the need to yearn for their salvation, as in Romans 10:1. As the Old Testament repeatedly confirms, God's election of the Hebrews did not forestall their judgment indefinitely (see, e.g., Amos 3:2). Instead, failure to respond obediently to God in covenant relationship provokes judgment, which is the next theme of Old Testament theology that calls for special attention with respect to world mission.

JUDGMENT

Indeed, judgment looms for God's people when they choose not to obey him. Thus the church must recognize that participation in the Great Commission is not a task that can wait until an imagined more convenient time in the future. The intent of Old Testament announcements of judgment on the people of God is not to instill a spirit of "judgment avoidance": aligning with God's will and his ways in order to escape his wrath. Indeed, God loves his people and prefers to relent from judgment as his people repent (see, e.g., Joel 2:12–14). God's people should love him in return (Deut 6:5). If that responsive love is true, it should compel Great Commission obedience.

The Old Testament theology of judgment is particularly helpful in clarifying that just as judgment on God's people is sure, so is his judgment on the nations. This surety of judgment bears directly on the question of the fate of the unevangelized. A misplaced sense of compassion—misplaced in the sense that humans presume that they can be more compassionate than God—leads some to suggest that God only holds the nations accountable to the degree that they have the opportunity to hear the gospel message.[66] According to this thought process, people without access to the word of God can rely on God to reveal himself through other

---

66. See the profile of pluralist and inclusivist views of salvation of unevangelized people in Robert A. Altstadt and Enoch Wan, "The Salvation of the Unevangelized: What the Literature Suggests," *Global Missiology* 2, no. 2 (2005): 1–21. Note the authors' fronting of the need for compassion in engagement with the issue of the unevangelized at the top of page 2.

means such as through philosophical musings on the beauty of nature, sparks of insight received through world religions, or even postmortem confrontations with God himself. Thoughts such as these may have fleetingly coursed through Naomi's mind at the outset of the book of Ruth. Naomi urges her two daughters-in-law to return to Moab and the embrace of the Moabite god Chemosh rather than follow her to Bethlehem in the land of God's people (Ruth 1:1–18). In the contemporary instance of world mission, explicit and clear communication of the gospel indeed incurs a responsibility to respond. However, if other salvation-gaining avenues exist, this responsibility to respond affirmatively to the specific message of the gospel is not primarily a welcome blessing but a burdensome liability. Thus the good news transforms into bad news in this distortion of biblical teaching.

Old Testament prophecy counters the misconception that God maintains some alternative program for the nations other than covenant relationship with him. In this regard it is important to recall that the proclamation of almost every Old Testament prophecy about the fate of gentile nations was to Hebrews, not gentiles. As mentioned previously, these prophecies were indirect speech acts, reminding God's people not to compromise their faith through allying with foreign peoples. Yet prophecies against the nations were also direct speech acts to God's people, announcing the objective fact that the nations stand under God's judgment.

An application of both indirect and direct aspects of these prophecies to missiology generates a reminder that world mission is not interfaith dialogue. God will judge the nations. With or without access to the gospel, the nations are accountable to him. The book of Ruth dramatizes this accountability, in that Ruth 1:14 narrates the moment Orpah kisses Naomi goodbye and begins returning home. For Orpah this is the kiss of death.

In startling contrast, Ruth clings to Naomi.[67] Ruth then vocalizes her seemingly unreasonable decision to remain a destitute widow with her mother-in-law, famously stating, "Your people shall be my people, and your God my God" (Ruth 1:16). In Hebrew there is no capital "G" to

---

67. For a critical treatment of the significance of Ruth's "clinging," see Scott N. Callaham, "But Ruth Clung to Her: Textual Constraints on Ambiguity in Ruth 1:14," *TynBul* 63 (2012): 179–97.

distinguish between gods, thus perhaps allowing the reader to conjecture that life circumstances require Ruth merely to trade one god for another that is a rough equivalent. Yet then Ruth calls specifically on "the LORD" in the following verse, marking a definitive transfer of allegiance that requires specific knowledge of Israel's God. Over several verses of Biblical Hebrew narrative, the sisters-in-law Orpah and Ruth act out the predicament of the nations. As Moabite women they both stand under God's judgment, but in the crucial moment of decision Ruth sets out on the path of life by grasping hold of the God who will never loosen his hold on her.[68]

NEW CREATION

Finally, the Old Testament theology of new creation bears directly on the task of world mission. The new heavens and new earth is the setting that the prophets envision for the new covenant to come into full fruition and for God's redemption of the remnant of the nations to take place. The New Testament book of Hebrews states that Jesus is the mediator of this new covenant, thus further connecting new covenant and new creation (Heb 9:15; 12:24).[69]

A recovery of new-creation theology in mission work faces a preliminary challenge: the need to recover new-creation theology among missionaries and their sending churches. That is to say, the prevailing present state of thinking about eschatology in churches needs to change in order to regain a biblical footing. Specifically, for any number of reasons, one could only wish that somehow Christians would agree to a moratorium on attempts to divine details about God's future unfolding of history. Perhaps one reason is sufficient for the present discussion: the disrepute the church lamentably accrues when apocalyptic predictions reliably prove false.

---

68. Joüon succinctly characterizes the spirit of the book of Ruth by stating that the author wrote "with love." See Paul Joüon, *Ruth: Commentaire philologique et exégétique* (Rome: Pontifical Biblical Institute, 1924), 12.

69. The phrase "new covenant" appears earlier in Heb 8:8 and 8:13, referring to the new covenant of Jer 31:31–34. See the many references to Jesus as mediator and even "guarantor" of the new covenant in Scott W. Hahn, "Kinship by Covenant: A Biblical Theological Study of Covenant Types and Texts in the Old and New Testaments" (PhD diss., Marquette University, 1995).

As for "last things" in the personal realm, popular evangelical Christian thinking attaches almost singular importance to the idea of going to heaven after death, and this emphasis is readily apparent in evangelistic presentation scripts, songs, movies, and multiple accounts of people claiming to possess extrabiblical revelation, for they have visited heaven and returned. Yet contrastingly, the specific idea of individual believers going to heaven after death does not seem to be a major concern in Scripture. Instead of dwelling on death, the Bible celebrates life: bodily resurrection, which will take place in God's renewed creation.[70] The incredible idea of resurrection—so central to the gospel and so relevant to the eternal destiny of believers on the mission field, who, like all humans, ponder the injustice of death—begins in the new-creation theology of the Old Testament. Missionaries should welcome the work of new creation already begun in themselves in their rebirth through the power of the Holy Spirit. Then, as they baptize new brothers and sisters in Christ on the mission field, they should announce that God's new creation is drawing near. The redemption of the nations has begun!

---

70. See N. T. Wright, *The Resurrection of the Son of God*, Christian Origins and the Question of God 3 (Minneapolis: Fortress, 2003), 121-27.

2

NEW TESTAMENT THEOLOGY
AND WORLD MISSION

Wendel Sun

INTRODUCTION

The New Testament is at heart a collection of *missional* texts produced in the context of mission. That is, the documents were written as the early church expanded into new areas and contexts, often in response to the challenges faced by young churches.[1] More fundamentally, as Michael Goheen writes, "the biblical books are products of God's mission."[2] Throughout this chapter, I will argue that Jesus came as a missional Messiah and that his people are to be a missional people. Fittingly, the creation of texts that testify about this Messiah took place within the context of mission. Moreover, these texts were written to carry on the mission of the Messiah. The New Testament documents were intended by the authors to be persuasive accounts of the story of Jesus and the church (Gospels and Acts) or letters to spur on faithfulness to the Messiah (the Epistles). Despite the differences in genre, each document was written with missional purposes: to persuade readers (or hearers) of the truthfulness of the gospel message and to call them to repentance and faith. N. T. Wright aptly summarizes the point: "The purpose of the NT emerges from the

---

1. I. Howard Marshall, *New Testament Theology: Many Witnesses, One Gospel* (Downers Grove, IL: InterVarsity Press, 2004), 34–35.

2. Michael W. Goheen, "A History and Introduction to a Missional Reading of the Bible," in *Reading the Bible Missionally*, ed. Michael W. Goheen (Grand Rapids: Eerdmans, 2016), 3–27, esp. 26.

entire missional agenda of the early church."[3] In other words, in both content and intent, the New Testament is thoroughly missional.

In this chapter we will examine the foundation for all New Testament missional activity: the mission of Jesus. I will argue that the authors of the New Testament understood his mission in Old Testament terms. A significant part of this mission is to (re)create the people of God as those who are united to Jesus the Messiah. Union with Christ entails entering into his story such that his story becomes our story. Consequently, I will argue for a participatory view of the church's mission; the people of God in Christ are to participate in and carry on the mission of Jesus.

THE MISSION OF THE KING

We begin with a brief analysis of Jesus' mission using four major Old Testament themes: Adam, the seed of Abraham, Moses, and Messiah. While many other themes could be selected, I believe these are significant because (1) they occupy a significant place in New Testament theology, and (2) they provide a well-rounded view of Jesus' mission.

JESUS IS THE LAST ADAM WHO RESTORES THE IMAGE OF GOD

While most readers of the New Testament are familiar with Paul's use of Adam in Romans 5 and 1 Corinthians 15, Adamic themes are much more prevalent than is often realized. The following survey will highlight some of the ways the New Testament authors make use of the Adam narratives in explaining the identity and mission of Jesus.[4]

Matthew 1:1 begins the New Testament with an allusion to creation in the words literally translated "book of genesis" (Βίβλος γενέσεως),[5] a phrase found only twice in the LXX: Genesis 2:4 and 5:1. Of particular interest is Genesis 5:1, where the phrase heads Adam's genealogy. Thus Matthew opens his Gospel with reference to origins, presenting the genealogy of Jesus as that of a new Adam. While many rightly note the pattern of Israel's story within Matthew, echoes of Adam feature prominently in

---

3. N. T. Wright, "Reading the New Testament Missionally," in Goheen, *Reading the Bible Missionally*, 175–93, esp. 176.

4. For a fuller treatment of Adamic themes in the Gospels, see Brandon D. Crowe, *The Last Adam: A Theology of the Obedient Life of Jesus in the Gospels* (Grand Rapids: Baker, 2017).

5. R. T. France, *The Gospel of Matthew*, NICNT (Grand Rapids: Eerdmans, 2007), 28.

the opening verses. As Richard Hays notes, "This genealogy prepares the reader to interpret Jesus as the heir of the promises to Abraham, the consummation of Israel's epic story that began in the patriarchal narratives of Genesis."[6] It is unsurprising, then, that Matthew begins Jesus' story similarly to the beginning of Israel's story: the creation/Adam narratives.[7] Interestingly, Luke's genealogy explicitly links Jesus to Adam (Luke 4:38), thus confirming that the connection of Jesus to Adam was a matter of theological reflection in the early church.[8]

Following the explicit mention of Adam in chapter 3, Luke then tells of Jesus' temptations in an Adamic pattern.[9] A face-to-face encounter with Satan has clear similarities to the early chapters of Genesis, but other clues also point to an Adamic background. First, Satan twice challenges Jesus with the words "if you are the Son of God" (4:3, 9). As noted above, Luke also calls Adam the Son of God. Moreover, the serpent's challenge to Eve in Genesis 3 likewise tempts the first couple to question their relational status with God when he claims that only by eating the fruit will they be "like God" (Gen 3:5). Thus the use of "Son of God" functions on a literary level by implicitly stating that Jesus is the Son of God and on a theological level by connecting Jesus' temptation to that of Adam.

Second, like Adam, Jesus is first tempted with food. Unlike Adam, Jesus has no other food and is in the wilderness instead of a garden, yet does not sin.[10] Third, the third temptation (worship me and I'll give you the world's kingdoms) recalls the desire of Adam and Eve to rule independently of God. Satan promises the primeval couple that eating will give them God-like knowledge such that they will be their own authority.

---

6. Richard B. Hays, *Echoes of Scripture in the Gospels* (Waco, TX: Baylor University Press, 2016), 110.

7. For textual similarities between the Old Testament Adam and Israel stories, see Seth D. Postell, *Adam as Israel: Genesis 1–3 as the Introduction to the Torah and Tanakh* (Eugene, OR: Pickwick, 2011), who argues for close textual connections between the two narratives. Jewish reflection on Adam in the Second Temple period most often pictured Adam as a Jewish ancestor and his story as a part of Israel's story. See John R. Levison, *Portraits of Adam in Early Judaism: From Sirach to 2 Baruch*, Journal for the Study of the Pseudepigrapha Supplement Series 1 (Sheffield: JSOT, 1988).

8. While John includes no genealogy, John 1 carries explicit creational themes.

9. G. K. Beale, *A New Testament Biblical Theology: The Unfolding of the Old Testament in the New* (Grand Rapids: Baker Academic, 2011), 391.

10. Darrell L. Bock, *Luke 1:1–9:50*, BECNT (Grand Rapids: Baker Academic, 1994), 371.

Similarly, Satan tempts Jesus with authority apart from the Father, which Jesus rejects.[11] Fourth, the last temptation evokes Satan's words to Eve: "you will not surely die." Satan encourages Jesus to jump from the highest point of the temple knowing that he will not die. Finally, and in sharp contrast to the first Adam, Jesus is victorious over the enemy, marking the beginning of Jesus' continuous battle—and triumph—over Satan, evoking the promise of Genesis 3:15. In short, numerous subtle allusions to the early chapters of Genesis picture the temptation narrative as a recapitulation of Eden with Jesus as the new, faithful Adam.[12]

While some of the above references to Adam in the Gospels are subtle and may be unfamiliar, Paul explicitly refers to Jesus as a new or last Adam.[13] The first of these (in canonical order) is found in Romans 5. Through the progression of thought within Romans, Paul argues that all people, Jew and gentile alike, are bound up in Adamic sin.[14] In Romans 5:12–21, he contrasts Adam and Christ in order to magnify the work of Christ and adequately to root the identity of the Roman church, Jew and gentile together, in him. Our discussion focuses on the mission of Christ over against the Adamic background. One key observation is that when Paul points to the sin of Adam, he most likely refers to more than fruit eating. Adam's sin is his failure to fulfill the human vocation of caring for God's world under his rule.[15] Moreover, Adam and Eve are tasked with

---

11. David E. Garland, *Luke*, ZECNT (Grand Rapids: Zondervan, 2012), 188.

12. Matthew's account is similar, but seems more clearly to echo Israel's wilderness wanderings than Adam's story. Mark adds a couple of interesting details that potentially support an Adamic reading. First, Mark describes Jesus as being in the wilderness "with the wild animals" (μετὰ τῶν θηρίων), possibly recalling Adam in Eden with the animals. Second, following the temptations, angels come to minister to Jesus. By contrast, the angels in Eden block Adam's way to the tree of life (Gen 3:24).

13. An additional important Adamic thread in the Gospels that cannot be adequately explored here is Jesus' self-referential use of "Son of Man." As Beale, *New Testament Biblical Theology*, 83–84, 390–401, and N. T. Wright, *The New Testament and the People of God*, Christian Origins and the Question of God 1 (Atlanta: Augsburg Fortress, 1992), 291–97, argue, Jesus' use of the term most likely alludes to Dan 7, where the "Son of Man" is given an everlasting kingdom. The text of Dan 7 echoes Gen 1–2, thus giving an Adamic flavor to "Son of Man" language. For an analysis of interpretive options of the term, see Mogens Müller, *The Expression "Son of Man" and the Development of Christology: A History of Interpretation* (London: Equinox, 2008).

14. Although space does not allow a full argument here, I believe Paul alludes to the Adam narrative at least four other times in Romans: 1:18–32; 3:23; 7:7–12; and 8:18–21, 29. See Wendel Sun, *A New People in Christ: Adam, Israel, and Union with Christ in Romans* (Eugene, OR: Pickwick, 2018), 40–105.

15. N. T. Wright, "Romans," in *NIB* 10:393–770, esp. 526.

"multiplying" and "filling the earth" with the image of God. That is, God's people are to fill God's world with reflections of his glory. As G. K. Beale argues, "God's ultimate goal in creation was to magnify his glory through-out the earth by means of his faithful image-bearers inhabiting the world in obedience to the divine mandate."[16] Thus Adam's sin is ultimately a fail-ure in *mission*.

Paul draws attention to this failure in Romans 5:12–14 by arguing that sin entered the world through Adam and therefore death spread to all through sin. Instead of filling the earth with God's glory, Adam's sin led to a world saturated with sin and death. The obedience of Jesus leads not simply to a reset, but to justification and eternal life that far exceed the effects of Adam's disobedience. The link between Adam and Jesus is the fact that their actions have serious consequences for those iden-tified with them. Jesus not only obeys where Adam failed, but he fulfills and escalates Adam's mission. Jesus reigns as Lord, and those rightly identified with him reign alongside him. Indeed, Christ comes as the true image of God to conform believers to that true image (Rom 8:30).

In 1 Corinthians 15, Paul touches on similar themes with regard to Adam and Christ. The primary theological topic of 1 Corinthians 15 is res-urrection, which leads Paul to emphasize the resurrection of Christ over against the sin of Adam with their respective consequences: "In Adam all die, so also in Christ shall all be made alive" (1 Cor 15:22). Paul again picks up and develops the theme in 15:45. Here Paul creatively quotes and interprets Genesis 2:7, linking the creation of Adam with the life-giving resurrection of Jesus.[17] For our purposes, it is important to note the restor-ative work of Jesus. Though we now bear the (fallen) image of Adam, we will bear the true (restored) image of God in Christ. While Adam's failure brought death and destruction, Jesus brought life and restoration.

What are the implications of Christ's work of restoration for under-standing his mission? First, the Adamic background of Christ's mission alerts us to its scope. Christ came to restore God's people and God's world. He lives as the true human being and thereby restores God's image and

---

16. G. K. Beale, *The Temple and the Church's Mission: A Biblical Theology of the Dwelling Place of God* (Downers Grove, IL: InterVarsity Press, 2004), 82.

17. See the discussion in Gordon D. Fee, *Pauline Christology* (Peabody, MA: Hendrickson, 2007), 114–19.

allows those in him to become all God created humanity to be. By completing Adam's failed mission, Jesus moves creation toward the goal of filling the earth with God's glory, or, as Beale argues, becoming a worldwide temple.[18]

Second, Christ as the *resurrected* new Adam inaugurates the new creation. John 20 echoes much of the creation story of Genesis 1–2 and pictures Jesus' resurrection as new creation. The theme of renewed creation runs throughout John's story, climaxing with the resurrection account.[19] Paul clearly argues similarly in 1 Corinthians 15, as we noted above. The biblical story culminates with the new heavens and the new earth, which Revelation pictures in Edenic terms (Rev 21–22). Christ's mission, then, was largely about new creation.[20]

Third, the Adamic background undergirds the kingly mission of Christ. Created in God's image, Adam was to have dominion over all creation under God's rule (Gen 1:28). In his rebellion, Adam fails in this rule and allows creation (the serpent) to rule over him. As the last Adam, Christ restores humanity's rule over creation (demonstrated in the nature miracles) and takes up Adam's failed mission. It is significant that in many New Testament passages that allude to Adam, kingship themes are in the near context. Indeed, as Hans Hübner notes, kingship "is the central idea of Christology" in 1 Corinthians 15.[21] Christ is the resurrected King who rules over all creation.

JESUS IS THE SEED OF ABRAHAM
WHO FULFILLS COVENANT PROMISES

From the opening chapter of the New Testament, it is clear that the authors believe Jesus to be the promised seed of Abraham. Indeed, Matthew 1:1 identifies Jesus as υἱοῦ Ἀβραάμ (son of Abraham), immediately linking the story Matthew will tell with the promises given to the patriarch. Luke

---

18. Beale, *Temple and the Church's Mission*, 387.

19. Jeannine K. Brown, "Creation's Renewal in the Gospel of John," *Catholic Biblical Quarterly* 72 (2010): 275–90. See especially 279–83 for Brown's analysis of possible allusions to Genesis in John 20.

20. See J. Richard Middleton, *A New Heaven and a New Earth: Reclaiming Biblical Eschatology* (Grand Rapids: Baker, 2014), 155–77.

21. Hans Hübner, *Biblische Theologie des Neuen Testaments* (Göttingen: Vandenhoeck & Ruprecht, 1990–1995), 3:200.

likewise mentions Abraham at the beginning of his Gospel, but gives even more weight to the significance of the covenant promises. Two important characters, Mary and Zechariah, understand the events in Luke 1 as fulfilling promises. First, Mary concludes the Magnificat with praise to God for his help and for remembering his mercy (μνησθῆναι ἐλέους) to Israel, "as he spoke to our fathers, to Abraham and to his offspring forever" (Luke 1:55). Mary has just heard the news of her pregnancy and that of her cousin Elizabeth, which she believes to be in fulfillment of God's covenant promises to Abraham. Moreover, the use of ἔλεος is significant, as it is a common LXX translation of חֶסֶד ("loving kindness"). For example, Psalm 98:3 (97:3 LXX), to which Luke 1:54 probably alludes, proclaims that God "has remembered his steadfast love (חֶסֶד; ἔλεος) and faithfulness to the house of Israel." For Mary, the vindication of Israel is on the basis of God's covenant faithfulness, which is ultimately displayed in the coming of the Messiah.[22] Within Luke's Gospel, a pattern is established to set the story of Jesus within the wider story of Abraham and Israel.

Second, when Zechariah's mouth is opened following the birth of his son John, he also praises God for "remember[ing] his holy covenant" (μνησθῆναι διαθήκης ἁγίας αὐτοῦ) with Abraham (Luke 1:72–73) to bring about the rescuing of his people that leads to service (Luke 1:74).[23] The narrative pattern of barrenness and the birth of a son in old age may have evoked the memory of Abraham and Sarah in early readers and hearers.[24] Like Mary, Zechariah believes the birth of his son, which is the prelude to the coming of the Messiah, to be God's great fulfillment of these promises. As Darrell Bock notes, "The idea of remembering is not merely cognitive, but refers to God's bringing his promise into operation."[25]

The significance of God's keeping covenant promises extends beyond ethnic Israel. Luke's emphasis on Abraham in his opening chapter is probably intended to evoke the wider promises to the patriarch, not least the

---

22. David W. Pao and Eckhard J. Schnabel, "Luke," in *Commentary on the New Testament Use of the Old Testament*, ed. D. A. Carson and G. K. Beale (Grand Rapids: Baker, 2007), 262.

23. Note also the use of ἔλεος in 1:72.

24. Joel B. Green, "The Problem of a Beginning: Israel's Scriptures in Luke 1–2," *BBR* 4 (1994): 61–86.

25. Bock, *Luke 1:1–9:50*, 184.

promise to bless "all the families of the earth" (Gen 12:3; 22:18).[26] The theme of salvation for all nations features significantly in Luke-Acts. Throughout both volumes, the blessing of the nations rests on God's fulfillment of his promises to Abraham through the life, death, and resurrection of Jesus. Though but one example among many, Peter's sermon in Acts 3 clearly connects the spread of the gospel to the covenant promises given to Abraham, with particular emphasis on blessing the nations. In Acts 3:13 Peter introduces Jesus as one glorified by "the God of Abraham, the God of Isaac, and the God of Jacob." Then, picking up the "ends of the earth" from Acts 1:8, Peter emphasizes the covenant promises to bless the nations, which are now enacted in the resurrection of Jesus (Acts 3:25).[27] This point is further developed in Paul's letters, but also formed a significant part of Luke's understanding of the gospel.[28]

Paul argues strongly for the fulfillment of covenant promises to Abraham through Jesus in Romans 4 and Galatians 3. Having claimed that God is the God of all, Jew and gentile alike, in Romans 3:29–30, Paul extends the argument further in Romans 4 by defining the family of Abraham on the basis of faith. For our purposes, it is important to note quotations from the Abraham narratives. While Genesis 15:6 features prominently throughout the chapter, Paul twice quotes Genesis 17:5, in which God promises that Abraham will be the "father of many nations" (Rom 4:17–18). In 4:18 Paul also draws on Genesis 15:5, where God promises that Abraham's family will be as numerous as the stars. The precise means of blessing is withheld until the end of the chapter, but is crystal clear: "[Christ] was delivered up for our trespasses and raised for our justification" (Rom 4:25). While there are exegetical difficulties with this verse,[29] Paul undoubtedly wants to communicate that the blessing of Abraham comes

---

26. Hays, *Echoes of Scripture in the Gospels*, 198–99.

27. Thomas R. Schreiner, *New Testament Theology: Magnifying God in Christ* (Grand Rapids: Baker, 2008), 296.

28. From a historical perspective, there is possible Pauline influence on Luke, as Luke accompanied Paul on some missionary journeys (Acts 16:10–17; 20:5–15; 21:1–18, 27–28; Col 4:14). It is also possible that Luke's readers would have been familiar with Paul's writings. See Stanley E. Porter, "Luke: Companion or Disciple of Paul?," in *Paul and the Gospels: Christologies, Controversies, and Convergences*, ed. Michael F. Bird and Joel Willitts (London: T&T Clark, 2011), 146–68.

29. See the discussion in Richard N. Longenecker, *Epistle to the Romans*, NIGTC (Grand Rapids: Eerdmans, 2016), 535–37.

to the gentiles by faith in the crucified and resurrected Messiah, thereby creating Abraham's worldwide family.

In Galatians 3, Paul similarly draws on the Abraham story in order to argue for a multiethnic people of God not by "works of the law" but through faith/faithfulness.[30] For Paul, these are questions of primary identity. Are God's people to be marked ethnically? Or is there some other mark that constitutes their fundamental identity? Paul argues that the Scriptures are clear. God's people are marked by faith (Gal 3:6), a result of the work of the faithful Messiah (Gal 3:13, 22), which in turn brings the blessings of Abraham to the nations (Gal 3:14). The covenantal promises still stand, but are only fulfilled in Christ.[31] Jesus is the true seed of Abraham, and those rightly connected to him become the family of Abraham. Moreover, Paul argues that the inclusion of the gentiles in the family of faith is at the very heart of the gospel. In Galatians 3:8, Paul claims that God proclaimed the gospel to Abraham in the promise "in you shall all the nations be blessed."

How does the above analysis help us understand the mission of the Messiah? Several points are worth mentioning. First, Jesus came to bring the promised blessing of Abraham to God's people. While much New Testament scholarship has focused on the nature of justification by faith, it is clear that Paul was more concerned with the blessing of Abraham coming to the gentiles in fulfillment of the covenant promises. Jesus' death and resurrection fulfills God's covenant promises by calling all people to faith in the faithful Messiah. Thus, Jesus came on a covenant-fulfilling mission. Christ's fulfillment of covenant promises to Abraham overlaps with the Adamic background of his mission, since the covenant with Abraham was closely tied to creation. That is, when God promised to bless Abraham and, through him, the world (Gen 12:1–3), he was promising to restore the creational blessings given to Adam and Eve (Gen 1:28). Simultaneously evoking both Adam and Abraham places heavy emphasis on the faithfulness of God to his creational intentions and his covenantal promises.

---

30. On the πίστις Χριστοῦ debate, see Michael F. Bird and Preston M. Sprinkle, eds., *The Faith of Jesus Christ: Exegetical, Biblical, and Theological Studies* (Peabody, MA: Hendrickson, 2009).

31. Udo Schnelle, *Theology of the New Testament*, trans. M. Eugene Boring (Grand Rapids: Baker, 2009), 332.

Second, the Abrahamic foundation of Christ's mission underscores that the Messiah comes for "all nations." It is very significant that the New Testament authors in the Gospels, the Pauline Epistles, and Acts (Peter's sermon) draw explicit attention to the promise to bless all nations through Abraham as they reflect on the mission of Jesus.[32] It is not just that Jesus is the true seed of Abraham, but that as the true seed, he is the one through whom God brings blessing to all peoples.

Finally, the connection between the Abrahamic covenant and the mission of Jesus redefines the family of Abraham around Jesus. For most societies, including that of the first-century Greco-Roman and Jewish worlds, family identity is fundamental.[33] Thus one can scarcely overstate the importance of the New Testament's reorientation of family identity, such that Abraham's true family members are those rightly related to Jesus. The mission of Jesus was to give a new identity to his people based not on ethnicity, but on faith.

JESUS IS THE PROPHET LIKE MOSES WHO LEADS THE NEW EXODUS

In addition to a new Adam and the seed of Abraham, the New Testament also presents Jesus as the prophet like Moses promised in Deuteronomy 18.[34] The "new exodus" theme emerges in the Gospels, and Jesus is pictured as the one who leads it. The launch point is again Matthew 1. Mixed in the Abraham narrative background and the Davidic kingship themes are also allusions to exodus themes. Even the basic pattern of the Matthean narrative reflects a Mosaic background.[35] The messianic mission statement in Matthew 1:21 ("he will save his people from their sins")

---

32. Though not mentioned above, the inclusion of gentile women in the genealogy of Matt 1 probably hints at the "all nations" nature of Christ's mission. If so, the subtle but significant appearance of gentiles in Matt 1 forms a nice bookend with the Great Commission in Matt 28. See Hays, *Echoes of Scripture in the Gospels*, 112.

33. Larry W. Hurtado, *Destroyer of the Gods: Early Christian Distinctiveness in the Roman World* (Waco, TX: Baylor University Press, 2016), 77-104.

34. Richard Bauckham, *The Testimony of the Beloved Disciple: Narrative, History, and Theology in the Gospel of John* (Grand Rapids: Baker, 2007), 213-21, surveys Second Temple Jewish expectations of a messianic prophet like Moses.

35. Dale C. Allison Jr., *The New Moses: A Matthean Typology* (Eugene, OR: Wipf & Stock, 2013), 140, claims that the birth and infancy narratives are "permeated with Mosaic motifs."

may hint toward exodus-like rescue. As Moses led his people in rescue, so Jesus will rescue his people from their sins.[36]

The similarities to Moses' birth narrative are many and obvious. In both accounts, there is an evil king (Pharaoh and Herod) who seeks to kill male Israelite babies. In both stories, parents are forced to hide a child, and both babies are rescued by God's intervention. Furthermore, the allusions move beyond similar narrative patterns. Matthew quotes Hosea 11:1 in Matthew 2:15 and pictures Jesus' return from Egypt as a new exodus. Thus Jesus repeats Israel's exodus while inaugurating the promised new exodus.[37] While the accent is on Jesus as Israel (see below), this does not exclude echoes of Moses.[38] The Lord's words to Joseph in Matthew 2:20 (τεθνήκασιν γὰρ οἱ ζητοῦντες τὴν ψυχὴν τοῦ παιδίου; "for those who sought the child's life are dead") confirm the point as they are a direct quotation of the LXX of Exodus 4:19 (τεθνήκασιν γὰρ πάντες οἱ ζητοῦντές σου τὴν ψυχήν).[39] In the context of Exodus 4, the Lord is calling Moses to send him to Egypt to lead the first exodus. Matthew mirrors the language of Moses' call, suggesting that Jesus will lead the new exodus.

The Sermon on the Mount evokes memories of Moses receiving the law from the Lord on a mountain.[40] Moreover, the content of the sermon as an authoritative interpretation of the law pictures Jesus as a new and superior Moses.[41] Matthew's account of the transfiguration contains striking parallels to Moses in Exodus 24.[42] After six days of the glorious cloud covering the mountain, Moses goes up with three others (Exod 24:9, 15–16). Jesus

---

36. In context, the rescue from sin is most likely a reference to national sins that led to exile. Matthew's genealogy presents the coming of the Messiah as the end of exile, which fits with the new-exodus motif.

37. Ulrich Luz, *Matthew 1–7*, Hermeneia (Minneapolis: Fortress, 2007), 121. On the use of Hos 11:1 in Matt 2:15, see John H. Sailhamer, "Hosea 11:1 and Matthew 2:15," *WTJ* 63 (2001): 87–96; and G. K. Beale, "The Use of Hosea 11:1 in Matthew 2:15: One More Time," *JETS* 55 (2012): 697–715. While differing on the details, both Sailhamer and Beale argue that Matthew's use is derived from the wider context of Hosea.

38. Allison, *New Moses*, 142.

39. Charles L. Quarles, *A Theology of Matthew: Jesus Revealed as Deliverer, King, and Incarnate Creator* (Phillipsburg, PA: P&R, 2013), 36–37. The wider context suggests further parallels. See Allison, *New Moses*, 142–44.

40. The words ἀνέβη εἰς τὸ ὄρος ("he went up on the mountain") in Matt 5:1 probably allude to Moses' ascent of Mount Sinai in Exod 19:3 (ἀνέβη εἰς τὸ ὄρος).

41. Quarles, *Theology of Matthew*, 37.

42. Quarles, *Theology of Matthew*, 42–43.

goes up to the mountain with Peter, James, and John "after six days" (Matt 17:1). Jesus is transfigured, shining forth divine glory. In Exodus 34, Moses also shines with divine glory. In both stories, God speaks from the cloud (Exod 24:16; Matt 17:5). Moses (along with Elijah) appears at the transfiguration, further linking the two. Luke adds that Moses and Elijah speak with Jesus concerning his ἔξοδος (exodus; Luke 9:31). Thus, the Evangelists present Jesus as a new, but better Moses. While Moses could merely reflect divine glory, Jesus himself is divinely glorious. The divine command to "listen to him" in Matthew 17:5 identifies Jesus as the prophet like Moses (Deut 18:17–18).

Jesus is also presented as the prophet like Moses in John's Gospel. A full treatment is not possible here, but a few clear references will suffice.[43] The prologue, while clearly focused on the new creation through the coming of the Messiah, sets up the Moses-Christ connection in 1:17. Jesus, like Moses, is a mediator; however, what he mediates is superior to what Moses mediated: grace and truth rather than the law.[44] Philip most likely has the prophet-like-Moses theme in mind when he claims to have found the one about whom Moses wrote (John 1:45). Additional hints to Jesus' Moses-like mission are found in John 3:14–15, where Jesus compares himself to the bronze serpent lifted by Moses in the wilderness, and in John 4:19, where the Samaritan woman recognizes Jesus as a prophet.[45] While the reference in John 3:14–15 is to the serpent rather than Moses, I suggest that the contrast with Moses remains. While Moses lifted the serpent, Jesus himself will be lifted up and bring a greater healing. Indeed, this healing is for "all who believe."

Twice in John's Gospel people respond to Jesus' ministry and teaching by suggesting that he could be "the Prophet" (John 6:14; 7:40). Clearly such a claim is pregnant with eschatological meaning derived from Deuteronomy 18. As Richard Bauckham notes, both instances take place around Jewish festivals that arouse hope for a coming prophetic leader:

---

43. See David W. Coker, "Jesus as the Prophet like Moses in the Fourth Gospel" (ThM thesis, Southeastern Baptist Theological Seminary, 2012).

44. Andreas J. Köstenberger, *John*, BECNT (Grand Rapids: Baker, 2004), 48.

45. See Hannah S. An, "The Prophet like Moses (Deut. 18:15–18) and the Woman at the Well (John 4:7–30) in Light of the Dead Sea Scrolls," *The Expository Times* 127 (2016): 469–78.

Passover (John 6) and the Feast of Tabernacles (John 7).[46] The contexts of the two instances lend further weight to the identity of Jesus as the prophet like Moses. In John 6:1-5, Jesus feeds a crowd in the wilderness, echoing the gift of manna given to Israel in the wilderness. Nevertheless, Jesus is greater than Moses because while Moses could not give the bread himself, Jesus *is the bread of life* (John 6:30-40). In John 7 the crowd is divided over Jesus, with some believing him to be "the Prophet." They respond to his claim to give water that eternally alleviates thirst, evoking Moses giving water to the Israelites in the wilderness. John explains that this water refers to the Spirit, further demonstrating Jesus' superiority to Moses.[47]

John 12:44-50 is a significant passage in which Jesus reflects on his messianic mission. Jesus comes as a light to rescue those who dwell in darkness (John 12:46). The main emphasis is on the words of Jesus. Those who reject these words do so to their own detriment, as Jesus' words are the very words of God. John 12:47-50 alludes to Deuteronomy 18:18-19, where God promises to send a prophet like Moses. God will put his words into the mouth of this prophet, and those who do not obey them will be held accountable. Thus, Jesus understood his own mission in prophet-like-Moses terms.[48]

In several letters, Paul describes salvation in Christ as a new-exodus experience. One clear example is Galatians 4:1-11. Paul is addressing a church mired by the temptation to add to the gospel. Here, at the heart of the letter, he encourages the Galatians to live in light of their new identity as the people of God in Christ. He uses the exodus story to do so and thereby claims that a new exodus has taken place in Christ. In Galatians 4, the believers were formerly "enslaved" (Gal 4:3, 8) but have now been set free through the sovereign action of God. God sent his Son to redeem slaves and lead a new exodus (Gal 4:4-5).[49] As the people of Israel were called God's son (Exod 4:23; Hos 11:1), so those set free in Christ are sons in the Son and therefore heirs (Gal 4:6-7). Having been set free, they should

---

46. Bauckham, *Testimony of the Beloved Disciple*, 222.

47. Bauckham, *Testimony of the Beloved Disciple*, 222. Bauckham notes the allusion to Ps 78:16, which reflects on the water from the rock.

48. Köstenberger, *John*, 394.

49. N. T. Wright, *Paul and the Faithfulness of God* (Minneapolis: Fortress, 2013), 656-58.

not turn back to "Egypt" like the Israelites (Gal 4:9–11; see also Num 14:1–4). Rather, they should follow the Spirit given to lead them as the cloud and fire led Israel in the wilderness.[50]

In sum, two points seem particularly noteworthy with regard to Jesus' mission. First, Jesus as the new Moses comes on a *prophetic* mission. Moses was the mediator of God's word to Israel. Jesus is the Word made flesh (John 1:14) and the authoritative interpreter of the law (Matt 5–7). Moses was a prophet; Jesus is the prophet like Moses who perfectly speaks God's words. Jesus is the final and fullest revelation of God (Heb 1:1–4). Moses gave God's commands to Israel; Jesus commands his followers to take his words to the nations (Matt 28:16–20). Jesus is the true prophet.

Second, as the new Moses, Jesus *leads the new exodus*. Christ came on a mission of redemption from the slavery to sin that encumbers all people. He leads the new exodus through his death and resurrection, fulfilling the Isaianic promises of new exodus leading to new creation.[51] As Michael Bird puts it, "The God of the exodus has brought a new exodus through Jesus' resurrection, which is testified in Israel's sacred traditions as the long-awaited goal that God had been promising his people."[52] Thus, the mission of Jesus includes the redemption from sin and the establishment of those who believe in him as the new-exodus, new-covenant people of God.

JESUS IS ISRAEL'S MESSIAH WHO CREATES THE NEW PEOPLE OF GOD

In many ways, this last category encompasses the above three. That is, Jesus' messianic mission includes his work as the new Adam, the seed of Abraham, and the new Moses. Indeed, the above aspects of Christ's mission can be seen as subsets of the overarching messianic mission. Nevertheless, we bring in this last identifier—Messiah—in order to round

---

50. Similar themes are expounded in Rom 8. See Sylvia C. Keesmaat, "Exodus and the Intertextual Transformation of Tradition in Romans 8.14–30," *Journal for the Study of the New Testament* 54 (1994): 29–56.

51. See Rikki E. Watts, "Consolation or Confrontation: Isaiah 40–55 and the Delay of the New Exodus," *TynBul* 41 (1990): 31–59; and Watts, "Echoes from the Past: Israel's Ancient Traditions and the Destiny of the Nations in Isaiah 40–55," *JSOT* 28 (2004): 481–508.

52. Michael F. Bird, *An Anomalous Jew: Paul among Jews, Greeks, and Romans* (Grand Rapids: Eerdmans, 2016), 125.

out our examination of the mission of Jesus. Thus, this section will focus more narrowly on the messianic mission to create a new people of God.[53]

The four canonical Gospels clearly present Jesus as the promised Messiah.[54] The more pressing question relates to the nature of Jesus' messianic mission. Here we focus on the restorative mission of Jesus with regard to God's people. Having introduced Jesus as the Messiah, the son of David (Matt 1:1, 17), Matthew defines the messianic mission via the words of the angel: "he will save his people from their sins" (Matt 1:21). The term λαός ("people") typically refers to historic Israel, but the context points to a more universal meaning.[55] Not only has Matthew linked this mission to the Abrahamic promises, but he also includes gentile women in Jesus' genealogy.[56] Moreover, Matthew links this mission to the prophecy of Isaiah 7; this child is "God with us." God himself, in the coming of the Messiah, is completing his own mission of restoration. It is also no accident that this definition of the mission closely follows on the mention of exile (Matt 1:17). In short, the Davidic King has arrived in the birth of Jesus, the one who will restore his people. It is understandable, therefore, that one of Jesus' primary teaching topics is the kingdom of God. He is the King who brings the kingdom.

We noted above that Matthew presents Jesus as a new Israel in the early narratives of the Gospel. The narrative sequence of return from Egypt (Matt 2:13-23), baptism (Matt 3:13-16), and temptation in the wilderness (Matt 4:1-11) closely parallels the story of Israel. These events, combined with the repeated references to Jesus as the Son of God (Matt 2:15; 3:17; 4:3, 6) as well as "king of the Jews" (Matt 2:2), identify Jesus as

---

53. This emphasis does not deny all the contours of the term "Messiah" in both Second Temple Judaism and the NT. It is merely to limit the scope of the investigation to a single aspect of the messianic mission.

54. There were varying understandings of "Messiah" in Second Temple Judaism. See John J. Collins, *The Scepter and the Star: The Messiahs of the Dead Sea Scrolls and Other Ancient Literature* (New York: Doubleday, 1995); Matthew V. Novenson, *Christ among the Messiahs: Christ Language in Paul and Messiah Language in Ancient Judaism* (New York: Oxford University Press, 2015), 12-33; Wright, *New Testament and the People of God*, 307-20. My purpose here is limited to the view of Jesus' messianic mission in the New Testament in regard to the restoration of God's people.

55. Contra Luz, *Matthew 1-7*, 95, who believes the term has no immediate application to the church.

56. Hays, *Echoes of Scripture in the Gospels*, 111-12.

the Messiah-King. He calls twelve disciples, matching the twelve tribes of Israel (Matt 10:1–4). Thus, Jesus represents Israel as the long-awaited king who reconstitutes his people. He does so by recapitulating Israel's history, succeeding where Israel failed.[57]

Similar restoration themes can be found in direct connection to Jesus' messianic ministry in the other Gospels. Mark opens his Gospel with the identification of Jesus as Messiah (Mark 1:1), and the rest of the Gospel fills out just what kind of messiah he is. In Mark 1:14–15, Jesus begins his ministry with the announcement of the arrival of the kingdom of God and a summons to repent and believe. Jesus the Messiah-King has arrived, and with him the kingdom of God. As Robert Stein notes, "Jesus surely taught a great deal more than the fifteen words making up his message in 1:15, but Mark wants his readers to see Jesus's announcement of the kingdom's coming and the necessity of repentance and faith as the heart of Jesus's preaching."[58] The call to repent evokes the many prophetic exhortations to Israel to end the exile through repentance.[59] As such, the arrival of the Messiah marks the end of Israel's exile via repenting and believing the gospel: the proclamation of Jesus as the Messiah-King.

The arrival of the messianic kingdom is marked at once by the defeat of the powers in Jesus' exorcisms (Mark 1:21–28) and the healing of disease (Mark 1:39–45). Yet Peter's confession of Jesus as Messiah is a major turning point in Mark's Gospel (Mark 8:29). Though correct in broad terms, Peter scarcely understands exactly what he confesses. Jesus immediately provides clarification: the true Messiah is the Son of Man who suffers, dies, and rises from the dead (Mark 8:31), an announcement Jesus will make two more times in the near context (Mark 9:30–32; 10:32–34). Thus the restoration comes about through his cross and resurrection. Thus the messianic mission is restoration through resurrection.

The messianic mission extends beyond the geographic and ethnic boundaries of Israel. Indeed, Israel's vocation was to be a "kingdom of priests and a holy nation" (Exod 19:6). That is, they were to bring God's

---

57. Frank Thielman, *Theology of the New Testament: A Canonical and Synthetic Approach* (Grand Rapids: Zondervan, 2005), 95–96.

58. Robert H. Stein, *Mark*, BECNT (Grand Rapids: Baker, 2008), 70.

59. N. T. Wright, *Jesus and the Victory of God*, Christian Origins and the Question of God 2 (Minneapolis: Fortress, 1996), 248–49.

blessing to the world. Thus, Jesus as the new Israel has the nations as his end goal, which relates closely to the other missional themes discussed above. Nevertheless, it bears repeating here: Israel's Messiah is also the Savior of the world. As Goheen has aptly noted, this concept fits perfectly within the narrative trajectory of the Bible: "The movement of God's mission is from one place (Israel) to the ends of the earth, and from one nation (Israel) to all nations."[60] Jesus is not just Israel's king; he is the king of all nations.

Another clear indication that Jesus is the Messiah who restores God's people is the scene of the Last Supper. With his humiliation mere hours away, Jesus shares the Passover meal with his disciples. At the meal he institutes the Lord's Supper, which served as a reminder of Christ's death for the coming generations of believers. Two points are particularly significant for our purposes. First, the Passover setting is crucial for understanding the meaning of the Supper. The Passover was celebrated in remembrance of Israel's rescue from Egypt, which established the nation as God's chosen people. Likewise, the Supper marks the restoration of God's people through the death and resurrection of Jesus. Second, Jesus explicitly announces that his blood will inaugurate the new covenant. Israel's hope in exile was the future new covenant (Jer 31:31–34). Jesus proclaims that this hope has become reality in his death. Thus, the death and resurrection of the Messiah marks the making of the new covenant through which God's people are restored.

Paul also identifies Jesus as Israel's Messiah who has come to restore God's people (including the gentiles). Romans 1:1–4 is one of Paul's clearest statements on the gospel and highlights the role of Jesus as Messiah. Indeed, Paul is the servant of "Messiah Jesus" (Χριστοῦ Ἰησοῦ). For our purposes here, I want to emphasize the kingship of Jesus. The gospel is about the Son of God who is of the seed of David. The title "Son of God" alone carries royal connotations, most likely drawing on Psalm 2:7 ("You are my Son").[61] Further emphasizing the kingly status of Jesus, Paul includes a parallel statement that Jesus is "descended from David."[62] While these

---

60. Goheen, "History," 22.

61. Schnelle, *Theology of the New Testament*, 173–74.

62. Larry W. Hurtado, "Jesus' Divine Sonship in Paul's Epistle to the Romans," in *Romans and the People of God*, ed. Sven K. Soderlund and N. T. Wright (Grand Rapids: Eerdmans, 1999), 217–33, esp. 225–27.

terms have garnered much scholarly discussion, Paul unambiguously defines the gospel in royal terms: Jesus is Israel's promised Messiah-King.[63] Moreover, the gospel is about the Son of God who was designated (ὁρισθέντος) as such by the Spirit through his resurrection. Paul includes Christ's resurrection as an important part of the gospel message because the resurrection confirms Jesus' status as Messiah, Son of God. For Paul, this is particularly important as the resurrection of Jesus marks the beginning "of God's long-promised new age," as Wright puts it.[64]

Many more passages could be mentioned, but the point is clear. Jesus is Israel's Messiah who restores God's worldwide people among all nations (see also Phil 2:6–11; Eph 1:20–23). Like the other themes explored above, this theme yields significant implications for understanding the mission of Jesus. First, as Israel's Messiah, Jesus came on a *corporate* mission. That is, he comes to restore the people of God. Of course, the restoration of a people necessarily involves the redemption of individuals, but the corporate aspect remains primary. Second, Jesus comes on a mission of *fulfillment*. That is, he completes the vocation originally given to Israel (and Adam). Finally, the Messiah completes his mission through *suffering, death,* and *resurrection*. This Messiah shockingly brings about restoration through suffering. He (re)creates a people through his own death.

CONCLUSION

The above categories are intended to help us view the mission of Jesus from various angles and should not be understood as different "parts" of the mission. It would not be possible to separate the words and works of Christ into these categories. Rather, Old Testament themes give a fuller picture of his mission. Reflecting on the baptism of Jesus, Beale strikes each of the above notes of the messianic symphony:

> Jesus's baptism signifies not only the beginning of a new exodus but also a new creation, since he has come to reverse the curses of the fall (through his healings, cross, and resurrection). . . . Jesus

---

63. Fee, *Pauline Christology*, 242. Contra Joseph A. Fitzmyer, *Romans: A New Translation with Introduction and Commentary,* Anchor Bible 33 (New York: Doubleday, 1993), 235, who claims "Son of God" has no messianic connotation.

64. Wright, "Romans," 419.

steps directly into the land of promise to begin his new creation/ exodus mission after his baptism, which . . . is but a foreshadowing of the ultimate promised land of the new creation. Thus, Christ begins to rule over the powers of evil in beginning fulfillment of the Adamic commission to rule.[65]

A number of additional themes could be probed to complete the portrait of the Messiah's mission, but the above are some of the most significant in the New Testament.[66] Moreover, these missional contours drawn from the Old Testament ought to shape the church's mission.

THE MISSION OF THE KING'S PEOPLE

In the above section, I argued that the New Testament authors present the mission of Jesus in a number of Old Testament terms. While others could be mentioned, the four themes noted above are central to the New Testament presentation of Jesus and his mission. A fundamental question follows on from this discussion: What, if any, impact does comprehending Jesus' mission have on our understanding of the mission of the church? In short, the church's mission is to participate and continue Christ's mission on earth.

THE KING'S PEOPLE: THOSE "IN CHRIST"

In recent years, interest in union with Christ has increased among New Testament scholars.[67] The widespread use of ἐν Χριστῷ ("in Christ"), διὰ Χριστοῦ ("through Christ"), and related phrases alerts readers to the importance of union themes, especially in Paul's letters. For our purposes, we need only to highlight the use of the concept to (re)define the people of God. This way of identifying God's people will have significant implications for understanding the mission of the church.

---

65. Beale, *New Testament Biblical Theology*, 414.

66. For example, Brant Pitre, *Jesus the Bridegroom: The Greatest Love Story Ever Told* (New York: Image, 2014), argues persuasively that Jesus comes in the role of bridegroom to join the people of God to himself.

67. See, for example, Constantine R. Campbell, *Paul and Union with Christ: An Exegetical and Theological Study* (Grand Rapids: Zondervan, 2012); and Grant Macaskill, *Union with Christ in the New Testament* (Oxford: Oxford University Press, 2014).

While the Synoptic Gospels clearly define the people of God as those rightly related to Jesus, union themes are more implicit than explicit.[68] John's Gospel and the Pauline Epistles contain much more explicit union language and will therefore be the focus of our study. In what follows, we will sample a few key passages in John and Paul that define the people of God as those united to Christ.

Central to John's theology of union is the vine-and-branches discourse of John 15. Here Jesus describes the connection between himself and his followers in the most intimate of terms. Of course, the primary point is that branches must remain joined to the life-giving vine. Yet, the nature of the relationship is also important. As Andreas Köstenberger notes, Jesus' teaching "elaborates on the organic unity between him and his followers that will be sustained subsequent to his exaltation with the Father in and through the Holy Spirit."[69] The image of vineyard is an important theme in the Old Testament, used to describe Israel as God's covenant people. For example, Psalm 80:8–11 describes Israel as a vine removed from Egypt and planted in the promised land.[70] It is important to note that Jesus uses an Old Testament theme related to the covenant people of God to describe his followers and does so in terms of union. That is, the true branches are those united to the true branch. Jesus defines God's covenant people as those ἐν ἐμοί ("in me").

The vine-and-branches image further builds on Jesus' words regarding the Spirit in John 14 and anticipates his additional teaching on the Spirit in John 15–16. As Grant Macaskill rightly argues, "the state of abiding in Jesus, which is equated with Jesus abiding in the believer or in the church (John 15:4), is itself equated with the presence of the Spirit."[71] All of this imagery and teaching fits within and contributes to John's broader understanding of salvation, which is consistently pictured as being rightly related to Jesus the Messiah through faith. In John's Gospel,

---

68. For example, see the family themes in Matt 5:44–48; Luke 6:35–36; 20:36, all of which identify God's family as those who follow/obey Jesus.

69. Andreas J. Köstenberger, *A Theology of John's Gospel and Letters* (Grand Rapids: Zondervan, 2009), 241.

70. Macaskill, *Union with Christ*, 262. Macaskill lists Isa 5:1–7; 27:2–13; Jer 2:21; 12:10–17; Ezek 15:1–8; 17:1–21; 19:10–14; Hos 10:1–2 as other examples.

71. Macaskill, *Union with Christ*, 262.

Jesus invites people to turn from their sin and enter the kingdom of God through faith in him (for example, John 1:12; 3:16, 36; 5:24; 10:1–18; 14:6). Especially clear are the participatory notes in John 6:47–51, where salvation is found through eating the "bread of life." This striking imagery connotes the most intimate of unions between Jesus and those who follow him. Finally, Jesus prays in John 17:23 that his followers will know unity with God and each other in the same way he is united to the Father. This unity in love summarizes the mission of Christ in John. Bauckham aptly summarizes the point:

> By the end of chapter 17, we know that this love of God for the world comprises the whole movement of God's love that begins in the mutual loving communion between the Father and the Son, entails the Son's mission to include humans in that divine love, creates the loving community of disciples of Jesus, and thereby reaches the world.[72]

Paul's letters contain the most robust development of union themes in the New Testament. As Paul unfolds his theology in reflection on the Old Testament and in light of the coming of the Messiah, union with Christ is central to numerous theological themes. Constantine Campbell argues, "Union with Christ is the 'webbing' that holds [Paul's theology] all together."[73] As such, union with Christ, while an important theological theme itself, links all the threads of Paul's theology, not least soteriology, Christology, and ecclesiology.

Space will not allow a full treatment of union with Christ in Pauline theology. Instead, I will focus on Paul's identification of the people of God as those who are united to Christ. In Romans, Paul uses union with Christ to unite the Roman church(es) in their common identity in Christ. Union with Christ, while not setting aside ethnicity, becomes the new primary identity for followers of Jesus.[74] Thus, the church is to

---

72. Richard Bauckham, *Gospel of Glory: Major Themes in Johannine Theology* (Grand Rapids: Baker, 2015), 41.

73. Campbell, *Paul and Union with Christ*, 441.

74. For the ethnic composition of the audience of Romans, see Richard N. Longenecker, *Introducing Romans: Critical Issues in Paul's Most Famous Letter* (Grand Rapids: Eerdmans, 2011), 75–91. Longenecker argues (rightly in my view) that the church(es) in Rome included both Jewish and gentile believers in Christ.

be united in diversity by their shared common identity in Christ. Paul argues that while all people were formerly united to Adam, believers are now united to Christ (Rom 5:12–21). In fact, all those baptized are baptized "into Christ Jesus" (εἰς Χριστὸν Ἰησοῦν), which demonstrates their identification with him in new, resurrection life (Rom 6:1–5). The mention of Christ's life, death, and resurrection is evocative of Jesus' story. Thus, Paul is saying that baptism incorporates believers into the story of Jesus; his story is our story. In Christ there is no condemnation, and those in Christ have the Spirit within, building them into the community of faith as God's children (Rom 8:1–17). The numerous allusions to the Old Testament present union with Christ as the fulfillment of God's covenant promises, as those in Christ are the new-covenant people of God.

Other Pauline letters similarly push the recipients to unity in Christ through reframing their corporate identity as the people of God in Christ. Union with Christ is the sign of "new creation" (2 Cor 5:17). That is, participation in Christ marks participation in the new creation. As Herman Ridderbos argues, "When [Paul] speaks here of 'new creation,' this is not meant merely in an individual sense . . . but one is to think of the new world of the re-creation that God has made to dawn in Christ, and in which everyone who is in Christ is included."[75] The eschatological people of God are created in Christ and therefore participate in the new creation. One can immediately see the connections with the contours of Christ's mission explored above.

We noted above that Paul believes the seed of Abraham to be those united to Christ (Gal 3:27–4:7). This terminology builds on Paul's language of co-crucifixion in Galatians 2:19–20. Thus what has been accomplished in Christ is an "absolute transformation of identity," as Macaskill puts it.[76] The majestic praise of Ephesians 1 is filled with "in Christ" language, which sets the stage for Paul's argument for the unity of God's people in Christ in Ephesians 2:11–22, the body of Christ imagery of Ephesians 4, and the marriage analogy of Ephesians 5. Thus, in Paul's writings, union with Christ defines the identity of God's people, sums up the salvific

---

75. Herman N. Ridderbos, *Paul: An Outline of His Theology*, trans. John Richard de Witt (Grand Rapids: Eerdmans, 1975), 45.

76. Macaskill, *Union with Christ*, 221.

consequences of the Christ event, and provides the fundamental motivation for ethical community life.

The above analysis is a mere sampling of union themes in the New
Testament. Participation in Christ plays a more significant role than is
often realized. We have noted some important passages in John and Paul,
but union with Christ is important in other books as well.[77] More could be
mentioned, but the point is clear: the people of God are those in Christ.
Being in Christ means identification with him, entering his story, and
being in covenant bond with him through faith.[78]

THE MISSION OF THE KING'S PEOPLE
AS PARTICIPATION IN HIS MISSION

The identity of God's new-covenant people as those who are "in Christ"
has significant implications for our understanding of the mission of the
church. If union with Christ entails an entrance into the story of Jesus
such that his story becomes our new story, it is safe to assume that this
union entails entrance into his mission. That is, *the mission of God's new-
covenant people is to participate in and continue the mission of Jesus.* Indeed,
Jesus himself calls his followers to a mission mirroring his own. In
Mark 3:13–19, Jesus ascends the mountain and calls apostles to himself
in order to (1) be with him, (2) send them to preach, and (3) have authority
to cast out demons. Attentive readers will realize that these three points
are a short summary of Jesus' ministry in Mark 1–3. As noted above, that
Jesus calls twelve apostles is significant, as Jesus "viewed himself as God's
agent for covenant renewal and the eschatological restoration of Israel,"
as Mark Strauss puts it.[79] It is very significant that in choosing the Twelve
to represent the restoration of Israel, Jesus immediately gives them a mission that is at its heart a participation in his own mission.[80]

---

77. See Macaskill, *Union with Christ*.

78. Faith itself is participatory in the New Testament. See David M. Hay, "Paul's Understanding of Faith as Participation," in *Paul and His Theology*, ed. Stanley E. Porter (Leiden:
Brill, 2006), 45–76; Douglas A. Campbell, "Faith and Participation in Paul," in *"In Christ"
in Paul*, ed. Michael J. Thate, Kevin J. Vanhoozer, and Constantine R. Campbell (Tübingen:
Mohr Siebeck, 2014), 37–61.

79. Mark L. Strauss, *Mark*, ZECNT (Grand Rapids: Zondervan, 2014), 159.

80. See also the sending out of the disciples in Mark 6:7–13 and the parallel passages in
Matthew and Luke.

Similarly, John records a postresurrection commissioning of the disciples in John 20:21: "As the Father has sent me, even so I am sending you." The sending language connects to the multiple similar uses related to Jesus' understanding of his mission throughout John's Gospel. Jesus came to "do the will of him who sent me" (John 4:34; 5:30; 9:4), to call people to believe his words and the one who sent him (5:24; 6:29; 11:42), to teach the words of the one who sent him (7:16; 12:49; 14:24), and to reveal the Father (12:45; 13:20). Jesus' prayer in John 17 demonstrates that the sending is closely related to the union between Jesus and the Father, and this same unity exists between believers and Christ through the work of the Spirit. Thus, as Köstenberger writes, "Jesus' mission as the sent Son significantly entails the gathering of the new messianic community and its commissioning for its mission to the world. . . . In this respect Jesus' union with the Father forms the basis for believers' union in their mission."[81] The community of faith carries on the mission of Jesus in union with him just as Jesus, in union with the Father, was sent into the world on the messianic mission.

It is clear, then, that the Gospels picture the mission of the messianic community as participation and continuation of Jesus' own mission.[82] In the remainder of this chapter, we will reflect on the church's mission as participation in the various contours of Jesus' mission explored above. That is, since our mission is derived from our union with Christ, the missional and christological themes that mark out Christ's mission ought also to mark out our mission. Indeed, I will argue below that the Great Commission of Matthew 28 in various ways alludes to each of the christological themes we have explored.[83]

UNION WITH THE NEW ADAM

First, *united to the new Adam, the people of God are to be the renewed humanity on earth.* As the new Adam, Christ came on a mission of restoration:

---

81. Köstenberger, *Theology of John's Gospel*, 540–41.

82. It should be clear that I am not saying the church can replicate Jesus' mission in its entirety. Rather, I am saying that the concept of union with Christ should help shape the contours of the church's mission.

83. Schnelle, *Theology of the New Testament*, 435, rightly argues that in the final scene of Matthew draws together all the narrative threads of the Gospel. We should expect, then, to see the various themes related to the messianic mission within the Great Commission.

restoration of God's people and God's world. Likewise, the new-covenant people of God must be agents of restoration through the gospel.

I argued above that though Matthew's Gospel places heavy emphasis on Jesus as the new Israel and new Moses, there are clear allusions to Adam in the first chapter. The Great Commission (Matt 28:16–20) functions as a bookend to the Gospel with additional hints toward an Adamic mission. R. T. France convincingly argues that the closing words of Matthew allude to the LXX of Daniel 7:14.[84] Both Jesus and the Son of Man of Daniel 7 are given authority (Matt 28:18: ἐδόθη μοι πᾶσα ἐξουσία; Dan 7:14: ἐδόθη αὐτῷ ἐξουσία). The Son of Man's authority extends to "all nations" (πάντα τὰ ἔθνη), while Jesus sends the apostles to make disciples of "all nations" (πάντα τὰ ἔθνη). Within Daniel, the "Son of Man" seems to represent the people of God: Israel. However, early Jewish interpretations in 1 Enoch and 4 Ezra take the passage to refer to the Messiah.[85] Jesus seems to identify himself as the Danielic Son of Man in Matthew 26:64.[86] Hays notes the significance: "The disciples' mission to the Gentiles actually constitutes the fulfillment of the triumph of the Son of Man."[87] Indeed, through preaching the gospel, the church brings about the fulfillment of the vision that "all peoples, nations, and languages should serve him" (Dan 7:14).

Crucial to the present argument is the observation that the Son of Man passage in Daniel alludes to Adam. The Son of Man in Daniel 7 is pictured as a new Adam, given the dominion that Adam surrendered in sin. The near context includes additional clues that Adam is in the background of the passage.[88] Moreover, the "Son of Man" is probably an innerbiblical allusion to Psalm 8, which itself echoes the creation narrative.[89] The point is that as Jesus takes up the role of the Son of Man, he also brings to completion Adam's vocation. In sending his followers to "all nations," Jesus commands them to continue in the Adamic mission. Restoration comes

---

84. France, *Matthew*, 1112–13.

85. Ernest C. Lucas, *Daniel*, Apollos Old Testament Commentary (Downers Grove, IL: InterVarsity Press, 2002), 185.

86. See also Matt 16:28; 19:28; 24:30–31; 25:31–34.

87. Hays, *Echoes of Scripture in the Gospels*, 184.

88. Beale, *New Testament Biblical Theology*, 83–84.

89. Lucas, *Daniel*, 187.

to the world through the making of disciples. Thus, the mission of the church is to participate in the mission of the new Adam.

In addition to Matthew 28, other New Testament passages indicate that the church is to carry on Christ's Adamic mission of restoration. While many could be mentioned, 2 Corinthians 5:16–21 seems very appropriate for our present discussion. In the first fifteen verses of the chapter, Paul recalls his previous letter, reminding the Corinthians of hope beyond death (see also 1 Cor 15). Indeed, "if anyone is in Christ, he is a new creation" (2 Cor 5:17). Notice the clear connection between union with Christ and new creation. The next verse draws us into the story of reconciliation as Paul proclaims, "All this is from God, who through Christ reconciled us to himself and gave us the ministry of reconciliation." The narrative from creation ("all this is from God") to new creation ("reconciliation") is clear, with believers drawn into the story ("the ministry of reconciliation"). The rest of the passage fills out the details of this ministry. We continue the work of God in Christ as his ambassadors for reconciliation through the proclamation of the word of reconciliation. We have this ministry because of Christ's death as a sin offering (2 Cor 5:21). Through this ministry God displays his faithfulness; the church exists as the righteousness of God and as we participate in the reconciliatory work of Christ.[90] Thus, for Paul, the mission of the church must include the restorative work of new creation.

Finally, knowing the end of the story provides the motivation for mission. The Bible ends with a description of new creation, where Christ rules as King and where his people dwell with him forever. Since the story's conclusion is certain, the church's mission must be shaped accordingly. Thus, we are to be involved in the ministry of restoration, taking the gospel to the ends of the earth so that people move from allegiance to the old Adam to allegiance to the last Adam. Christ inaugurates the new creation in his resurrection. We participate in new creational ministry through proclamation of the gospel. Christ culminates the new creational mission in his return.

---

90. Michael J. Gorman, *Becoming the Gospel: Paul, Participation, and Mission* (Grand Rapids: Eerdmans, 2015), 249. Paul is probably referring to his own ministry in the first instance, but extending the same ministry to the church as the righteousness of God seems reasonable.

UNION WITH THE SEED OF ABRAHAM

Second, *united to the seed of Abraham, we become the seed of Abraham in new-covenant community.* After the debacle of Babel, God calls Abraham, blesses him, and promises that through him all the families of the earth will be blessed (Gen 12:1–3). The church's mission is to participate in the ongoing fulfillment of this promise as God's new-covenant community. That is, the church is to *be* the new-covenant community and to *make* the new-covenant community.

The Great Commission alludes to this aspect of the church's mission in two ways. First, the command to make disciples of all nations points to the Abrahamic covenant promises that through Abraham and his seed "all the families/nations of the earth shall be blessed" (Gen 12:3; 22:18). The LXX of Genesis 22:18 uses the same phrase (πάντα τὰ ἔθνη) as Matthew 28:19, making the allusion all the more probable.[91] Throughout Matthew's Gospel, Jesus' mission focuses almost exclusively on the "lost sheep of the house of Israel" (Matt 10:6; 15:24). Nevertheless, as noted above, there are numerous hints that the nations will also enter the kingdom. The hints give way to commission as the Gospel concludes. The mission of the church is to extend to "all nations." As such, the blessing of Abraham is at last reaching the nations through the making of disciples.

Second, the commission ends with the promise of the ongoing presence of Jesus with the disciples, recalling the promise of Yahweh to be with Isaac as he was with Abraham (Gen 26:3). Moreover, Yahweh promised to be Abraham's and his offspring's God (Gen 17:7–8). The divine presence is presented as the greatest blessing given to Abraham. Intriguingly, Jesus promises something in Matthew 28:20 that only Yahweh is able to do: be always present with his people. This window into Matthew's high Christology has significant implications for our understanding of mission. Jesus, the true seed of Abraham, has taken his rightful place as covenant head and now commissions his people to carry on his covenant-fulfilling mission through his powerful presence.[92]

In addition to the Great Commission, a number of other New Testament passages point to the covenant-fulfilling mission. In Romans 1:5,

---

91. Note the same phrase in the LXX of Dan 7:14, as noted above.

92. Jesus also fulfills the Immanuel promise of Matt 1:23 (citing Isa 7:14).

Paul reveals the goal of his ministry to be "the obedience of faith for the sake of his name among all the nations" (εἰς ὑπακοὴν πίστεως ἐν πᾶσιν τοῖς ἔθνεσιν ὑπὲρ τοῦ ὀνόματος αὐτοῦ). Given that Paul draws explicitly on the Abraham narrative in Romans 4, he probably has the covenant promises in mind in Romans 1:5 as well. Paul wrote Romans in part to invite the Roman church to join him in this mission to the gentiles.[93] Thus, the church is to participate in the covenant-fulfilling ministry by both being the faithful seed of Abraham in Christ and joining in Paul's apostolic ministry.

A further implication of the covenant-fulfilling ministry among all nations is the creation of multiethnic communities of faith. In Ephesians 1:9-10, Paul praises God for the "mystery of His will . . . to unite all things in [Christ]." He explains further in chapters 2 and 3, arguing that in Christ, those who were not God's people have become God's people, bringing together separate peoples, resulting in the creation of "one new man" (2:15). Paul's mission is to proclaim the revealed mystery of the gospel to the gentiles that in Christ, the multiethnic church might display God's "manifold wisdom" (Eph 3:10). In the early church, ethnic problems primarily centered on conflicts between Jews and gentiles. However, the principle extends more broadly to modern missions. The gospel brings together people of various ethnicities in Christ for the establishment of multiethnic communities that display God's power and wisdom to those outside. Such communities are signposts of the gospel's beauty: the peacemaking power to bring together those formerly at enmity. Peacemaking is inherent to the gospel; gospel communities "become the gospel of peace," as Michael Gorman puts it, by displaying the peace of the gospel and taking this peace to the world.[94] I am not arguing that the New Testament demands a multiethnic membership for every church. Some churches are located in monoethnic communities or communities in which linguistic differences make multiethnic worship impossible. Churches in such situations are not unhealthy due to a lack of ethnic diversity. Instead, I am arguing throughout this chapter that socioeconomic and/or cultural

---

93. So Michael F. Bird, "The Letter to the Romans," in *All Things to All Cultures: Paul among Jews, Greeks, and Romans*, ed. Mark Harding and Alanna Nobbs (Grand Rapids: Eerdmans, 2013), 177–204.

94. Gorman, *Becoming the Gospel*, 181–211.

backgrounds are not to be the primary identifiers for those united to Christ. In multiethnic settings, a church's identity in Christ supersedes such differences, and the unity found in Christ is a beautiful reflection of the gospel.

UNION WITH THE NEW MOSES

Third, *united to the new Moses, we bring the prophetic word of the gospel to the ends of the earth, thereby leading people out of slavery.* I argued above that Jesus as the new Moses shapes the messianic mission in two ways: the messianic mission is prophetic and leads the new exodus. As a people united to the new Moses, the church in its mission must also include these two components. The Great Commission alludes to the Mosaic shape of Jesus' mission in a number of ways, and the commission extends this mission to Jesus' disciples.[95] Similarly to the Sermon on the Mount and the transfiguration stories, Jesus, like Moses, goes "to the mountain" (εἰς τὸ ὄρος), where he gives his final commandment to the disciples. The disciples are to teach others to obey all that he commanded, just as Israel was to obey all that God commanded through Moses.[96] While there are similarities, the differences point to Jesus as a new, yet greater Moses. Moses conveyed the Lord's commands; Jesus himself has authority to issue commands. Moses led the people in worshiping the Lord; Jesus accepts worship. Moreover, while Moses' ministry was mostly limited to ethnic Israel, Jesus commands his disciples to participate in his mission by taking his words to the ends of the earth. Thus, Jesus' Mosaic mission extends beyond the boundaries of Israel.

It should be clear that the Great Commission entails both aspects of the Mosaic shape of Jesus' mission. The prophetic aspect of the mission is continued through the proclamation of the gospel. The disciples, and by extension the church, are to teach the nations "to obey all that I have commanded." As the disciples were taught by Jesus, the new Moses, so they

---

95. W. D. Davies and Dale C. Allison, *The Gospel according to Matthew*, The International Critical Commentary (Edinburgh: T&T Clark, 1989–1997), 2:678.

96. Grant R. Osborne, *Matthew*, ZECNT (Grand Rapids: Zondervan, 2010), 1077, notes that several commissioning passages in the Old Testament (Exod 7:2; Josh 1:7; 1 Chr 22:13) focus on the Mosaic law and are structured similarly to Matthew's account of the Great Commission.

are to teach his words to the world. The prophetic aspect is also the means by which the new-exodus aspect is continued. The nations are freed from slavery to sin as they hear and respond to the gospel.

The Mosaic-shaped ministry of the church is seen in the narrative of Acts. David Pao argues that the new-exodus motif, mediated through Isaiah, provides a "hermeneutical paradigm" for the whole of Luke-Acts, with the quotation of Isaiah 40:3–5 in Luke 3:4–6 as the "hermeneutical key" to understanding the entire narrative.[97] Pao argues that Isaiah's new exodus stands behind the programmatic statement of Acts 1:8, which alludes to several passages in Isaiah. First, the phrase "to the end of the earth" (ἕως ἐσχάτου τῆς γῆς) alludes to the LXX of Isaiah 49:6, which uses this exact phrase. Luke quotes Isaiah 49:6 in its entirety in Acts 13:47, a central text in narrating the movement of the gospel outside Israel. Second, Pao sees Isaiah 32:15 behind the promise of the Spirit. There the Lord promises that the Spirit will be "poured out" on God's people. Finally, Pao believes "you will be my witnesses" (ἔσεσθέ μου μάρτυρες) has antecedent texts in Isaiah 43:10 (γένεσθέ μοι μάρτυρες) and 43:12 (ὑμεῖς ἐμοὶ μάρτυρες). Thus, Pao concludes that the coming of the Spirit and the command to be witnesses for Jesus "signifies the dawn of the Isaianic New Exodus."[98] The expansion of the church in the rest of Acts is the outworking of this new exodus as Jews and gentiles are freed from sin and become members of the new-covenant people of God.[99] Thus, the early church carried on Jesus' new-Moses mission through proclamation of the word, which led to the new exodus.[100]

As noted above, the new-exodus theme is also prominent in Paul's letters. Here we mention only one example, related to Paul's understanding of his ministry (and, consequently, the church's mission). In 2 Corinthians 3, Paul describes his ministry as belonging to the new covenant. New-covenant ministry is more glorious than that of Moses because it is the ministry "of the Spirit" that leads to righteousness and endures forever (2 Cor 3:7–11). The ministry of the Spirit brings (new exodus) freedom

---

97. David W. Pao, *Acts and the Isaianic New Exodus* (Eugene, OR: Wipf & Stock, 2016), 249.

98. Pao, *Acts and the Isaianic New Exodus*, 91–93.

99. Pao, *Acts and the Isaianic New Exodus*, ch. 4.

100. Pao, *Acts and the Isaianic New Exodus*, ch. 5.

(2 Cor 3:17) and the unabated view of glory within the church (2 Cor 3:18) as believers are "transformed into the same image" (τὴν αὐτὴν εἰκόνα μεταμορφούμεθα), the image of Christ (see 2 Cor 4:4). The presence of glory in the church alludes to the church as the new temple. The holiness of the new temple and the concept of transformation speak to the ethical dimension of the mission; the church is to live as the justified people of God.[101] Therefore, the church is the new-exodus people, and the ministry of this people is to carry on the new exodus.

UNION WITH ISRAEL'S MESSIAH

Finally, *united to Israel's messiah, we proclaim the gospel of King Jesus and live under his glorious rule.* The concept of Messiah sums up all the various aspects of Jesus' mission. As Israel's Messiah, he is the new Adam, the seed of Abraham, and the new Moses. He comes as the promised Davidic king, restoring his people and establishing the kingdom of God on earth. The Great Commission alludes to the messianic status of Jesus and extends his mission to his people. First, the claim to absolute authority both on earth and heaven is a claim to sovereign kingship. As we have seen, there is an allusion to Daniel 7, but it is clear that the Son of Man is the Messiah-King. Second, he sends the disciples to the ends of the earth as his royal emissaries, again taking the role of king. He sends his people, not with their own authority, but by Christ's authority so that the nations will be his royal inheritance (Ps 2:8).

Beale rightly argues that the Great Commission contains an allusion to 2 Chronicles 36:23,[102] which states, "Thus says King Cyrus of Persia: The LORD, the God of heaven, has given me all the kingdoms of the earth, and he has charged me to build him a house at Jerusalem, which is in Judah. Whoever is among you of all his people, may the LORD his God be with him! Let him go up" (NRSV). There are at least three connections between the two texts: authority, the command to go, and the promise of divine accompaniment. However, the Great Commission is greater than Cyrus' edict, in that Jesus has greater authority, the goal is greater than the land of Israel, and Jesus himself promises to be with his disciples. Moreover,

---

101. Gorman, *Becoming the Gospel*, 281–82.
102. Beale, *Temple and the Church's Mission*, 176–77.

Cyrus is called "[the LORD's] anointed" (τῷ χριστῷ) in Isaiah 45:1, as he is used by the Lord to begin the restoration of Israel after the exile. However, Jesus, the true Messiah, actualizes the restoration through his death and resurrection. Finally, it is significant that the edict of Cyrus occurs at the close of the Hebrew Bible, while the Great Commission closes Matthew's Gospel. In other words, as the Old Testament ends like a book without a conclusion,[103] so Matthew's conclusion is not the end of the story; the followers of Jesus continue his messianic mission by proclaiming him as king to all nations. Beale notes one further significant implication of the allusion to 2 Chronicles 36. The edict of Cyrus allows the Israelites to return in order to rebuild the temple. As such, the Great Commission implies the command to build the true temple (the church) among all nations. I would add that Jesus' death and resurrection, along with the worldwide mission of the church, therefore brings about the true end of exile.

Beyond the Great Commission, there are numerous New Testament texts that picture the church's mission as the continuance of the messianic ministry of Jesus. Romans 15:8–21 is a clear example. Paul moves from the mission of Israel's Messiah (Rom 15:8) for the purpose of bringing the gentiles to glorify God (Rom 15:9–13) to his own mission to the gentiles (Rom 15:14–21). Thus, Israel's Messiah is King, not just of the Jews, but also of the gentiles. Paul's desire is to proclaim his kingship to all nations. By implication, Paul wishes to encourage the same missional attitude within the Roman church.

As the early church spread, persecution and suffering arose. Given the violent death suffered by the church's Lord, persecution was an expected outcome of the growth of the church. Within the context of suffering, Peter writes to "elect exiles" (1 Pet 1:1) in order to encourage them to remain faithful through their suffering. In so doing, Peter often links their story to that of Jesus. As Jesus first suffered and then received glory (1 Pet 1:11), so their suffering will lead to glory (1 Pet 1:7). Jesus, as Israel's Messiah, is restoring the true people of God through his death and resurrection (1 Pet 1:2, 3, 11, 19–21; 2:5, 21–25; 3:18–22; 4:1–2, 13). As

---

103. Stephen G. Dempster, *Dominion and Dynasty: A Theology of the Hebrew Bible*, NSBT 15 (Downers Grove, IL: InterVarsity Press, 2006), 227.

the Messiah's people, the church is the true new-covenant people of God. Thus, Peter applies Old Testament descriptions of Israel to his (mostly gentile) audience. In 1 Peter 2:9, Peter draws on Exodus 19 to label the church as "a chosen race, a royal priesthood, a holy nation, a people for his own possession." This special status is for a clear purpose: "that you may proclaim the excellencies of him who called you out of darkness into his marvelous light." Thus, the church's mission includes living holy, faithful lives while proclaiming his glory among the nations. This is the continuance of Jesus' own messianic ministry.

CONCLUSION

The church's mission is christological in both shape and content. Christ's mission ought to serve as the model for the church's mission as we proclaim his story, the gospel. We enter his story, and therefore his mission, via our union with Christ. Jesus came on a mission of rescue and restoration. As a people united to the new Adam, the seed of Abraham, the new Moses, and Israel's Messiah, we exist for the purpose of carrying on his mission unto the glory of the Father.

Moreover, as the church participates in Christ's mission, this should result in the planting of new-covenant communities across the globe. The task of carrying on Christ's mission is given to the church as the new people of God in Christ. As such, the goal of the church's mission cannot be the mere proclamation of the gospel message, though this is a crucial part of the mission. Rather, the goal is the gathering of believers into new churches with equipped leadership, ready to serve the risen Lord. The Great Commission compels the church to fill the earth with the God-glorifying, Messiah-worshiping, Spirit-filled churches who themselves participate in the mission.

3

BIBLICAL THEOLOGY
AND WORLD MISSION

Wendel Sun

INTRODUCTION

The God of the Bible is a missionary God. From creation to new creation, all God's works and words are saturated with missional intent and content. As David Bosch explains, "Mission is, primarily and ultimately, the work of the Triune God, Creator, Redeemer, and Sanctifier. . . . Mission has its origin in the heart of God." Therefore, "to participate in mission is to participate in the movement of God's love toward people, since God is the fountain of sending love."[1] Mission starts in the being of God; the Father sends the Son and the Spirit (John 14:16; 20:21). Thus, mission is not fundamentally an activity of the church, but an attribute of the Trinitarian God.[2] John Piper has influentially written, "The goal of missions is the gladness of the peoples in the greatness of God."[3] Yet this principle applies to God as much as the church. God's mission is to magnify his greatness among all nations, for the sake of his holy name (Ezek 36:22).

Recent studies in biblical theology and mission have argued that the Bible tells a unified grand narrative.[4] In this chapter, I will argue that the biblical story is framed by the biblical covenants, and these covenants

---

1. David J. Bosch, *Transforming Mission: Paradigm Shifts in Theology of Mission* (Maryknoll, NY: Orbis, 1991), 390, 392.

2. Lesslie Newbigin, *Trinitarian Theology for Today's Mission* (Eugene, OR: Wipf & Stock, 2006).

3. John Piper, *Let the Nations Be Glad! The Supremacy of God in Missions*, 3rd ed. (Grand Rapids: Baker, 2010), 35.

4. Christopher J. H. Wright, *The Mission of God: Unlocking the Bible's Grand Narrative* (Downers Grove, IL: InterVarsity Press, 2006). See also Craig G. Bartholomew and

most clearly display the mission of God in the world. In the history of biblical theology, many have argued that the biblical covenants serve as the organizing theme of the biblical story line.[5] Indeed, the various covenants—with Noah, Abraham, Israel, David, and the new covenant—naturally divide the biblical revelation into manageable parts while holding together a basic unity.[6] To be sure, there are many ways to approach a basic covenantal understanding of biblical theology. In this chapter, there is little need to argue for or against these differing approaches. Instead, we are going to explore the role of the biblical covenants in fulfilling the mission of God with a view toward understanding the overall shape of God's mission and the way in which this covenantal shaping might affect the mission of the church. As Herman Bavinck notes, the plight of humanity requires that if humanity is to be rescued, God must come down in covenant love. He writes,

> If there is truly to be religion, if there is to be fellowship between God and man, if the relation between the two is to be also . . . that of a master to his servant, of a potter to clay, as well as that of a king to his people, of a father to his son, of a mother to her child, of an eagle to her young, of a hen to her chicks and so forth; that is, if not just one relation but all relations and all sorts of relations of dependence, submission, obedience, friendship, love, and so forth among humans find their model and achieve their fulfillment in religion, then religion must be the character of a covenant. For then God has to come down from his lofty position, condescend to his creatures, impart, reveal, and give himself away to human beings; then he who inhabits eternity and dwells in a high and

---

Michael W. Goheen, *The Drama of Scripture: Finding Our Place in the Biblical Story*, 2nd ed. (Grand Rapids: Baker, 2014).

5. See, for example, Peter J. Gentry and Stephen J. Wellum, *Kingdom through Covenant: A Biblical-Theological Understanding of the Covenants* (Wheaton, IL: Crossway, 2012).

6. "Covenant theology" in the modern sense developed after the Reformation, particularly from the works of John Calvin, Johannes Cocceius, and others. However, the concept of covenant was present in early church writings. See Andrew A. Woolsey, "The Covenant in the Church Fathers," *Haddington House Journal* 5 (2003): 25–52.

lofty place must also dwell with those who are of a humble spirit (Isa 57:15).[7]

In other words, humanity's only hope is covenant because in covenant, the king of the universe comes down to rescue and restore his people.

In this chapter, I am arguing that the biblical story is the story of God's mission enacted through the covenants. It may be helpful at this point to summarize the story line of the Bible before moving into an examination of the covenants with special emphasis on the mission of God. I would summarize the biblical story as follows: God, the Creator King, is reestablishing his kingdom in the world through keeping his covenant promises to Abraham, Israel, and David in the life, death, and resurrection of his Son Jesus Christ, who will reign forever in the new creation with his new-covenant people.

This one-sentence summary attempts to set out both the basic trajectory of the biblical story and the fundamental theological elements of the story. In what follows, we will trace the use of covenants in moving the missional story toward the final goal: the eternal magnification of God's glory in the new creation. In our examination of each of the major covenants, we will focus on mission from two perspectives: God's mission and the mission of God's people.

CREATION AND FALL

THE MISSION OF GOD

God's mission *in the world* begins with creation (his mission being eternal). If we are to understand the mission of God as the magnification of his glory, then for several reasons we must view the act of creation as a missional act. First, creation takes place at God's initiative. Biblically and theologically speaking, God was under no outward constraint to create the world. That is, creation is not a necessary act, but a voluntary act of God. Second, in creation, God acts for the purpose of his glory. Thus it may be said that the creation itself has a purpose of proclamation: "The heavens declare the glory of God" (Ps 19:1). Third, the mission of God can be most

---

7. Herman Bavinck, *Reformed Dogmatics*, vol. 2, *God and Creation*, trans. John Vriend (Grand Rapids: Baker, 2006), 569.

clearly seen in the creation of humanity. At creation (before sin entered the world), God speaks to his created people (Gen 1:28–30; 2:16–17) and endows them with a mission. These facets of the creation account point to a missional purpose: God acts in the creation of the world for a particular purpose, namely, his own glory.

John Sailhamer has argued that "formless and void" (תֹהוּ וָבֹהוּ) in Genesis 1:2 describes the earth "in its 'not-yet' state—in its state before God made it 'good.'" According to Sailhamer, this should be understood in relation to humanity; the land in 1:2 is "a place not yet humanly inhabitable."[8] As such, the rest of the creation story pictures God as preparing the earth for humans. Though some may disagree on the details of Sailhamer's exegesis, the trajectory of the narrative displays the earth moving from "formless and void" (תֹהוּ וָבֹהוּ) to "good" (טוֹב) in Genesis 1, all of which takes place through God's initiative and power alone. Two conclusions can be drawn from this observation. First, the narrative of the creation account portends missional activity by God. That is, the opening chapter of the Bible identifies the one true God as the God of all creation. The creation, like the Creator, is not random, but purposeful. That God himself prepares good land for his people suggests missional action. Second, the creation story sets the stage for all missional thinking. God graciously enters the world to accomplish his purposes. The story of creation displays God's care for his people and his world, a care that leads to his mission. Thus, apart from God's missional activity, mission in its true sense does not exist.

Having argued that the creation account is missional in nature, we now turn to some of the specific missional action of God. We have already noted the preparation of the land for humanity, but there are other features of the *missio Dei* in Genesis 1–2 that must be noted. First, God's *word* holds a significant place in the creation account.[9] God speaks the world into being and personally addresses his creatures. His word is the powerful means

---

8. John H. Sailhamer, *The Pentateuch as Narrative: A Biblical-Theological Commentary* (Grand Rapids: Zondervan, 1992), 85. Sailhamer notes similar themes in relation to the wilderness wanderings and Canaan in Deut 32 as well as the exile and return in Jer 4.

9. In fact, as Stephen G. Dempster, *Dominion and Dynasty: A Theology of the Hebrew Bible*, NSBT 15 (Downers Grove, IL: InterVarsity Press, 2006), 33, notes, each of the three major sections of the Hebrew Bible (Torah, Prophets, and Writings) begins with an emphasis on God's word (Gen 1; Josh 1; Ps 1).

of his creational mission. Moreover, God speaks a word of blessing over his created people. The prominence of "blessing" in the creation account as well as the subsequent narratives in Genesis suggests that God's mission of magnifying his glory includes graciously blessing his people. In fact, it might be said that blessing is God's "mission strategy"; he glorifies his name *through* blessing. Second, the creation is God's *world*. Here we find a broadening of God's missional purposes; the entire creation is the scope of his mission. This broadness of God's purposes is significant for a robust understanding of mission in the Bible. Third, God's *way* is essential in missional thinking. That is, the creation account is framed by the sovereign actions of a King (God) who creates his kingdom (the world) and fills the kingdom with his people (humanity). While God's kingly activity may not initially seem "missional," this basic worldview building block is essential for the missional trajectory of the Bible. For example, Psalm 93:1 links creation and kingship: "The LORD reigns; he is robed in majesty; the LORD is robed; he has put on strength as his belt. Yes, the world is established; it shall never be moved." Mission in the world is based on God's identity as the King of creation.

Of course, the biblical story does not remain in the garden of Eden. The first humans rebel against the Creator-King and are banished from the garden. Despite the rebellion, God triggers the next stage of his glorious mission: the restoration of his world and his people. Though I argue above that the mission of God is broader than the redemption of humanity, the biblical story places the salvation of people at the center of God's missional activity. Strikingly, the promise of redemption follows immediately after sin. In Genesis 3:15, God promises that the seed of the woman will one day defeat the enemy and thereby restore God's people and God's world. Thus, though God's people rebel, God himself is no less committed to the fulfillment of his purposes. Indeed, his glory is displayed through the restoration of his people. From the perspective of the entire Bible, we know that God's original intentions for creation are only satisfied in the coming seed, who is Christ. As Herman Bavinck eloquently explains, God graciously

> puts enmity between the seed of the serpent and the woman's seed, brings the seed of the woman—humanity, that is—back to

his side, hence declaring that from Eve will spring a human race and that that race, though it will have to suffer much in the conflict with that evil power, will eventually triumph. From this point on, the road for the human race will pass through suffering to glory, through struggle to victory, through the cross to a crown, through the state of humiliation to that of exaltation.[10]

MISSION OF ADAM AND EVE

The creation account establishes a pattern of God's missional engagement in the world. As noted above, the creation story reveals God's missional nature. Therefore, it would seem to follow that people created in the image of God would also be missional. Indeed, immediately after creating them, God gives his people a mission. As Richard Middleton puts it, "Humanity in Genesis 1 is called to be the representative and intermediary of God's power and blessing on earth."[11] Missional activity, then, is inherent to (true) humanity.

G. K. Beale has persuasively argued that the blessing/command given to the first humans in Genesis 1:28 implies that Adam and Eve are to expand the garden of Eden to fill the earth.[12] God commissions the first couple to "subdue" the earth—the whole created world—and have dominion over it. The geographical note—from Eden to the whole earth—implies the expansion of the garden. Of course, the expansion includes not only land, but also people. They are to multiply, reproducing people created in God's image. As Beale puts it, "God's ultimate goal in creation was to magnify his glory throughout the earth by means of his faithful image-bearers inhabiting the world in obedience to the divine mandate."[13] Moreover, several scholars have noted the similarities between the garden of Eden

---

10. Herman Bavinck, *Reformed Dogmatics*, vol. 3, *Sin and Salvation in Christ*, trans. John Vriend (Grand Rapids: Baker, 2006), 199.

11. J. Richard Middleton, *The Liberating Image: The* Imago Dei *in Genesis 1* (Grand Rapids: Brazos, 2005), 111.

12. G. K. Beale, *A New Testament Biblical Theology: The Unfolding of the Old Testament in the New* (Grand Rapids: Baker, 2011), 30–33.

13. G. K. Beale, *The Temple and the Church's Mission: A Biblical Theology of the Dwelling Place of God* (Downers Grove, IL: InterVarsity Press, 2004), 82.

and the later tabernacle and temple.[14] Thus, Adam the priest-king is to expand the creational temple to fill the entire world.

Genesis 2:15 is significant for understanding both Adam's commission and the trajectory of humanity's mission throughout the Old Testament. The Lord God places Adam in the garden "to work it and keep it" (לְעָבְדָהּ וּלְשָׁמְרָהּ). While these terms certainly carry agricultural meaning, they are used later in the Pentateuch to describe religious activity, especially that of the Levites. For example, in Numbers 18:7, Aaron and his sons are commissioned to "guard (שמר) your priesthood" and "serve" (עבד): the same two Hebrew verbs used in Genesis 2:15 to describe Adam's work. Reflecting on this observation, Gordon Wenham concludes, "If Eden is seen then as an ideal sanctuary, then perhaps Adam should be described as an archetypal Levite."[15] Strikingly, this description of Adam's role is followed immediately by a prohibition, linking his commission with obedience to God's word.[16] Thus, Adam's commission is priestly, mediating God's word and blessing to the world. Humanity's dominion over the earth—Adam's mission—is obtained only in service to God.[17]

COVENANTAL SHAPING OF THE CREATION ACCOUNT

While the term "covenant" appears for the first time in Genesis 6:18, many have argued that the creation story implies the existence of a covenant between God and Adam. Of course, scholars construe the particulars of the creational covenant in many different ways. I will not attempt to argue for the existence of a covenant here. Rather, my intentions are more modest. I argue that the creation story, particularly as related to the mission of humanity, has covenantal shaping.[18] First, the covenantal

---

14. See especially Beale, *Temple and the Church's Mission*, and John H. Walton, *The Lost World of Genesis 1: Ancient Cosmology and the Origins Debate* (Downers Grove, IL: InterVarsity Press, 2010).

15. Gordon J. Wenham, "Sanctuary Symbolism in the Garden of Eden Story," in *I Studied Inscriptions from before the Flood: Ancient Near Eastern, Literary, and Linguistic Approaches to Genesis 1–11*, ed. Richard Hess and David Toshio Tsumura (Winona Lake, IN: Eisenbrauns, 1994), 399–404, esp. 401.

16. Sailhamer, *Pentateuch as Narrative*, 101.

17. William J. Dumbrell, *The Search for Order: Biblical Eschatology in Focus* (Eugene, OR: Wipf & Stock, 1994), 26.

18. For an analysis of all the covenantal elements in the creation account, see Jeffrey J. Niehaus, *Biblical Theology*, vol. 1, *The Common Grace Covenants* (Wooster, OH: Weaver, 2014), 38–50.

shaping of the narrative is a rather obvious implication of God's kingship. That is, since God is presented as King of all creation, his relations with creation should be viewed as covenantal.[19] As Gordon Spykman argues, covenant and kingdom go hand in hand: God's kingship is covenantal, and the covenant flows from his kingship.[20] Second, the intimate relationship between God and humanity is best understood in covenantal terms. Not only is God pictured as King; he is also pictured as Father, one who cares for his created children. Indeed, God appears first in the genealogy of Genesis 5.[21] Third, there are demands, blessings, and consequences laid on humanity. Since these elements are common to the other biblical covenants, we can at least say that the relationship between God and the first humans was covenantal in type even if not formally proclaimed as such. Finally, the multiple similarities between the creation narrative and Israel's story imply that the two were each intentionally shaped to reflect the other.[22] Since the Sinai covenant is central to Israel's story, it is reasonable to assume that Adam's story is similarly covenantal. In short, whether or not an actual covenant between God and Adam existed, there is a covenant-like quality to the creation story. This concept of covenantal creation will prove important as the biblical story of God's mission moves forward.

IMPLICATIONS

To review: First, mission is not primarily a human activity. Mission did not originate with people, nor did God delegate it to humans as their sole responsibility. Rather, mission is most fundamentally *God's work*. To be sure, we have seen that humanity was created with missional purposes. However, the mission of humanity must be seen as participation in the mission of God. Second, the fact that mission is rooted in creation implies the universal scope of God's mission. The whole earth

---

19. William J. Dumbrell, *Covenant and Creation: A Theology of the Old Testament Covenants* (Carlisle, UK: Paternoster, 1984), 34.

20. Gordon J. Spykman, *Reformational Theology: A New Paradigm for Doing Dogmatics* (Grand Rapids: Eerdmans, 1992), 257–58.

21. Adam is also referred to as the "son of God" in Luke 3:38.

22. See Seth D. Postell, *Adam as Israel: Genesis 1–3 as the Introduction to the Torah and Tanakh* (Eugene, OR: Pickwick, 2011).

was created for God's glory; the goal of mission is for the world to be filled with God's glory. Third, all missional activity must be understood within the creational framework. The creation story of Genesis 1–2 is foundational for a biblical worldview, and this worldview must shape mission theory and practice.

THE COVENANT WITH NOAH

Like the promise of Genesis 3:15, the covenant with Noah comes in the context of judgment: this time the judgment of the whole world through the flood. The juxtaposition of covenant with judgment alone boldly proclaims the gracious missional activity of God in his world. Following the sin of Adam and Eve in Genesis 3, the world became full of sin and evil rather than being filled with the glory of God as originally intended. The rebellion of humanity against the Creator-King is met with judgment, but also with grace. God's mission is carried on through Noah and his family.

While the Noachian covenant typically receives less attention than other biblical covenants, it is essential for understanding the mission of God in the biblical story. In fact, the covenant with Noah can be seen as a hinge that links together creation and the rest of the covenant narrative of the Bible. Aaron Chalmers rightly summarizes the point:

> The testimony of the Noahic covenant to God's commitment to creation and the preservation of life on earth forms the foundation or basis for the covenant story of redemption. In short, without the Noahic covenant there could be no history, and hence no salvation history. Thus the Noahic covenant is absolutely essential to the metanarrative of Scripture.[23]

THE MISSION OF GOD

Not surprisingly, the mission of God is clearly seen in the details of the Noachian covenant. First, the close connections with the creation narratives link the covenant with Noah to God's creational purposes. In addition to the similar covenant promises, the flood narrative is pictured as a new

---

23. Aaron Chalmers, "The Importance of the Noahic Covenant to Biblical Theology," *TynBul* 60 (2009): 207–16, esp. 212.

creation. Bruce Waltke notes the parallel narrative structure, moving from precreation conditions in Genesis 1:2 and Genesis 8:1-2 through creation (or re-creation) in Genesis 1:3-31 and Genesis 8-9 to the blessing of Genesis 1:28 and Genesis 9.[24] These connections between the two stories alert attentive readers to the continuity of God's purposes. Though humanity, following Adam and Eve, has rebelled against him, God will fulfill his creational intentions.

Second, the covenant with Noah seals God's purposes in a binding agreement. That is, God's purposes will surely come to pass as he has bound himself covenantally to these promises. I argued above that the creation account is covenantal in nature. The covenant with Noah should probably be understood as a renewal of the creation covenant, but even if one rejects the concept of a covenant with Adam, it is clear that the Noachian covenant renews God's commitment to creation. What is implied in the creation account is explicit in the flood story; God binds himself in covenant to bring his creational purposes to fruition. Moreover, the promise never again to destroy the earth with a flood (Gen 9:11) ensures that creation will continue to its intended goal.

Finally, the Noachian covenant also demonstrates the universal purposes of God. The covenant is made not just with Noah, but "with you [Noah] and your offspring after you, and with every living creature that is with you" (Gen 9:9-10). As noted above, God's purposes in creation are universal, as God commands Adam and Eve to multiply and fill the entire earth. Here again, the covenantal intentions with Noah are universal in nature. The covenant includes all people and the creation itself.

THE MISSION OF GOD'S PEOPLE

Intriguingly, the Noachian covenant includes no conditions laid on humanity. This fact intimates that the goal of the covenant—blessing— will be accomplished, as the responsibility is God's alone. However, this should not be taken to mean that humanity's missional mandate is completely absent from the text. We have noted throughout this section that

---

24. Bruce K. Waltke and Charles Yu, *An Old Testament Theology: An Exegetical, Canonical, and Thematic Approach* (Grand Rapids: Zondervan, 2007), 293–94. Waltke notes numerous other connections between the two stories. See also Warren Austin Gage, *The Gospel of Genesis: Studies in Protology and Eschatology* (Winona Lake, IN: Carpenter, 1984).

there are numerous connections between the flood account and the creation story. These commonalities not only suggest that the covenant with Noah renews humanity's trust in God's commitment to his own mission, but also imply that Adam's original commission is passed on to Noah and his progeny. Indeed, the terms of the covenant with Noah repeat all parts of the creational mandate given to Adam.

Genesis 9:1–17 details the covenant God makes with Noah. As with Adam, the covenant begins with blessing (Gen 9:1). Blessing explicitly links the purpose of this covenant with that of creation. Twice God commands Noah to "be fruitful and multiply" (Gen 9:1, 7), using the exact words spoken to Adam and Eve in Genesis 1. This repetition places special emphasis on the command and confirms that although humanity as a whole has rebelled against him, God is intent on fulfilling his creational purposes through his people. Noah is therefore pictured as a new Adam.[25] Nevertheless, there shall be no return to Eden. Noah and his family fail to bring about the worldwide blessing, yet the passing along of God's commission ensures that God will eventually bring it to pass. Indeed, a new start is simply not enough to fix the mess humanity has made through sin.[26] The covenant assures humanity that God himself will provide the needed solution.

Finally, it should be noted that Noah, like Adam, serves as a priest. As noted above, Adam served in the garden as a priest tasked with serving God, protecting the sacred space, and mediating God's word to the world. It is interesting that Noah, as a new Adam, offers a sacrifice immediately upon leaving the ark.[27] Like the creation account, there seems to be a close link between the creational commission and worship. Indeed, Beale notes that a common feature in narratives involving divine commissions is the building of "small sanctuaries," including altars built by the patriarchs, the tabernacle, and eventually the temple.[28] This observation suggests

---

25. Waltke, *Old Testament Theology*, 296.

26. Waltke, *Old Testament Theology*, 296.

27. On the nature of Noah's sacrifice, see John H. Sailhamer, *The Meaning of the Pentateuch: Revelation, Composition, and Interpretation* (Downers Grove, IL: InterVarsity Press, 2009), 592–601.

28. Beale, *Temple and the Church's Mission*, 96–99.

that the original commission to Adam is passed on to Noah (and all people) and includes the (re)building of the creational temple.

THE COVENANT WITH ABRAHAM

The context of the Abraham narratives, like the previous two stories we have examined, displays the missional nature of the covenant. Abraham's call (Gen 12:1–3), which many identify as the central missional text of the Old Testament, follows yet another story of judgment. Though the flood of Genesis 6–9 is pictured as a new creation, a simple restart cannot bring about the restoration of God's world and God's people. Following the flood, people again rebel against God by refusing to spread out and fill the earth. Instead they construct the tower of Babel and again incur God's judgment. In the midst of this chaos, God calls Abraham.

The call of Abraham is a pivotal moment in the story of God's mission. In fact, so central are the promises of God to Abraham that Paul identifies the promise to bless all nations through Abraham as "the gospel" itself (Gal 3:8). The promise of blessing to the nations is repeated six times in Genesis and sets the stage for all later biblical reflection on God's purposes.[29] The centrality of blessing also links the call of Abraham to both the Noachian covenant and, significantly, the creational blessing. William Dumbrell draws attention to the similarities between the call of Abraham and the creation account and surmises that the call of Abraham "is tantamount to the language of new creation."[30]

The biblical pattern of moving from the particular to the universal is clearly illustrated through the call of Abraham. While Genesis 1–11 focuses on the universal events of creation, fall, flood, and Babel, the rest of Genesis zooms in on one family. However, the election of this family is for the benefit of the world. Moreover, the repetition of the word "blessing" in Genesis 12:1–3 links the Abraham story to creation; the purpose of Abraham's call is to restore the original blessing on humanity. As Sailhamer argues,

> Abraham is here represented as a "new Adam," the "seed of Abraham" as a "second Adam," a new humanity. Those who "bless" him,

---

29. Christopher J. H. Wright, *Mission of God*, 328.
30. Dumbrell, *Covenant and Creation*, 58.

God will bless; those who "curse" him, God will curse. The way of life and blessing which was once marked by the "tree of the knowledge of good and evil" (2:17) and then by the ark (7:23b), is now marked by identification with Abraham and his seed.[31]

Thus, like the Noachian covenant, the covenant with Abraham will have significant links to creation, as it will be the means through which God fulfills his creational purposes.

THE MISSION OF GOD

The covenant with Abraham vividly displays the mission of God. While this entire chapter could examine the Abrahamic covenant alone, space allows only a cursory analysis of God's mission in the covenant. As noted above, the call of Abraham is inherently missional, as God condescends once again into the chaos of human sin. The extraordinary grace of God is evident as he not only calls one man out of the chaos of Babel, but also promises to bless the entire world through this one man and his family. Indeed, the calling and covenant of Abraham provide a global trajectory of redemption and restoration that the authors of the New Testament saw fulfilled in Christ.

Having promised to make Abraham into a great nation and to bless the world through this nation, God leads Abraham on a journey of faith. The twists and turns of the Abraham story highlight the faithfulness of God. When Abraham in fear lies about his relationship with Sarah, God steps in to rescue Sarah and protect his promise (Gen 12:10–20; 20:1–18). Having promised in covenant to provide offspring for Abraham, God again renews the covenant with Abraham following an unwise decision to gain offspring through Hagar (Gen 16–17). Many more examples could be noted, but the point is clear. The Abraham story beautifully displays God's faithfulness to his covenant promises, and therefore his mission to bless the world.

In Genesis 15, God approaches Abraham in a moment of despair, seemingly because he is unsure how God will keep his promises. God leads

---

31. Sailhamer, *Pentateuch as Narrative*, 139–40. See also Dempster, *Dominion and Dynasty*, 77, and John Goldingay, *Old Testament Theology* (Downers Grove, IL: InterVarsity Press, 2003–2009), 1:213–14.

Abraham outside and tells him to count the stars and assures Abraham that his offspring will be as vast as the constellations. There is yet another connection to the creation here, as God is the Creator of the stars (Gen 1:16). The point is that if God is able to call stars into being, he is certainly able to give Abraham a child. The reader is also alerted to the fact that the Creator of the universe is able to fulfill his creational intentions through Abraham.

The making of the covenant in Genesis 15 is similar to other covenant-making stories. It begins with a reminder of who God is: "I am the LORD who brought you out from Ur of the Chaldeans to give you this land to possess" (Gen 15:7) and moves into promises. However, there is a covenant ceremony in which animals are divided into halves. God alone passes through the animals, intimating that the covenant fulfillment rests on him alone. The covenant promises include offspring (Gen 15:13-16) and land (Gen 15:18-20). While not explicit in Genesis 15, the intention of universal blessing through the seed of Abraham is undoubtedly implied, since the promise to bless the world is central to the call in Genesis 12 and repeated several times throughout the story. While God had made the same promises earlier to Abraham, they are now sealed in the covenant.

In Genesis 17, the covenant with Abraham is renewed with a few additional promises.[32] First, the promise that kings will come from Abraham is certainly related to nationhood, but there is perhaps a clue here to the eventual fulfillment of covenant promises through the kings that come from Abraham. Of course, we also argued that Adam is presented as a king (under God's universal rule) in Genesis 1, so there is a connection to Adam's commission as well. In relation to God's mission, it is important to recognize that God is the one providing the kingly offspring. Second, God confirms that the covenant with Abraham is an "everlasting covenant" (Gen 17:7). It is now unmistakable that God will carry on the promise through the generations until all has been fulfilled. Third, one may well

---

32. Paul R. Williamson, *Sealed with an Oath: Covenant in God's Unfolding Purpose* (Downers Grove, IL: InterVarsity Press, 2007), 84–91, believes that Gen 15 and 17 represent two distinct covenants. However, given the overwhelming similarities in the covenant promises, it seems best to take Gen 17 as covenant renewal with additional stipulations added rather than a separate covenant. See the response to Williamson's view in Gentry and Wellum, *Kingdom through Covenant*, 263–80.

ask what circumcision has to do with mission. In this case, circumcision and mission are intimately related. God has bound himself in covenant to fulfill his own mission through Abraham and his offspring. It is not coincidental that circumcision stands as the covenant sign. Abraham's body is marked on the offspring-producing organ as a constant reminder of God's promise.[33] Thus, circumcision is, at least in part, a mark of God's mission to be completed through his people.

Outside these two covenant-making chapters, the rest of the Abraham narrative continues to display God's mission through Abraham. People are blessed through Abraham (such as Lot and Abimelech), Isaac is given, and God emphatically restates the covenant promises after Abraham's obedience in Genesis 22. In 22:16–18, God says to Abraham,

> By myself I have sworn, declares the LORD, because you have done this and have not withheld your son, your only son, I will surely bless you, and I will surely multiply your offspring as the stars of heaven and as the sand that is on the seashore. And your offspring shall possess the gate of his enemies, and in your offspring shall all the nations of the earth be blessed, because you have obeyed my voice.

Note the emphasis on offspring and blessing; blessing to the nations will come through the offspring. Again, even in the climactic story of Abraham's obedience, the mission of God to bless the world takes center stage.

THE MISSION OF GOD'S PEOPLE

Though God promises to fulfill his creational intentions in the Abrahamic covenant, God also places demands on his covenant partners. These demands provide the instructions for proper participation in God's mission. In other words, Abraham and his family must follow God's way in order for them to be a blessing to the nations. While much could be said, I note here two primary points. First, the multiple connections between the Abraham narratives and the creation story imply that the mission of Adam and Eve has been passed to Abraham and his family. After surveying

---

33. Goldingay, *Old Testament Theology*, 1:201.

the repeated promises of blessing and multiplying through the stories of Abraham, Isaac, and Jacob, N. T. Wright concludes,

> Thus at key moments—Abraham's call, his circumcision, the offering of Isaac, the transitions from Abraham to Isaac and from Isaac to Jacob, and in the sojourn in Egypt—the narrative quietly makes the point that Abraham and his family inherit, in a measure, the role of Adam and Eve. The differences, however, are not insignificant . . . the command ("be fruitful . . .") has turned into a promise ("I will make you fruitful . . .").[34]

This observation is significant. It means that God has not forgotten his original intentions for humanity. He has simply chosen to bring about restoration and the consummation of his intentions through Abraham's family. Moreover, God has placed the burden of fulfillment on himself: "*I will* make you fruitful . . ." Nevertheless, Abraham and his offspring have a significant role to play. They are to live as the true, renewed humanity in covenant relationship with the Creator.

Second, while the covenant is the result of God's gracious act, Abraham and his family are called to obedience and faith. The story begins with the demand for obedience as God calls Abraham to leave his family and go to a land God will show him. As Victor Hamilton argues, the promises of blessing depend on Abraham's obedience to the call to leave. He must go in order to be blessed and be a blessing.[35] The pattern of obedience and faith continues throughout the narrative as Abraham responds to God's grace. Genesis 12:4 shows Abraham immediately obeying the initial call. In Genesis 22:3, Abraham leaves early in the morning in obedience to God's demand that he sacrifice Isaac. Of course there are moments of doubt, but overall, Abraham is pictured as faithful through his obedience to the Lord.

The demand of faith is not merely an implication of the narrative; it is a demand explicitly placed on Abraham. The requirement of faith is especially clear in Genesis 17 and confirmed in Genesis 22. In Genesis 17:1-2,

---

34. N. T. Wright, *The Climax of the Covenant: Christ and the Law in Pauline Theology* (Minneapolis: Fortress, 1991), 22.

35. Victor P. Hamilton, *The Book of Genesis, Chapters 1-17*, NICOT (Grand Rapids: Eerdmans, 1990), 373-74.

God says to Abraham, "I am God Almighty; walk before me, and be blameless, that I may make my covenant between me and you, and may multiply you greatly." The command to "walk before me, and be blameless" includes faithfulness and fidelity in covenant with God and the obligation to moral uprightness. The demand on Abraham can be summarized as "being whole or complete; being totally dedicated to God," as Paul Williamson puts it.[36] In faithful obedience, Abraham and his family will be a blessing to the nations. As Robin Routledge notes,

> God promises to bless Abraham so that he and the nation that come from him will in turn be the means by which divine blessing will extend to the whole world. That blessing flows from Abraham's covenant relationship with God, and to share the blessing, the nations must also be brought to share the relationship. Thus the extension of divine blessing anticipates also the extension of the covenant relationship with God to all peoples. The relationship between God and creation may have been broken by sin, but God's commitment to his world, embodied in the earlier covenant with Noah, opens the way for a renewed relationship with God and the blessings associated with it to be established.[37]

THE COVENANT WITH ISRAEL

The book of Exodus begins with the announcement that God has kept his covenant promise to make Abraham into a great nation (Exod 1:1–7). Moreover, as Dempster says, the "multiplying" of Israelites in the land "loudly echoes" the creation story, where God commands Adam and Eve to multiply.[38] However, the fulfillment of the covenant promise soon leads to suffering; the Egyptians fear the growing nation and enslave them, which is a threat to their continuing existence as a people. If the Israelites are extinguished, God's promises to bless the world through Abraham's seed will fail. Thus God sets the stage for his quintessential missional action in the Old Testament: the exodus. Keeping his covenant

---

36. Williamson, *Sealed with an Oath*, 87.

37. Robin Routledge, *Old Testament Theology: A Thematic Approach* (Downers Grove, IL: InterVarsity Press, 2008), 167.

38. Dempster, *Dominion and Dynasty*, 93.

promises to Abraham (Gen 15:12-16), God rescues his people through judging their enemies. In a magnificent display of his power, God leads his "son" (Exod 4:23) out of slavery to Sinai in order to make them into a nation: God's nation.

For our purposes, it is important to note the close connections between the exodus story and the creation narrative.[39] Exodus 14–15 clearly presents the exodus as a whole, and the crossing of the sea in particular, as acts of new creation. A brief look at Exodus 14:20-22 will suffice to demonstrate the point. In this passage, the crossing of the sea is described using the interplay of darkness and light (Exod 14:20; Gen 1:3), water and dry land (Exod 14:21-22; Gen 1:9-10), as well as the wind (רוּחַ) blowing over the water (Exod 14:21; Gen 1:2).[40] In short, the exodus is pictured as a sort of new creation. As such, we should expect that the covenant terms will carry forward God's creational intentions.

THE MISSION OF GOD

The entire exodus event powerfully displays the mission of God. The rescue of Israel is so that all people "shall know that I am the LORD" (Exod 6:7; 7:5, 17; 8:22). This display of power is to magnify the glory of God's name as the only true God. As John Goldingay argues,

> Simply to pluck the Israelites from Egypt by supernatural means would have liberated Israel as effectively, though it would perhaps not have so impressed Yahweh's power on either Israel or Egypt, or not impressed it in the same way. This is Yahweh's way of getting honor by or with the Egyptians. . . . It is by the demonstration of awesome power at the Red Sea that the Egyptians will thus come to acknowledge Yahweh.[41]

Thus even the punishment of Israel's enemies has missional intent.

While much could be said about God's mission through the exodus and wanderings narratives, we are focusing on the covenantal mission

---

39. Terence E. Fretheim, *God and World in the Old Testament: A Relational Theology of Creation* (Nashville: Abingdon, 2005), 110, argues that creational theology suffuses the whole of Exodus.

40. The Song of Moses in Exod 15 is also full of creational motifs.

41. Goldingay, *Old Testament Theology*, 1:321.

of God. This focus is appropriate, as the exodus was always for the purpose of leading Israel to covenant fellowship with the Lord. Strikingly, even this covenant fellowship is for a greater purpose: God's worldwide mission. There are clues to this worldwide intention throughout the first eighteen chapters of Exodus. As noted above, Exodus 1 connects the story of Exodus to the patriarchal narratives of Genesis. It is also significant that God's self-identification in Exodus links the exodus event directly to the Abrahamic covenant: "I am the God of your father, the God of Abraham, the God of Isaac, and the God of Jacob" (Exod 3:6; see also 3:15, 16; 4:5). The repetition of this identifier places the rescue from Egypt and the Sinai covenant within the narrative world of the Abrahamic covenant. Moreover, in Exodus 6:2–8 God explicitly tells Moses that in rescuing Israel from Egypt, he is keeping his covenant promises to Abraham. Further, as argued above, the central promise of the Abrahamic covenant is blessing to the world. Thus the exodus and the covenant with Israel are means by which God will not only make Israel his people, but through Israel, will fulfill his creational intentions.

The terms of the covenant also display the mission of God. Interestingly, the most significant missional aspects are the demands laid on Israel. That is, God clearly intends to complete his own mission through Israel. Nevertheless, God's own mission to display his glory to the world is clearly seen in several details of the covenant-making story. First, the scene at Sinai is a vivid revelation of the glory of God and stands as something of a microcosm of the goal of God's mission: the worldwide display of his glory. The thunder, lightning, loud trumpets, fire, and smoke of Sinai (Exod 19:16–20) are to elicit awe and faith in the people of Israel (Exod 19:9). Likewise, the awe and faith produced in Israel are to be passed to the nations so that the world will be filled with God's glory (Ps 72:19).

Second, God graciously gives the tabernacle to Israel, representing his missional presence. The purpose of the tabernacle is so that God can dwell with his people (Exod 25:8). The tabernacle is a reminder of Eden, where God dwelt with Adam and Eve. The command to build a tabernacle and the instructions for its construction come directly from God himself. The precise details of the tabernacle mirror Eden, for the decorations depict garden-like features, and the ark, like Eden, is guarded by cherubim.[42] While the tabernacle undoubtedly implies that Israel is to be a new Adam, that the tabernacle's design comes through God's initiative places emphasis on God's missional purposes.

Third, one purpose of the law is to create a missional people. While there are multiple purposes of the law, one is undoubtedly to define the means by which Israel will be God's missional people. Thus, the law displays the mission of God because God uses the law to shape Israel into a people who will display his holiness to the nations. Michael Goheen clarifies:

> If we are to understand the missional calling of Israel and the church, we must give attention to the tie of law to creation. God's mission since Eden had been to restore the good creation from its sinful pollution: he has made the promise to Adam and set out on the long road of redemption to accomplish it. Israel becomes the bearer of that promise, embodying God's commitment to renew the creation. Thus the life of Israel points back to the creational design and intention for human life. It also points forward, to God's final goal of a restored creation.[43]

More could be said, especially related to God's faithfulness to Israel through their rebellion, but the point is clear. The covenant with Israel is the means by which God will fulfill his creational mission. Like the previous covenants, God's sovereign activity in covenant making shows his commitment to his mission through his chosen people.

THE MISSION OF GOD'S PEOPLE

Like the previous covenants, the role of the God's covenant partner has direct links to God's creational intentions for humanity. The term "serve" (עבד) in the story of Israel's exodus recalls the commission given to Adam in Genesis 2:15, in which the same term appears.[44] This key term is repeated in Exodus 3:12; 4:22; 7:16; 9:1, 13; 10:3, 24–26, suggesting that

---

42. Dempster, *Dominion and Dynasty*, 103.

43. Michael W. Goheen, *A Light to the Nations: The Missional Church and the Biblical Story* (Grand Rapids: Baker, 2011), 40.

44. Scott W. Hahn, "Canon, Cult, and Covenant," in *Canon and Biblical Interpretation*, ed. Craig Bartholomew et al. (Grand Rapids: Zondervan, 2006), 207–35, esp. 215.

Israel is to take up Adam's commission. Just as Adam was to "serve" in the garden, so Israel is to "serve" the Lord following the exodus. We have noted the numerous connections between the creation and exodus stories, making the repetition of this key verb all the more significant. Indeed, in spelling out Israel's role within the covenant, Exodus 19:5–6 links directly to Adam's commission.

Exodus 19:5–6 in fact stands as the central text in defining the mission of Israel in covenant with God.[45] First, God begins with a reminder of his identity; he is the God who brought Israel out of Egypt (Exod 19:4). Significantly, God says that he brought them "to myself." This expression implies an intimate relationship with Yahweh, which was the goal of the exodus. Second, obedience to the covenant is commanded (Exod 19:5). Here the Sinai covenant looks much like the covenant with Abraham. The central demands are faith (Exod 19:9) and obedience.[46] We have already noted the close connection between the Abrahamic covenant and creation. The similar demands laid on Israel suggest an Adamic (and Abrahamic) shaping to Israel's covenant as well.

These observations lead into the defining of Israel's role in Exodus 19:5–6. They are to be a "kingdom of priests and a holy nation." These two primary descriptors are parallel and complementary.[47] That is, the way Israel will serve as priests to the nations is by *being* a holy nation. As Dumbrell states, "Israel's primary role in this connection [as a kingdom of priests] consisted in attracting the world to her form of government (i.e., the kingdom of God) by her embodied holiness."[48] John Davies argues that the essential role of the priest is to serve before the Lord in the tabernacle/temple rather than serve others.[49] However, priesthood does not rule out missional purposes. In fact, it is the access to the one true

---

45. John A. Davies, *A Royal Priesthood: Literary and Intertextual Perspectives on an Image of Israel in Exodus 19.6*, JSOTSup 395 (London: T&T Clark, 2004), 35, argues convincingly for a chiastic structure for Exod 19:1–8, with 19:5–6 at the center.

46. Sailhamer, *Meaning of the Pentateuch*, 386. Sailhamer further argues that the Mosaic law was added because of the failure of Israel to trust and obey the Lord. He writes, "Something more was needed to keep them loyal to the covenant."

47. Gentry and Wellum, *Kingdom through Covenant*, 318.

48. William J. Dumbrell, *The Faith of Israel: A Theological Survey of the Old Testament* (Grand Rapids: Baker, 2002), 38.

49. Davies, *Royal Priesthood*, 98–100.

God in covenant relationship that is displayed to the nations that should attract them to worship. Of course, centripetal attraction of the nations all depends on Israel being the "holy nation" they are intended to be. As Christopher Wright remarks, "Obedience to the covenant was not a condition of *salvation*, but the condition of their *mission*."[50]

The identity of Israel as a *kingdom* of priests further links Israel's vocation to that of Adam. Adam was given dominion over the whole of creation and was to execute this dominion through obedience to the LORD, his Creator. Likewise, Israel is to be a kingdom—a people with a kingly role—but only through obedience to the LORD, her Creator. Dempster explains, "Instead of being a kingdom of a particular king, it will be a kingdom marked by priesthood; that is, service of God on behalf of people and *vice versa*. . . . Israel will thus redefine the meaning of dominion—service."[51] Adam and Eve lost their dominion in rebellion against God. Israel is tasked with restoring that dominion through obedience and service: the precise demands laid on Adam. If they are successful, they will bring the blessings of creation and Abraham to the nations.

The tabernacle plays a central role in this mission. The presence of God is the distinguishing mark of Israel (Exod 33:16).[52] We have already noted that the tabernacle represents God's missional presence among his people. For Israel, it is a constant reminder not only that God is with them, but also of their priestly mandate. As Peter Gentry and Stephen Wellum put it, "The tabernacle is also a replica of the garden of Eden and a representation of the universe, so just as Adam was to fulfill his mandate by devoting himself to worship as a priest in the garden sanctuary, so Israel as a new Adam is to fulfill her mandate by devoting herself to worship as a priest in the tabernacle and later the temple."[53] Thus, the tabernacle symbolizes the Adamic mission given to Israel. They are to be a people marked by God's presence, filled with God's holiness, displaying God's beauty to the nations.

---

50. Christopher J. H. Wright, *Mission of God*, 333.

51. Dempster, *Dominion and Dynasty*, 101–2.

52. Christopher J. H. Wright, *Mission of God*, 335.

53. Gentry and Wellum, *Kingdom through Covenant*, 322.

These points illustrate that Israel's missional identity is inseparably linked to missional activity. That is, the fundamental missional task given to Israel is *to be the people of God among the nations*.[54] Deuteronomy 4:6–8 summarizes the point:

> Keep them and do them, for that will be your wisdom and your understanding in the sight of the peoples, who, when they hear all these statutes, will say, "Surely this great nation is a wise and understanding people." For what great nation is there that has a god so near to it as the LORD our God is to us, whenever we call upon him? And what great nation is there, that has statutes and rules so righteous as all this law that I set before you today?

Thus, the obedience of Israel was for missional purposes.[55] While the law is given to a particular people, it has universal intent: blessing for the nations.

THE COVENANT WITH DAVID

The story of Israel plays out much like the story of Adam: failure to be the people God intended them to be. They do not keep the covenant and fulfill their mission as the kingdom of priests. However, despite their rebellion, God remains faithful to his creational and covenantal intentions. This faithfulness is displayed in the final two covenants: the Davidic covenant and the new covenant.

Unsurprisingly, David's story and the covenant made with him come on the heels of yet another moment of crisis. After the death of Moses and the exodus generation in the wilderness, Joshua leads the people into Canaan. There God gives their enemies into their hands, and they acquire the land promised long before to Abraham. However, within one generation, Israel turns away from following the Lord (Judg 2:10). During the period of the judges, the pattern of sin and rescue repeats as a seemingly unending cycle. The last judge, Samuel, faithfully leads Israel to return to the LORD, but they soon demand a king "like all the nations" (1 Sam 8:5).

---

54. Dean E. Flemming, *Recovering the Full Mission of God: A Biblical Perspective on Being, Doing, and Telling* (Downers Grove, IL: InterVarsity Press, 2013), 27–28.

55. Christopher J. H. Wright, *Mission of God*, 336.

God gives them a king like the nations—Saul—whose failures lead to further misery. In this time of national crisis, God raises up David, the man after his own heart (1 Sam 13:14). Of course, the David narratives move through many twists and turns, but the story climaxes in covenant.

THE MISSION OF GOD

The mission of God is featured prominently in the David narratives. God's choice of David, protection of him, and enthronement of David all demonstrate divine power to fulfill his mission. God again condescends to his people and promises to be with them and to fulfill his purposes through them, this time focusing on the royal family line. God's mission is therefore central in the Davidic covenant. The details of the covenant support this claim.

The promises of the Davidic covenant are strikingly familiar; they echo the Abrahamic covenant. In fact, as Gerhard von Rad observes, the context of the covenant-making story links it to the patriarchal narratives. In 2 Samuel 6:23, David's wife Michal is barren, yet the central promise of the Davidic covenant is offspring who reign forever.[56] Thus, the promise of offspring combined with barrenness parallels the stories of the patriarchs, linking the covenant of 2 Samuel 7 to that of Abraham. Moreover, the promises given to David are nearly identical to those given to Abraham.[57] Note the following:

	Abraham	**David**
Name	Gen 12:2: "I will . . . make your name great"	2 Sam 7:9: "I will make for you a great name"
Victory	Gen 22:17: "And your offspring shall possess the gate of his enemies"	2 Sam 7:11: "And I will give you rest from all your enemies"
Relationship	Gen 17:8: "I will be their God"	2 Sam 7:14: "I will be to him a father, and he shall be to me a son"

---

56. Gerhard von Rad, *Old Testament Theology*, trans. D. M. G. Stalker (New York: Harper, 1962–1965), 1:312.

57. Williamson, *Sealed with an Oath*, 144.

	Abraham	David
Seed	Gen 17:6: "I will make you exceedingly fruitful, and I will make you into nations, and kings shall come from you"	2 Sam 7:12: "I will raise up your offspring after you"
Obedience	Gen 18:19: "I have chosen him that he may command his children . . . to keep the way of the Lord"	2 Sam 7:14: "When he commits iniquity, I will discipline him"
Eternal	Gen 17:7: "an everlasting covenant"	2 Sam 7:13: "I will establish the throne of his kingdom forever"
Blessing for the Nations	Gen 22:18: "in your offspring shall all the nations of the earth be blessed"	Ps 72:17: "May people be blessed in him, all nations call him blessed!"

These textual similarities suggest that God is going to keep his covenant promises to Abraham through the Davidic covenant, through the king that will come through David's family. The goal is the same: blessing for the nations through the chosen seed. Further, since the Abrahamic covenant is so closely connected to God's original intentions for creation, the Davidic covenant is also God's means for completing his creational mission.

This understanding of God's intentions in the Davidic covenant is supported through the many prophetic promises related to David. A few examples will suffice to make the point. Jeremiah 33:14–26 links together creation, the Abrahamic covenant, the Sinai covenant, and the Davidic covenant, suggesting that all the covenant promises will be fulfilled through the offspring of David. The point is that the promises to David are sure and bind together all the future hope for Israel.[58] In context, these promises are probably intended to be connected to the new covenant (Jer 31:31–34).

---

58. Dempster, *Dominion and Dynasty*, 167.

Likewise the prophecies of Isaiah 9 and 11 offer hope in the coming Davidic king who will rule not just Israel, but the world. In particular, Isaiah 11 pictures the new king's rule as a worldwide "Edenic paradise."[59] Many other examples could be mentioned, but the point is sufficiently clear. The coming king will fulfill God's creational purposes.

THE MISSION OF GOD'S PEOPLE

The demands of the Davidic covenant are similar to those of the Abrahamic covenant: obedience and faith. David and his seed are to live obediently before the Lord. However, like the Abrahamic covenant, the promises will be fulfilled, even when David's seed rebels (2 Sam 7:14–15). David's response to the covenant in 2 Samuel 7:18–29 reveals his understanding of the covenant. David humbly praises God as the one true God (2 Sam 7:22), the God of the exodus (2 Sam 7:23), and the God who made Israel his people (2 Sam 7:24). Of significance is 2 Samuel 7:19, where David claims that the covenant God has made with him is "instruction for mankind." That is, the seed of David will bring the word of God to the whole world. Gentry and Wellum explain:

> Therefore, as the divine son, the Davidic king was to effect the divine instruction or torah in the nation as a whole and was, as a result, a mediator of the Mosaic Torah. However, since the God whom the Davidic king represented was not limited to a local region or territory, but was the creator God and Sovereign of the whole world, the rule of the Davidic king would have repercussions for *all* the nations, not just for Israel. . . . Thus, faithfulness on the part of the Davidic Son would effect the divine rule in the entire world, much as God intended for humanity in the covenant of creation as indicated by the divine image.[60]

In short, the Davidic king will take up Adam's commission and bring it to fulfillment through his faithfulness to God.

---

59. Dempster, *Dominion and Dynasty*, 175.
60. Gentry and Wellum, *Kingdom through Covenant*, 400.

THE NEW COVENANT

The exile was the height of national disaster for Israel. They lost their land, their temple, their glory, and seemingly their place in God's story. They broke the covenant, faithlessly worshiping idols. Not only had they failed to bring God's blessing to the nations, but they had also lost their national blessing. However, even in their exile, God remains faithful to his creational and covenantal promises. One of the central aspects of hope in exile is the promise of a new covenant. The hope for a new covenant is not new to the exile period. In Deuteronomy 30, Moses already hints at the need for and eventual provision of a new covenant.[61] Moses knows that the people will break the covenant, but he points forward in hope to a new covenant in which God "will circumcise your heart and the heart of your offspring, so that you will love the LORD your God with all your heart and with all your soul, that you may live" (Deut 30:6).

The prophets draw on this hint from Deuteronomy in holding out hope for Israel after exile. Since the exile was the result of Israel's covenant failure, something more than simply a do-over is needed. In fact, nothing short of a new covenant is needed: a covenant in which God will change the hearts of his people. Thus a complete change of heart is precisely what God promises. For our purposes, it is important to note that the promise of a new covenant provides not only hope for Israel, but also hope for the world. For the exile was as disastrous for the nations as it was for Israel, even if the nations did not realize it. If Israel is not restored, the nations have no hope of knowing the one true God, since God has bound himself in covenant to bless the nations through Israel. *As long as Israel remains in exile, the nations remain "exiled" from God.* Therefore, the new covenant is hope for both Israel and the world.

THE MISSION OF GOD

The mission of God is the central focus of the new-covenant promises in the Old Testament. Of course, the restoration of Israel is a necessary part of God's mission to the nations, but there is another aspect of God's mission that is proclaimed in the Old Testament promises. The nations

---

61. Scholars debate the dating of Deuteronomy as a literary document. Nevertheless, even with a later date, the point here stands.

themselves will be included in the new covenant. In Isaiah 42:6, Yahweh speaks to the servant, saying, "I will give you as a covenant for the people, a light for the nations." The servant will be the center of the new covenant and this new covenant is not just for Israel, but for the nations.[62] Strikingly, the context draws on creational themes (42:5) and exodus themes (49:7), intimating that the new covenant will bring God's creational purposes to fruition.

The most prominent new-covenant text in the Old Testament Prophets is Jeremiah 31:31–34. Here God promises to make a "new covenant" with Israel and Judah. This covenant will be different from the covenant made with the exodus generation because in the new covenant, the Lord will write his law on the hearts of the people. As a result, all covenant members will know the Lord, and their sins will be forgiven. The focus on the heart is significant, as it connects with the words of Moses in Deuteronomy 30:6. The writing of the law on the heart is the circumcision of the heart. In fact, one of the central promises of the new covenant is change of heart. In Ezekiel 36:26, God promises to give his people a new heart, with the result that they will obey his word. Again, forgiveness of sins is mentioned, and Ezekiel adds the promise of the Spirit (Ezek 36:27). In the context of both Jeremiah and Ezekiel, the promise is for the restoration of the people of God. This restoration will include the removal of sin and the making of the new covenant.

The centrality of heart change is significant for at least two reasons. First, God himself is the one performing the heart surgery. In each of the promises, God says "I will . . ." and never commands the people of the new covenant to change their own hearts, which would be an impossible task. Rather, the new-covenant promises display God's mission in that he actively pursues his people and performs the necessary work of changing their hearts.[63] Second, heart change is the only means by which new-covenant members can be faithful. As Gentry and Wellum note, "The new covenant does not mean a change in God's standards of righteousness, of right and wrong, of what is appropriate in a covenant relationship. No, what is new about the new covenant is the ability of both

---

62. See also Isa 49:8.

63. Von Rad, *Old Testament Theology*, 2:213.

partners to keep the covenant."[64] Humans can at last keep covenant because the missional God graciously gives his covenant partners the ability to be faithful through changing their hearts. Thus, the new covenant will bring about that which God intended from creation: a people faithful to him, displaying his glory.

The unity of the covenants is also clearly seen in the promises of the new covenant. While it is a new covenant and not simply a renewal of the Sinai covenant, there are remarkable similarities such that the new covenant is presented as the fulfillment of all former covenants. I noted above that Jeremiah 33:14–26 links the Davidic covenant with creation and the Abrahamic covenant by promising that the Davidic scion will fulfill the covenant promises. Isaiah 55 explicitly brings together the promises to David with the new covenant. In 55:3–5, God promises,

> I will make with you an everlasting covenant,
>   my steadfast, sure love for David.
> Behold, I made him a witness to the peoples,
>   a leader and commander for the peoples.
> Behold, you shall call a nation that you do not know,
>   and a nation that did not know you shall run to you,
> because of the LORD your God, and of the Holy One of Israel,
>   for he has glorified you.

These are new-covenant promises that come through the new David. While the ESV translates Isaiah 55:3b as "my steadfast, sure love for David," many scholars have noted that the most likely meaning is the "steadfast love of David" (חַסְדֵי דָוִד).[65] In this case, the "everlasting covenant" is equated with the "steadfast love of David." Dempster notes the significance:

> These are not the promises of mercies to David but of David's mercies extended to others. But who can this David be? He cannot be the historical David, who is long since dead. He is none other than the David promised in the first half of Isaiah, Jeremiah's righteous scion, and Ezekiel's "my servant David." . . . It is this

---

64. Gentry and Wellum, *Kingdom through Covenant*, 506.
65. See Gentry and Wellum, *Kingdom through Covenant*, 407–10.

new David who has fulfilled the covenant requirements, made atonement and established an everlasting covenant with all who accept his free offer to partake of his covenant meal (Isa 55:1-2). It is he who will be a witness to the peoples, and their leader and commander. He will bring the knowledge of the Torah and of the covenant to the nations (Isa 42:4-6).[66]

In short, during the exile, God promises to make a new covenant through a new David that will result in forgiveness of sin and the restoration of God's people.

While the mission of God through the new covenant is promised in the Old Testament, the New Testament story shows the fulfillment of this promise through Jesus and in the church. The Gospels present Jesus as the Davidic seed who is the promised eternal king (Matt 1:1).[67] Luke's birth narrative is filled with covenant themes as he presents Jesus as the covenant-fulfilling Messiah (Luke 1:72-73).[68] As the Davidic king, Jesus inaugurates the new covenant. Indeed, Jesus himself interprets his death as a covenant-making event. In Matthew 26:28, Jesus tells his disciples that the cup is "my blood of the covenant." Here Christ is combining the language of Exodus 24:8 with the concept of new covenant from Jeremiah 31.[69] That the concept of new covenant is intended is confirmed by Luke's addition of "new" in the parallel passage (Luke 22:20). Thus, Jesus is teaching that his death inaugurates the new covenant and thus re-creates the people of God. Jesus' mission, then, is a covenantal mission that completes the mission of God begun at creation. Moreover, the resurrection of Jesus points forward to the new creation, in which God's creational intentions are fully realized.

As an apostle of Christ, the new covenant-making Messiah, Paul understands his ministry as new-covenant ministry.[70] While many texts

---

66. Dempster, *Dominion and Dynasty*, 180-81.

67. See the section titled "Jesus Is Israel's Messiah Who Creates the New People of God" in chapter 2 of this book.

68. Williamson, *Sealed with an Oath*, 183-84.

69. R. T. France, *The Gospel of Matthew*, NICNT (Grand Rapids: Eerdmans, 2007), 994.

70. The theme of covenant was also very important in Second Temple Jewish writings. See N. T. Wright, *The New Testament and the People of God*, Christian Origins and the Question of God 1 (Minneapolis: Fortress, 1992), 260-62. Of course, there is much debate on this issue, especially since the seminal work of E. P. Sanders and his concept of "covenantal nomism."

could be mentioned, we need only sample a few important passages. First, in Romans 2, Paul alludes twice to the new covenant, providing a new-covenant context for the entire epistle.[71] In Romans 2:15, Paul alludes to Jeremiah 31:33, arguing that those who obey the word of God through the gospel are new-covenant members. At the end of the chapter, Paul alludes to multiple new-covenant passages, including Deuteronomy 30 and Ezekiel 36, showing that the true people of God are those with circumcised hearts. Thus for Paul, the coming of the Messiah has resulted in the redefinition of the people of God as those covenantally united to Christ, Jew and gentile alike. In the gospel, God has kept his covenant promises to Abraham (Rom 4) and David (Rom 15), thereby fulfilling his mission through Jesus.

Second, in 2 Corinthians 3:6, Paul explicitly labels his ministry as that of a "new covenant" (καινῆς διαθήκης). The new-covenant ministry is far better than the old-covenant ministry of Moses because it is a ministry of the Spirit rather than of the letter. As such, the glory of the new covenant exceeds that of the old covenant (2 Cor 3:7–11). This is the ministry of the promised new covenant "written on tablets of human hearts" (ἐν πλαξὶν καρδίαις σαρκίναις). Paul's wording in 2 Corinthians 3:3 draws together the promises of Jeremiah 31:33 (ἐπὶ καρδίας αὐτῶν γράψω) and Ezekiel 36:26, where God promised to give his people a "heart of flesh" (LXX καρδίαν σαρκίνην). Thus, in the gospel, to which Paul was called as a minister, God is completing his mission of restoration.

Outside Paul's writings, Hebrews is another important new-covenant text. The author twice quotes Jeremiah 31 (Heb 8:8–12; 10:15–18), arguing primarily that the new covenant in Christ is better than the old covenant. It should be noted that the text does not intimate that the old covenant was inherently bad. Rather, it was insufficient because of the weakness of the human partners to keep the covenant. In this regard, the new covenant is simply better. It is better because it is administered by a better high priest who ministers from his heavenly throne (8:1–5). The new covenant also

---

See N. T. Wright's many works as well as the more critical response in D. A. Carson, Peter T. O'Brien, and Mark A. Seifrid, eds., *Justification and Variegated Nomism*, 2 vols. (Grand Rapids: Baker, 2001–2004).

71. See Wendel Sun, *A New People in Christ: Adam, Israel, and Union with Christ in Romans* (Eugene, OR: Pickwick, 2018), 118–32.

offers better promises, specifically the change in heart that the old covenant was unable to produce (8:6–7). The new covenant is inaugurated by
a better sacrifice—Christ's—and results in "eternal redemption" (9:12).
His sacrifice was made once for all (10:12), bringing God's mission to a
climax. By the death of Christ, humanity is renewed and enabled to be the
new-covenant people of God.

THE MISSION OF GOD'S PEOPLE

In the two sections immediately above, we have emphasized the work of
God in the new covenant. The Old Testament promises highlight God's gracious initiative through the repetition of promises ("I will . . ."). The New
Testament continues the same line of thought with particular emphasis on the work of Christ in inaugurating the new covenant through his
death and resurrection. Thus, in both promise and fulfillment, the new
covenant is the work of God alone. However, the unconditional nature
of God's commitment does not mean that the new covenant is devoid of
demands for the human covenant partners. In chapter 2 of this book, I
argued that the mission of the church is to participate in and continue
the mission of Christ. The church should carry out the covenantal aspects
of mission as well. In short, the church is called to carry on the new-
covenant mission of Christ by being the new-covenant community and
by sharing the good news of the new covenant with the nations.

During his ministry on earth, Jesus called disciples to follow him in
faith and obedience. At the beginning of his ministry, Jesus announces,
"the time is fulfilled, and the kingdom of God is at hand; repent
and believe in the gospel" (Mark 1:15). Jesus' new-covenant ministry includes calling people to enter the kingdom of God through faith
in the gospel. The kingdom-shaped message demands a turning from
former allegiances and giving full allegiance to Jesus the King. The
call is simple: follow Jesus in faith and obedience. In this way the new-
covenant demands are similar to all previous covenants. The Gospels are
filled with similar calls to allegiance (Matt 10:34–39; Luke 9:23–27). The
point is clear. Though the new covenant is entirely the work of God,
the demand on human partners is faith and obedience. The glory of the
new covenant is that the ability for such faith and obedience is given by
God through the Spirit.

Paul believed the goal of his ministry to be "the obedience of faith . . . among all the nations" (Rom 1:5). By calling the nations to "the obedience of faith," Paul sought to create new-covenant communities that embody the gospel and proclaim it to those around them. This is the sign of new creation (2 Cor 5:17): people in Christ living in new-covenant holiness. As N. T. Wright argues,

> [Paul] saw the church as a *microcosmos*, a little world, not simply as an alternative to the present one, an escapist's country cottage for those tired of city life, but as a prototype of what was to come. That is why, of course, unity and holiness mattered. And, because this *microcosmos* was there in the world it was designed to function like a beacon: a light in a dark place, as again Jesus had said.[72]

Thus, the new-covenant church is to be a picture of new creation, living holy lives by the power of the Spirit to display the glory of God throughout the world.

First Peter paints the picture of the missional life of the new-covenant community. Written to believers suffering because of their faith, Peter encourages these believers by deepening their understanding of their identity as the new-covenant people of God. In 1 Peter 2:9–10, Peter draws on three Old Testament texts to make a biblical argument for the identity of the church as the new-covenant community. He writes,

> But you are a chosen race, a royal priesthood, a holy nation, a people for his own possession, that you may proclaim the excellencies of him who called you out of darkness into his marvelous light. Once you were not a people, but now you are God's people; once you had not received mercy, but now you have received mercy.

Here Peter alludes to Exodus 19:5–6; Isaiah 43:20–21; and Hosea 2:23. These texts define the church as the new-covenant, new-exodus people of God. Exodus 19, as noted above, is one of the defining texts for Israel and is here applied to the church. They are the royal priesthood, proclaiming the glory of God to the surrounding nations. Both Isaiah 43 and Hosea 2

---

72. N. T. Wright, *Paul and the Faithfulness of God*, Christian Origins and the Question of God 4 (Minneapolis: Fortress, 2013), 1492.

are filled with new-exodus themes. Peter argues that the church has experienced the new exodus, since they have been led out of darkness into the light of being the people of God. With this identity in mind, Peter calls the church to holy living, even as they suffer. In this way, they follow the example of Jesus (1 Pet 2:21–25). Thus the mission of the church in 1 Peter—the call of the new covenant—is to live out the church's identity as the chosen people of God and thereby proclaim his glory.

CONCLUSION

In this chapter we have traced the biblical story of God's covenantal mission to display his glory among all nations. The covenantal view of mission has emphasized several points that should influence the church's understanding and practice of mission. Here I mention two. First, understanding God's mission through the covenants highlights the sovereignty of God in mission. Mission is, above all, God's mission. Mission is *from* God and *for* God. As redeemed humanity, the church participates in God's mission. God's chosen strategy is covenant making, calling people to restorative relationship with him. He fulfills his original intentions for humanity in covenant faithfulness, creating a worldwide people for his glory.

Second, the covenantal view of mission as presented in this chapter should serve as a reminder to the church that being the people of God in Christ is perhaps the most missional activity the church can perform. As Christopher Wright has said, "There is no biblical mission without biblical holiness."[73] I would add that there is no biblical mission without new-covenant unity in the church. Indeed, the primary call of the new covenant is to live holy lives of faithfulness together in community in order to display the glory of God to the nations. Mission is as much being as it is doing. Of course, mission as a state of being does not limit the church's engagement with the nations for the sake of the gospel. Proclamation of the gospel is a fundamental task of the church. However, the covenantal shape of mission reminds us that we must demonstrate the power of the gospel in the new-covenant communities in order to proclaim the truth of the gospel effectively. Craig Bartholomew aptly summarizes the point:

---

73. Christopher J. H. Wright, *The Mission of God's People: A Biblical Theology of the Church's Mission* (Grand Rapids: Zondervan, 2010), 126.

"A missionary encounter occurs when the church believes the Bible to be the true story of the world and thus embodies or 'indwells' the comprehensive claims of that story as a countercultural community over against the dominant cultural story."[74] As such, the new-covenant church lives as the renewed humanity, showing and proclaiming the glorious gospel in anticipation of the return of her king, who will consummate the new creation and dwell forever with his people from every tribe, tongue, people, and nation.

---

74. Craig G. Bartholomew, *Introducing Biblical Hermeneutics: A Comprehensive Framework for Hearing God in Scripture* (Grand Rapids: Baker, 2015), 72.

II

WORLD MISSION STRATEGY

*All authority in heaven and on earth has been given to me.
Go therefore and make disciples of all nations, baptizing them
in the name of the Father and of the Son and of the Holy Spirit,
teaching them to observe all that I have commanded you. And
behold, I am with you always, to the end of the age.*

Matthew 28:18b–20

"Disciples, make disciples!" This is the command of the Lord. Indeed, in the original Greek of the New Testament "make disciples" is the only imperative verb form in the Great Commission. On one hand, it is possible to make too much of this fact, glossing over the Great Commission's own explanation of what "making disciples" means. On the other hand, it is possible to write hundreds of pages on the subject of world mission strategy without any consideration of the role of disciple making as the core, the center, the heart of Great Commission obedience.[1]

While the specific shape of organizational strategies among churches and mission agencies naturally varies, we contend that Christians should look to the Great Commission itself to identify the irreducible, necessary components of what it means to obey it. Thus the leading chapter of this second major section of our book engages directly with the meaning of discipleship in Matthew's Great Commission, the other three Gospels,

---

1. See for example Edward R. Dayton and David A. Fraser, *Planning Strategies for World Evangelization* (Grand Rapids: Eerdmans, 1980).

and the rest of the New Testament, with consultation of the Old Testament as background. The chapter then reflects on how the biblical theology of discipleship addresses disciple making today.

Of course, the direct object of "make disciples" in the Great Commission is "all nations." Thus the second chapter of this major section approaches the "who" of discipleship through an extensive evaluation of the phrase "all nations" throughout the Bible. This chapter pays special attention to an often-overlooked text in Galatians 3:8, where Paul writes that "the gospel" has to do with the blessing of "all nations."

The remaining two chapters of this section on world mission strategy deal with the "how" of discipleship according to Jesus' teaching in the Great Commission. First, obeying the Great Commission means that Jesus' followers must baptize new disciples. Accordingly, the chapter on baptism asserts not only that baptism is an integral component of world mission, but also that Scripture presents a clear biblical theology of baptism. Baptism uniquely and powerfully preaches the gospel.

To conclude this major section, we present a chapter on the crucial role of theological education in world mission. Many missionary-sending churches rightly expect their missionaries to receive theological training in order to ensure faithfulness to Scripture on the mission field. Yet according to the Great Commission, disciple making on the mission field also requires teaching *all* that Jesus commands.[2]

A clear implication follows from the careful studies presented in the four chapters of this section on world mission strategy: obeying the Great Commission requires making disciples of all nations, which *at a minimum* must include the practices of baptism and theological education in accordance with Scripture. This by no means implies that all other acts of missionaries constitute disobedience, only that missionaries should direct their energies through all their varied tasks toward the support of disciple making as defined by the Great Commission. May God receive great glory, and may the work of world mission advance all the more in the power of the Holy Spirit, through reorienting contemporary mission work toward Great Commission obedience!

---

2. In Greek the term for "all" in "*all* I have commanded you" is the same as the "all" word in "*all* authority," "*all* nations," and in the expression for "*always*, to the end of the age." Simply put, "all" indeed means "all." A minimal subset of teachings is clearly not in view.

4

DISCIPLESHIP AS INTEGRAL COMPONENT OF WORLD MISSION STRATEGY

Stephen I. Wright

INTRODUCTION

The so-called Great Commission (Matt 28:18–20) is the most familiar of all New Testament mandates for Christian mission, and it begins with the simple words: "As you go, *make disciples* of all nations" (28:19a; my translation). The purpose of this chapter is to explore just what is meant by this command to "make disciples" and to locate Jesus' words within the sweep of a biblical theology of discipleship that can and should inform world mission today.[1]

We will begin by discussing how Matthew presents the nature of disciples and disciple making, giving the reader the clues needed to understand the command in Matthew 28:19a. We will compare Matthew's presentation to those of the other Gospels, and Acts, in order to highlight the distinct contributions of each. We will then survey the theme of discipleship as it emerges in the rest of the New Testament and within the wider compass of the whole biblical canon, demonstrating that the new commission issued by Jesus is consistent with the purposes of Israel's God as revealed in the Old Testament. Finally, we will suggest some possible implications of our study for contemporary world mission.

---

1. A more thorough overview of the New Testament material than is possible in this chapter is given in Richard N. Longenecker, ed., *Patterns of Discipleship in the New Testament* (Grand Rapids: Eerdmans, 1996).

DISCIPLESHIP IN MATTHEW

When Matthew reports Jesus' closing command to the Eleven to "make disciples," he expects his hearers/readers to know what that means from the story he has told. He has given them—including us—a graphic story of what being a disciple of Jesus entailed while Jesus was physically present. Indeed, like the other Evangelists, Matthew does not so much teach a *concept* of discipleship as tell a *story* of disciples of Jesus. It is important to grasp the nature of Matthew's account of discipleship as *story*, because there is a danger that in our contemporary mission and ministry practices we make "discipleship" sound rather abstract. We cannot reduce it to schemes, formulae, or a syllabus of instruction. It is vitally significant that discipleship rooted in the pattern of the gospel concerns real, complex, many-sided people learning what it means to be loyal to a real person: Jesus Christ, for it is logically impossible to be a "disciple" in general terms; you have to be a disciple of someone or something. Part of the drama of the Gospels is the way that the disciples of Jesus gradually become a distinct and recognizable group.

Matthew's hearers/readers would have known of the concept of a "disciple" (μαθητής in Greek). Although it surfaces quite rarely in the Old Testament (see section The Old Testament Background of Discipleship below), the Jewish historian Josephus writes of Elisha as a disciple of Elijah (*Ant.* 9.33), of the disciples of Elisha (*Ant.* 9.68) and of disciples of the Pharisees (*Ant.* 13.289; 15.3).[2] In the wider Hellenistic world, the word could be used of a pupil of a living philosophical or religious teacher, or a follower of one who was dead. The relationship entailed an element of personal commitment and imitation.[3] The rabbinic literature—later in its present form than the Gospels but no doubt reflecting Jewish practice going back, in some cases, into the first century AD—shows that the rabbis had disciples, passing on to them the "Oral Torah": the traditional interpretations of the law of Moses. The Gospels themselves indicate that Jesus was not unique in having disciples. John the Baptizer had them (e.g., Matt 9:14; John 1:35). The Pharisees proclaim themselves disciples of

---

2. See BDAG, s.v. μαθητής.

3. Michael J. Wilkins, "Disciples and Discipleship," in Joel B. Green, Jeannine K. Brown, and Nicholas Perrin, eds., *Dictionary of Jesus and the Gospels: A Compendium of Contemporary Biblical Scholarship*, 2nd ed. (Downers Grove, IL: InterVarsity Press, 2013), 202–12, esp. 203.

Moses (John 9:28), while Matthew and Mark, like Josephus, both write of the Pharisees themselves having disciples (Matt 22:16; Mark 2:18).

Any study of what it meant to be a disciple of Jesus according to the Gospels will focus on the Evangelists' use of the word μαθητής and its related forms, but must extend much more widely to the picture of the disciples communicated by the narratives as a whole. Our focus here is particularly on the sense of identity implied by being a disciple of Jesus, and the trajectory of his disciples' story.

THE DISCIPLES' IDENTITY:
CALLED TO THE SERVICE OF GOD'S KINGDOM

Matthew is an orderly writer, so it is important to note carefully how he begins his account of Jesus' ministry. He tells us that after John the Baptizer has been arrested, Jesus begins to proclaim, "Repent, for the kingdom of heaven has come near" (Matt 4:17).[4] Jesus then called the fishermen Simon and Andrew by the Sea of Galilee, saying, "Follow me, and I will make you fish for people" (Matt 4:18–22). After this, Matthew records, Jesus went all over Galilee, "teaching in their synagogues and proclaiming the good news of the kingdom and curing every disease and sickness among the people" (Matt 4:23), drawing great crowds (Matt 4:24–25). At that point, "When Jesus saw the crowds, he went up the mountain; and after he sat down [the usual posture of a teacher], his disciples came to him" (Matt 5:1). This is the first mention of "disciples" in the Gospel. So who are they?

As readers, we are surely right to assume that Simon and Andrew, who have been introduced shortly before, are among them. Yet the number and extent of "disciples" are here, as often in the Gospels, left vague. Sometimes it is suggested that when Matthew and Mark use the word "disciples" they are referring only to the inner circle of twelve (on the basis of the usage "the twelve disciples" in Matt 10:1; 11:1).[5] But it is better to see these references to disciples as deliberately ill-defined, because for

---

4. Unless otherwise specified, Scripture quotations in this chapter follow the NRSV.

5. This is asserted, for instance, by Dan Nässelquist, "Disciple," in *The Lexham Bible Dictionary*, ed. John D. Barry (Bellingham, WA: Lexham Press, 2012–2015). R. T. France gives a more nuanced view: *The Gospel of Matthew*, NICNT (Grand Rapids: Eerdmans, 2007), 328–29, 375.

Matthew, like the other Evangelists, historical precision is often not as important as the significance of the history for the ongoing life and mission of the church. And in this short section near the start of his Gospel he is surely teaching us foundational elements of what it entails to be a disciple of Jesus—the kind that he wants to have, in the future, among "all nations" (Matt 28:19).

First, discipleship entails adherence to Jesus—the Jesus who announced that God's kingdom is at hand. Jesus' general proclamation (Matt 4:17) is the context for his call of individuals (Matt 4:18–19). The disciples are seen as those who are not simply drawn to a man, but gripped by the truth of what he is saying.[6] The reality of God's kingdom drawing near precedes the phenomenon of being Jesus' disciples. Any use of the "Great Commission" as a basis for world mission must remember this, for the nearness of God's kingdom requires "repentance," a radical reorientation of outlook and life (Matt 4:17). Being a disciple of Jesus means, fundamentally, allowing that reorientation to take place.

Second, disciples are implicitly defined here as those who respond to the call of Jesus to be with him, whatever cost is involved, and share in his work. The way in which Simon and Andrew immediately leave their trade, their father, and their livelihood (no doubt causing consternation among their family) pictures the complete commitment Jesus calls for. Being a disciple of Jesus is in some ways unique when compared to the idea of "discipleship" with which people may have been familiar. Jesus' disciples are not simply apprenticed to a master to learn a trade, nor simply pupils of a teacher learning a philosophy of wisdom. They are summoned to radical personal commitment to him. Moreover, unlike the disciples of the rabbis who normally chose their teacher, Jesus seems often to have taken the initiative in inviting people to become disciples (in Matthew, see 4:18–22; 9:9; 11:28–30).[7] Jesus' action underlines that the community

---

6. Thus James D. G. Dunn rightly begins his helpful book *Jesus' Call to Discipleship* (Cambridge: Cambridge University Press, 1992) with a chapter on "The Call of the Kingdom," 6–31.

7. Nor, as Best points out with reference to Mark, do the Gospels envisage the possibility that the disciples of Jesus will ever become "Christs" in the way that the disciples of rabbis or philosophers could themselves in due course become rabbis or philosophers. See Ernest Best, *Following Jesus: Discipleship in the Gospel of Mark*, Journal for the Study of the New Testament Supplement Series 4 (Sheffield: JSOT, 1981), 248–49.

of disciples is not something that arises in a merely haphazard way; it is Jesus' deliberate intention to form it. Since he is not an authorized teacher, amassing a group of disciples requires outgoing initiative. Of course, people can also join the group on their own initiative (Matt 8:19).

As we shall see, it is possible to be genuinely a disciple without physically accompanying Jesus. Moreover, Jesus' healing of Peter's sick mother-in-law (Matt 8:14–17) shows us that the call to leave one's old life does not imply a lack of care for those left behind. Yet the situation of these first disciples is surely meant as a paradigm by Matthew. Responding to Jesus' call to be with him and share in his work, "fishing for people," means making the choice to leave a settled lifestyle and embark on one of great vulnerability. Being with Jesus enables them also to observe his life and actions at close quarters. It is revealing that when the high priest's servant girl sees Peter in the courtyard while Jesus is inside being tried, she accuses him of having been "with" Jesus (Matt 26:69, 71): one of the simplest and most powerful pictures of what being a disciple means (see also Mark 3:14). As they go with him, the disciples learn what is entailed in drawing people to the God whose kingdom Jesus proclaims.

Third, this opening series of scenes in Matthew shows us that a disciple can be defined as one who listens to Jesus. It is the disciples to whom the first great collection of Jesus' teaching in Matthew, known as the Sermon on the Mount, is addressed (Matt 5:1). The second, fourth, and fifth collections of Jesus' teaching in Matthew are also addressed to disciples (Matt 10:1–5; 18:1; 24:1). Additionally, the third collection, Matthew 13:1–53, has private teaching to the disciples inserted within addresses to "crowds." Matthew thus presents the disciples as those who are learning from Jesus' teaching. They must go on attending to learning from Jesus, as the voice from the cloud when Jesus is transfigured makes plain to the innermost group of three: "This is my Son, the beloved; with him I am well pleased; listen to him!" (Matt 17:5). Matthew presents Jesus as the one with unique authority to reveal God's will (Matt 28:18; see also 7:29). So discipleship means, quite simply, learning from Jesus to do the will of God. Matthew has gathered much of the core teaching of Jesus into thematic blocks that will help the new disciples, those "made" by the original ones, to go on learning from Jesus when he is no longer visible.

This three-sided definition of discipleship—adherence to Jesus as he proclaims and embodies God's kingdom, responding to his call to be with him and share in his work, listening to and learning from him—is visualized as we follow the disciples' story through Matthew. In the process, we see that those identified as disciples are a remarkably inclusive group. Matthew repeats Jesus' warnings against those who would try to "purify" the group prematurely, in the story of the wheat and the weeds with its interpretation (Matt 13:24-30, 36-43) and the urging to restore the "lost" (Matt 18:1-35), as well as the vision of the sheep and the goats at the last judgment, when there are surprises in store for both groups (Matt 25:31-46). The corollary of Jesus' teaching is that even the closest and most loyal of disciples are presented as needing constantly to learn, and they should not presume that their closeness gives them special status above other disciples. At the same time, the division between those who are responsive and those who are resistant to Jesus' announcement of God's kingdom, which becomes clearer as the narrative of Jesus' ministry progresses, is manifest on a much wider scale than the division between those who are literal followers of Jesus and those who are not. In Jesus' words, the "field" in which God's kingdom is becoming manifest is "the world" (Matt 13:38), not merely—as we might say—"the church"; the disciples bear witness to God's kingdom, but they are not simply identified with it. Let us now trace the main outlines of the story.

THE DISCIPLES' STORY: LEARNING FROM JESUS

Matthew gives no indication in Matthew 5:1 of how many disciples gather to listen to Jesus' teaching. At the close of the "sermon" in Matthew 7:28, he mentions "crowds" rather than disciples. Matthew's choice of terms could imply that on some occasions, Jesus started speaking to a small group (perhaps just the Twelve), then others gradually crept up to eavesdrop. But perhaps Matthew deliberately leaves the relationship between "disciples" and "crowds" ambiguous at this point; he simply wants to identify disciples as those who come to hear Jesus.

The possibility of intermingling "disciples" and "crowds" is strengthened by the beginning of the sermon with announcements that seem to have a wide intended audience. Rather than being instructions for a small group, they are blessings and assurances—directed toward giving hope to Israel's poor, those who realize that they must look to God alone for rescue. Those who are pronounced blessed (Matt 5:3–12) are precisely the kinds of people of whom, it seems, those drawn to Jesus were made up. The calling of Matthew the tax collector and the subsequent feast with others of his kind (Matt 9:9–13) demonstrate the desire of Jesus to make disciples of the "poor in spirit" and their ready response to that call. Thus the way in which Matthew has structured this collection of Jesus' words suggests that rather than being a manual for the wise and experienced, the sermon is to be seen as good news for the needy. The first step in discipleship is readiness to accept Jesus' message of hope: hope that God's kingdom is indeed dawning for the blessing of all who at the moment seem most downtrodden and oppressed. That Jesus begins his sermon with these startling statements of fact illustrates that being a disciple is about a reorientation of the mind to God's surprising truth before it is about obeying specific commands.

On the basis of this good news, Jesus seeks to establish a group identity among the disciples (as in Matt 5:13, "You are the salt of the earth"; Matt 5:14, "You are the light of the world"). He shows how his followers are to be marked out from others, specifically from the dominant Pharisaic approach in the land at the time (Matt 5:17–6:24). Here Jesus seems to have his sights on a group larger than a handful; his language suggests he is seeking a renewal of God's people Israel as a whole. He also warns that superficial enthusiasm is not the same as true obedience: "Not everyone who says to me, 'Lord, Lord,' will enter the kingdom of heaven, but only the one who does the will of my Father in heaven" (Matt 7:21). The crowds may be astounded at his teaching (Matt 7:28), but will they be those who act on it, thus building their "house" on the rock (Matt 7:24–27)? Here Matthew sets up the tension that will continue throughout his narrative. The listeners may already be called disciples, but who among them will truly learn?

As the story proceeds, we see the disciples becoming more visible as a group distinguished from other groups, such as the disciples of John or those of the Pharisees (Matt 9:14). When Jesus breaks conventional mores and has dinner with tax collectors and "sinners," the disciples are with him (Matt 9:10). Like Jesus, they do not fast (Matt 9:14); and, presumably imitating Jesus, they pluck heads of grain as they walk through the grain

fields on the Sabbath (Matt 12:1). They further draw the Pharisees' attention by not taking part in ritual washings before eating (Matt 15:2).

The vaguely defined group called "disciples" in Matthew 5:1 is
replaced in the next block of teaching by "his twelve disciples" (Matt 10:1),
more commonly called "the twelve apostles" (Matt 10:2). These are
those known by Matthew's congregation in the early church as the first
Christian leaders (with the exception of Judas Iscariot) and appear in
the Gospels as the inner core of disciples. They are those who persevere
longest in Jesus' company, though even they abandon him in his hour of
greatest need (Matt 26:56). It is these eleven (now without Judas) who
will gather once again on a mountain in Galilee (Matt 28:16) to receive
Jesus' final commission, after their female companions have run to tell
them about the resurrection (Matt 28:1–10).

In Matthew 10:5–39, Jesus sends out the Twelve "to proclaim the
good news" and demonstrate the signs of God's kingdom (Matt 10:8).
The instructions he gives them apply to the immediate situation, while
Jesus himself is still engaged in his ministry, but also look ahead to the
situation after he has gone. The Twelve become a representative group
in Matthew's narrative, not (as we have seen) because they are in any
way superior to other disciples, for they are case studies in the need to
learn and grow in faith. Rather, it is because they are those who most
nearly exhibit the radical commitment Jesus calls for and because in
simple fact they are the visible remnant at the end of the story to whom
Jesus can entrust his ongoing work. In their number, parallel to Israel's
twelve tribes, they very likely symbolize Jesus' understanding that God
had called him to renew Israel itself. Jesus' mission to renew Israel lends
meaning to his promise that these disciples will sit on thrones, judging
the twelve tribes (Matt 19:28).

While the visible group of disciples narrows to a tiny number at the
time of Jesus' death, it is clear that even in the time of Jesus' ministry, not
all those to be regarded as disciples are literal followers. Anyone who is
committed to the kingdom announced by and embodied in Jesus may be
regarded as a disciple, which becomes very clear in Matthew 12:49–50.
Jesus points to his disciples and says, "Here are my mother and my brothers! For whoever does the will of my Father in heaven is my brother and
sister and mother." Here Jesus makes two crucial equations. First, he says

(by his gesture) that *his disciples* are family; the bond that ties him to them is closer than blood kinship. Being a "disciple of Jesus," then, is no part-time hobby, but a relationship with Jesus and other disciples. Yet, second, he says that those who do the will of his Father are family. Thus he makes the possibility of discipleship universal, implying that it does not depend on physical proximity to him. This saying also reflects the continued possibility that those who *are* in physical proximity to him, indeed those who seem very eager to follow him, may not all do the Father's will consistently. And in his portrayal of those who are visible disciples of Jesus, Matthew shows us the two sides of the coin; here are people who *do* learn, who *do* share in Jesus' work, yet can also be slow and have "little faith."

Accompanying Jesus gives opportunity for the disciples to learn from his ways as well as his words and to put that learning into practice within a fellowship of followers. It enables them to ask questions of Jesus and receive his answers (e.g., Matt 13:10–23, 36–43; 19:1–12; 19:16–20:16). Some are close eyewitnesses of Jesus' transformative dealings with individuals, which helps prepare them for their own future ministry. They are with Jesus when he goes to the house of Jairus, raising his daughter and healing a woman with hemorrhages on the way (Matt 9:18–26). Not only does Jesus trust his closest associates with proclaiming and enacting the good news among "the lost sheep of the house of Israel" (Matt 10:5–42). He also enlists their help in feeding the crowds (Matt 14:13–21; 15:32–39), arranging for his entry into Jerusalem (Matt 21:1–11), and preparing for the Passover meal (Matt 26:17–19). These occasions prepare us (as they no doubt prepared the disciples themselves) for hearing about the ongoing mission they were to exercise under Jesus' authority, once his physical presence was gone (Matt 28:18–20).

The other side of the disciples is seen when they are afraid on the storm-struck lake, and Jesus rebukes them for their little faith (Matt 8:23–27; see also 14:22–36). On another occasion, they urge Jesus to send away a Canaanite woman shouting for help (Matt 15:23); Jesus himself seems initially reluctant to help (Matt 15:24), but relents, and his praise for the woman's faith acts as an implied rebuke to their attitude (Matt 15:28). The incidents of the epileptic boy (Matt 17:14–20) and the cursing of the fig tree (Matt 21:18–22) provide further object lessons in faith. Matthew encourages us today with this realistic picture of the disciples' misunderstandings and slow learning.

Matthew's third block of teaching (Matt 13:1-53) shows how Jesus' message is dividing his hearers between those who accept it and those whose ears are dull to its urgency. In particular, the parable of the sower with its interpretation (Matt 13:1-8, 18-23) pictures varying degrees of responsiveness to the "word of the kingdom." It is addressed to the crowds (Matt 13:2), which implies that Jesus believes there are some among them who may yet turn out to be seed on good soil (Matt 13:8, 23). Yet in this chapter the disciples—those who, at least for the moment, demonstrate receptivity to the word—emerge more starkly as a group marked out from the crowd. They come and ask Jesus about the parables (Matt 13:10, 36). In his response Jesus draws a contrast between the resistance of the dull-hearted, as in Isaiah's time (Matt 13:13-15), and the disciples, who are blessed because they see and hear (Matt 13:16-17). At the end of this teaching section the disciples affirm that they do indeed understand (Matt 13:51), and Jesus calls them scribes "trained [literally 'discipled'] for the kingdom of heaven." As Matthew's narrative proceeds, the division between those who "understand" and those who do not becomes starker still. Jesus' home synagogue is offended by him (Matt 13:54-58).

As the narrative moves to its climax, Matthew highlights the disciples' own lack of comprehension—and ultimately, loyalty—more intensely. Having pronounced Peter blessed for his God-given insight into Jesus' identity, Jesus rebukes him for his complete failure to understand its implications (Matt 16:22-23). It is telling that it is his *disciples* to whom Jesus addresses the words, "If any want to become my followers, let them deny themselves and take up their cross and follow me" (Matt 16:24). As events will show, they are willing to go so far, but not to the very end.

It is therefore fitting that the fourth collection of teaching (Matt 18:1-35), as well as material in the subsequent chapters, focuses especially on the attitudes appropriate to Jesus' disciples as they become a fledgling community. When the disciples ask Jesus who is the greatest in the kingdom of heaven (Matt 18:1), he responds that they are to be humble like children (Matt 18:2-4), and do everything possible to guard others and themselves from "stumbling" and win them back when they have strayed (Matt 18:5-35). In this chapter, Jesus refers to "these little ones"

(Matt 18:6, 10) as those who "believe in me" (Matt 18:6), as well as to "your brother or sister" (Matt 18:15; see also v. 21, "my brother or sister"). These are clearly equivalent phrases to each other as well as descriptions of "disciples." The reason that Matthew does not use the word "disciple" in these contexts is probably that, as often, he is recording Jesus' teaching with an eye to the postresurrection Christian communities of his own time. When Jesus was no longer physically present, the language of family and "little ones" perhaps came more readily to describe his followers than the language of discipleship.

The necessity for this teaching is acted out when they try to turn away those bringing little children to him and Jesus has to correct them (Matt 19:13–15), when they argue about who is the greatest (Matt 20:20–28), and when they are angry at a woman's "waste" of ointment on Jesus (Matt 26:6–13). Such incidents illustrate the unconventional attitudes that truly accepting God's kingdom requires, and the welcome to all kinds of people that is inherent in the kingdom's presence.

In the final block of teaching (Matt 23:1–25:46), after warning them against the scribes and Pharisees for being "blind guides," Jesus points his disciples to the time of national and cosmic judgment ahead and the suffering for his followers that will accompany it. They are to be wise and watchful. The block concludes with the vision of the nations gathered before the Son of Man on "the throne of his glory" (Matt 25:31), that is, his God-given place of authoritative judgment. Here we find that Jesus is essentially making the possibility of discipleship a worldwide one. This passage is important for Matthew's presentation of discipleship, in two ways.

First, people do not have to encounter Jesus in the flesh to find themselves on the right side, the side of the sheep, on the day of judgment. They are judged, rather, on their response to "the least of these brothers and sisters of mine" (Matt 25:40; see also 25:45, "the least of these") — that is, his disciples. We note the more widely accessible family language again, rather than that of "discipleship."

Second, people may not recognize that in serving his brothers and sisters, they are serving Jesus. Both those who have done so and those who have not express surprise at the king's verdict (Matt 25:37–39, 44). This teaching again throws open the possibility of discipleship very widely; even knowledge of the name of Jesus, it seems, is not required, just the (probably costly) business of caring for, and thus identifying with, those who are his "brothers and sisters."[8]

In common with other passages (e.g., Matt 7:21), Matthew 25 makes it clear that we should not equate discipleship with simple profession of faith. It is those who do the will of the Father whom the Father welcomes into his kingdom and who are in fact identified by Jesus as his brothers and sisters (Matt 7:21; 12:50; 25:34–36). As Jesus says earlier in Matthew's Gospel, anyone who even gives a cup of cold water "to one of these little ones" because they bear the name "disciple" will have a reward (Matt 10:42). This statement raises the further question of how Jesus expects his brothers and sisters, his disciples, to be recognized. Again his teaching earlier in Matthew is plain: "You will know them by their fruits" (Matt 7:20). Thus the idea of being a disciple becomes equivalent to being "righteous"; "whoever welcomes a righteous person in the name of a righteous person will receive the reward of the righteous" (Matt 10:41).[9]

The closeness of the disciples, and especially the Twelve, to Jesus through his ministry contrasts with their withdrawal from him as his death approaches. In describing Jesus' prayer in Gethsemane, Matthew, alone among the Evangelists, specifically uses the word "disciples" on two of the occasions when Jesus returns to Peter, James, and John and finds them sleeping, as if to underline that those closest to him are no longer "with him" in spirit. Judas's betrayal (Matt 26:47–50), Peter's denial (Matt 26:69–75), and the desertion of all the male disciples (Matt 26:56) leave Jesus a lonely figure indeed, though supported by many women who look on from a distance as he dies (Matt 27:55–56) and tended by a disciple whom we have not previously encountered, Joseph of Arimathea, after death (Matt 27:57–60).

In the Gospel, the story of the disciples ends where it began, with God's gracious gift. As Jesus took the initiative to call them (Matt 4:19), and the first words Jesus uttered to his gathered followers were words of blessing

---

8. There has been much debate about the identity of the "least of these," the "brothers and sisters" in this passage. Some have drawn the conclusion that Jesus identifies himself here with all who are poor and needy. Undoubtedly the Gospels testify to Jesus' compassion for and alignment with the marginalized, but in Matthew the "little ones" or "brothers and sisters" seems to refer explicitly to disciples, those who owe allegiance to Jesus (whether during his lifetime or afterwards).

9. Other passages in which Matthew emphasizes "righteousness" include Matt 1:19; 5:6, 10, 20; 6:33.

(Matt 5:1–12), so it is plain that only the gracious forgiveness of God, extended through Jesus, could have commissioned for service those whose loyalty to Jesus has faltered in his hour of greatest need. The promise of his presence "to the end of the age" (Matt 28:20) is what sustains all disciples still.

Matthew, then, portrays the disciples as those who respond to Jesus' proclamation that God's rule has drawn near. They are those who observe his life and help to carry out his work. They are those who learn from Jesus as they listen to his words. Matthew is happy to use the word "disciple" quite inclusively; he is clear that the first disciples, including the inner circle, frequently failed and had much to learn. However, he is also clear that full-blooded discipleship entails commitment and perseverance. For some it may entail death itself (Matt 16:24). That commitment is equated with doing the will of God (Matt 7:21; 12:49–50). Literal following is not a requirement of discipleship. In the story, those who do literally follow fail at the end and can only be commissioned for future service because Jesus does not count that failure as final. Yet the commitment and perseverance demonstrated at least partially by the Twelve gives to all future disciples, those whom the Twelve will "make," the pointer for the life of complete dedication to God, which is now thrown open to all people. Disciples of Jesus have an awesome responsibility, because it is through their attitude to Jesus' disciples that people reveal their attitude to Jesus himself. Undergirding all this teaching on discipleship is the gracious initiative, forgiveness, and presence of this Jesus.[10]

DISCIPLESHIP IN MARK, LUKE–ACTS, AND JOHN

Let us now briefly turn from Matthew to see how the other Evangelists give us their unique perspectives on Jesus' disciples.

MARK

Mark's presentation of the disciples is similar to Matthew's. In particular, he underlines Jesus' warning against exclusivism with the saying

---

10. The centrality of discipleship to Matthew's view of mission is discussed in detail in David J. Bosch, *Paradigm Shifts in Theology of Mission*, 20th anniversary ed. (Maryknoll, NY: Orbis, 2011), 74–84.

"Whoever is not against us is for us" and the incident that prompts it, in which John forbids someone from casting out demons in Jesus' name because he is not a literal follower (Mark 9:38–39; see also Luke 9:50).

One of the most obvious differences is that although Mark certainly highlights Jesus' role as a teacher, his Gospel contains comparatively little of the content of Jesus' teaching, and thus brings the actions and sufferings of Jesus into comparatively greater prominence. The way Mark describes the appointment of the twelve apostles is characteristic. He does not even use the word "disciple": "And he appointed twelve, whom he also named apostles, to be with him, and to be sent out to proclaim the message, and to have authority to cast out demons" (Mark 3:14–15). As in the other Gospels, the Twelve function in the story as representative disciples, displaying both that closeness to Jesus and also that slowness to learn that, for the Gospel writers, were clearly at the heart of the experience of discipleship. But here in Mark the emphasis is not so much on the content of what Jesus teaches them as on their "being with" Jesus and being caught up into sharing in his powerful work.

The other key difference is that whereas Matthew represents the disciples as those who—at least in part—understand the revelation being given to them through Jesus (Matt 11:25; 13:51; 16:17), Mark's picture is bleaker. He includes none of these positive affirmations and underlines that they do not understand Jesus' words about his impending death (Mark 9:32). We might say that while Matthew shows the disciples as, to some extent, representatives of the postresurrection church, Mark shows them as representatives of all the unresponsive humanity for whom Jesus died. The way of the cross disciples must tread thus entails crucifying all naively optimistic self-evaluation. Yet the picture is hopeful. In Ernest Best's words summarizing Mark's view of discipleship: "If the journey is open-ended because the cross is not just something reached and left behind but is ever present, it is also open-ended because it is a journey in mission. It is a journey beyond the cross into the resurrection; it is a journey of expansion in search for others."[11]

---

11. Best, *Following Jesus*, 249.

LUKE–ACTS

Luke in some respects defines discipleship more radically than Matthew and Mark. Matthew and Mark both record Jesus' warnings to his disciples that to follow him means to take up the cross, but as we saw, Matthew 16:24 (see also Mark 8:34) recognizes that one might still have the identity of a "disciple" even if one chooses not to take up the cross and follow Jesus to the end. Luke's equivalent verse (Luke 9:23) is similar, but there Jesus' words are addressed to "all." It is a universal call to radical discipleship rather than (as in Matthew and Mark) a warning to existing disciples about how hard true allegiance to Jesus will be. And in Luke 14:27 Jesus' words come over more bluntly: "Whoever does not carry the cross and follow me cannot be my disciple." In the same section, "hating" one's family and giving up all one's possessions are also said to be conditions of discipleship (Luke 14:26, 33). Similarly austere is the description of disciples in Luke's version of the Beatitudes as "you who are poor" (Luke 6:20). In Matthew it is explicitly a disciple who says to Jesus, apparently on his own initiative, "Lord, first let me go and bury my father" (Matt 8:21). In Luke it is just "another," who says it in response to Jesus' command, "Follow me" (Luke 9:59). Luke defines discipleship more simply as radical following, while Matthew gives more recognition to the distinction between having the identity of a disciple and going the full distance in urgent, literal following.

Yet Luke also extends the process that is also apparent in Matthew and Mark, of telling the stories in such a way that they will be demonstrably applicable after Jesus in his physical person has gone. Indeed, Luke's inclusion of the word "daily" after "take up their cross" in Luke 9:23 seems designed to underscore that the call of discipleship is not just for a specific time (the weeks and months leading up to Jesus' crucifixion). "Hating" (i.e., putting in second place) one's family and giving up all one's possessions sound extreme enough, and yet they are also ways of expressing, at any point in history, that readiness to die that is required of only a few.

Other incidents, unique to Luke, also point to the wide sphere in which "discipleship" may be worked out, even when, as far as we can tell, the people concerned do not literally follow Jesus. Thus Mary is surely to be taken as an exemplary disciple as she "sat at the Lord's feet and listened to what he was saying" (Luke 10:39). So, indeed, is Martha in her hospitality (Luke 10:38), though Jesus chides her for her anxious distractedness

(Luke 10:41). They show their discipleship in their own home. Similarly, Jesus declares that salvation has come to Zacchaeus' house (Luke 19:9); he gives evidence of his discipleship through declaring that he will give half his goods to the poor and giving fourfold restitution to those he has cheated (Luke 19:8). In no sense does Jesus, or Luke, chide Zacchaeus because he has not given away *all* his possessions (see Luke 14:33), or make their affirmation of him conditional on his following Jesus all the way to the cross.

Another detail unique to Luke worth noting here is the information about the women who accompany Jesus along with the Twelve (Luke 8:1-3). This text and others in Luke especially highlight the role of women and Jesus' regard for them, thus making clear the universal possibility of discipleship. These texts in Luke also display the practical implications of discipleship, in that many women contribute to the common fund out of their own means.

Perhaps Luke's most striking contribution to our understanding of what it means to be a disciple of Jesus, though, is the structuring of his central section as a journey narrative in which Jesus makes his way to Jerusalem (Luke 9:51-19:28). By presenting this journey as one in which Jesus is constantly teaching his disciples, even as he continues to engage with the various crowds and individuals he encounters, Luke evokes the early Christian image of discipleship as "the Way" (Acts 9:2).[12] Through attending and responding to the teaching given on the journey, Luke's readers may also—it is implied—be genuine followers of this "Way" even though they cannot see Jesus in the flesh. This journey is also the setting for a second "mission" of the disciples, this time involving seventy acting as heralds of Jesus (Luke 10:1-12, 17-20), rather than just the Twelve as in the first one (Luke 9:1-6; see also Matt 10:1-42, Mark 6:7-13).[13] This sending of the Seventy foreshadows the wider mission of the fledgling Christian movement, described in Acts.

---

12. Mark also offers glimpses of this, as when he tells us that the healed Bartimaeus "followed [Jesus] on the way" (Mark 10:52). For an excellent comparison of Mark and Luke on this theme see Best, *Following Jesus*, 247.

13. Whether there are seventy disciples in Luke 10:1 and 17 or seventy-two is a matter of debate in New Testament textual criticism. See Bruce M. Metzger, *A Textual Commentary on the Greek New Testament*, 2nd ed. (Stuttgart: Deutsche Bibelgesellschaft, 1994), 150-51.

Luke uses the word "disciple" less than Matthew in his Gospel, but perhaps that is because he wants to use it extensively in Acts. So although Luke does not use "disciples" in his version of the Great Commission (Luke 24:46–49), saying instead that "repentance and forgiveness of sins"[14] must be proclaimed in Jesus' name to all nations, he certainly demonstrates its outworking in terms of which Matthew would have heartily approved. In Acts the early Christians are regularly simply designated "disciples" (see Acts 6:1, 2, 7; 9:1, 10, 19, 25, 26, 38; and a number of other places through the book). It is interesting that the first of these references, Acts 6:1 (and also 6:7), tells us that the disciples are "increasing in number." The disciples are making more disciples, as per Matthew 28:19. "Disciple" (along with "believer") seems to be a normal term for "Christian." It is, therefore, critical that Christians today take with the utmost seriousness what this biblical term means.

JOHN

John mentions disciples frequently and in a distinctive way. In particular, he recounts personal encounters of disciples with Jesus in much more detail than the synoptic Evangelists. Jesus' meetings with Simon, Andrew, Philip, and Nathanael in John 1:25–51 and his appearances to various disciples after his resurrection in John 20:1–21:23 are prominent examples of this. It is notable that his long discourse on the night of his betrayal is punctuated by questions from named disciples: Simon Peter (John 13:36), Thomas (John 14:5), Philip (John 14:8), and Judas (John 14:22). All this helps the individual reader or hearer of the Gospel to grasp the personal quality of relationship to Jesus that discipleship entails. To an even greater extent than the other Gospels, John enables his readers to identify with the disciples in their excitement and puzzlement, in their loyalty and their failure.

Like the other Gospels, John makes it plain that the disciples face the fundamental challenge of whether they will continue with Jesus. Starting out with him is no guarantee that they will stay the course till the end. If

---

14. Repentance and forgiveness are prominent motifs in Luke. Perhaps repentance is his equivalent to Matthew's emphasis on "righteousness," which he partly shares (see 116n9). Both terms stress the challenge for disciples to be more than just listeners or hangers-on, even if that is where they have begun.

any will be "truly" Jesus' disciples, they must "continue in my word" (John 8:31). Uniquely, John records that after Jesus' difficult teaching about his being "the bread of life," many disciples turn back (John 6:66), and Jesus asks the Twelve whether they also wish to go away (John 6:67). Simon protests his loyalty (John 6:68–69), but Jesus reveals his knowledge that one of them is a "devil" (John 6:70—Is this a suggestion that Judas Iscariot, before his betrayal of Jesus, will try to tempt him aside from the path he knows he must take?).

The question of whether disciples will stay with Jesus is a central example of how John brings the division between discipleship and opposition to Jesus into starker relief than the other Evangelists. From early in John's Gospel, we get a sense of the competing allegiances to which the residents of Palestine might be drawn. One of John (the Baptist)'s disciples reports that Jesus is now baptizing, and "all"—presumably those who might up to that point have gone to John for baptism—"are going to him" (John 3:26). Ominously, the Pharisees hear about this too (John 4:1), although John (the Evangelist) qualifies the information by saying, "It was not Jesus himself but his disciples who baptized" (John 4:2), giving a picture of their strong group identity and shared activity, which points ahead to the mission of the early postresurrection Christians. In John 9:27 the man born blind (and now healed) taunts the Jewish leaders, "Do you also want to become his disciples?" The newly healed man's question provides the opportunity for the leaders to draw the line between their group and that of Jesus: "You are his disciple, but we are disciples of Moses" (John 9:28).

Throughout his Gospel John paints the contrast between light and darkness, belief and unbelief, belonging to Jesus and not belonging to him, in vivid colors. Explicitly and implicitly, he shows the disciples as those who believe (John 2:11), who come to the light (John 3:21), who are his sheep (John 10:27), though the disciples' positive response should not cause any to become complacent, as Jesus clearly thinks it necessary to ward off the danger of any "stumbling" (John 16:1).

The sense of the close bond between Jesus and his disciples reaches its climax shortly before Jesus' death. After Jesus' final summons to the crowds to belief in the light while they have the light (John 12:35–36, 44–50), interwoven with John's note that many continue not to believe, while others believe but are afraid to admit it (John 12:37–43), John's Last Supper scene shows us Jesus' absolute commitment to "his own" (John 13:1) as he washes their feet (John 13:3–11). Jesus' closeness with his disciples is not a warrant for their remaining in a closed huddle, because it is through their love for one another, stemming from his love for them, that "all people" will know that they are his disciples (John 13:35). The discourse that follows in chapters 14–16 is full of assurance for them about the future as well as a sense of the opposition they will face from "the world," understood as all that stands against the will of God the Father. Jesus' love for "his own" is sealed in the prayer that he prays for them (John 17:1–26).

John thus brings to the surface that which is partly latent in the other Gospels: that discipleship is a matter of absolute and ultimate commitment by Jesus to his followers and his followers to him. To be sure, John still shows us the disciples growing and learning, failing and falling. But his portrayal of them both reflects and seeks to direct the life of the early church, in which loyalty to the community of believers—and to Christ in and through that community—was a costly yet vital choice. Against this backdrop, the personal touch with which John shows us Jesus' disciples is warmly encouraging.

The common yet varying emphases of the four Gospels may be illustrated by the story of Joseph of Arimathea. In Matthew he is called a disciple (27:57), in John a secret disciple (19:28), while in Mark (15:43) and Luke (23:51) he is "waiting expectantly for the kingdom of God." Mark and Luke seem to retain the flavor of uncertainty and vagueness that must have characterized the time of Jesus' actual ministry on the question of who exactly can be called a disciple. Matthew and John use the word "disciples" in a more thoroughgoing way and thus narrate Jesus' ministry in a manner that reflects the establishment of the disciples as a distinct and continuing group, in contradistinction to others. At the same time, Luke makes the practice of discipleship widely accessible by using more general terms for Joseph: "a good and righteous man" (Luke 23:50).[15]

---

15. Note that this echoes the words of the centurion about Jesus in Luke 23:47 as well as the characterization of Zechariah and Elizabeth at the beginning of the Gospel, before Jesus is even born (Luke 1:6).

DISCIPLESHIP IN THE
REST OF THE NEW TESTAMENT

Strikingly, the word "disciple" does not appear in the New Testament out-side the Gospels and Acts. This fact suggests its authenticity as a desig-nation for those who followed Jesus while he was physically with them and in the aftermath of his resurrection. It also reflects the natural devel-opment of a range of fresh terminology that sought to do justice to the full dimensions of belonging to the risen Lord and being indwelled by his Spirit—most notably, the Pauline notion of being "in Christ."

However, the concept of "learning" that lies at the heart of disciple-ship continues to be important in the Letters, and the word μανθάνω, "learn," occurs quite often. Discipleship requires holistic, transforma-tional learning, not mere absorption of information: "It implies accep-tance of Christ himself, rejection of the old existence and beginning the new life of discipleship in him."[16] The phrase "That is not the way you learned Christ" (Eph 4:20) especially captures the disciple's kind of learn-ing. Often "learning" relates to specific Christian teaching that has been, or is being, handed on (e.g., Rom 16:17; 1 Cor 4:6; 14:31, 35; Col 1:7; 1 Tim 2:11; 2 Tim 3:7, 14). For Paul and the other New Testament writers, such teaching is always rooted in the grace received through Christ (e.g., Titus 3:4–7) while showing the response that grace calls for—"learning to devote themselves to good works" of various kinds (Titus 3:14).

It is also important to note that the "learning of Christ" expected of disciples in the early churches was mediated partly by other disciples. They did not have a physical Jesus to accompany, but they had other Chris-tians, who, albeit imperfectly, modeled the way of Jesus. Thus we find the language of imitation, which is closely related to that of discipleship. Not only are Christians called to "be imitators of God, as beloved children" (Eph 5:1). Other Christians, especially leaders, are to be imitated. Paul can say, "Be imitators of me, as I am of Christ" (1 Cor 11:1; see also 1 Cor 4:16; Phil 3:17; 1 Thess 1:6; 2 Thess 3:7, 9; Heb 13:7). More widely, Paul commends the Thessalonian church for becoming "imitators of the churches . . . in Judea" in their willing suffering for Christ (1 Thess 2:14). In Philippians,

---

16. C. Blendinger, D. Müller, and W. Bauder, "Disciple, Follow, Imitate, After," in *NIDNTT* 1:480–94, esp. 486–87.

not only does Paul make extensive use of his own example (see especially Phil 3:1–14); he specifically commends the example of other, named individuals to the Christians' attention: Timothy (Phil 2:19–24), Epaphroditus (Phil 2:25–30), and even, though he urges them to be united, Euodia and Syntyche (Phil 4:2–3).[17]

In general, although the language may differ, there are strong continuities between the picture of disciples and discipleship within the Gospels and Acts on the one hand, and the rest of the New Testament on the other. The members of the early churches prove themselves just as fallible as the disciples in the Gospels, just as much needing to depend on God's grace in Jesus, and often having just as much to learn. Those who are genuinely learning often give evidence of this in their readiness to suffer, as Jesus did. Second Corinthians, Hebrews, and Revelation in particular highlight this theme.

THE OLD TESTAMENT
BACKGROUND OF DISCIPLESHIP

The word μαθητής occurs only twice in the Greek Old Testament (LXX), and then only as a variant reading (Jer 13:21; 20:11).[18] Isaiah apparently has a group of "pupils" (28:16 MT; translated "disciples" by NRSV. The LXX reading does not give a direct translation of the MT here), but the most we can say about other prominent figures is that they have personal assistants, "servants." Moses has Joshua (Exod 24:12), Elijah has Elisha (1 Kgs 19:21), Elisha has Gehazi (2 Kgs 4:12), and Jeremiah has Baruch (Jer 32:12–15).[19]

As Dietrich Müller points out, there is a simple reason for this lack of "disciples" in the Old Testament narrative: no prophet or teacher, however great, was regarded as a direct mediator with God in the way that Jesus came to be recognized.[20] The Torah itself was God's word to which his people were subject; Moses, the priests, the prophets, and wisdom

---

17. Paul S. Cable, "*Imitatio Christianorum:* The Function of Believers as Examples in Philippians," *TynBul* 67 (2016): 105–25.

18. See BDAG, s.v. μαθητής.

19. Blendinger, Müller, and Bauder, "Disciple, Follow, Imitate, After," 485. Note, however, that Josephus wrote of the disciples of Elisha (see above). See also Wilkins, "Disciples and Discipleship," 202.

20. Blendinger, Müller, and Bauder, "Disciple, Follow, Imitate, After," 485.

teachers were but servants of that word, to communicate and apply it in different circumstances. And yet the grand pattern of the Old Testament narrative, and a key theme within it, point very suggestively to the New Testament concept of discipleship.

First, the story of Israel itself foreshadows the story of Jesus' disciples in the Gospels. Israel, like the disciples, is called and taught. Like the disciples, the Israelites often fail truly to learn and need to be forgiven. They too are called into an uncertain, itinerant lifestyle, in which they are to model particular behavior. Second, the theme of "the way" is an important Old Testament image for the direction of one's life, whether following the path of wickedness or that of Torah (Ps 1 and many other places). There is an obvious connection here with "the Way" as a name for the early Christian movement (Acts 9:2) as well as the journey narrative in Luke (see above). At times of both wandering and being settled, Israel is called to a path of life marked by the character of the God who has set it apart as holy (Lev 19:2).

These links between Old Testament and New Testament should not be taken as implying that the disciples "replace" Israel in any sense. Rather these links imply that the path of trust and obedience set out before God's people from ancient times is continuous with the path to be trodden by Jesus' disciples. Jesus reveals the path and opens the borders of Israel beyond ethnic lines. As Christopher Wright argues, the Great Commission itself (Matt 28:18-20) has the character of a covenant established by God. It marks the development, not the annulment, of God's gathering and shaping of a people for himself.[21]

BIBLICAL DISCIPLE MAKING TODAY

How, then, should we summarize the implications of a biblical theology of discipleship for world mission today? First, Matthew 28:19 leaves us in no doubt of the biblical centrality of the task of making disciples. Although "mission" cannot simply be defined as "disciple making," disciple making is at its heart. Moreover, "disciple" is overwhelmingly the main category used in the Gospels and Acts for the followers of Jesus.

---

21. Christopher J. H. Wright, *The Mission of God: Unlocking the Bible's Grand Narrative* (Downers Grove, IL: InterVarsity Press, 2006), 354–55, 391, 512.

Different though our situations are from theirs, Jesus' first disciples continue to act as exhibits of what it means to follow him, in their failures as well as their dedication. The Old Testament, despite the rarity of discipleship language, shows us that human beings are called to learn the ways of God and follow them. The New Testament shows us the one who not only has all authority to teach these ways, but has brought to life again the possibility of obeying them.

Second, we should take seriously the need for learning, which is implied in the concept of discipleship. All those engaged in Christian mission should remind themselves that Jesus does not command his disciples to make converts, but to make disciples. In the nature of the case, that can never be an overnight process. It entails discovering through study, practice, and experience what it is to follow the way of the Lord. The union of intellectual and practical dimensions in learning Christ is summed up in Paul's call for us to offer our *bodies* as a living sacrifice, being transformed by the renewal of our *minds* (Rom 12:1–2). Therefore both a long-term challenge and great patience are entailed in making disciples. We are to be prepared not merely to proclaim, expound, and apply the truth of Christ, which is vital, but to model the way of Christ, whose name we bear, so that others may over time learn his ways too. We are to be realistic about the fact that every disciple faces many forks in the road, which test their commitment to continue humbly learning from Jesus. Conversely, just as Matthew seems to use the term "disciple" quite inclusively, we should not despise those whose interest or commitment may seem embryonic, nor those who are doing similar things to us, but not as part of our group.

Third, disciples are those who join themselves in visible, explicit ways to Jesus and join with fellow disciples in doing so. (This principle need not deprecate the witness, nor cast doubt on the integrity, of those who, through the threat of danger, must temporarily keep their discipleship secret; Joseph in John 19:28 may act as an encouragement to such brothers and sisters.) It is in such communities, small or large, official or unofficial, that the practicalities of following Jesus are worked out. Just as the question of who is the greatest would probably not have arisen if James and John had not been part of a group of twelve with Jesus, so the beautiful dynamics of mutual loving service cannot be experienced in solitude.

Such communities should not be led in authoritarian ways that seek to impose tight controls on disciples' thinking and practice. The stories of Jesus with his disciples suggest that they should be arenas where no question is seen as too foolish or dangerous to ask, and thus where genuine learning can take place. They should be environments of grace where forgiveness is exercised for lapses "seventy times seven" (Matt 18:22). They should be spheres of love and truth where honest rebukes can be given and discipline exercised, but always in the spirit and aim of restoration to fellowship, the place of safety where the "little ones" can be brought back and helped to stay on the way (Matt 18:10–20).

No particular model of the church is implied by the concept of discipleship, and we should be wary of attempts to impose such a model as if it were the only one guaranteed to form true disciples. Some kinds of church are very good at displaying the inclusive dimension of discipleship; people of all kinds feel very welcome to join the fellowship and learn from Jesus in a gradual and informal way, asking questions and expressing doubts freely.[22] Other kinds of church are very good at displaying the teaching and discipline that always keep before disciples the challenge of Jesus to love God with all one's heart, mind, soul, and strength (Mark 12:29–31), and one's neighbor as oneself. Both kinds are equally radical and authentic in their way, and of course ideally it does not have to be an either/or choice. Both kinds are also susceptible to veering away from the Master's spirit: the one through underplaying the cost of discipleship, the other through underplaying the generous welcome of Jesus to all.

Finally, the concept of discipleship may sometimes have been downplayed, for fear that it should undermine the truth that salvation is given by the free grace of God alone, received by faith alone. I hope that all I have said here will show that that is a groundless fear. Yet it is worth stressing once more that the story of the disciples as presented in the Gospels is supremely a story of grace. Jesus announces the reality of God's kingdom and invites people to discover it and share in its expression and extension. In the archetypal accounts of people starting to follow, it is Jesus who takes the initiative to call them (Matt 4:18–22; Mark 1:18–20).

---

22. Dunn expresses well the "openness" of the community of discipleship as seen in the Gospels in *Jesus' Call*, 111–13.

Jesus remains committed to them despite their slowness to catch on to his teaching and manner of life. In the end they desert him, but in his risen person he graciously restores them. Without grace, there would have been no disciples, and there would certainly have been no disciple making after the resurrection. Disciples today also depend on the grace of God, made known in Jesus, from start to finish.

Conversely, however, it is a truncated and subbiblical gospel that proclaims Jesus' salvation without his lordship, initial commitment without ongoing learning, "decisions" without discipleship. Undoubtedly, such one-sided proclamation has sometimes been in reaction to versions of Christianity that appear to present Jesus' way as a pilgrimage with an uncertain destination, a hard slog that depends largely on human effort. But we should not separate what God has joined. Faith and obedience are more deeply intertwined than often imagined, in both Old and New Testaments (see Rom 1:5, and the entire argument of Romans, if in doubt about this). Hebrews, which presents Jesus more clearly than any other biblical book as the supreme and final sacrifice for sin, also presents him unequivocally as the pioneer we are called to follow (Heb 12:1-2). And Jesus' own invitation to come to him and find rest (Matt 11:28) is bound up with the call to take his yoke upon us, and *learn* from him, for his yoke is easy, and his burden is light (Matt 11:29-30).

5

FOCUS ON "ALL NATIONS" AS INTEGRAL COMPONENT OF WORLD MISSION STRATEGY

Jarvis J. Williams and Trey Moss

INTRODUCTION

Missionaries take the gospel to the ends of the earth so that people will become disciples of Jesus Christ and be transformed by the power of the gospel. Christian mission is an important topic of discussion in New Testament scholarship.[1] Christian writers, preachers, and churches have labored to make disciples of all nations since Jesus commanded his original disciples to do so through the Great Commission after his resurrection. While Christians generally grasp the paramount importance of taking the gospel to and making disciples of the ἔθνη ("nations") and πάντα τὰ ἔθνη ("all nations"), the precise meaning of ἔθνη and πάντα τὰ ἔθνη at times seems less certain.

Much contemporary missiological theory assumes a modern social-scientific definition for ἔθνη, which is to say that the focal point of mission efforts is finely delineated "families of mankind—tongues, tribes, castes, and lineages of men."[2] This line of thinking results in casting world mission primarily in terms of engaging socioculturally differentiated "people groups." Yet one could well question the legitimacy of interpreting the Great Commission through the controlling lens of

---

1. For examples, see the detailed work of Schnabel and the bibliography in Eckhard J. Schnabel, *Early Christian Mission: Jesus and the Twelve* (Downers Grove, IL: InterVarsity Press, 2004); and Schnabel, *Early Christian Mission: Paul and the Early Church* (Downers Grove, IL: InterVarsity Press, 2004).

2. Donald A. McGavran, *Understanding Church Growth* (Grand Rapids: Zondervan, 1970), 62.

modern anthropology. Simply put, does Jesus indeed command his followers to disciple all *nations*, meaning analytically defined people groups? Or does Jesus command his followers to disciple *all nations*—all people in every place? We believe that clarity can come to this debate through a return to interpreting the meaning of biblical texts in context, then applying biblical teaching to the contemporary practice of world mission.

Discovering the meaning of ancient words in ancient texts and then expressing those meanings accurately in modern languages presents a challenge for contemporary believers.[3] Even so, grammatical-historical interpretation of the Bible is always a worthwhile challenge, for the concept of biblical authority requires that the teachings of God's word remain paramount in Christian faith and practice. In this essay we focus on the meaning of ἔθνη and πάντα τὰ ἔθνη in Galatians 3:8 (a central text for understanding the gospel message) and Matthew 28:19 (the Great Commission). Our thesis is that ἔθνη can carry either a universal meaning that includes both Jews and gentiles, or a specific meaning that exclusively refers to gentiles (i.e., non-Jews) in certain texts. However, Paul's use of ἔθνη and πάντα τὰ ἔθνη in Galatians 3:8 and Matthew's use of πάντα τὰ ἔθνη in Matthew 28:19 most plausibly refer to Jews and gentiles—all of humanity—scattered throughout the world. We support this thesis in four ways. First, we survey a few uses of ἔθνη in selected texts in the Septuagint and the New Testament. Second, we argue that Paul's uses of ἔθνη in Galatians primarily refer to non-Jewish people in general. Third, we discuss the meaning of ἔθνη and πάντα τὰ ἔθνη in Galatians 3:8. Fourth, we consider the meaning of πάντα τὰ ἔθνη in Matthew 28:19. Finally, we conclude the essay with an urgent exhortation to Christians to pursue mission to all people near and far as God leads.

---

3. For a few examples of different ways authors understand ἔθνη and πάντα τὰ ἔθνη, see arguments and bibliography in James M. Scott, *Paul and the Nations: The Old Testament and Jewish Background of Paul's Mission to the Nations with Special Reference to the Destination of Galatians* (Tübingen: Mohr Siebeck, 1995); John Piper, *Let the Nations Be Glad!: The Supremacy of God in Missions*, 3rd ed. (Grand Rapids: Baker, 2010).

ΕΘΝΗ IN SELECTED TEXTS
FROM THE SEPTUAGINT

Within the Pentateuch, the term ἔθνη often identifies those who are not God's people.[4] Ἔθνη at times specifically refers to the nations that God drove out before Israel entered the promised land (Exod 23:18, 27; Deut 7:1). The term also refers to non-Jews in general (Exod 15:14; 33:16; Num 24:8; Deut 7:6). In Numbers 14:14–16, the people (λαός) of Israel are contrasted with the ἔθνη, whom the Lord has not chosen as his own: "And will you destroy this people [λαόν] as one man, and the nations [ἔθνη] who heard your name will say, He destroyed them because it is beyond the ability of the Lord to bring this people [λαόν] into the land which he swore to them" (LXX Num 14:15–16).[5] In Deuteronomy 7:6, the phrase πάντα τὰ ἔθνη distinguishes Israel from non-Jewish people in general. Moses says to Israel, "Because you are a holy people to the Lord your God, and the Lord your God chose you to be to him a chosen people from all the nations [πάντα τὰ ἔθνη] which are on the face of the earth." Thus, the term ἔθνη functions in the above texts to distinguish non-Jewish people from Yahweh's covenant people.[6]

Certain prophecies in Isaiah concern the relationship of Israel with the ἔθνη (Isa 2:2–3; 8:9; 10:7; 11:10, 12; 14:2, 12, 26; 16:8; 17:13; 25:7; 30:28; 33:3, 12; 34:1–2; 37:26; 40:15, 17; 41:5; 42:4; 43:9; 45:1; 49:1, 22; 51:5; 52:15; 54:3; 55:5; 60:2–3, 12; 62:2, 10; 64:1; 66:18–19). While Israel is still distinct from the ἔθνη, Isaiah prophesies the ἔθνη will come to Zion to learn the ways of the Lord (Isa 2:3; 60:11, 12; see also Isa 11:10, 12; 12:4; 42:4; 43:9; 49:1, 6; 51:5; 62:2). Promises of salvation for the ἔθνη intertwine with pronouncement

---

4. For a few examples, see LXX Exod 15:14; 23:18, 27; 33:16; 34:24; Lev 18:24; 26:33; Num 14:15; 24:8; Deut 7:1, 6–7. As Scott (*Paul and the Nations*, 58) has shown, ἔθνη can at times refer to all the nations of the world, including Israel. Our analysis in this section is not intended to be exhaustive, but we simply make the point here that the term can refer to non-Jewish people in general. For a detailed analysis of ἔθνος in the Old Testament, Jewish sources, and Paul's letters, see Scott, *Paul and the Nations*. For a recent study of ἔθνος and γένος with regard to race and Paul's identity, see Love L. Sechrest, *A Former Jew: Paul and the Dialectics of Race* (New York: Bloomsbury T&T Clark, 2009). Sechrest analyzes thousands of occurrences of γένος and ἔθνος in a variety of ancient sources.

5. This is the author's translation. The words λαός and λαόν are the same word in the original language. The morphological difference between the two words is a result of their grammatical function in the sentence. Λαός is a subject and λαόν an object.

6. The distinction between λαός as Israel and ἔθνη as gentiles is also found in the book of Acts (see Acts 26:17, 23; 28:17).

of judgment (see Isa 34:2). Thus within the book of Isaiah, we see a shift from the exclusion of the ἔθνη to their inclusion within God's eschatological and soteriological purposes for the Jewish people.

The contrast between Israel and the ἔθνη is also evident in the apocryphal books of Tobit and 1 Maccabees.[7] The two books differ in their stance toward the ἔθνη, yet both works employ ἔθνη as a general reference to non-Jews. For the purposes of our argument, we focus here on Tobit 13–14. Tobit prophesies that if Israel, while in exile, should turn to the Lord with all their heart and soul, then the Lord will turn to them, gather them from the ἔθνη (13:5), and show his might and power to the ἔθνη sinners (13:6). Tobit prophesies that if these sinners turn to God, he may perhaps have mercy on them. In his farewell address to his son as an old man (14:3–11), Tobit prophesies that God will have mercy on his people and bring them back from exile (14:5–7). Tobit asserts that after the faithful Israelites rebuild the temple and the city of Jerusalem, all the nations (πάντα τὰ ἔθνη) will fear the Lord (14:5).

The perspective of the author of Tobit concerning the nations' rejection of idolatry to serve and fear the one true God coheres with the prophetic visions of Jeremiah and Isaiah (Jer 14:6–7; Isa 2:2–3; 60:2–3). The book of Tobit envisions the return of Jews from the diaspora to Palestine in conjunction with the gentiles turning to the Lord (Tob 13:6–11; see Isa 11:12; 43:5–7; 54:7; Jer 29:13–14; 31:7–10; 32:37; Zech 14:16).[8] Like the Old Testament prophets, the book of Tobit paints an optimistic picture of Jews and gentiles worshiping the Lord in harmony.

First Maccabees expresses a less sanguine perspective toward the destiny of the ἔθνη. Written as a history of the Maccabean revolt against the Seleucids' dominance over the land of Israel (175–143 BC), the book presents the ἔθνη as a threat to Jewish identity (1 Macc 1:42; 2:12, 18–19, 40, 44; 3:10, 25–26, 48, 52; 4:11, 14, 45, 54, 60; 5:1, 9–10, 19, 21, 38, 43, 57; 7:23; 12:53; 13:6; 14:36). Judas Maccabeus and his brothers revolt against King

---

7. For an overview of the books of Tobit and 1 Maccabees, see David deSilva, *Introducing the Apocrypha: Message, Context, and Significance* (Grand Rapids: Baker Academic, 2002), 63–84, 244–65. Tobit's presence at Qumran (4Q196–200), notably four copies in Hebrew and one in Aramaic, demonstrates its wide readership and popularity in the Second Temple period. So James C. VanderKam, *The Dead Sea Scrolls Today*, 2nd ed. (Grand Rapids: Eerdmans, 2010), 53; Daniel J. Harrington, *Invitation to the Apocrypha* (Grand Rapids: Eerdmans, 1999), 25.

8. deSilva, *Apocrypha*, 74, 80.

Antiochus Epiphanes IV's decree to hellenize all cultures throughout his kingdom, through which Antiochus bans the Jews from participating in Torah-compliant worship (1 Macc 1:42).

Mattathias, the patriarch of his family, bemoans the apostasy of Israel and the defiling of the temple by the ἔθνη (1 Macc 2:12). When officials from Antiochus come to Modein, the village where Mattathias and his sons live, he kills one of the officials and an apostate Jew who offers swine's flesh on an altar.[9] Mattathias' deathbed charge is that his sons must pay back the ἔθνη (1 Macc 2:68). Throughout the narrative, the ἔθνη threaten the Maccabeans with destruction. Yet the Maccabeans eventually overcome their oppressors. Simon, the oldest surviving brother, sets up an independent kingdom and removes the yoke of the ἔθνη from Israel (1 Macc 13:41; see Deut 28:48; Isa 9:3; 10:24–27; 14:24–27; Jer 30:4–8; Ezek 34:27–28).[10]

ΕΘΝΗ IN SELECTED NEW TESTAMENT TEXTS

Ἔθνη often means non-Jews in general in the New Testament.[11] In Matthew, Jesus contrasts the cares and concerns of the ἔθνη with his own followers, whom he commands to seek the kingdom of heaven and his righteousness (Matt 6:32). Jesus commends to his disciples a mission that at first excludes the ἔθνη. In Matthew 10:5, Jesus instructs his recently selected

---

9. The narrative compares Mattathias with Phinehas (Num 25:6–15; see Sir 45:23–24) with respect to their "zeal for the law."

10. Jonathan Goldstein, *1 Maccabees*, Anchor Bible 41 (New York: Doubleday, 1976), 477–78. The perception of the ἔθνη in 1 Maccabees is not monolithic. On one hand, the ἔθνη are portrayed as characteristically arrogant and foolish (1 Macc 1:3, 21, 24). On the other hand, the Hasmonean dynasty (the name of the Maccabean family's dynasty) forms alliances with the ἔθνη. These alliances help Israel establish political independence. For example, Rome and Sparta (two ἔθνη) are presented as allies of the Jewish people (1 Macc 8:23–32; 12:6–18). This alliance reveals that according to 1 Maccabees, there is a right and a wrong way for Jews and gentiles to interact. Interaction that does not threaten Jewish identity is encouraged. However, Jews who betray the covenant and align themselves with the Seleucid throne are castigated as "renegades" or "lawless ones" (1 Macc 9:23, 58, 68–69; 10:61). What is most essential for the authors of Tobit and 1 Maccabees is Jewish faithfulness to the covenant. Faithfulness to the covenant is the key for Maccabean deliverance from their oppressors and the future ingathering of the gentiles to Jerusalem for worship (Tob 13:11). This note on the perception of the ἔθνη in Tobit and 1 Maccabees is paraphrased from deSilva, *Apocrypha*, 263–64.

11. E.g., Matt 6:32; 10:5; 12:21; 20:25; Luke 2:32; 21:24; Acts 9:15; 13:46, 47; 15:7, 14, 23; 18:6; 21:11; 22:21; Rom 3:29; 9:24; 15:9, 10, 11, 12, 16; 16:26; Gal 2:9; 3:14; 2 Tim 4:17; Rev 14:18; 16:19; 19:15; 20:8; 21:24.

Jewish apostles to avoid going in the way of the ἔθνη and to avoid entering into the villages of the Samaritans. Instead Jesus urges his disciples to minister to the lost sheep of Israel. Later in the narrative, Jesus contrasts the leadership style of the rulers of the ἔθνη with the leadership style of the disciples of the kingdom (Matt 20:25; see also Luke 21:24).[12]

Also in Acts, the term ἔθνη can refer to non-Jews in general. Ananias describes Paul's mission as directed to "Gentiles [ἐθνῶν], kings, and the sons of Israel" (Acts 9:15). This statement indeed forecasts Paul's later ministry. When Jews reject Paul's message, he and his colleagues "turn to the ἔθνη" (Acts 13:46–47; see also Isa 49:6). The non-Jewish nuance of ἔθνη is evident in the account of the Jerusalem Council. Peter reminds those in attendance in Acts 15:7, "You know that from the earliest days among you that God chose the ἔθνη to hear and believe the word of the gospel through my mouth." Writing to the brothers of Antioch, Syria, and Cilicia (Acts 15:23), James' words support that ἔθνη could refer to non-Jewish believers who live in those regions.

In Romans 3:29, Paul uses ἔθνη to contrast Jews and non-Jews: "Is God only the God of the Jews? Is he not also the God of the ἔθνη? Yes, he is even the God of the ἔθνη."[13] The Jew-and-gentile binary opposition is found in the thesis statement of the letter: "I am not ashamed of the gospel, for it is the power of God for salvation to all who believe, both to the Jew first and to the Greek" (Rom 1:16). Ἔθνη is not used here. Instead, Paul uses the Greek word Ἕλληνι. Yet, when compared with Paul's comments in Romans 1:14 about Greeks and barbarians, ἔθνη appears often to be a broad Pauline term in Romans to describe multiple kinds of non-Jews (e.g., Rom 2:1–3:20; see also Eph 2:11–21). These non-Jews include barbarians (non-Greek speakers), Greeks (Rom 1:16; 3:9), and any other non-Jewish person (Rom 3:29–30).

In Romans 9:30–33, Paul returns to the question from Romans 3:29–30 regarding whether God is God of both Jews and gentiles (ἔθνη). In the former text, he considers the implications of God's sovereign choice prior to that person doing anything good or evil (see Rom 9:11). Paul's series of

---

12. Like Isaiah, both Matthew and Luke envision a time when the gentiles will turn to God (Matt 12:21; Luke 2:32).

13. Here the Greek word is the genitive plural ἐθνῶν ("of the Gentiles").

rhetorical questions beginning in Romans 9:30 sustains the Jew-gentile binary. The ἔθνη received the righteousness that is from faith, although they did not seek it (Rom 9:30). Israel sought righteousness from the law by works, but did not obtain it (Rom 9:31–32). In Romans 9:30, ἔθνη appears to refer to the totality of gentiles in general, not to specific groups of ἔθνη distinguished from Israel. In Romans 9:30–31, in contrast with the ἔθνη, Israel seems to refer to Jews in general since Paul identifies himself as a Christ-following Israelite in Romans 11:1 to support that God has not forsaken his people (i.e., Israel). Paul's remarks in Romans 11:25–27 support this interpretation of ἔθνη when he says that the fullness of the "Gentiles" (ἐθνῶν in Rom 11:25) will lead to the salvation of "all Israel" (Rom 11:25–26). The "deliverer will come from Zion" (Rom 11:26), he will turn ungodliness from "Jacob" (Rom 11:26; see Isa 59:20–21), and he will forgive "their sins" (i.e., Israel's sins; Rom 11:27).

Paul also cites Jesus as an example of selfless service for Jews and gentiles (Rom 15:7). Paul notes there is a difference between the relationship of Jesus' self-sacrificial service to gentiles and to God's purposes for Jews and gentiles. For the circumcision—Jews (Rom 15:8)—Jesus became a servant in order to confirm God's promises to the patriarchs (see Rom 9:1–11:36), but for the ἔθνη, Jesus became a servant for the sake of mercy in order to glorify God (Rom 15:9; see also Ps 17:50; Deut 32:43). Thus Paul uses ἔθνη in these texts in Romans to refer to non-Jews (i.e., gentiles).

ΕΘΝΗ IN GALATIANS 1–2

In Galatians 1–2, Paul primarily uses ἔθνη to designate non-Jews in general and to highlight the Jew-gentile binary.[14] However, in these chapters ἔθνη also occasionally has a universal nuance, referring to both Jews and gentiles. Though this universal nuance appears to be secondary in Galatians 1–2, the universal use of πάντα τὰ ἔθνη appears to be primary in Galatians 3:8 and 3:14. In Galatians 1:11–24, Paul recounts his apostolic call to the ἔθνη through a revelation from God about Jesus Christ (Gal 1:16). In Galatians 1–2, Paul highlights that his work focuses on the

---

14. For essays addressing various debates on Galatians, see Mark D. Nanos, ed., *The Galatians Debate* (Peabody, MA: Hendrickson, 2002). For a social-identity reading of Galatians, see Philip F. Esler, *Galatians* (London: Routledge, 1998).

ἔθνη, while Peter's work focuses on the Jews. His statements about his gospel for the uncircumcision and Peter's gospel for the circumcision highlight the gentile-Jew binary without using the term ἔθνη to identify the uncircumcision (Gal 2:7).

In Galatians 2:11–14,[15] Paul explicitly builds on the Jew-gentile binary and their unity in Christ by faith apart from works of the law, stating that Jewish Christians should not compel the ἔθνη to become Jews (Gal 2:14). In Galatians 2:12, ἐθνῶν (the genitive plural form of ἔθνη), the phrase "those from the circumcision," and a reference to Peter (a Jew) impress a gentile-specific (i.e., non-Jewish) meaning on ἔθνη in Galatians 2:11–14. The terms Ἰουδαῖος ("Jew/Judean"; Gal 2:14), ἐθνικῶς ("Gentile manner of life"; Gal 2:14), Ἰουδαϊκῶς ("Jewish manner of life"; Gal 2:14), and Ἰουδαΐζειν ("to live a Jewish manner of life"; Gal 2:14) manifest both the Jew-gentile binary and the ethnically specific reference to gentiles in Galatians 2:12. Paul says that Peter's act of separating from table fellowship with the ἐθνῶν led Barnabas (a Jew) and the rest of the Jews (Ἰουδαῖοι) to be complicit in Peter's hypocrisy (Gal 2:13). Their hypocrisy is out of step with the gospel (Gal 2:14). Thus Paul condemned Peter in the presence of "all" (Jews and gentiles; Gal 2:14). Peter stood condemned by his actions (Gal 2:11), because he was out of step with Paul's gospel that he received from God and which God commissioned him to preach as good news to the ἔθνη (Gal 1:1, 6–12, 16–24; 2:11, 14; see also 1:16).

In Galatians 1:10, Paul defends the gospel he preached to the ἔθνη against the distorted gospel of rival teachers in Galatia (see Gal 1:6–8).[16] Paul counters their distorted gospel, reminding the Galatians that his gospel comes from God (Gal 1:1, 10–12). Paul's gospel about God's Son for the ἔθνη contrasts with his previous manner of life in Judaism, which was marked by zealous adherence to the "traditions of the fathers" (Gal 1:14).[17]

---

15. Galatians 2:11–14 and the crisis in Antioch present different interpretive challenges. For a discussion of the issues in Gal 2:11–14, see commentary and bibliography in A. Andrew Das, *Galatians*, Concordia Commentary (St. Louis: Concordia, 2014), 196–231.

16. Scholars have offered various proposals concerning the identity of the agitators. For a discussion, see Das, *Galatians*, 10–14.

17. Similar to the way some of his Jewish ancestors violently responded to the threat of Israel's God being dishonored by gentiles (Phinehas [Num 25] and Mattathias and his sons [1 Macc 1–2]), Paul expressed his zeal for the traditions of his fathers through violence against Christ-following Jews (Gal 1:13–14; Acts 8–9).

The revelation of Jesus Christ he received from God commissioned him to announce God's Son as good news to the ἔθνη (Gal 1:13–14, 16).[18]

In Galatians 1:15–16 Paul uses similar language to that of Jeremiah in order to express his calling to announce the gospel of God's Son to the ἔθνη (LXX Jer 1:5).[19] God appointed Jeremiah to be a prophet to the ἔθνη (LXX Jer 1:5).[20] Ἔθνη in Jeremiah 1:5 includes Israel and other nations (ἔθνη). The Lord tells Jeremiah he will go to "all" to whom he should send him (LXX Jer 1:7). The Lord further says to Jeremiah he will set him over "nations" (ἔθνη) and "kingdoms" (βασιλείας; Jer 1:10). The coordination of ἔθνη and βασιλείας here suggests that ἔθνη in LXX Jeremiah 1:10 refers to both Jews and gentiles. Jeremiah's prophecy includes messages both to Israel and Judah and to other nations (see Jer 27–31).[21]

When Paul recounts his visits to Jerusalem, he mentions the visit he made to the Jewish "pillars" with Titus (a gentile) and Barnabas (a Jew; Gal 2:1–3). Paul emphasizes that during their meeting with the Jewish pillars, no one compelled Titus (a Greek) to be circumcised (the Jewish sign of the Abrahamic covenant). Despite the Jewish pillars' approval of Paul's gospel and mission to the gentiles, otherwise unknown (and likely Jewish) "false brothers" (Gal 2:4) secretly entered into their meeting to spy out the freedom Jews and gentiles have in Christ. Paul's mission to the ἔθνη (i.e., non-Jews) is affirmed by the Jewish pillars at Jerusalem. Paul's gentile

---

18. On the question of when Paul turned to the ἔθνη after God revealed this mission to him, see comments and bibliography in Michael F. Bird, *An Anomalous Jew: Paul among Jews, Greeks, and Romans* (Grand Rapids: Eerdmans, 2016), 85–87.

19. For a discussion of potential Old Testament allusions, see Martinus C. de Boer, *Galatians*, New Testament Library (Louisville: Westminster John Knox, 2011), 90–91. For an analysis of the presence and function of Scripture in Gal 1–2, see Roy E. Ciampa, *The Presence and Function of Scripture in Galatians 1–2*, WUNT 2 (Tübingen: Mohr Siebeck, 1998). For Isaiah as a background behind Paul's gospel in Galatians, see Matthew S. Harmon, *She Must and Shall Go Free: Paul's Isaianic Gospel in Galatians*, Beihefte zur Zeitschrift für die neutestamentliche Wissenschaft 168 (New York: de Gruyter, 2010).

20. God's appointment of Paul to announce his Son as good news to the ἔθνη in 1:16 may primarily emphasize gentiles (i.e., non-Jews), but Jeremiah's prophetic call seems to be a call to both Jews and gentiles. But if we read Gal 1:16; 3:8, 14 together, perhaps the function of ἔθνη in these two texts is a matter of emphasis: primarily a reference to gentiles in 1:16, but a universal reference to Jews and gentiles in 3:8a–b and 3:14. The latter point seems right in light of Paul's appeal to LXX Gen 12:3 (and 18:18) in Gal 3:8 and his comments about Jews and gentiles experiencing the blessing of Abraham in Gal 3:14.

21. Additional examples further support the universal nuance of ἔθνη in LXX Jer 1:5. The Lord promises disaster will come on "all of those who dwell upon the earth" (LXX Jer 1:14). The Lord calls "all the kingdoms of the north" against the cities of Judah (LXX Jer 1:15–16).

mission is contrasted with Peter's Jewish mission to the circumcision (see also Gal 2:7, 9b). Paul's specific reference to Titus's Greek identity in the presence of the Jewish pillars of the church as he presented to them his gospel that he preached to the ἔθνη (ἔθνεσιν in Gal 2:3) highlights the non-Jewish nuance of ἔθνη in Galatians 2:3.[22]

ΕΘΝΗ AND ΠΑΝΤΑ ΤΑ ΕΘΝΗ IN GALATIANS 3:8 IN THE CONTEXT OF GALATIANS 3:1–14

Galatians 3:1-14 is a dense text. In Galatians 3:1-14, Paul argues that ἔθνη[23]—non-Jews—do not need to be Torah observant in order to receive the promises of Abraham (Gal 3:1-29). In Galatians 3:8, Paul uses ἔθνη to express that God's promise to bless πάντα τὰ ἔθνη in Abraham is realized by the justification by faith of Jews and gentiles apart from works of the law (see Gen 12:3; 18:18; 22:18; 26:4; 28:14). Paul's certainty that the Abrahamic blessing extends to gentiles through a faith analogous to Abraham's is based on Christ's (Abraham's true offspring in Gal 3:16) death and resurrection (Gal 1:4; 3:1, 13-14).[24]

Paul uses ἔθνη and πάντα τὰ ἔθνη alongside a catena of multiple scriptural texts (see Gen 12:1-3; 15:6 within Gal 3:6-9, 16; Deut 21:23; 27:26; 28:58; 30:10 within Gal 3:10-14).[25] Genesis 15:6 emphasizes that Abraham (a gentile) received right standing in the presence of God by faith apart from observance of the law before he was circumcised (see Gen 17). He applies these passages to Jews and gentiles with faith in Christ in light of Jesus' death and resurrection (see Lev 18:5; Hab 2:4 with Gal 3:11-14).[26] God's universal work of justifying Jews and gentiles by faith apart from

---

22. Paul mentions that no one compelled Titus (a Greek) to be circumcised until the "false brothers" sneaked into the meeting and (presumably) urged Titus to be circumcised. This adds further evidence of non-Jewish nuance for ἔθνεσιν in Gal 2:3.

23. The word for gentiles (ἔθνη) appears frequently in the first three chapters of the letter. For a few examples, see Gal 1:16; 2:2, 8, 9, 12; 3:8, 14.

24. On how faith justifies, see Thomas R. Schreiner, *Galatians*, ZECNT (Grand Rapids: Zondervan, 2010), 197-98.

25. See Das, *Galatians*, 283.

26. For a work focusing on scriptural echoes, citations, and allusions in Paul, see Richard B. Hays, *Echoes of Scripture in the Letters of Paul* (New Haven, CT: Yale University Press, 1993). For a work focusing on Paul's hermeneutics of faith, see Francis Watson, *Paul and the Hermeneutics of Faith*, 2nd ed. (London: Bloomsbury T&T Clark, 2016).

works of the law fuels Paul's ensuing comments in Galatians 3:28 about the unity of Jews and gentiles in Christ. The ἔθνη and πάντα τὰ ἔθνη receive an equal share of the Spirit in Christ apart from works of the law (Gal 3:10–14). Jews and gentiles by faith in Christ receive an equal portion of Abraham's inheritance by faith (Gal 3:29), even as their distinct ethnic and social markers remain apparent (as in Gal 3:28).

THE MEANING OF ΕΘΝΗ AND ΠΑΝΤΑ ΤΑ ΕΘΝΗ IN GALATIANS 3:8

As our analysis has demonstrated, the terms Paul uses to categorize groups of people are flexible in the ancient sources.[27] That is to say, their meanings are fluid and can change markedly based on the context in which these terms appear. Thus in theory Paul could be employing the two mentions of ἔθνη in Galatians 3:8 in distinct ways. However, context suggests that he uses the term to emphasize gentile inclusion into the Abrahamic blessing along with Christ-following Jews. He appears to universalize ἔθνη in Galatians 3:8a by placing the adjective πάντα before ἔθνη in Galatians 3:8b to include both Jews and gentiles within the promise to Abraham. These gentiles (ἔθνη) have faith in Christ. As a result, they receive the blessing of Abraham by faith in Jesus Christ apart from works of the law (see Gal 2:16; 3:1–5), like Jewish Christians (Gal 2:16) and like Abraham (Gal 3:6; see LXX Gen 12:3). Paul applies the verse to Jews and gentiles who are justified and receive the Spirit by faith (Gal 3:8–9, 14).[28]

Paul's statement in Galatians 3:8 about God's promise of the justification of the ἔθνη appears to be a combination of texts from LXX Genesis 12:3 and 18:18 (see 22:18; 26:4). LXX Genesis 12:3 states that "all the tribes" (φυλαί) of the earth will be blessed, whereas Paul states all of the ἔθνη of the earth will be blessed (Gal 3:8). LXX Genesis 18:18 asserts all of the ἔθνη will be blessed "in him" (i.e., in Abraham). LXX Genesis 22:18a states all of the ἔθνη will be blessed in "your seed."[29] Jews and gentiles receive this

---

27. For examples, see Bird, *Anomalous Jew*, 69–107. Ἔθνη is one term among many that illustrates the complexity of defining the terms used to construct Jewish and gentile identity. See, for example, LXX Gen 10:32; 14:5; 17:6, 20; 18:18; 25:16, 23; 26:4; Exod 15:14; 23:18; 33:16; 34:24; Lev 18:24; Num 14:14–15; Deut 4:38; 7:1–7.

28. So also de Boer, *Galatians*, 214–15.

29. Abraham's "seed" emerges later in Paul's argument in Gal 3:16–29 (see Gen 26:4). For mention of these texts in the context of theological reflection on the ἔθνη, see Moisés Silva,

blessing "in Abraham" and in his offspring and not "in the law" (see Gal 2:16; 3:1–16).[30] A relationship with Christ extends the blessing of Abraham to Jewish and gentile Christians (see Gal 4:5–7).[31] God makes a promise to Abraham before his giving of the law at Sinai (Gen 12:3). Abraham, the previously uncircumcised "gentile," is the agent in whom and through whom God will bless πάντα τὰ ἔθνη (here, Jews and gentiles) and ultimately fulfill his promise to πάντα τὰ ἔθνη in Christ (Gal 3:8b; see LXX Ps 71:17).[32] "Those from faith" who are justified by faith in Christ refers to Jews and gentiles.[33] These distinct groups together are blessed along with faithful Abraham (Gal 3:9; see 2:16; 3:7–9, 11–12, 22), because of Jesus (Abraham's offspring, Gal 3:16).[34] Paul understands the promise to Abraham to bless

---

ed., "ἔθνος," *NIDNTTE* 2:89–93, esp. 90. LXX Isa 44:3 uses the plural "blessings." Both this text and Gal 3:14 appear to use "blessing" and "Spirit" synonymously. Other Jewish texts also connect blessing and the Spirit (Testament of Judah 24.2–6). The information in this note and its referring material above are paraphrased from Das, *Galatians*, 334–36.

30. For a discussion of whether ἐν σοὶ should be translated as locative or instrumental, see discussion and sources cited in Matthew V. Novenson, *Christ among the Messiahs: Christ Language in Paul and Messiah Language in Ancient Judaism* (Oxford: Oxford University Press, 2012), 126. For a short but insightful interaction with Novenson, see Peter Oakes, *Galatians*, Paideia: Commentaries on the New Testament (Grand Rapids: Baker, 2015), 107.

31. The above sentence was shaped by Douglas J. Moo, *Galatians*, BECNT (Grand Rapids: Baker, 2013), 214–15, esp. 215. Moo's comments are specifically related to Gal 3:14.

32. For the perspective that ἔθνη can refer to all people including Israel, see Scott, *Paul and the Nations*, 128–32.

33. Contra de Boer (*Galatians*, 191–93), who argues that "faith" in the phrase "those from faith" refers to Jesus's faithful death.

34. The blessing of Abraham is the fulfillment of the eschatological and soteriological promise that all of the families of the earth will receive the eschatological and soteriological inheritance of the Spirit (Gal 3:1–14; 6:15). Richard B. Hays correctly says that "Paul regards the promise to Abraham as being fulfilled in the church's experience of the Holy Spirit." See Richard B. Hays, "Galatians," in *NIB* 11:181–348, esp. 261. Yet as Douglas Moo states, "The evident presence of God's Holy Spirit in power among the believers constitutes clear evidence that the 'last days' have dawned (Acts 1:4; 2:33, 39)." See Moo, *Galatians*, 216. Jews and gentiles experience this inheritance by means of being justified by faith in Christ (Gal 3:8). Paul's point is not that God promised the Spirit to Abraham and his physical offspring, since God did not mention the Spirit in the original promise to Abraham and his offspring (see Gen 12–50). Rather, God fulfilled the promise to Abraham and his offspring in the eschatological and soteriological gift of the Spirit to Jews and gentiles. The many seed promised to Abraham are the many believing Jews and gentiles who have faith in his singular offspring, Jesus (Gal 3:16). The universal experience of the Spirit through justification by faith in Christ constitutes a new "Israel of God" consisting of Spirit-filled Jewish and gentile Christians (Gal 6:15–16). The kingdom of God (Gal 5:21), eternal life (Gal 2:16–21), justification (Gal 2:16–17; 5:2–6), and new creation (Gal 6:15) are realized by faith in Christ in this new age ushered in by the outpouring of the power of the Spirit (see Jer 30–31). The age of the Spirit was a prophetic anticipation in the Old Testament (LXX Joel 2:28–32). Some of the preceding

the ἔθνη and πάντα τὰ ἔθνη to be fulfilled in his christological gospel that universally blesses the ἔθνη and πάντα τὰ ἔθνη in Christ with the Spirit by incorporating them into Abraham's offspring (Gal 3:29).[35]

When God promises Abraham that he will bless πάντα τὰ ἔθνη in him, there are diverse peoples/clans/tribes of the earth (see LXX Gen 12–50), but there are no individual groups of people distinguished as Jews and gentiles in Abraham's lifetime.[36] Use of ἔθνη and πάντα τὰ ἔθνη in Galatians 3:8, then, possibly carries eschatological and soteriological significance. If so, Paul asserts that God's worldwide promise to Abraham to bless the ἔθνη and πάντα τὰ ἔθνη has been fulfilled in Jesus, and also in the gift of the Spirit that comes to all families of the earth via Jesus' death (and resurrection) and through justification by faith (Gal 1:1, 4; 3:8, 13–14).[37] Paul deftly transitions from ἔθνη in Galatians 3:8a to πάντα τὰ ἔθνη in 3:8b, suggesting that here he possibly universalizes ἔθνη to include both Jews and gentiles rather than distinguish Jews from gentiles.

In Galatians 2:11–15, Paul distinguishes between Jews and gentiles with ἔθνη ("gentiles"; Gal 2:12), τοὺς ἐκ περιτομῆς ("those from the circumcision"; Gal 2:12), Ἰουδαῖος ("Jew"; Gal 2:13–14), ἰουδαΐζω ("to Judaize"; Gal 2:14), ἐθνικῶς ("gentile-ishly"; Gal 2:14), and Ἰουδαϊκῶς ("Jewishly"; Gal 2:14). Yet as mentioned before, the term ἔθνη in Galatians 3:8a and the phrase πάντα

---

section is paraphrased from and influenced by Das, *Galatians*, 332. The new age introduces a time when "Gentiles would forsake their idols and turn to the LORD; they would join the eschatological procession to Zion and the final banquet" (Isa 25:6–10; 56:6–8; 60:1–22; Zech 8:20–22). See Das, *Galatians*, 330.

35. Against Sam K. Williams, *Galatians*, Abingdon New Testament Commentaries (Nashville: Abingdon, 1997), 87. Williams asserts, "The import of the gospel that Paul discerns in these conflated texts is ecclesial rather than Christological. The gospel proclaimed beforehand to Abraham announces the inclusion of all peoples in the people of God." Instead, we assert that Paul's point is ecclesial, christological, eschatological, and soteriological.

36. MT Gen 12:3 highlights the universal nature of God's promise to Abraham. With the word for tribes (φυλαί), LXX Gen 12:3 likewise supports that all of the ἔθνη universally refer to all of the different kinds of people/tribes/clans on the earth.

37. Similarly Schreiner, *Galatians*, 194. Schreiner specifically notes the order in which Paul cites texts about Abraham. He cites Gen 15:6 (Gal 3:6) before he cites Gen 12:3 and 18:18 (Gal 3:8). Schreiner insightfully suggests that "Gen 15:6 is the foundational text, indicating that Gen 12:3 (18:18) must be read through the lens of 15:6." Schreiner continues: "Gen 12:3 promises that all nations will be blessed in Abraham, and Paul identifies this promissory word as the gospel proclaimed to Abraham in advance. But it is precisely here that Gen 15:6 plays its axiomatic role, for in giving this promise (12:3) to Abraham, Scripture foresaw that God would declare the gentiles right in his sight by faith."

τὰ ἔθνη in Galatians 3:8b refer to both Jews and gentiles.[38] Ἔθνη seems primarily to highlight gentiles in Galatians 3:14b alone, but ἔθνη in Galatians 3:8 and Galatians 3:14a–b together refer to everyone (including Jews and gentiles), just as MT Genesis 12:3 and LXX Genesis 12:3 anticipate. In Galatians 3:8–14, Paul appears to identify all the people of the earth (i.e., Jews and gentiles) as ἔθνη to accentuate the fulfillment of the promise to Abraham in the death and resurrection of Jesus (Gal 1:4; 3:13–14; see LXX Ps 71:17), Abraham's seed/offspring (Gal 3:16).[39] Thus, all of those "in Christ" (Abraham's seed/offspring) are also the "seed/offspring of Abraham" and "heirs of the promise" (Gal 3:29).

ΠΑΝΤΑ ΤΑ ΕΘΝΗ IN MATTHEW 28:19

Πάντα τὰ ἔθνη appears in an especially significant place in Matthew's Gospel: in the Great Commission in Matthew 28:19.[40] After Jesus' resurrection, he meets his disciples at Galilee (Matt 28:16). With words similar to Daniel 7:14, Jesus commands his disciples that because "all authority in heaven and on earth" has been given to him (Matt 28:18), they must go to πάντα τὰ ἔθνη to make disciples (Matt 28:19). We assert that the phrase πάντα τὰ ἔθνη carries exactly the same meaning here as in Galatians 3:8b, in that it refers to both Jews and gentiles. We support this with two lines of argument. First, we argue this exegetically from selected texts in Matthew's Gospel. Second, we argue this through a comparative analysis of Daniel 7:14 and Matthew 28:19.

---

38. This might be why Paul says the blessing comes to the ἔθνη in Gal 3:14a. The blessing comes to the ἔθνη (Gal 3:8a, 14a), and "we" (i.e., Jews and gentiles) received the Spirit by faith (Gal 3:14b). See Scott's discussion in *Paul and the Nations*, 128–30. Paul's use of ἔθνη in Gal 3:8 in conjunction with Gal 3:14 suggests Jews and gentiles are the ἔθνη who receive the blessing of Abraham/the Spirit. We agree with those scholars who maintain that the first-person plural pronouns in Gal 3:13–14 refer to both Jewish and gentile Christians. For examples, see Moo, *Galatians*, 215. For a different reading, see N. T. Wright, *The Climax of the Covenant: Christ and the Law in Pauline Theology* (Minneapolis: Fortress, 1991), 154.

39. This point provides one reason Paul remarks there is neither Jew nor Greek, slave nor free, male nor female in the assemblies of Galatia (see Gal 3:28–29).

40. We have opted to analyze Matt 28:19 last because this Gospel was written later than Galatians. In contrast, Galatians is one of the earliest New Testament texts containing the phrase πάντα τὰ ἔθνη.

SELECTED TEXTS IN MATTHEW

Matthew identifies Jesus as the Messiah of both gentiles and Jews in Matthew 1:1. He calls Jesus the Christ (Matt 1:1), the Son of Abraham (Matt 1:1), and the Son of David (Matt 1:1). "Christ" is a Jewish title (see Pss 2; 110). Abraham was an uncircumcised "gentile" until Genesis 17 (see Gen 12:1-3; 17:1-14). David was a Hebrew and Israel's king (2 Sam 7:12-14). God made a covenant with Abraham (a gentile; Gen 12:1-3) and with David (a Hebrew; 2 Sam 7:12-13) by promising to give them both a "seed." Matthew 1:1 overtly signals that Jesus, the Christ, is their promised seed.

After Matthew identifies Jesus as the Son of Abraham and the Son of David, he then offers a genealogy with gentiles (Matt 1:2, 5) and Hebrews (Matt 1:6-16) intermixed. Throughout the Gospel of Matthew, Matthew prioritizes Jesus' mission to the Jews as the Jewish Messiah (Matt 1:18–2:15; 10:5-6; 15:24), as the new and perfect Israel (Matt 2:15), and as the new and better Moses (Matt 4:1-7:29), while showing that Jesus also took the gospel to the gentiles (Matt 15:21-28), though he restricted the Jews from taking the gospel to the gentiles until after his resurrection (Matt 10:5-6; 28:19).

The above pattern suggests that the Jewish and gentile elements of Jesus' messianic identity in the beginning of the Gospel are proclaimed publicly to "all" (Jews and gentiles without distinction) after his resurrection at the end of the Gospel.[41] Matthew has already anticipated this universal mission prior to Matthew 28:19 through his use of πάντα τὰ ἔθνη elsewhere.[42] Matthew uses πάντα τὰ ἔθνη in reference to the gospel as "a testimony to all of the nations" (Matt 24:14).[43] He also uses it in reference to the "universal hatred of his disciples" because of Jesus' name (Matt 24:9) and in reference to God's "universal judgment" of all of the ἔθνη (Matt 25:32).[44]

The Jewish disciples of Jesus fulfill Israel's mission of being a light to the nations by taking the gospel of the Jewish Messiah to both Jewish and

---

41. For scholars with an alternative reading of ἔθνη in Matt 28:19, see sources cited in David L. Turner, *Matthew*, BECNT (Grand Rapids: Baker, 2008), 689.

42. John Nolland, *The Gospel of Matthew*, NIGTC (Grand Rapids: Eerdmans, 2005), 1265.

43. Nolland, *Gospel of Matthew*, 1265.

44. Nolland, *Gospel of Matthew*, 1265.

gentile people.[45] Jesus' command to his disciples to take the gospel to πάντα τὰ ἔθνη is a messianic proclamation.[46] That is to say, it is a pronouncement of the messianic age that Israel will no longer be a "come and see" people to the ἔθνη but a "go and tell" people to πάντα τὰ ἔθνη (Isa 11:9–10; 42:6; 49:6).[47] As Grant Osborne puts it, Matthew 28:19-20 is "that messianic launch of that universal mission, and it constitutes the final word of the exalted Jesus to the disciples in Matthew."[48] This Jewish emphasis on proclaiming the gospel to πάντα τὰ ἔθνη was somewhat of a novel concept for Jews.[49] The impetus behind this novelty is the resurrection and Jesus' full authority as the Messiah.[50] As Acts 1:8 and the entire book of Acts suggest, after the resurrection and after the Spirit comes, the disciples indeed take his gospel to Jerusalem, Judea, Samaria, and to the ends of the earth. This geographic progression suggests that Jesus' resurrection and the pouring out of the Spirit now open up the mission of God to include Jews and gentiles within the people of God through the proclamation of the gospel by Jesus' disciples to Jews and gentiles alike (see Isa 40–66).

DANIEL 7:14 AND MATTHEW 28:18–19

In Daniel 7, Daniel sees a vision of the Ancient of Days (Dan 7:9-10) and of the Son of Man (Dan 7:13-14). The Ancient of Days is sitting triumphantly on his throne in a posture of sovereignty ready to judge the thousands before him (Dan 7:9-10). The Son of Man appears before the Ancient of Days (Dan 7:13). In the vision, the Ancient of Days gives authority ("dominion," "glory," and "a kingdom") to the Son of Man over the nations so that all "the peoples, nations, and languages should serve him" and so that his dominion will not pass away, nor his kingdom be destroyed (Dan 7:14).[51]

---

45. Similarly Turner, *Matthew*, 689.

46. Grand R. Osborne, *Matthew*, ZECNT (Grand Rapids: Zondervan, 2010), 1079.

47. Osborne, *Matthew*, 1079. For Jewish missionary activity in Second Temple Judaism, see bibliography and argument in Michael F. Bird, *Crossing Over Sea and Land: Jewish Missionary Activity in the Second Temple Period* (Grand Rapids: Baker, 2010).

48. Osborne, *Matthew*, 1079-80. A portion of Osborne's statement quotes Joachim Gnilka, *Das Matthäusevangelium*, Herders Theologischer Kommentar zum Neuen Testament (Freiburg: Herder, 1988), 2:501.

49. Nolland, *Matthew*, 1266.

50. Nolland, *Matthew*, 1266.

51. Cited passages refer to the ESV.

Matthew 28:18 uses some of the same words as LXX Daniel 7:14 to refer to Jesus' universal authority over πάντα τὰ ἔθνη. LXX Daniel 7:14 and Matthew 28:18 both use the word ἐξουσία ("authority"), the phrase πάντα τὰ ἔθνη (in Matt 28:19), and the verb ἐδόθη ("was given"). Daniel's interpretation of the vision in Daniel 7:15–27 focuses on the eternal inheritance of the eternal kingdom to be received by the saints of the Most High (Dan 7:18) and the temporary suffering of the saints of the Most High by the nations until the saints inherit the kingdom (Dan 7:21–27; see also Rev 6:9–11). Matthew's appropriation of Daniel 7:14 identifies Jesus as the messianic Son of Man.[52] The key point for our thesis is that the Son of Man in Daniel 7:14 and Jesus in Matthew 28:18–19 have universal authority over πάντα τὰ ἔθνη. The Ancient of Days gives the Son of Man authority over πάντα τὰ ἔθνη in LXX Daniel 7:14. God gives Jesus universal authority over πάντα τὰ ἔθνη in Matthew 28:18, and Jesus then gives authority to his disciples in 28:19–20 to make disciples of πάντα τὰ ἔθνη. The phrase πάντα τὰ ἔθνη, in both LXX Daniel 7:14 and Matthew 28:19 at least, refers to Jews and gentiles.[53]

CONCLUSION

God's promise and fulfillment of the justification of the peoples of the earth, by faith alone in Jesus Christ alone, should motivate Christians to preach the gospel to all people without ethnic distinction scattered throughout the world, with the belief and expectation that some from every tribe, tongue, people, and nation will believe the gospel and be saved. God has promised to bless all of the families of the earth (Jews and gentiles) through faith in Jesus Christ. Christians must therefore seek to make disciples of these families of the earth wherever they reside and wherever they are scattered with the saving message of Jesus Christ.

Taking the gospel to Jews and gentiles scattered throughout the world continues the Great Commission of Jesus given to his original disciples. As the gospel penetrates ethnic and racial barriers and as it crosses the various social, cultural, national, political, and geographic boundaries,

---

52. Jesus often applies the title "Son of Man" to himself in Matthew (e.g., Matt 8:20; 9:6; 11:19; 12:8, 32, 40; 13:37, 41; 16:27).

53. For the parallels between Dan 7:14 and Matt 28:18, see Craig L. Blomberg, "Matthew," in Commentary on the New Testament Use of the Old Testament, ed. G. K. Beale and D. A. Carson (Grand Rapids: Baker, 2007), 1–110, esp. 100.

Christians throughout the world from every tongue, tribe, people, and nation must labor to carry out Jesus' commission of making disciples of πάντα τὰ ἔθνη and participate in blessing the diverse peoples of the world through the messianic seed of Abraham. Christians do this by proclaiming the gospel to and making disciples of Jews and gentiles both near and far.

May God inspire Christians to continue to take the gospel to the ends of the earth across all boundaries. As some Christians advance the gospel wherever they are and as others intentionally commit themselves to take the gospel of Jesus Christ beyond their homelands, may we trust by faith that in Christ Jesus, God has fulfilled and will continue to bring to full realization his promise of blessing the families of the earth in and through Jesus, Abraham's offspring, by justifying the ἔθνη and πάντα τὰ ἔθνη by faith. According to the Bible, who are the ἔθνη and πάντα τὰ ἔθνη, and where in the world are they? They are diverse Jews and gentiles. The ἔθνη and πάντα τὰ ἔθνη are scattered throughout the world.

6

BAPTISM AS INTEGRAL COMPONENT OF WORLD MISSION STRATEGY

John Massey and Scott N. Callaham

INTRODUCTION

I n 1812 Adoniram and Ann Judson departed North America and set sail as missionaries to Asia. During the long sea voyage, Adoniram undertook a study of the Greek New Testament centering on baptism, for he anticipated that William Carey would challenge his views on their meeting in India. Unexpectedly, Adoniram came to the conviction that his doctrine of infant baptism could not be found in the New Testament. Ann eventually reached the same conclusion. Driven by a sense of personal integrity, they agreed to resign from their Congregationalist mission organization, cutting them off from financial support just as their work on the mission field began.[1]

The Judsons did what all missionaries and indeed all Christians should do: examine biblical teaching in order to understand and practice baptism in accordance with God's word. If Christ commanded baptism as an integral component of the church's worship and witness in the world, then missionaries are duty bound to embrace baptism within their practice of world mission. Accordingly, this chapter outlines the theology of baptism, explores the place of baptism within ecclesiology (the theology

---

1. Courtney Anderson, *To the Golden Shore: The Life of Adoniram Judson* (Valley Forge, PA: Judson University Press, 1987), 127–29, 143–48. The Judsons' change of conviction regarding baptism required four months of dedicated inquiry both before and after arriving in India. See Keith E. Eitel, "The Enduring Legacy of Adoniram Judson's Missiological Precepts and Practices," in *Adoniram Judson: A Bicentennial Appreciation of the Pioneer American Missionary*, ed. Jason G. Duesing (Nashville: B&H Academic, 2012), 129–48, esp. 130–31.

of the church), and applies principles drawn from the theology of baptism to current issues in world mission.

THEOLOGY OF BAPTISM

WHY THE THEOLOGY OF BAPTISM MATTERS

Ignited by the spark of the Protestant Reformation, fueled by revival fires, and sustained by a thoroughgoing sense of accountability to God for disciple making, vigorous contemporary expressions of evangelicalism manifest many positive attributes. Among the commendable characteristics of evangelical Christianity are a high view of Scripture and the drive to ground Christian cooperation on shared gospel witness. Accordingly, Great Commission obedience and maintaining a prophetic voice against the competing truth claims of culture have been long-standing priorities of evangelical Christians across denominational lines. "Unity in the gospel" is thus a concise expression of the spirit of transdenominational evangelicalism, and evangelical yearning for unity surely honors Jesus' prayer that his followers would be "one" even as he and the Father are "one" (John 17:21–22).

However, there is a cost to transdenominational unity as normally practiced. Those issues about which the various denominations of Protestantism differ most strongly—such as ecclesiology (the doctrine of the church)—recede to the background of theological thinking. Differences of emphasis on various doctrines naturally arise in all expressions of Christianity as believers live out their faith within specific historical and cultural settings. However, in the case of the current "consensus faith" of transdenominational evangelicalism, ecclesiology has arguably diminished in significance to the point of practical nonexistence. The consensus "agreement *not* to disagree" is unsustainable in the long term, for in practice it means refusal to think theologically about the church. Yet in contrast, it is quite obvious that the church as the "community of the Gospelized" is no small concern in the New Testament.[2]

---

2. Michael F. Bird, *Evangelical Theology: A Biblical and Systematic Introduction* (Grand Rapids: Zondervan, 2013), 701. The "community of the Gospelized" is Bird's evocative description of the church in the final section of his work.

The gaping hole left by neglect of the church in rigorous evangelical theological thinking carries profound and perhaps unexpected consequences. One consequence that bears on the focus of this chapter is the near-absence of reflection on baptism as a task of the church. This theological loss is lamentable enough by itself, yet the lack of theological thinking about baptism surreptitiously lances the very heart of evangelicalism—the doctrine of soteriology—for Scripture directly connects baptism with belief and salvation.[3] Further, weakness or lack of baptism theology even enervates the evangelical impulse toward Great Commission obedience, for baptism is an explicit element of Jesus' commission.[4]

BAPTISM IN THE GREAT COMMISSION

Matthew records the Great Commission as follows:

> But the eleven disciples proceeded to Galilee, to the mountain which Jesus had designated. When they saw Him, they worshiped Him; but some were doubtful. And Jesus came up and spoke to them, saying, "All authority has been given to Me in heaven and on earth. Go therefore and make disciples of all the nations, baptizing them in the name of the Father and the Son and the Holy Spirit, teaching them to observe all that I commanded you; and lo, I am with you always, even to the end of the age." (Matt 28:16–20)[5]

Claim to total authority in heaven and earth leads Matthew's account of Jesus' words in Matthew 28:18. David Dockery observes, "Matthew wants his readers to know that Jesus has taken his place along with the Father and the Spirit as the object of the disciples' worship and commitment."[6] That is to say, Matthew presents Jesus as one who exercises the power and prerogatives of God alone. If Christ, who has all authority in heaven and earth, commands the action of making disciples, then making

---

3. Thomas R. Schreiner and Shawn D. Wright, eds., *Believer's Baptism: Sign of the New Covenant in Christ*, NAC Studies in Bible & Theology (Nashville: Broadman & Holman, 2015), 26.

4. Bruce A. Ware, "Believers' Baptism View," in *Baptism: Three Views*, ed. David F. Wright, Spectrum Multiview Books (Downers Grove, IL: InterVarsity Press, 2009), 19–50, esp. 20.

5. English Bible references in this chapter are to the NASB, Updated Edition.

6. David Dockery, "Baptism," in *Dictionary of Jesus and the Gospels*, ed. Joel B. Green, Scot McKnight, and I. Howard Marshall (Downers Grove, IL: InterVarsity Press, 1992), 55–58, esp. 58.

disciples is what his followers must do. Quite obviously, Christ spoke his command to the eleven disciples standing with him. The book of Acts and the rest of the New Testament demonstrate, however, that the Great Commission is a task for the church at large.

To begin discerning the relationship between baptizing and making disciples in the Great Commission, it is first necessary to point out that the only imperative verb in Matthew 28:19-20 is "make disciples" (μαθητεύσατε). The leading "go" (πορευθέντες) in English translations is a participle of attendant circumstance, and "baptizing" (βαπτίζοντες) and "teaching" (διδάσκοντες) are participles of means that describe how to carry out "making disciples."[7] Thus both baptizing and teaching comprise the specific acts of obedience that Jesus requires. To draw out interpretive implications regarding baptism specifically, one could state that where there is no baptism, there is also no Great Commission obedience. Furthermore, according to Jesus' teaching, having received baptism is an irreducible component of the definition of what it means to be a disciple. Simply put, the New Testament does not envision the possibility that a disciple of Jesus will remain unbaptized.[8]

WHO RECEIVES BAPTISM

Since the Great Commission specifically designates baptism as an act of disciple making, the answer to the specific question "Who receives baptism?" actually rests on the answer to the broader question "Who is a disciple?" Eckhard Schnabel notes,

It is surely significant that baptism is mentioned after the winning of disciples: it is people who have been converted to faith in Jesus Christ who are baptized (not vice versa, baptized people being made into disciples by the teaching of the church). Baptism is not the means by which people become disciples. Rather, baptism

---

7. On attendant-circumstance participles, see Daniel B. Wallace, *Greek Grammar beyond the Basics: An Exegetical Syntax of the New Testament* (Grand Rapids: Zondervan, 1996), 640–45, esp. 645. On participles of means see 628–30.

8. It is perennially necessary to emphasize that baptism is a nonnegotiable element of Great Commission obedience, particularly in light of missiological theories and practices that repudiate biblical teaching on this matter, as surveyed in section Rejection of Baptism in Western Theories of World Mission below.

characterizes and explains the winning of disciples: disciples are people who follow Jesus, who have received purification from their sins and put Jesus's teaching into practice.[9]

Just as there is no category in New Testament theology for a perpetually nonbaptized disciple, likewise the New Testament does not envision nondisciple baptism. Yet many churches routinely baptize people whom no one claims to be disciples of Jesus: infants. It is certainly beyond the scope of this chapter to narrate the history of baptism in the Christian church and furthermore to rehearse the details of the various arguments crafted to justify this specific kind of nondisciple baptism. A common element of the various attempts to justify infant baptism through Scripture is often appeal to "household baptisms" in Acts such as that of Lydia in Acts 16:15 and the Philippian jailer in Acts 16:33. Yet to remain logically consistent, suggesting that household baptism allows nondisciple baptism in Acts 16:33 also requires allowing for "household salvation" and thus "nonfaith salvation" two verses before in Acts 16:31. That is to say, the jailer's faith in the Lord Jesus suffices to save both him and his whole household. Therefore, in the course of justifying infant baptism by pointing to Acts 16:33, one must also posit that nondisciples in the jailer's household are not only baptized but also saved without any reference to personal faith in Jesus.

Infant-baptizing churches also appeal to the authority of church tradition and various forms of systematic theology that usually not only allow but actually mandate infant baptism. Again, a full treatment of these competing systematic theologies is not possible here, but one can at least note how far these theological systems range from a grammatical-historical interpretation of the New Testament—especially the Great Commission. Straightforwardly, the New Testament does not advocate baptism based on an expressed *hope* in the *possibility* that a person *might* profess faith in Jesus and become a disciple at some point later in life. Instead, the consistent witness of the New Testament is that baptism is for those who are unreservedly already Jesus' disciples.

---

9. Eckhard Schnabel, *Early Christian Mission: Jesus and the Twelve* (Downers Grove, IL: IVP Academic, 2004), 357.

HOW ONE RECEIVES BAPTISM

The Mode of Baptism

The Greek verb βαπτίζω ("baptize"), found in the Great Commission and elsewhere in the New Testament, means to plunge, immerse, dip, or wash.[10] John the Baptist, Jesus' disciples, and the early church immersed new converts in water. Accounts of the circumstances of baptism in the New Testament offer every indication that the act was indeed immersion through the use of the verbs καταβαίνω ("go down," in Acts 8:38) and ἀναβαίνω ("go up," in Matt 3:16; Mark 1:10; Acts 8:39). Specifically, the act of baptism means κατέβησαν ... εἰς ("going down into" in Acts 8:38) water, then ἀνέβη ἀπό ("going up from" in Matt 3:16) or ἀναβαίνων ἐκ ("going up out of" in Mark 1:10) the water.

Unfortunately, as in the case of the English word "baptize," translations from New Testament Greek to other languages normally obscure the meaning of βαπτίζω through creation of a new loanword through transliteration. On one hand, this translational choice seems like a feasible compromise enabling the cooperation of immersing and nonimmersing Christians in Bible translation and pioneer mission efforts. On the other hand, once again, transdenominational cooperation exacts a price. Although typically the motivation for using words from other languages is to import the meaning of loanwords from one language into another largely intact, in practice, translational compromise over βαπτίζω results in stripping meaning away in order to create a meaningless transliterated word.[11] Then churches are free to shape the meaning of the newly

---

10. See BDAG, s.v. βαπτίζω. Incidentally, Septuagint employment of βαπτίζω in the sense of immersion seems relatively uncontroversial. See for example the translation of 4 Reigns 5:14 (2 Kgs 5:14) in the New English Translation of the Septuagint (NETS): "And Naiman went down and immersed [ἐβαπτίσατο] himself in the Jordan seven times, according to the word of Elisaie, and his flesh returned like the flesh of a small child, and he was cleansed." Here the Greek translator selected βαπτίζω to render the Hebrew verb for "dipping into," "diving into," or "plunging into." See HALOT, s.v. טבל.

11. See the discussion of the use of loanwords in Bible translation in John Beekman and John Callow, *Translating the Word of God: With Scripture and Topical Indexes* (Grand Rapids: Zondervan, 1974), 198–99. Interestingly, transliteration of βαπτίζω is not feasible in all languages. For example, although Chinese Bibles use the nonalphabetic Chinese writing system to render proper nouns and certain words such as "Emmanuel," "hallelujah," and "amen" phonetically, major Bible translations have never transliterated βαπτίζω. Instead, a more natural solution from the standpoint of Chinese linguistics is to create a new technical term

minted word for baptism to fit their existing traditions rather than critically assess whether their traditions actually cohere with the meaning of the word in the Bible. Thus the English word "baptism" can designate either a nonimmersion water rite for nondisciples or a ceremonial immersion in water for disciples only. Intentional lack of self-evident definition of baptism terminology in English and other languages perpetuates the mistaken impression among contemporary Christians that the baptism theology of the New Testament is similarly obscure.

In contrast, the literal meaning of Jesus' command to baptize is clear enough. Yet one might object that despite referring to a well-defined act in the Great Commission and certain other texts, the fuller meaning of baptism in the New Testament must take into account its employment as a metaphor, as in John the Baptist's assertion that Jesus will baptize with the Spirit and fire in Matthew 3:11.[12] Yet literary metaphors do not communicate effectively if readers do not grasp the semantics of the words they employ in a figurative manner. Thus "*immerse* with the Spirit and fire" means *something* to readers of English, however unclear that meaning may be without more contextual information. Yet it is difficult to claim that "*shijin* with the Spirit and fire" is an effective metaphor, because most English readers would not recognize the Mandarin Chinese verb for immersion. All this is to say that metaphorical uses of the concept of baptism in the New Testament actually spring to life as evocative, figurative language precisely due to their play on the literal meaning of baptism as immersion in water.

Regarding baptismal metaphors, there is yet one often left uncontemplated, perhaps because it is ultimately ineffable: too arresting for words to express adequately. A spirit of holiness descends in its actualization. A sense of intimacy with the divine pervades its expression.

---

that includes a character designating "ritual." However, technical terms by their nature specify meaning, unlike "meaningless" and malleable new transliterated words. Thus in the history of Chinese Bible translation, nonimmersing Christians actively suppressed the concept that baptism is an act of immersion by demanding the adoption of the deliberately vague term 洗礼 ("washing ritual") rather than 浸礼 ("immersion ritual"). See Clement Tsz Ming Tong, "The Protestant Missionaries as Bible Translators: Mission and Rivalry in China, 1807–1839" (PhD diss., University of British Columbia, 2016), 214–21.

12. Of course in Matt 3:11 John *the Baptist* also affirms the literal meaning of his title: one who immerses in water.

This metaphor of baptism is the message acted out through every immersion baptism of every disciple of Jesus. The disciple goes under the surface of the water, *buried* with Christ through baptism. Burial is for the *dead*, thus the lifeless corpse of the disciple before he or she met Christ lies in the watery tomb, forever to remain there. Yet God *resurrects* the disciple through his or her faith such that the death that sin brings is powerless to prevent the disciple from rising from the water to the new life in Christ (Rom 6:4; Col 2:12).

Baptism preaches the gospel. Baptism preaches the gospel message of Jesus' historical death for sinners, his historical burial in his tomb, and his historical resurrection that defeats the power of sin and death forever. Baptism preaches the gospel message of the very present death that sin brings to every sinner, the present burial of the sinner with Jesus, and the present resurrection of the disciple whom God sets free from the power of sin and death forever. Just as baptism preaches the gospel message in the historical past and the contemporary present, it also preaches the gospel with an eye to the future. Unless Jesus returns first, all disciples will physically die, and their bodies will physically return to the earth. Yet just as surely, they will also physically resurrect as God dwells with redeemed humanity for all eternity to come. Baptism is a drama of death, burial, and resurrection with Jesus Christ that encompasses the full span of past, present, and future. Baptism—immersion baptism of disciples of Jesus—preaches the gospel.

Baptism in the Name of the Father, the Son, and the Holy Spirit

According to the Great Commission, disciples should receive baptism "in the name of the Father and the Son and the Holy Spirit." These words comprise one of the clearest expressions of trinitarian theology in the New Testament, and they derive from the mouth of Jesus himself. This trinitarian baptismal formula announces a gospel truth. The disciple has relinquished all other allegiances and instead embraced the one true and living God as revealed in the person of Jesus Christ through the work of the Holy Spirit. Schnabel notes,

> The reality that baptism expresses is denoted in the phrase "in the name of" (εἰς τὸ ὄνομα). This phrase is a formula of transfer used

in legal and commercial texts as a technical term meaning "to the account of (over which the name stands)." This background indicates that new believers in Jesus Christ who are immersed in water "become the possession of and come under the dedicated protection of the one whose name they bear." The person who has come to faith in Jesus enters into a new relationship to God who now is Lord. The Christian belongs to God, his life is determined by Jesus Christ, and his behavior is ruled by the Holy Spirit.[13]

Explicitly affirming the lordship of Christ over one's life in baptism is an element of obedience to everything that Christ has commanded, and the act of receiving baptism proclaims that the disciple has turned from false notions of deity and has embraced Jesus Christ as Lord. Among the many people groups of the world for which sociocultural and religious identity fuse tightly together, baptism is a radical act. Baptism irrevocably triggers wide-ranging and often fearful familial, vocational, and societal consequences for the believer. At the same time baptism generates clear opportunities for witness to the power of God through the gospel. Baptism brings clarity to the disciple's new identity and loyalty that bursts the "wineskins" of one's old life and religious order.[14]

Baptism is a potent symbol of the gospel's power within predominantly Islamic cultures. One of the most significant barriers to a Muslim coming to Christ is the deity of Christ, expressed partly in the Trinitarian Sonship of Jesus, for the radical monotheism of Islam expressly excludes the deity of Jesus Christ and the Holy Spirit. Honesty and integrity in gospel witness requires sensitive and clear communication of biblical teaching. Becoming Jesus' disciple entails a conscious transfer of allegiance from Allah as envisioned in Islam to the Triune God of the Bible. Baptism proclaims this transfer of loyalty through words and actions. For Hindus, conversion and subsequent baptism require upending the entire Hindu tradition and belief system. Receiving Jesus as Lord requires something wholly different from merely adding him to a long list of equally legitimate expressions of deity.

---

13. Eckhard J. Schnabel, *Paul the Missionary: Realities, Strategies and Methods* (Downers Grove, IL: IVP Academic, 2008), 231.

14. See Matt 9:17; Mark 2:22; Luke 5:37.

Rather, faith in Christ requires embracing Father, Son, and Holy Spirit as the sole sovereign of the universe. For Buddhists, becoming Jesus' disciple requires overcoming the traditional belief that there is no God, and instead confessing Father, Son, and Holy Spirit as creator, redeemer, and sustainer of all. For African traditional religionists, becoming Jesus' disciple demands receiving the Father, Son, and Holy Spirit who is God Most High and specifically Jesus as the one mediator between God and humanity. Conversion in an African setting involves turning away from veneration of ancestral spirits, the acknowledgment of lesser deities, and fear of the trickster spirit that seeks to bring harm to one's life, family, and community. In any cultural and religious setting, no one should regard the Trinitarian baptismal formula as a mere motto or a *shibboleth*-style test of authenticity. Instead, baptism expresses a disciple's whole-life commitment to the God of Scripture, the God who reveals himself as Father, Son, and Holy Spirit.

WHEN ONE RECEIVES BAPTISM

Baptism in the New Testament immediately followed faith in Christ. Benjamin Merkle notes,

> When is a new convert ready for baptism? . . . In the early church, baptism normally occurred on the same day as conversion. There was not a long time of teaching and testing beforehand. If baptism is a symbol of death and resurrection with Christ and entrance into the body of Christ, it makes sense that baptism should be done as close to conversion as possible. Thus, in the early church, teaching followed baptism (cf. Mt 28:19-20).[15]

In contrast, many churches in the Majority World require a waiting period prior to baptism for new disciples who come out of religious traditions at great variance with biblical Christianity. Churches reason that they need time to teach new converts the essentials of the faith in order to ensure that their conversions are genuine. Then for administrative reasons some churches may schedule quarterly or even only annual baptism services, making baptism a relatively rare event.

---

15. Benjamin L. Merkle, "Paul's Ecclesiology," in *Paul's Missionary Methods: In His Time and Ours* (Downers Grove, IL: IVP Academic, 2012), 56–73, esp. 63.

Regarding the baptism of young people, churches face a special challenge. Children or adolescents who come to faith in Christ before their non-Christian parents are often faced with the dilemma of parental opposition to baptism. In such cases churches frequently counsel delaying baptism until adulthood.

Churches that decide not to baptize new disciples soon after they begin following Jesus should critically evaluate whether their contemporary circumstances justify a different approach to baptism from the one modeled in the New Testament. As for the issue of immediate baptism for an adult convert from a radically different faith, there was apparently no concern that the great persecutor of the church Saul of Tarsus lacked a period of catechetical instruction before he received baptism in Acts 9:18. In the case of a child who comes to faith before his or her parents (a situation not directly addressed in the New Testament), churches must always discern the Holy Spirit's guidance in wisely applying biblical principles within their various cultural settings. Part of that discernment process should take into account that baptism connects intimately with the theology of the church, the proclamation of the gospel, Christian discipleship, and obedience to the Great Commission. Intentionally departing from the New Testament's model of immediate baptism in any situation can indirectly communicate that other considerations take higher priority.

WHAT THE ACT OF BAPTISM
MEANS FOR BAPTIZED CHRISTIANS

Christians often do not make enough of baptism as a means of both worshipful obedience and proclamation of the saving grace of God. Unfortunately, the acted-out sermon of baptism can become a mere symbol rather than a meaning-rich metaphor, as if symbolic acts were somehow less meaningful than nonsymbolic ones. Of course this modern understanding of symbolism is strangely counterintuitive, for symbols by their very nature can carry far more meaning than deeds invested with no special meaning. After all, baptism is a symbol of union with Christ and his people (Rom 6:1–4; Gal 3:27–29), a public profession of repentance from sin and belief in Jesus Christ for salvation (Acts 2:38). Baptism is a sign that Christ has performed a circumcision of the heart, removing the body of sin connected with Adam (Col 2:11–12). Thus baptism is a symbol of purification (Acts 3:19; 22:16), and it acts out the victory of Christ over sin and the forces of evil (Col 2:12–15). Finally, as mentioned above, baptism in the name of the Father, Son, and Holy Spirit proclaims that new disciples have transferred their loyalty and entrusted their lives to the Triune God of the Bible (Matt 28:19).

Modern devaluation of symbolic acts can seem to clash with the experience of God's power in baptism, leading to questioning whether baptism is "more than" a symbol. Due to the influential work of G. R. Beasley-Murray certain British Baptists have begun answering in the affirmative, asserting that baptism is a "symbol with power."[16] Paul Fiddes states that "water is a place in the material world that can become a 'rendezvous' with the crucified and risen Christ." He further states, "Now, I want to stress here that the water in baptism is not merely a visual aid to help us understand various spiritual concepts: in its sheer materiality and 'stuffness' it actually communicates the presence of the transcendent God."[17] The desire for ecumenical engagement with non-Baptists has led to the surprising rise of a sacramental understanding of baptism among British Baptists.

Space constraints of this chapter do not allow a thorough exploration of the concept of sacraments, which according to sacramental theology are certain mediatory acts that impart special kinds of grace, usually performed by duly appointed officials of churches. It is only possible to mention two related problems that commonly arise in popular perception through the embrace of sacramental views of baptism. First, the idea that an act conveys grace implies that the act is necessary to receive that kind of grace, and one receives something from God and the church that one would not have received without that act. Since this reception of grace primarily has to do with the act, only a half-step away lies the notion that one can place trust in the act. Anecdotally, one's most frequent encounter with "baptismal regeneration" is not with Christians whose churches endorse the heterodox idea that baptism saves, but with those whose

---

16. For resurgent sacramental views of baptism among British Baptists see Stanley K. Fowler, *More than a Symbol: The British Baptist Recovery of Baptismal Sacramentalism*, Studies in Baptist History and Thought (Eugene, OR: Wipf & Stock, 2007). See also G. R. Beasley-Murray, *Baptism in the New Testament* (Grand Rapids: Eerdmans, 1973).

17. Paul S. Fiddes, "Baptism and Creation," in *Reflections on the Water: Understanding God and the World through the Baptism of Believers*, ed. Paul S. Fiddes, Regents Study Guide 4 (Oxford: Regents Park College, 1996), 47–68, esp. 57–58.

description of their faith begins with, "I was baptized [insert denomination name here], therefore . . ."

Since impartation of grace through an act focuses on the act rather than the recipient, sacramental thinking about baptism also encourages nondisciple baptism, such as for infants. Various understandable pressures in church history such as high rates of infant mortality encouraged family members to seek all the grace from God that they could get for their loved ones before their untimely departure from the present life. In this line of thinking, baptism ensured that God would receive infants into his presence upon their deaths.

In view of such widespread misunderstandings of biblical teaching, one should discourage transferring trust from God to the act of baptism even to the slightest degree. Any transfer of trust to the act of baptism, as in the extreme but familiar case of trusting baptism for one's salvation, is lamentable. Similarly, sacramental justification of nondisciple baptism not only contradicts the plain reading of Scripture that baptism is for disciples of Jesus, but also detracts from the rationale for the nondisciple to become a disciple in the future.

Any placement of trust in baptism highlights the underlying and most grievous problem with popular embrace of a sacramental view of baptism: stealing glory that belongs to God alone. Thus to take a strong stand against sacramentalism and for the grammatical-historical interpretation of baptism in the New Testament at its heart is not a matter of denominational distinctives. Instead, baptism promotes discipleship and fans the flames of faith in the God whom baptism glorifies as a vital part of the witness of the church to the world.

BAPTISM AND ECCLESIOLOGY

BAPTISM IS AN ORDINANCE OF THE LOCAL CHURCH

Augustus H. Strong defines "ordinance" as "those outward rites which Christ has appointed to be administered in his church as visible signs of the saving truth of the gospel."[18] Although some definitions of "sacrament"

---

18. Augustus H. Strong, *Systematic Theology: A Compendium Designed for the Use of Theological Students* (Valley Forge, PA: Judson University Press, 1907), 930.

seem essentially identical with this formulation, ordinarily motives for use of the term "ordinance" include specifically denying that God conveys special grace through the act.

A less-appreciated facet of ordinances is that they are ordinances *of the church.* That is to say, Christ has *ordained* that the *church* baptize all believers as a mark of discipleship. Thus to draw out specific implications for the practice of world mission, baptism is an ordinance neither for individuals, nor for mission organizations, nor for parachurch ministries. None of these people or structures have authority to baptize apart from the church.[19] It is necessary to draw special attention to these implications because Westerners tend to read the New Testament much more individualistically than non-Westerners and thus gloss over the ecclesiological context of the Great Commission. That is to say, the Great Commission is a communal act: a priority the church should carry out intentionally, strategically, and cooperatively rather than in an atomistic manner through independent, uncoordinated individuals.

The drawing together of one-time baptism and ongoing teaching within the Great Commission demonstrates this ecclesiological principle. When the church makes disciples through proclamation and living out the gospel message, the church, following the pattern of the New Testament, should baptize new disciples immediately and welcome them into fellowship. New Testament practice does not contemplate birthing new believers and then abandoning them to their own devices. Instead, new believers need their new family of faith for instruction and nurturing in the Lord. At first glance the conversion and Philip's subsequent baptism of the Ethiopian eunuch in Acts 8:26–40 appears to be an exception to the rule that baptism is an ordinance of the church, for "the church" was not present for the baptism, and Philip never saw the eunuch again. Yet interestingly, Ethiopian Christianity is one of the forms of world Christianity with the most ancient history. It is possible that the eunuch's baptism marked the beginnings of the African church.

---

19. In view of some contemporary theories of missiology, it is unfortunately necessary to elaborate further. If missionaries act under the authority of a church, mission organizations may not *forbid* missionaries to baptize new disciples.

WHO SHOULD BAPTIZE FOR THE CHURCH

Since baptism is an ordinance of the church, those who perform baptisms do so for the sake of the church. Thus it is the church alone that decides who should baptize new disciples. Their decision should take into account the theology of baptism, including the close connection of baptism and discipleship within the context of the church. As a result of the great significance of baptism, some churches decide that only ordained ministers should baptize new disciples. In reaching such a decision churches should take into account that the concept of an ordained professional ministry only developed after the New Testament era; thus it would be anachronistic to claim that the Bible itself mandates that only ordained ministers should baptize. In fact, in light of 1 Corinthians 1:10–17, it appears that Paul did not reserve baptism solely for himself at his apostolic level of authority, but encouraged others to baptize and furthermore not divide into factions based on who baptized whom. Following Paul's example, missionaries should at times baptize new disciples when appropriate, and in other situations encourage local believers to do so.

On the subject of missionaries themselves performing baptism, once again missionaries should remember that the ordinance of baptism belongs to the church rather than to them individually. Thus they should carry out their ministries in accountability to their church in their home countries, much like Paul and Barnabas did in relationship to the church in Antioch that sent them out.[20] Furthermore, when possible, they should actively participate in the ministries of churches on the mission field as well. Accordingly, missionaries should baptize under the authority of mission-field churches for the sake of serving them and building them up toward further Great Commission obedience.

THE UNITY OF THE CHURCH IN BAPTISM

All believers enter the church bearing the distinctive sociological marks that cultures use to divide and classify people, such as ethnicity and social class. Yet strikingly, Jesus' Great Commission states that at the moment of entry into the church, there is only one visible mark of the disciple:

---

20. Acts 14:27 relates that Paul and Barnabas gave an account of their work to the Antioch church after they returned from their first missionary journey.

baptism. Ephesians 4:4–6 elaborates: "There is one body and one Spirit, just as also you were called in one hope of your calling; one Lord, one faith, one *baptism*, one God and Father of all who is over all and through all and in all." God intends for the church to be a new kind of humanity—a redeemed humanity—incorporating believers of every nation, tribe, people, and language (Rev 7:9).

Baptism is indeed a great unifier of God's people, symbolizing the gracious activity of God in his redemption of people from all nations and backgrounds through the cross of Christ, integrating them into one new people. It represents the mystery of the gospel, God's plan from all ages, hidden in the past but now revealed through apostles and prophets, that believing gentiles are fellow heirs with believing Jews. Baptism is a dramatic demonstration that all who call on the name of the Lord will be saved by God's grace through faith, and furthermore that they have identical standing with God. Thus the church must follow through with this conviction and treat new disciples as valued and equal members of Christ's kingdom, teaching them all to obey Jesus' commands in every aspect of life.

BAPTISM AND THE "HARD CASES"

Baptism is an unparalleled, potent act of gospel proclamation. Every moment is thick with spiritual significance. Due to the presence and activity of the Holy Spirit, even non-Christians may breathe in the atmosphere of intense anticipation at the baptism of a new disciple. Since baptism is a category all its own among human experiences, it is unsurprising that the practice of biblical baptism stimulates emotionally charged, reactive opposition. These responses are remarkably consistent, and they almost always immediately propose one or more "hard cases" with the intention of challenging the legitimacy or consistent application of biblical baptism.

The first kind of hard case has to do with the availability of water. In the most extreme posited scenario there is no water, thus prompting the suggestion that one "baptize" using some other material such as sand.[21]

---

21. Byzantine monk John Moschos relates an account of baptism with sand in John Moschos, *The Spiritual Meadow*, trans. John Wortley, Cistercian Studies 139 (Kalamazoo, MI: Cistercian, 1992), 144–46.

However, since water is necessary for survival, for this situation one might point out that theological speculation should cease and the task of finding water should begin! Thus the slightly less extreme next hard case concerns scarcity of water; there is simply not enough available to immerse.[22] Returning to the desert setting of the first hard case, one could ask why one feels the pressing need to baptize when it is not possible to carry out baptism according to the biblical pattern. Indeed, is Great Commission obedience not worth the effort of fetching sufficient water, or even traveling to some location where there is enough water to baptize?

The second category of hard case is much more sensitive in that it concerns the felt and expressed needs of human beings. This hard-case story line strongly implies that the practitioner of biblical baptism is unreasonable for valuing biblical teaching over the desires of a person. The first of these cases is most common; a recipient of nonbiblical baptism (such as infant baptism) wants to join a church but refuses to receive the biblical baptism of a disciple of Jesus. So the question arises: Why should a church rebaptize someone, especially someone who professes faith in Christ? From the standpoint of ministry, patient explanation of biblical teaching is key in reframing the question. First, the term "rebaptize" does not apply, in that there was no biblical baptism before. Thus one could proceed to inquire about willingness to preach the gospel through what should be the first act of obedience of a disciple of Jesus: baptism according to the Bible. In light of biblical teaching, why would a disciple of Jesus, who continually offers him- or herself as a "living sacrifice" (Rom 12:1) to God, remain adamantly opposed to simple obedience? Who is unreasonable, the church or the individual disciple who demands that the church abandon biblical convictions in order to accept him or her as a member?

The emotional intensity of hard-case objections then typically climaxes in desperate personal scenarios: the dying baby on one hand, or the elderly or otherwise seriously infirm on the other. The tragic experience of infant mortality lies in the background of infant baptism in

---

22. In the judgment of Thomas Aquinas, water scarcity and certain other hard-case conditions permit deviation from what he terms "safer," "more ordinary," "more frequently in use," and "more commendable": baptism by immersion. See *Summa Theologica* 3.66.7, found in Thomas Aquinas, *The "Summa Theologica" of Thomas Aquinas*, trans. Fathers of the English Dominican Province (London: R. & T. Washbourne, 1912–1925), 17:108–10.

church history and thus need not require further comment now. So turning to the penitent in the hospital bed, who would deny a measure of comfort through some symbolic application of water in "baptism"? Once again, the premises of such a question are not in line with biblical teaching. One should instead ask, What is prompting desire for baptism in the present dire circumstances that do not permit immersion? Most likely it is the influence of sacramental theology, the belief that an act will confer a special grace that one would not otherwise receive without the act. As mentioned before, no one should encourage this line of thinking, which transfers trust to an act rather than God, thus stealing his glory. Instead, the best comfort one can offer in dire circumstances should be the gospel! Should a person depart this life and face God trusting in a sacrament or in Jesus? This is the right question in the midst of the most heart-wrenching hard-case scenarios.

Let us offer a parting thought about hard cases, recognizing from a pastoral perspective that the intensity of emotion that accompanies the positing of these scenarios can actually signal that the Holy Spirit is confronting human pride with biblical truth. We suggest that real-life testimonies of hard-case situations can encourage laying aside resistance to biblical teaching in favor of a God-glorifying faith response. So, for example, we may return to the "worst of the worst" hard case. Before we rush to conclude that baptism by immersion is absolutely impossible for the physically ill, we should think again. During a particularly memorable day of worship, a church in Singapore baptized a wheelchair-bound elderly man. Deacons and a nonbelieving daughter surrounded him and then lowered him *and his wheelchair* into and under the water. This new convert to Christ insisted on receiving baptism in the way Christ prescribed: by immersion as a profession of his faith in Jesus. He wanted to make his faith known to all through baptism.[23]

---

23. Through believer's baptism by immersion on Christmas Day 2006 at Calvary Baptist Church of Singapore, Ang Chong Kuan, then eighty-five years old, testified that Jesus Christ is Lord (Pastor Koh Kok Chuan, personal communication).

BAPTISM AND CURRENT
ISSUES IN WORLD MISSION

BAPTISM IN GLOBAL CONTEXT

The various denominations of Western Christianity participated in the initial advance of the gospel across Asia, Africa, and Latin America, bringing with them differences over ecclesiology and baptism. With non-Western national churches presently taking deeper root in a new phase of church history, faithful local Christian leaders of every denomination are now in a position to reevaluate the traditions and theologies they have inherited from the West. The need for thoroughgoing rethinking of theology is particularly acute in light of the decisive turn of many Western churches away from biblical authority and toward theological liberalism.

One option for non-Western churches to defend against imported theological liberalism is to champion the kind of "consensus evangelicalism" mentioned previously in this chapter. Yet consensus evangelicalism, with its intentional suppression of differences in favor of unity in the gospel message, indeed represents a defensive position in theological thinking. Rather than maintain a fixed reference point in biblical authority, consensus evangelicalism rallies around the dynamic of consensus: pragmatically motivated suspension of disagreement. Church history dramatically illustrates that human nature mandates shifts in consensus, and pragmatism almost never moves toward acknowledgment of the sovereignty of God expressed through his authoritative word.

As a review of church history from the New Testament onward demonstrates, baptism by its nature is a radical act of discipleship that plays an integral role in world mission. James Garrett notes,

> In the New Testament era, in the Pre-Constantinian patristic age, in the sixteenth century and later for the Anabaptists, in the seventeenth century and after for English Baptists and early American Baptists, in most nations of Asia and Africa during the nineteenth and twentieth centuries, and in the U.S.S.R., China, and Eastern Europe for much of the twentieth century, Christian baptism was *contra-cultural*. It marked a radical break with family, past religion, state religion, tribe, and/or clan. To submit to Christian baptism was to make a

costly decision of an irreversible and consequential nature. Within European Christendom for many centuries and to a great extent in North American Protestantism and in South and North American Roman Catholicism, however, Christian baptism has been an act that has had the *sanction* of the *culture* and was almost an expression of culture. Hence it was a less decisive and less costly step. Herein lies one of the major challenges vis-à-vis baptism today.[24]

As non-Western churches grow larger than their Western forebears and more and more distinct from them in ethos, in the face of Western rejection of biblical authority they may yet choose to reconstruct their theology from the ground up. Thus it is possible that the non-Western church can lead the rediscovery and renewal of baptism theology for worldwide Christianity.

REJECTION OF BAPTISM IN
WESTERN THEORIES OF WORLD MISSION

Despite the possibility and hope of renewal of baptism theology within the global church, new theories of world mission developed by Western missionaries leave biblical-theological thinking behind altogether, even to the point of discouraging baptism. These are variations of Insider Movements (IM) missiology, which hold that Christ followers to some significant degree should remain in their previous religious and cultural contexts.

"Christward Movements"

A type of insider movement in India called "Christward movements" affirms believers' abstention from baptism. A *Christianity Today* article written by Jeremy Weber cites Richard Howell of the Asia Evangelical Alliance based in Delhi:

> "Christward movements are culturally Hindu yet Christian in faith," says Howell. Members read the Bible and pray openly, but they meet on Saturdays in homes, not churches, in order to avoid "the impression that Christianity is Western." Their biggest break

---

24. James Leo Garrett, *Systematic Theology: Biblical, Historical, and Evangelical* (Grand Rapids: Eerdmans, 1995), 2:585–86.

is not with the Western church as much as the historic church: They don't perform baptisms.

The article continues,

> Howell supports their abstention. He estimates that 70 percent of Christians in India are of Dalit background, and thus constrained by the Scheduled Caste welfare regulations. "They worship no god but Jesus," he says. "But they don't take baptism because they will lose their jobs and families, because their benefits will be taken away by the government. The church is not equipped to help them. If they take baptism, millions would be out of jobs. What would we do?" The abstention is strategic, not syncretistic, he says.[25]

These Christward movements in India pose a challenge to missionaries in a position to influence such movements. The critical questions raised by these movements are twofold. First, can the gospel actually take root among a people without creating the church? Second, can people refuse baptism and still be Jesus' disciples? The New Testament clearly presents a radically different baptism theology from that of Christward movements.[26] Awareness of the New Testament pattern does not necessitate condemning such movements toward Jesus altogether, but should prompt Christians to serve as Aquilas and Priscillas for the movement to point toward the biblical path of discipleship.

"Churchless Christianity"[27]

Talman and Travis offer a sympathetic view of insider movements in their edited work, *Understanding Insider Movements: Disciples of Jesus within Diverse Religious Communities*. Though noted for their observations on the Muslim world, they also examine IMs outside Islamic contexts. Their review of IMs in India cites the work of Lutheran missionary Herbert

---

25. Jeremy Weber, "Outpacing Persecution: Why It's the Best of Times and the Worst of Times for India's Burgeoning Churches," *Christianity Today* 60, no. 9 (2016): 38–47, esp. 46.

26. Of course there is lamentable irony in the title "Christward movements." Eschewing baptism means that would-be Jesus followers cut short their "movement" toward Jesus at the most elementary stage of obedience.

27. Herbert Hoefer, *Churchless Christianity* (Pasadena, CA: William Carey Library, 2002).

Hoefer, who "stumbled upon some Hindu Christ followers in South India, whom he labelled 'non-baptized believers in Christ.' "[28] Hoefer said that they referred to themselves as "devotees of Jesus" or "*Jesu bhaktas*." In reference to Hoefer's work, H. L. Richard states, "For the high-caste non-baptized believer in Christ (NBBC), however, the issue is social. His family and social group are far removed culturally from 'Christian' society, and cannot understand conversion in anything but sociological terms." Richard quotes Hoefer's final analysis:

> It is clear, furthermore, that the communalized nature of the church exists quite apart from baptism. Even among the non-sacramental churches where baptism is considered unnecessary (as among the Salvation Army) or merely symbolic (as among the Baptists) the church is just as exclusively communal as among those churches who emphasize the necessity of baptism. . . . *The character of the church is formed by the structure of the society irrespective of the theology or practice of baptism.* Therefore, the primary questions raised for us by the phenomenon of non-baptized believers in Christ around us are not about their authenticity but about ours. The questions are about our recognition of sociological realities in ecclesiastical structures and mission planning. The questions are about developing a style of church fellowship and ministry which make the call of Christ and gift of His Spirit available to all in the fullest possible freedom and power.[29]

The highlighted sentence in this quote from Hoefer reflects his observation of nonbaptized believers in India and seems to urge readers to accept a sociologically defined minimalist ecclesiology. That is to say, according to Hoefer, baptism is not the visible mark of the church; societal structures mark the church most significantly. Review of Hoefer's work by Richard indicates that he too views the NBBC movement as a

---

28. Harley Talman and John Jay Travis, eds., *Understanding Insider Movements: Disciples of Jesus within Diverse Religious Communities* (Pasadena, CA: William Carey Library 2016), 13.

29. H. L. Richard, "Christ Followers in India Flourishing—but outside the Church: A Review of Herbert E. Hoefer's *Churchless Christianity*," in *Understanding Insider Movements: Disciples of Jesus within Diverse Religious Communities*, ed. Harley Talman and John Jay Travis (Pasadena, CA: William Carey Library, 2016), 150, emphasis ours.

valid form of Christianity that missiologists should celebrate and pro-mote in various settings across the world. Richard notes,

> Herbert Hoefer's study documenting the existence and vitality of faith in Christ outside the institutional church may well be the most significant missiological publication related to India to have appeared in the second half of the twentieth century. On the basis of experiential findings, followed up with careful research, Hoefer challenges the assumptions and practices of established church and mission structures. He calls for a paradigm shift in thinking about service for Christ in India, and for radical adjustment of min-istry models to deal with a significant but ignored work of the Holy Spirit in our midst. In the years since the publication of *Churchless Christianity*, little notice seems to have been taken, debate has not been stirred, and, *most tragically, ministry strategies that affirm and empower the NBBC have not been born*.[30]

With the final, highlighted phrases above, Richard departs from review and evaluation in favor of advocacy. Indeed, Richard apparently thinks that Hoefer does not go far enough. He later qualifies his praise for Hoefer's work by stating, "Nonetheless, one must question whether Hoefer in the end is either too traditionally attached to the church or just not careful enough to define what he means in saying that this churchless Christianity needs the church."[31]

Some IM theorists allow for both rejecting baptism and for baptizing according to nonbiblical patterns, all due to the felt need to accommodate the doctrinal sensitivities of other religions such as Islam. For example, John Travis notes that there are a variety of practices related to baptism among "Jesus-following Muslims."

> Most Jesus-following Muslims practice some form of water bap-tism as well, *not to indicate a change of religious affiliation, but as a sign of identifying with Jesus*, who has opened the way for the cleans-ing of sin and for new life through him. Some Muslim disciples of Jesus who do not yet practice outward water baptism consider

---

30. Richard, "Christ Followers in India Flourishing," emphasis ours.
31. Richard, "Christ Followers in India Flourishing."

themselves to have been baptized spiritually because of their relationship with Christ, who baptizes with the Holy Spirit.[32]

As mentioned earlier in review of the theology of baptism, biblical baptism is in the name of the Father, the Son, and the Holy Spirit. Transfer of loyalty to the Triune God of the Bible could not stand more at odds with Islam; therefore "change of religious affiliation" is always necessary. One must leave Islam. Problems with the accommodationist NBBC view of baptism also include overlooking the ecclesiological dimension of baptism, in that baptism does not just represent the believer "identifying with Jesus" but also with the people of Jesus: the church. Rebecca Lewis writes,

> In "insider movements," therefore, there is no attempt to form neo-communities of "believers-only" that compete with the family network (no matter how contextualized); instead, "insider movements" consist of believers remaining in and transforming their own pre-existing family networks, minimally disrupting their families and communities. These believing families and their relational networks are valid local expressions of the Body of Christ, fulfilling all the "one another" care seen in the book of Acts, and so they do not need to adopt the meeting and program structures common in Western aggregate churches.[33]

In essence, IM missiology rejects biblical ecclesiology, including the theology of baptism. Baptism is a radical act of obedience signifying the disciple's willing identification with Jesus Christ in his death, burial, and resurrection, and thus with the body of Christ, the church. Baptism symbolizes absolute transfer of loyalty to a new Lord and a new family. Jesus offers a sober reminder in Luke 14:26 to those who would follow him that "If anyone comes to Me, and does not hate his own father and mother and wife and children and brothers and sisters, yes, and even his own life, he cannot be My disciple." In other words, in comparison to one's love

---

32. John Jay Travis and J. Dudley Woodbury, "When God's Kingdom Grows like Yeast: Frequently Asked Questions about Jesus-Movements within Muslim Communities," *Mission Frontiers* 32, no. 4 (2010): 24–30, esp. 29, emphasis ours.

33. Rebecca Lewis, "Promoting Movements to Christ within Natural Communities," *International Journal of Frontier Missiology* 24 (Summer 2007): 75–76.

for Christ, love for one's family will appear as hate. In Matthew 10:32–39, Jesus states,

> Therefore everyone who confesses Me before men, I will also confess him before My Father who is in heaven. But whoever denies Me before men, I will also deny him before My Father who is in heaven.
>
> Do not think that I came to bring peace on the earth; I did not come to bring peace, but a sword. For I came to SET A MAN AGAINST HIS FATHER, AND A DAUGHTER AGAINST HER MOTHER, AND A DAUGHTER-IN-LAW AGAINST HER MOTHER-IN-LAW; and A MAN'S ENEMIES WILL BE THE MEMBERS OF HIS HOUSEHOLD.
>
> He who loves father or mother more than Me is not worthy of Me; and he who loves son or daughter more than Me is not worthy of Me. And he who does not take his cross and follow after Me is not worthy of Me. He who has found his life will lose it, and he who has lost his life for My sake will find it.

The demands for discipleship as set forth by Christ are rigorous. They were demanding in Jesus' day for Jews who received Christ as the Messiah. Jewish believers lost favor with family, culture, and religious leaders, and were ejected from synagogues. Ancient Near Eastern culture highly valued family and closely tied together culture and religion, just like most contexts in the present-day Majority World. For Jews, becoming Jesus' disciple meant the loss of everything once held near and dear. The demands for discipleship were equally rigorous for gentile believers. Christians willingly turned their backs on the cult of the emperor, calling Jesus κύριος ("Lord"), instead of Caesar. Paul commends the Thessalonian believers because they turned from idols to serve the true and living God. The church in the Roman Empire refused to worship other deities, and they endured governmental and societal persecution as a result.

In non-Christianized cultures and in multireligious contexts, non-Christians frequently do not consider professions of faith in Christ to be serious until the new convert undergoes baptism. In accordance with biblical teaching, baptism requires that the disciple "out" him- or herself publicly as a follower of Jesus. Immersing in the water of baptism proclaims the disciple's willingness to die to the ways of the world and instead to identify with Christ and his people at all costs. One of the grievous oversights of the IM paradigm is lack of a biblical and historical understanding that persecution, suffering, and death of God's people are often means by which God advances his work in the world through the gospel.

As they present the clear biblical demands of discipleship, of course missionaries from a Western context normally stand under far less jeopardy than national believers. In the case of organized religious persecution, national governments may merely revoke missionaries' visas and send them away. In contrast, persecution for a national believer may indeed entail incurring harm societally, culturally, and physically in ways that would stagger the imagination of comfortable Westerners. Therefore, as in the sharing of all biblical truth, gentleness should be a defining characteristic of the teaching ministry of the missionary (Heb 5:2). With nationals who are struggling with the decision to receive baptism and proclaim their faith in Christ within a hostile culture, missionaries can only share what Christ has commanded, encourage obedience, and pray for the Holy Spirit's work in the hearts of new disciples according to the word of God.

To review, IM missiology redefines ecclesiology according to the dictates of the structures of society in order to make discipleship more hidden. According to IM thinking, hidden discipleship is most effective in permeating a culture. The desire for Christianity to spread through a culture like yeast through dough is laudable (see Matt 13:33), but the IM movement advocates that the personal preferences and experiences of national Christians take precedence over the New Testament. IM-influenced strategy also seeks to diminish the ostracizing of new converts from their families and communities and thereby distorts the demands of discipleship clearly set forth in the New Testament. Ironically and tragically, although developed to champion indigenous expressions of Christianity, IM missiology is yet another Western-developed philosophy foisted on the global church.

CONCLUSION

The central command of Christ in his Great Commission (Matt 28:16–20) to the church is to make disciples of all nations, baptizing them in the name of the Father, Son, and Holy Spirit and teaching them to observe all that he has commanded. Baptism according to the Great Commission is necessary for disciples' obedience to Jesus; it is not optional. Baptism plays a central and nonnegotiable role in the gospel-centered, disciple-making, church-planting mission of the church to all nations. Baptism is the one-time act of obedience that dramatizes the new disciple's salvation and incorporation into a local church.

Baptism preaches the gospel to both the church and the world. Thus baptism is a herald of salvation—a sign of gospel advance—and an objective measure of the church's faithfulness to the Great Commission. While profession of faith is essential, proof of the reception of the gospel often lies in the new believer's submission to baptism, incorporation into the body of Christ, and faithful adherence to the teachings of the Bible.

7

THEOLOGICAL EDUCATION AS INTEGRAL COMPONENT OF WORLD MISSION STRATEGY

Sunny Tan and Will Brooks

INTRODUCTION

Purposeful training of church leaders is rooted in the New Testament and founded on Jesus' words: "teaching them to obey everything I have commanded you" (Matt 28:20).[1] Those words express a threefold concern: for the task of teaching itself, that a revealed body of knowledge be transmitted, and that obedience be the desired outcome.[2] Thus, theological education and mission are intricately woven together since the burden for training leaders grows out of the Great Commission itself.

To explain the relationship between theological education and mission we can ask two questions. The first question starts with missionaries in mind and asks, "What role does theological education play in the missiological task of the church?" The second question focuses on theological educators and asks, "How does a biblical-theological understanding of

---

1. Unless otherwise noted, Bible quotations derive from the NIV (1984).

2. This chapter is not overly prescriptive, but it does point theological education in a direction it should be heading. The approach of this chapter is inspired by Bill Lawson's choice of the phrase "ears to hear" as the rubric for his course on biblical interpretation at Malaysia Baptist Theological Seminary. In the preface to his textbook he states, "The purpose of this guide is to provide principles, methods, and procedures for Christians as they seek to hear God speak through the Bible." William H. Lawson, *Ears to Hear: A Guide for the Interpretation of the Bible* (Penang, Malaysia: Institute for Biblical Interpretation, 1994), 5. In the phrase "ears to hear," we have in a nutshell a significant motivation for Christian mission: that every person will hear and obey the Triune God. The hearing encounter with God may begin with the gospel call, but then it must continue in the disciple's life. In linking the phrase "ears to hear" with the proper handling of the Bible, we see the reason for the command to "teach" in the Great Commission. Disciples must be taught God's word if they are to hear, obey, and be transformed.

mission shape the task of theological education?" This chapter answers these two questions in turn.

THE IMPORTANCE OF THEOLOGICAL EDUCATION TO MISSIONS STRATEGY

Missionaries love to discuss strategy. Those discussions, however, seldom address the critical role of theological education in the missional task. This section will attempt to remedy that oversight by considering missionaries, their work among the nations, and why theological education must be an integral part of their strategy.

HOW THEOLOGICAL EDUCATION RELATES TO AN OVERALL MISSIONS STRATEGY

At this point we can consider the foundational question, "What role does theological education play in the missiological task of the church?" To answer that question, we need to consider what the goal of the church's mission is. As other chapters in this book show, God the Father desires that his name be magnified among all the nations of the earth. This exaltation happens as the gospel of the Son is proclaimed by Spirit-empowered sent-out ones. We see a picture of this end goal of missions in Revelation 7:9, when people from every tribe, nation, and language gather together in worship. God desires all people to know and worship him.

How does theological education, then, help the church to reach this goal? We can define theology as the study of God and his nature, character, attributes, and work to redeem the created world. Therefore theological education aims at teaching people to know God, his attributes, and his story in such a way that leads to life transformation. We often associate formal theological education with the academy. The second half of this chapter will show how a biblical-theological understanding of mission should shape the work of existing institutions of higher learning. At the same time, however, we need to recognize that theological education plays an important role as the gospel advances to areas where its light has not previously shined.

On its most basic level, world mission strategy is concerned with faithful believers being sent out from the local church, crossing cultural boundaries, and proclaiming the life-changing truth of the gospel to people within that new context. In time people accept the gospel, and missionaries then disciple those people and gather them into churches. Preliminarily, of course, theological training is a necessity for missionaries themselves since they must share the gospel, disciple people, and equip local believers for healthy church formation: all theologically inclined tasks. Missionaries must balance the pastoral calling of discipling these young believers to maturity with the apostolic calling of raising up local leaders and eventually moving on to another context.

Yet before moving on, the missionary should plant a healthy church. To reach this goal, the missionary must equip the local leadership to implement biblical forms of preaching, giving, worship, leadership, fellowship, prayer, and of course evangelism and missions. Like the early work of the missionary upon entering a new field and sharing the gospel in a culturally appropriate way, these tasks are also profoundly theological. Coming alongside local believers and training them to perform these tasks requires a commitment to providing rigorous theological training.

In the early stages of church planting, theological training will likely not be formal and highly academic. Instead, theological training will largely consist of the missionary modeling and teaching biblical interpretation to new believers. It will include theological discussions of what Scripture says about God's nature and character. It will also involve setting the biblical-theological foundation for *why* believers evangelize, not just the practical training of *how* to evangelize. Moreover, it will also involve the *what* of evangelism, ensuring that believers are sharing the true gospel. The priority of a firm understanding of the gospel message is what motivated Paul to begin many of his letters with teaching on the gospel.

These comments are not an attempt to dichotomize nonformal and formal types of theological education, nor are they an attempt to criticize one or the other. Rather, each method of theological education should complement the other, with nonformal theological training naturally leading to more formal types of training. Some have criticized traditional models of theological education because they require too many allegedly "impractical" or "irrelevant" courses such as Biblical Hebrew.[3] Studying

---

3. Perry Shaw, *Transforming Theological Education: A Practical Handbook for Integrative Learning* (Carlisle, UK: Langham Global Library, 2014), 10–11; Larry Caldwell, "How Asian Is Asian Theological Education?," in *Tending the Seedbeds: Educational Perspectives on Theological*

Hebrew may not be necessary for every single believer, yet this fact does not mean that biblical language study is irrelevant to all believers and therefore should be jettisoned from all theological education. Instead we should recognize that the various stages of the missionary task require training tailored to those stages. Yet a more fundamental consideration that embraces both nonformal and formal methods of theological education at every level is this: Missionaries should tirelessly labor to ensure national believers receive the highest quality training in the word of God that is possible. Training in the biblical languages, ideally conducted through the local language medium rather than English, liberates the biblical text from the unavoidable defocusing effects of translation.[4] Treating national believers as true brothers and sisters—as co-laborers on God's harvest field—entails doing everything we can to throw open for them the gates of access to Scripture. The missionary's vision should be that national leaders will teach and preach in the power of the Holy Spirit, such that the word of God will burn with the Spirit's fire. Missionaries' hearts for national leaders should beat to the rhythm of Arnold Dallimore's meditation, inspired by the life of George Whitefield:

> Yea . . . that we shall see the great Head of the Church once more . . . raise up unto Himself certain young men whom He may use in this glorious employ. And what manner of men will they be? Men mighty in the Scriptures, their lives dominated by a sense of the greatness, the majesty and holiness of God, and their minds and hearts aglow with the great truths of the doctrines of grace. They will be men who have learned what it is to die to self, to human aims and personal ambitions; men who are willing to be "fools for Christ's sake," who will bear reproach and falsehood, who will labor and suffer, and whose supreme desire will be, not to gain earth's accolades, but to win the Master's approbation when they

---

Education in Asia, ed. Allan Harkness (Quezon City: Asia Theological Association, 2010), 23–45, esp. 35. For a more balanced perspective see Stephen J. Andrews, "Some Knowledge of Hebrew Possible to All: The Value of Biblical Hebrew for the Church," *Midwestern Journal of Theology* 17 (2018): 28–51, as well as the chapter "Language and World Mission" in this book.

4. See reflections on teaching Biblical Hebrew through the medium of Chinese in Scott N. Callaham, "Biblical Hebrew in Chinese: Fostering the Rethinking of Teaching Method through Language Defamiliarization," *HHE* 19 (2017): 103–19.

appear before His awesome judgment seat. They will be men who will preach with broken hearts and tear-filled eyes, and upon whose ministries God will grant an extraordinary effusion of the Holy Spirit, and who will witness "signs and wonders following" in the transformation of multitudes of human lives.[5]

Theological education is about imparting a biblical worldview, helping believers to know God such that he transforms their lives. Before they can embrace biblical lifestyles, though, they must learn to look at God, themselves, and the world in a different way. This transformative process starts with thoughts, progresses to beliefs and values, and only then affects behaviors. Deep, lasting change does not move in the opposite direction, with habituated behaviors generating altered beliefs and values that change one's whole manner of thinking. Instead, worldview transformation includes both conversion (a single point in time) and sanctification (an ongoing process).[6]

Accordingly, in terms of theological training, missionaries are not simply striving to disseminate information. Their goal is life transformation, which first begins with thought transformation. For missionaries to plant a healthy church, they must equip local believers to think in biblical ways. The church and its leaders must be able to understand Scripture beyond a superficial level such that they can apply its truth to the pressing issues of the local context. Kang-San Tan describes this goal as "nurturing contextual theologians in residence"; that is, theological education should focus on developing leaders who think clearly about God and how his truth relates to their world.[7] This goal cannot be accomplished through passing along a set of predetermined lessons with minimal critical thinking about contextualization.

Unfortunately, many missionaries and mission organizations have traditionally approached discipleship and leadership training in a fairly

---

5. Arnold Dallimore, *George Whitefield: The Life and Times of the Great Evangelist of the 18th Century Revival* (Carlisle, PA: Banner of Truth, 1970–1980), 1:16.

6. Paul G. Hiebert, *Transforming Worldviews: An Anthropological Study of How People Change* (Grand Rapids: Baker, 2008), 319.

7. Kang-San Tan, "In Search of Contextualised Training Models for Chinese Christian Diaspora in Britain," *Transformation* 28 (2011): 29–41, esp. 36–37.

uniform, process-centric fashion. New believers are considered discipled because they have completed some series of lessons. In the same way, some church leaders are pronounced equipped simply because they attended several training sessions, often based on curriculum translated into the local language with insufficient regard for cultural context. As a simple example of this cultural oversight, consider the spiritual challenges of animism and ancestor worship. Although pervasive across many cultures in the world, these issues seldom appear in systematic theology textbooks used in Western theological education. Further, since most Western missionaries never learn about these topics in seminary, they arrive on the field ill-equipped to answer the most fundamental worldview questions of the people they are seeking to engage and equip. Using translated Western curricula, textbooks, or evangelistic tracts is not sufficient to meet real-life challenges effectively on the mission field. Missionaries themselves need strong theological foundations to be able to develop materials that address the worldview issues of their target contexts.

A second problem with this "direct translation" approach is more pedagogical. With the goal of being rapid and reproducible, the missionary relays content while the local believer fills in the blanks in a workbook. The missionary then expects that the local leader, notes in hand, will be able to teach the same material with an identical level of theological precision. In almost every case, however, the local leader is not allowed the same amount of time that the missionary had to internalize and process the material. The missionary may prepare the lessons several months in advance, but even prior to lesson preparation has likely had years of daily Bible reading and perhaps extensive theological training. Yet the local leader is expected to learn the material and be able to teach it to others after just a few hours of study.

Theological education is not about the learning or memorizing a key set of facts. Nor is the goal of theological education to answer every possible question. It is about equipping people to think biblically, and this goal should influence *how* we teach and disciple. It means that instead of telling others what a text means, missionaries teach them how to interpret. Instead of telling local believers what the Bible teaches about baptism, they lead them to the Scriptures and help them to discern its meaning. Instead of giving these young leaders sermons to preach, missionaries teach them the process for going from text to sermon. Thus theological education is fundamentally not about transmitting facts and materials that local leaders can easily disseminate. The missionary's goal is to teach local leaders so that they produce their own theologically sound content.

This vision of theological education is a bit like the old adage that giving a man a fish will feed him for a day, but teaching him to fish will feed him for a lifetime. To be sure, this type of theological education takes longer and is often messier than the fill-in-the-blanks approach. The old adage glosses over the fact that fisherman will find it far easier and less time consuming to catch the fish than it will be for him to teach someone else how to fish. In the end, the fisherman's apprentice may even choose to adopt a method of fishing differing from that of the fisherman. Both the deeper investment required in quality theological education and the possibility that national leaders may choose different paths of ministry make missionaries nervous.

Nonetheless, when considering the missiological task and the planting of a healthy church among a target population, missionaries should not merely seek what is easy or what can be accomplished quickly. Speed should not be the driving concern in missiology. It is for this reason that Paul emphasizes that believers must take care in how they plant and lead churches built on the foundation of Christ (1 Cor 3:10). He goes on to explain that at Christ's return "the fire will test the quality of each person's work" (1 Cor 3:13). *Quality matters.* Thus missionaries must take the time to disciple believers at the deep level of worldview. They must also equip church leaders with the theological skills they will need to lead their churches for years to come. Missionaries must labor with the long-term health of the church in mind.

Although theological education of nationals is primarily informal during the early stages of the missionary task, situationally appropriate informality of training need not imply that traditional modes of theological education are unhelpful or even unnecessary. Formal theological education such as seminary training is not only necessary but critical to the long-term health of the church. Not only does this type of training produce indigenous pastors and missionaries with strong exegetical and theological skills, but it also produces indigenous scholar-teachers, who are able to continue the work of training future leaders long after the missionary has moved on.

HOW THEOLOGICAL EDUCATION
ADVANCES THE CAUSE OF MISSIONS

How does this worldview-transforming model of theological education serve to advance the cause of missions? If it is messier and more time consuming, why should missionaries take the time to develop indigenous thinkers rather than just tell them what to think? We suggest four reasons.

First, developing indigenous interpreters of Scripture is biblical. It is important to remember that the Great Commission commands us to "make disciples of all nations" (Matt 28:19). That command is accomplished in part by "teaching them to obey everything I have commanded you" (Matt 28:20). Wendel Sun asserts the importance of the discipleship component of the Great Commission: "The missionary task is incomplete without advanced theological education."[8] Sun does not mean the Great Commission can only be completed when certain degrees from theological institutions are conferred on a given number of people. What he does mean is that the church needs leaders with strong theological foundations for the gospel to take root in some specific context.

We certainly see this truth displayed in Paul's missionary endeavors. He was deeply concerned not just for the existence of churches but also for their theological fidelity. In fact, Sun makes the case that in Romans Paul primarily uses a biblical-theological argument to instruct the Roman church.[9] His letters to the churches at Colossae and Corinth demonstrate how Paul applies biblical theology to the pressing issues of those contexts. Paul did not merely use simple, reproducible teaching techniques; rather, he taught complex theology even to new believers. At least on one occasion, he taught for so long that one believer fell asleep, tumbled out an open window, and died (Acts 20:9). Another example comes from Paul's relationship with the church at Thessalonica. Though

---

8. Wendel Sun, "Biblical Theology and Cross-Cultural Theological Education: The Epistle to the Romans as a Model," *Global Missiology* 4, no. 12 (2015): 1–14, esp. 1.

9. Sun, "Biblical Theology and Cross-Cultural Theological Education," 6.

he was only with them for three Sabbaths, he covered everything from election (1 Thess 1:4), to the need for holy living (1 Thess 4:1–6), to the return of Christ (1 Thess 5:1–2), and even the person and work of the antichrist (2 Thess 2:5).[10]

Paul's pastoral heart was intertwined with his apostolic calling. He did not teach new believers in a way that made them dependent on him. To the contrary, he sought to equip leaders because he knew that he would not be with them forever. His letters to Timothy are saturated with verses emphasizing the importance of doctrine. They also display that Paul has taught Timothy *how* to teach. He encourages him to "follow the pattern of the sound words that you have heard from me" (2 Tim 1:13 ESV). Having been mentored by Paul and having traveled with him for years, Timothy learned a process for teaching others. Thus he was not repeating exactly what Paul said word for word. He learned the biblical story well and learned how to teach in a way that built up others and equipped them to become teachers themselves (2 Tim 2:2).

Another reason the vision of deep investment in theological education is critical is that it helps ensure that missionaries will plant healthy churches. The work of missions has an ecclesiological intention. That is, sharing the gospel in missional contexts should lead to churches being planted in those locations. The notion of an individual Christian living totally separate from other believers is foreign to the New Testament.[11] Discipleship takes place in the context of a local church, and for this reason Paul planted churches in all the cities he visited. As we said above, when Paul planted churches, he was concerned for the health and vitality of those churches. This concern led him to return to them, write letters, and send coworkers to help them.

Like Paul, contemporary missionaries also need to be concerned for the overall health of the churches they plant. Because missionaries yearn for the spread of the gospel, they at times define church health solely in

---

10. We owe this series of insights into Paul's relationship with the church at Thessalonica to Preston Pearce, personal communication.

11. For a missiologically oriented argument that in certain contexts people can follow Christ without ever being baptized or joining a local church, see Herbert E. Hoefer, *Churchless Christianity* (Pasadena, CA: William Carey Library, 2001).

terms of a church's ability to reproduce.[12] We have already mentioned the importance of believers knowing not just the *how* but also the *why* of evangelism. Articulating the reasons for the church's evangelistic burden requires strong theological foundations. Moreover, as critical as evangelism is to the overall health of a local church, a healthy church does more than evangelize. It is for this reason that the International Mission Board developed twelve characteristics of a healthy church to help guide their missionaries in their church-planting efforts.[13] Theological education equips leaders to implement and lead their church toward biblical forms of teaching, worship, tithing, and other important activities.

Third, theological education equips the Christians of newly planted churches to think theologically. Theology is about far more than just the exposition of doctrines that someone may study in a systematic theology course. Theology is about knowing God. In that sense, teaching theology enables forming a biblical worldview and knowing the biblical story so well that Christians are able to respond to the situations of life in ways that align with biblical truth. Theological education seeks to equip people with the exegetical and theological skills to apply Scripture to their contexts.

When the missionary begins to disciple those who have responded to his preaching, these new believers will raise a host of practical questions. These include, "How does our belief in Christ affect participation in our traditional rituals and festivals and approach to life's many challenges?"

---

12. For two examples of this tendency, consider V. David Garrison, *Church Planting Movements: How God Is Redeeming a Lost World* (Bangalore: WIGTake Resources, 2004), 172–200; Stephen R. Smith and Ying Kai, *T4T: A Discipleship ReRevolution* (Bangalore: WIGTake Resources, 2011), 252–57. While both books emphasize the need for teaching on church health, their explanations show that the purpose of this teaching is to foster church reproduction at a faster rate. Thus multiplication becomes the defining metric of church health, and is the standard by which all aspects of church life are evaluated. For example, Garrison promotes lay leadership because lay leaders need minimal training and therefore are able to reproduce quickly. To be fair, many models of church health are lacking in that they do not emphasize sending (especially in terms of the cross-cultural communication of the gospel) or in that they *only* emphasize sending. For a comparison of various healthy church models with the biblical data in Acts, see William P. Brooks, "From Healthy Church to Healthy Church: Why Sending and Planting Models Are Insufficient," paper presented at the annual meeting of the Evangelical Missiological Society, Southeast Region, April 2016.

13. Editorial Staff, imb.org, "12 Characteristics of a Healthy Church (A Summary of David Platt's Teaching)," August 31, 2016, https://www.imb.org/2016/08/31/2016083112 -characteristics-healthy-church/.

and "In what ways does God's mercy to us affect how we respond to the poor in our society?" Make no mistake; these are theologically oriented questions. Encounter with the Triune God will affect their actions and behaviors and will ultimately change how they view the world. Theological training equips believers to think in fresh and biblical ways about their cultural context.

Further, particularly while the church is in its very early stages of growth, it is highly likely that specific and complex theological questions will arise for which no one has previously sought an answer. Western systematic theology textbooks will not likely address those questions. The missionary must train new believers in exegetical skills in order to apply Scripture to those questions.

Also, following the missionary's eventual departure, new questions will arise that the missionary did not envision but for which the church must provide a thorough theological response. If theological education is simply "answering all their questions" or teaching the local believers to disseminate the limited content provided by the missionary, the church will respond ineffectively to new challenges. From the earliest stages of evangelism, discipleship, and church formation the missionary must equip the local believers with the necessary exegetical and theological tools such that, long after the missionary leaves, the church can continue the process of applying the unchanging truth of the gospel to the changing cultural context.

A fourth reason that theological education is an important component of a missiological strategy is that it enables the church to persevere. In 2 Corinthians 11:28, Paul speaks of the "daily pressure of my concern for all the churches." What anxiety or pressure did he feel? First Thessalonians 3:5 explains Paul's fears, "that in some way the tempter had tempted you and that our labors might have been in vain." Paul's great anxiety and fear is that the churches he planted will fall away and not persevere. If that happens, he will consider his work in those areas to have been in vain.

Contemporary missionaries can relate to Paul's anxiety. No one wants to go through the trials of leaving home, learning another language, adjusting to a new culture, communicating the gospel, and planting a church, only to have the believers fall away and the church cease meeting together when the missionary leaves. No one wants such work to be carried out in vain. What was Paul's remedy to this potential danger? *He taught theology.* He sought to equip the churches he planted not just to understand the depths of the gospel but also to know it in such a way that they could apply it to their contexts and teach it to others.

Paul's letters to Timothy and Titus emphasize the importance of doctrine (1 Tim 1:3, 10; 4:6; 6:3). For Paul, doctrine is more than mere head knowledge. For this reason, he speaks of Timothy's faith dwelling in him (2 Tim 1:5) and of the connection between the teaching, his conduct, and aim of life (2 Tim 3:10). Along the same lines, studying doctrine involves more than just memorizing facts. He speaks to Timothy of the importance of "rightly handling the word of truth" (2 Tim 2:15 esv) and of the need for leaders to "give instruction in sound doctrine and also to rebuke those who contradict it" (Titus 1:9 esv). These are all skills that require a significant investment of time and preparation. No one learns them by accident, nor by repeating or memorizing a prepackaged set of lessons.

In his letter to the church at Ephesus, Paul explains the connection between doctrine and the long-term health of the church (Eph 4:11–16). He writes that God gave leaders to the church for the purpose of equipping the saints for the work of ministry. This equipping process focuses on their being strengthened and united in the common faith and on growing in the knowledge of the Son of God. This process continues on until the church reaches maturity. Paul's entire description in 4:11–13 points to the importance of doctrinal fidelity and strong theological foundations for every believer. Especially important to Paul's argument is the purpose clause in 4:14, which states that the equipping happens so that the saints will not be "tossed back and forth by the waves, and blown here and there by every wind of teaching." Paul knows that churches need strong theology if they are going to persevere and not be overcome by false doctrine.

Some might argue that this type of theological training best happens organically, in the context of everyday life, and not as part of an institution or formal degree program. Much of twentieth-century missiology emphasized the need for viewing the church as a dynamic movement that spreads through a segment of society. This idea is set against the model of the church as a static institution. Some elements of truth exist here. Once the gospel penetrates a population segment, we hope it will spread in such a way that it touches every portion of that people.

At the same time, we need to recognize that more formal and institutionalized types of theological education provide a greater degree of stability to the church. Tim Keller explains the need for institutions to stabilize and strengthen movements.[14] Movements are guided by a compelling vision, but for that vision to be effective, it cannot change on a daily basis. Thus the vision naturally leads to structure. He explains, "Institutions are necessary and helpful, providing established, reliable systems and frames for accomplishing what needs to be done." He continues, "Institutions bring order to life and establish many of the conditions for human flourishing and civilized society."[15]

When theological education is more formalized and institutional, it provides stability and longevity to the gospel's movement within a society. Institutions, if they can maintain their health and focus, last longer than movements and will be around to continue training future generations of leaders. Moreover, when such training is accredited and culminates in a seminary degree, these are marks of quality, depth, stability, and accountability. Quality theological education equips pastors and church leaders with a deep understanding of the overarching message of the Bible and enables them to recognize the false claims of heretical movements. Formal theological education also provides church leaders with the necessary tools to preach expository sermons, and by extension to teach congregations how to interpret the Bible. Accredited theological education fosters the stable, long-term growth of the church because it does not attempt to reinvent the wheel. Rather, it builds on the theological lessons that the church has learned in many locations throughout its history. Moreover, accreditation ensures accountability to similar institutions and governing bodies. Standardized processes for research, reflection, writing, and so on found in accredited institutions are critical to the equipping of leaders who will persevere in the long term.

Some people criticize formal theological education, claiming that it slows down the spread of the gospel because it removes people from their context and requires them to relocate to a seminary campus. This view is outdated. In today's world, with the abundance of online and

---

14. Timothy Keller, *Center Church* (Grand Rapids: Zondervan, 2012), 337–42.
15. Keller, *Center Church*, 339.

extension-type programs, seminary training is more accessible than any other time in church history. Even in the West, more and more seminaries are using modular and online formats so that potential students can remain in their current ministry contexts and pursue a course of study. High-quality institutions are constantly evaluating their learning environments and adjusting delivery methods accordingly.

At the same time, the idea of setting aside time to prepare for future ministry is a biblical one. In the New Testament alone we see Jesus himself waiting until he is thirty to begin his ministry and being led into the wilderness for forty days of preparation through temptation. Even during his ministry, he moves away from the crowds for private reflection and prayer. Peter, John, and the other disciples spend three years walking with Jesus and learning from him before starting their own ministries. Paul spends time in Arabia before beginning his ministry.

Emerging leaders (and current ones) need time to think, reflect, process, and internalize the truths of Scripture. A time of focused preparation in the context of a seminary or formal theological institution may remove leaders from ministry for a season, but it will also strengthen and equip them to stay faithful for a long time. Such a perspective is like the woodsman who was asked what he would do if he only had five minutes to cut down a tree. He responded that he would spend the first two and a half sharpening his ax. Theological preparedness not only makes one more effective, but it also leads to perseverance. That said, given that accrediting agencies require that practical ministry training be a key component in all ministry degree programs, formal theological education rarely leads to full withdrawal from ministry. More often, emerging leaders experience seasons during which they commit more time to being equipped while giving slightly less time to equipping others.

HOW UNDERSTANDING THEOLOGICAL
EDUCATION SHAPES THE MISSIONARY

What, then, does this type of theological education mean for the missionary? First, missionaries must recognize that discipleship requires more than just teaching people how to evangelize. Since missionaries love the spread of the gospel, they tend to emphasize the aspects of discipleship that accomplish that goal. As we have noted, some have even defined church health solely in terms of a church's ability to start new churches. Evangelism and missions are certainly critical aspects of church health, but they are not the only factors contributing to the spiritual vitality of churches. To plant healthy churches that persevere, missionaries must ensure that those churches have strong biblical and theological foundations. They must help these new believers to understand the biblical story. They must equip leaders with the exegetical and theological skills to apply Scripture to their contexts.

Second, reproducibility should not be the primary standard by which we judge and evaluate training tools. Reproducibility is often described as the need for indigenous Christians to be able to carry out the missionary's modeled task in a short period of time, sometimes after as little as six months. Of course proponents of this type of reproducibility do not assert that new believers need to do *all* that a missionary can do. Instead, a concern for reproducibility drives the missionary to simplify the processes used and limit the amount of teaching provided so that lesson concepts are simple enough for new believers to learn and implement quickly. The critical problem with this approach is that it does not prioritize a biblically oriented vision of healthy discipleship: training people to think in biblical ways. Healthy discipleship is concerned with equipping disciples to interpret Scripture in ways that are faithful to the original authors' intent.[16]

In reproducible forms of theological training, lectures are typically written out (in fill-in-the-blank style) and thus, upon completion of the course, students carry with them a complete record of all of the course's material. The student then has the ability to "reproduce" or teach verbatim from those notes. Training systems based on a standard such as this are clearly not training disciples to think in biblical ways. The purpose of programs of theological education is not for missionaries to provide indigenous believers with a preformulated set of answers and then teach them how to disseminate that content to others. In contrast, training people to think biblically calls for missionaries to invest their limited resources of time and effort more deeply and strategically. Therefore the

---

16. For a deeper treatment of the importance of biblical interpretation for missiological strategy, see the chapter "Grammatical-Historical Exegesis and World Mission" in this book.

question missionaries should ask is not "Is this material easily reproducible?" Instead, what they should ask is "Does this material equip leaders to lead a healthy church in my absence?" This second question encourages missionaries to focus on equipping leaders rather than just directing local leaders to distribute the missionary's content.

Redirecting emphasis away from content distribution does not imply that content or so-called head knowledge is bad by definition. Rigorous theological education that leads to overall church health requires that a certain amount of information be communicated. Our point here is simply that it matters *how* we convey that content. Pedagogy is critical. Simply because a group of believers can quote our statements verbatim or carry our notes in their hands does not mean they have learned. Missionaries must implement training systems that equip leaders to think, to apply Scripture to their context, and one day to contribute to the global theological conversation. Doing so not only fosters healthy reproduction by allowing local leaders the necessary time to think, learn, process, and reflect on complex theological concepts, but it also advances beyond reproduction by equipping the local leaders to exceed the missionary's more limited ability to communicate cross-culturally.

A third implication of this vision of theological education is that missionaries themselves need ongoing theological education. When considering missionary qualifications, organizations sometimes reflect on the practical question, "How much, if any, seminary training do missionaries need?" For many reasons, this is the wrong question to ask. Instead of focusing on the minimum requirements for missionaries as this question does, organizations should consider what best equips missionaries for long-term service. If missionaries are going to be able to plant healthy churches that practice biblical modes of preaching, stewardship, worship, and so on, they need rigorous theological preparation. If they want to train church leaders to know the gospel well, and if they are going to equip church leaders to interpret and apply Scripture to the local context, then they need to be equipped with such knowledge and skill themselves. Otherwise, how will they train others for future ministry when they have not been trained? How will they encourage others to prepare for the work to which God is calling them when they have not personally set aside the time for preparation?

In more ways than one, missionaries must be lifelong learners. This truth certainly applies to the missionary's need to study language and culture. It also applies to missionaries' commitment to theology. Doing theology in a foreign context is inherently more complicated than thinking theologically in one's native context. Furthermore, especially in the early stages of their ministry, missionaries often do not understand the target cultural context as well as their native one. In some situations the missional burden of responsibility seems far weightier than what the missionary's own capabilities can bear. After all, the missionary could be the first person to attempt to communicate the gospel to a certain people group, for no one has ever previously applied biblical truths within that context. This reality requires missionaries to possess significant theological acumen. They need to have the skills and abilities to apply Scripture to complex culturally contextualized issues. They must also work with local believers and churches to answer questions never previously asked. Moreover, missionaries must teach with sound pedagogical methods so that they do not merely become the answerer of questions. Rather, they must teach the local believers in a way that the indigenous church develops the ability to use Scripture to answer their own questions.

Finally, as a missionary writing to missionaries, let me state a final point as directly as possible. Brothers and sisters, theological education is not about us.[17] Equipping and empowering local leaders is not about increasing numbers on a ledger. Discipleship and theological training are not about us deciding the content that others need to learn. Theological education focuses on God, not us. D. T. Niles once defined evangelism in simple terms as "one beggar telling another one where to find food."[18] He went on to explain that when the Christian speaks to the non-Christian, "It is not *his* knowledge of God that he shares, it is to God Himself that he points."[19] In the same way, the missionary does not own theology any more than he or she owns Scripture or the biblical message. When missionaries disciple indigenous believers, they must point those believers to the very fount from which their own theology flows: the Bible.

---

17. This paragraph is a personal appeal from Will Brooks.

18. D. T. Niles, *That They May Have Life* (New York: Harper & Brothers, 1951), 96.

19. Niles, *That They May Have Life*, 96, emphasis added.

THE IMPORTANCE OF MISSION IN
SHAPING THEOLOGICAL EDUCATION

HOW MISSION SHAPES THE CHURCH'S
UNDERSTANDING OF THEOLOGICAL EDUCATION

While the previous section focused on the missionary, this section shifts attention to the academy and provides a perspective that distinguishes contemporary theological education from the educational processes carried out in the local church. No doubt education in the church is also *theological* (in the sense that it is about God), but here "theological education" refers to the academic discipline of theology as well as to the way of thinking that undergirds all the courses taught in the process. The argument below presents theological education in terms of (1) those responding to a call, (2) the formation of a theological mind, and (3) teachers transmitting knowledge that forms community.

Those Responding to a Call

Education in the church is mainly aimed at maturing disciples in a life of obedience, but formal theological education seeks to equip those convinced that God is calling them to fulfill his mission through a particular kind of service dedicated to him.[20] These disciples are convicted to do something in line with God's mission through their work, gifting, and sphere of influence and to seek academic training that will equip them to do that very thing.[21] Theological schools respond to this need by providing education for a better understanding of God and preparation for the work required. Theological schools should review their curricula regularly to respond to the kind of missional tasks needed in changing societies.[22] Hence theological education should free itself from a strictly

---

20. Noelliste argues that theological education is "education of the whole people of God," but he clarifies that there is a place for the singling out of a smaller group within the wider body of Christ for special attention. See Dieumeme Noelliste, *Toward a Theology of Theological Education* (Seoul: WEF Theological Commission, 1993), 14.

21. The concept of divine calling here may also be explained in terms of "spiritual gifting" for a certain task, as in the case of Timothy, who is to "fan into flame the gift [χάρισμα] of God, which is in [him]" (2 Tim 1:6).

22. Since children now comprise a large portion of many contemporary societies, note the Holistic Child Development Program of Malaysia Baptist Theological Seminary as an example of a strategic pivot in theological education to meet an emergent need.

clerical paradigm in order to offer academic programs that provide theological foundations for a wide variety of ministries. Individual theological schools may opt to specialize (thus training only pastors, missionaries, counselors, etc.), but theological education per se is for all who can testify to a call to a task.

The Formation of a Theological Mind

The preaching of the gospel of Jesus Christ, according to the apostle Paul, should take place while taking "captive every thought to make it obedient to Christ" (2 Cor 10:5). It follows that when a person becomes a disciple, the theological education process aims at the "renewing of [the] mind" so that the new disciple acquires the skill to "test and approve what God's will is" (Rom 12:2). The Bible is the primary textbook to enable striving toward that end. The Bible, however, must be read and interpreted rightly for that goal to be achieved.[23] As a book that is translatable into any language yet still retains its nature as Scripture, the Bible is especially susceptible to misunderstanding and misrepresentation (see 2 Pet 3:16, 2 Tim 2:15).[24] Hence, training in the proper interpretation of the Bible is necessary as part of the educational process of the church. Theological education seeks to build on what the church has begun and further seeks to form the disciple's mind *theologically*.

Thinking theologically is an attempt to discern the connection between the human and the divine. A theological mind is thus characterized by "an expanded field of vision," as David Gill puts it.[25] A theological mind is also

---

23. The point here also serves to explain why focus on the Bible is one of the key concerns of this chapter and why it readily stands in for the phrase "everything I have commanded you" in the Great Commission. While at the moment of speaking Jesus was not referring to inscripturated commandments, the Bible is the means of transmitting Jesus' commands to the church. It is significant that God entrusted the church with an authoritative book to teach that transmits the Christian faith. Klaus Bockmuehl observes, "Apart from the incarnation of His Son and next to oral preaching, God has chosen the medium of the book in order to proclaim His goodness to us. In a conspicuous manner the book has become a prominent tool for God's plan of salvation with the world." See Klaus Bockmuehl, *Books: God's Tools in the History of Salvation* (Vancouver: Regent College, 1986), 7.

24. In contrast to the scriptural texts of religions that require access through a certain language (such as the Classical Arabic of the Qur'an), the Bible is itself multilingual and inherently translatable. The Bible's translatability is a significant factor in Christian formation.

25. David W. Gill, *The Opening of the Christian Mind: Taking Every Thought Captive to Christ* (Downers Grove, IL: InterVarsity Press, 1989), 65.

able to think critically, as there is an ongoing conflict between truth and falsehood.[26] A discerning mind has to be formed according to the revealed truths in the Bible. In short, Christian theology comprises the distinct content of theological education. Christian theology is an academic discipline and a way of thinking derived from the "one story" of the Bible. The emphasis on the one story of the Bible is vital, as it implies that the logic of the Christian faith, the logic for understanding and accessing the true and the real, must align with the one story that unfolds from Genesis to Revelation. It is this one story of the God-human relation that conflicts with other worldviews.[27]

Teachers Transmitting Knowledge That Forms Community[28]

Education involves a teacher as a knower facilitating transference of knowledge to students who are potential knowers. As those who are enrolled in theological schools are preparing themselves for God-assigned

---

26. Critical thinking here is distinguished from a mind that is "closed" because of mere indoctrination. The issue of indoctrination is a serious issue in religious settings. Merkle refers to it when he affirms that theological education is for strengthening believers for ministry and "not about controlling the local believers or even indoctrinating them." See Benjamin L. Merkle, "The Need for Theological Education in Missions: Lessons Learned from the Church's Greatest Missionary," *SBJT* 9, no. 4 (2005): 50–61, esp. 59. Harkness observes, "Historically, [indoctrination] has been a positive term, similar to some of the common meanings of education. Within religious settings, it has meant teaching doctrine, or instructing in religious belief. However, in contemporary educational usage indoctrination has a negative stigma, with a meaning akin to 'unreasonable manipulation.' " See Allan Harkness, "Indoctrination," in *Encyclopedia of Christian Education*, ed. George Thomas Kurian and Mark A. Lamport (Lanham, MD: Rowman & Littlefield, 2015), 2:630–33, esp. 630.

27. N. T. Wright contends, "By opening the Bible and reading it for all its worth the Church will be unable to avoid the fact that it challenges and subverts other world views. An integrated missionary strategy, which takes the Bible seriously, will need to become increasingly clear about these challenges. For, when we begin to face and engage with these challenges, we can move from a position of largely groping in the dark towards an effective placing of the biblical narrative in the public arena as a source of truth and hope for our world." See N. T. Wright, "The Book and the Story," *The Bible in TransMission*, September 1, 2001, http://www.biblesociety.org.uk/uploads/content/bible_in_transmission/files/2001_special_edition/BiT_Special_2001_Wright.pdf.

28. This section is based on Sunny Boon-Sang Tan, "Community-Building: A Formative Principle in Theological Education (With Special Reference to the Baptist Theological Seminary, Malaysia)" (ThM thesis, Regent College, Vancouver, 1994). The term "community-building" is basically used in opposition to "individualism," and in the biblical sense of bringing people together in a way that reflects God as Triune. In mission there is the presupposition that community is essential and necessary. The emphasis in this section is on the attitude to be formed and not on the actual work of building a community. This concept is based on Stanley J. Grenz's work on community as the framework for doing theology.

work, then, the body of knowledge to be transferred may be expected to be both practical and useful. Knowledge certainly contributes to application, but the obedience required by the gospel and by the God who calls is ultimately about relationships, both with the Triune God and between disciples. Reality in the Christian view is relational because God exists as a divine community. God also teaches humans to relate to him and to participate in his community.[29] God's mission as revealed in Jesus Christ is stated in relational terms (such as "God so loved," "be reconciled with God," "becoming children of God"), and Jesus' command to teach disciples to obey assumes their incorporation into a church community. Furthermore, biblical knowing is relational in character, so a claim to know and to possess knowledge should be evident in conduct that brings people together. Therefore, educators should not treat knowledge as an end in itself without any bearing on relationships and communities to build up.

One particular tendency that teachers in theological schools have to guard against is the temptation that "knowledge puffs up" (1 Cor 8:1b). Such is the temptation of knowledge in a fallen world that even so-called spiritual knowledge may incite pride in the one who possesses it. This problem is unavoidable in the academic process. A common criticism leveled against theological schools is that graduates cannot fit into local churches, as their learning has distanced them from congregations. The apostle Paul's response to such a temptation is to practice love (that is, the love that "builds up" in 1 Cor 8:1c). Here, love is not set in opposition to knowledge. Rather, one who knows must also love in order that the knowledge is properly employed to help others. In other words, because of love, knowledge is transferred by the teachers to build relationship and community. In the context of this chapter, theological education needs to carry out the work of teaching in such a way that its graduates contribute to the mission of reconciliation, of relationships in Christ, and of the building up of churches that practice genuine community.

---

29. The apostle Paul reminds the Thessalonians that they "have been taught by God to love each other" (1 Thess 4:9). The teaching act in the Christian framework is theological through and through; we teach because God teaches. We also imitate the divine motivation to teach.

In summary, what is formal theological education? The answer points to a particular kind of education practiced by the disciples of Jesus Christ to equip those whom God calls. Theological education may be offered at various academic levels, but at whatever level, it gives priority to the formation of disciples' minds according to the one story of the Bible, for the sake of building up relationships and genuine communities. As such, formal theological education may be regarded as significant for world mission, especially when the additional emphases discussed next are taken into consideration.

HOW MISSION SHAPES THE
GOALS OF THEOLOGICAL EDUCATION

Jesus' command to make disciples includes the key component of teaching obedience.[30] Thus theological education is essentially subsumed in mission; God's mission is *the* referent and *the* evaluative criterion for the practice of theological education. From such a perspective, theological education is carried out with the primary aim of preparing disciples to be involved in God's mission. This perspective, however, is not to claim that all theological disciplines have to be understood within a missional framework or to propose that theological schools should teach only mission courses.[31] Instead, the essential connectedness between theological education and mission has to do with developing God-centered lives offered up to further God's mission.[32] How is this connection worked out in theological education? The answer proposed here is in terms of three intrinsic

---

30. Blomberg comments, "Teaching obedience to all of Jesus' commands forms the heart of disciple making." Craig L. Blomberg, *Matthew*, NAC (Nashville: Broadman, 1992), 433.

31. On the debate over the place of mission within theological education curricula see David J. Bosch, "Theological Education in Missionary Perspective," *Missiology* 10 (1982): 13–33. On one hand Greenman proposes a radical shift from a professional to a missional paradigm for theological education. See Jeffrey P. Greenman, "Mission as the Integrating Center of Theological Education," in *The Bible in World Christian Perspective: Studies in Honor of Carl Edwin Armerding*, ed. David W. Baker and W. Ward Gasque (Vancouver: Regent College Press, 2009), 193–210. On the other hand, Guder argues that if theological education intentionally forms students to follow the footsteps of the early apostles (that is, having an apostolic vocation), there would no longer be need for a discrete "missional" focus. See Darrell L. Guder, "*Missio Dei*: Integrating Theological Formation for Apostolic Vocation," *Missiology* 37 (2009): 63–74, esp. 66.

32. Much like the term "theological education," the word "mission" is also a modern construct. The word "mission" as it appears in some English Bibles (as in Acts 12:25) is a translation of the Greek word for "service" (διαχονία).

components present in the practice of theological education and mission: work, wisdom, and words.

The Work of Redemption and Transformation

God's mission may be understood in terms of a twofold work: his work to redeem and to transform. The work of redemption deals squarely with the problem of sin. This work is supremely revealed in Jesus Christ; thus it is from a Christ-centered framework that the word "redeem" and its cognates are to be understood with respect to Christian mission. When God's mission is presented on the basis of the Great Commission, the emphasis is on this redemptive aspect of God's work. That is to say, people hear the gospel and become disciples of Jesus Christ. However, becoming a disciple is not an end in itself, as the Great Commission requires disciples' lifelong obedience. This obedience transforms, matures, and sanctifies. Hence the apostle Paul speaks of being "transformed . . . with ever-increasing glory" when beholding the glory of Jesus (2 Cor 3:18).

The work of transformation may also be viewed as already initiated with God's creation of humankind. From the beginning, God's plan is that people participate in a process of becoming and being transformed as they live out their lives according to his will. Thus, the apostle Paul speaks of "the natural" as coming first and then "the spiritual" (1 Cor 15:46). The first two chapters of Genesis depict God and humankind relating to each other, and humans are entrusted with the responsibility to transform the world by working it (Gen 1:28). Though not clearly spelled out in those two chapters, it is implied that people will themselves be transformed as they carry out God's plan. Thus, the apostle Paul's words that disciples are "God's handiwork, created in Christ Jesus to do good works" (Eph 2:10a) may be interpreted as also embracing the original divine intention for human participation in God's mission of doing good in the world, and not just in the church.

Theological schools design their curricula according to the tasks needed to carry out God's mission. For much of the history of theological education, the tasks have been understood in terms of service to the church. The task of pastoring requires a certain body of knowledge, and the task of serving as a church educator requires another set of appropriate knowledge. Then specialization in church and mission work inevitably leads to even greater proliferation of varied theological curricula. Such a development has led to criticism of fragmentation in theological education.[33] However, expansion and development of contemporary theological education efforts need not be viewed negatively as long as the commitment toward the twofold work of redemption and transformation remains the controlling vision. Theological education, as described earlier, is for all who are ready to participate in God's mission either by entering a full-time ministry or by using their occupation and position of influence to carry out the task God assigns.

Wisdom for Living and Doing

From the perspective of the Bible, humans live either wisely or foolishly. Wise living is in obedience to God, while foolish living ignores him. The church is called to be a people who demonstrate practical wisdom based on the fear of God and in doing so make "the teaching about God our Savior attractive" (Titus 2:10). The godly living exemplified by disciples has to be noticed as to have "value for all things, holding promise for both the present life and the life to come" (1 Tim 4:8). Mission as such may be understood as promoting a wisdom that contributes to wise ways of living on earth, which in turn causes people to seek God.[34]

The wisdom literature of the Bible is a subject of study in theological schools, but wisdom per se is not in the curriculum. Yet wisdom is a major theme of the Bible, and its readers are encouraged to seek it from the Creator God. The apostle Paul asserts that the "Holy Scriptures . . . are able to make [one] wise for salvation" (2 Tim 3:15). The word "wisdom" ($\sigma o \phi i \alpha$) is linked to the Scriptures and to a desired outcome in missions, that is, finding salvation. Disciples are to seek the "wisdom that comes from heaven" (Jas 3:17) embodied in Jesus Christ. Jesus himself is declared the "wisdom of God" (1 Cor 1:24). Jesus defines a wise man as one who hears his words and acts on them (Matt 7:24). When he sends out his disciples to preach

---

33. Regarding fragmentation in theological education see Edward Farley, *Theologia: The Fragmentation and Unity in Theological Education* (Philadelphia: Fortress, 1983). Farley proposes community building in theological formation to counter this fragmentation.

34. The apostle Paul's sermon to the Athenians in Acts 17:22–31 may be considered as using a wisdom approach. He points out the foolishness of having idols and the wisdom of seeking God through inferences drawn from creation.

the kingdom of God, he says they are as "sheep among wolves" and so they have to "be as shrewd [φρόνιμος] as snakes and innocent as doves" (Matt 10:16). Thus, theological education is not only about imparting knowledge and skills but also in assisting students to be wise in living and doing in the context of a fallen world. Gordon T. Smith's proposal that wisdom be the "unifying principle" for theological schools is relevant here.

> The objective of the academy, then, would be to enable men and women to become wise. Wisdom is a helpful point of reference because it incorporates the development of knowledge and understanding as well as the formation of character. Wise people are mature in both their understanding and their behavior. Further wisdom assumes the integration and appropriation of truth—we both understand and live the truth.[35]

Words as Method for God's Mission

The Bible is composed of inspired words to be read, understood, and obeyed. The Christian faith is based on the claim that God speaks. Creation exists because God spoke, and creation is good because it is according to

---

35. Gordon T. Smith, "Spiritual Formation in the Academy: A Unifying Model," *TE* 33 (1996): 83–91, esp. 86. Enns argues for training in wisdom from the perspective of intercultural theological education. Her fundamental assertion is that education is for wisdom, and the uniqueness of the education that is rooted in the Bible is that "(1) wise people interpret experience theologically; (2) they 'fear the Lord' and live with 'whole holiness' or 'holy wholeness' within the framework of Israel's covenantal life; and (3) ultimately, they follow Jesus Christ, who is wisdom's cruciform embodiment." See Marlene Enns, "Educating to Become Wise: Intercultural Theological Education," in *The Old Testament in the Life of God's People: Essays in Honor of Elmer A. Martens*, ed. Jon Isaak (Winona Lake, IN: Eisenbrauns, 2009), 55–72. Charry urges a return to wisdom theology. According to her, "sapience includes correct information about God but emphasizes attachment to that knowledge. Sapience is engaged knowledge that emotionally connects the knower to the known. In the West, knowledge of God's grandeur and wrath inculcated a strong sense of sinfulness in the individual who contrasted him or herself with God. In this view, growth in the Christian life turned on the ability to trust God as a father rather than fear him as a master. In the East, the emphasis was on likeness to God, by means of which we turn to him from less worthy pursuits. Both traditions, however, insisted that God is the origin and destiny of human happiness, that knowing and loving God are the foundation of human self-knowledge and direction, and that life's goal is conformation to God." See Ellen T. Charry, *By the Renewing of Your Minds: The Pastoral Function of Christian Doctrine* (New York: Oxford University Press, 1997), 4. See also Treier's proposal for "theology as wisdom" in Daniel J. Treier, *Virtue and the Voice of God: Toward Theology as Wisdom* (Grand Rapids: Eerdmans, 2006).

the spoken divine word (Gen 1).[36] Human beings are created to "live on bread" and by "every word that comes from the mouth of the LORD" (Deut 8:3). The fall stems from listening to false words (Gen 3). One becomes a disciple of Jesus by hearing "the message of truth" (Eph 1:13). Disciples are built up by the "word of [God's] grace" (Acts 20:32). Carrying out the redemptive and transformative task of mission requires truthful words to be delivered to human hearers. Such truthful words are normally not delivered by supernatural beings but by human agents. Philip has to speak to the Ethiopian (Acts 8:26–39) and Peter to Cornelius (Acts 10). Paul almost persuades Agrippa to become a Christian by his words (Acts 26:28). Christians are to be ready to "give the reason for the hope" in them (1 Pet 3:15). Jesus was the Word incarnate, and in his incarnation he affirmed the connection between words, materiality, and conduct. Truthful words are for the here and now, and so "false prophets" are known by "their fruit" (Matt 7:15–20). Since falsehood and illusory words dominate human societies, it is the task of disciples to counter them with truthful words. Words that are according to and from God are like a sword that cuts deeply (Heb 4:12), and are like seed (Luke 8:11) and food (Heb 5:12–14) that promotes life.[37]

A theological school may be viewed as the agency charged with the responsibility of paying attention to use of words with reference to God. Teachers are to model to the students the importance of words in the Christian faith. The apostle Paul in exhorting Timothy to "correctly" handle "the word of truth" compares him to a workman who knows how to use his tools properly (2 Tim 2:15). Faithfulness cannot be understood without taking into consideration words heard and spoken. Words and conduct must align in faithful discipleship. Jesus declares that it is the words from the heart that finally indicate whether a person is clean or

---

36. Note that Adam is not created by words spoken but by God's action of forming and breathing. Divine words encounter Adam only *after* he becomes "a living being" (Gen 2:7). Words heard and internalized then become the means of human transformation. However, the kind of words received becomes a matter of life or death: "true" words from God bring life, and "false" words bring death.

37. The term "word" at times serves as a metaphor for "language." The one story in the Bible provides a particular religious language for accessing the truths proclaimed by it. See Edmond La Beaume Cherbonnier, "The Theology of the Word of God," *Journal of Religion* 33 (1953): 16–30.

unclean (Matt 15:16–20). Thus, teachers should train their students on the proper use of words as tools.[38] Training in theology includes learning to communicate to people the written word *of* God, truthful words *about* God, and wise words *from* God; and also to teach them to speak sincere words *to* God. Hence, along with community building as a knowledge paradigm in theological education, training in the proper use of words, especially in the speaking of truthful words, prepares students to engage in God's mission.

CONCLUSION

Jesus' Great Commission directive to teach disciples "to obey everything I have commanded you" thoroughly integrates theological education with world mission strategy. The preceding discussion reflects on the pressing need for theological education to prepare cross-cultural missionaries to carry out their biblical mandate in accordance with scriptural teaching. Furthermore, as missionaries lead locals to faith in Christ, baptize them, and gather them into churches for discipleship, they must begin carrying out informal theological education in order to ground the next generation of church leadership in Scripture. Missionaries should also selflessly encourage more formal types of theological education—even to higher levels than they possess themselves—for nationals whom God prepares for such challenges. Quality theological education instills a biblical worldview, a thoroughly biblical ethos for all aspects of life, thus facilitating the planting of healthy churches that naturally transition from receiving missionaries to sending missionaries. May all levels and methods of theological education continue to fuel single-minded devotion to God and his word, for his glory, in all nations!

---

38. Theological schools typically require preaching courses for pastoral candidates and a cross-cultural communication course for those preparing to be missionaries. Perhaps there is also a need to equip students in what Piper calls "Christian eloquence." Piper observes that Paul's warning on eloquence in 1 Cor 1:17 has been misunderstood. "When we take care to create a beautiful way of speaking or writing about something beautiful, the eloquence—the beauty of the form—reflects and honors the beauty of the subject and so honors the truth." See John Piper and Justin Taylor, eds., *The Power of Words and the Wonder of God* (Wheaton, IL: Crossway, 2009), 80.

III

CURRENT ISSUES IN WORLD MISSION

O n a certain day in 1807 Henry Martyn, single and in ill health, poured himself into his Persian translation work. He started in the morning and persevered long into the night. To contemporary readers, such a life makes little sense. Why would someone willingly sacrifice both the chance to be with the woman he loved and the opportunity for a successful academic career? And why would he then move to a foreign country where he knew no one and labor endlessly to translate some book into another language? In his journal that day Martyn penned words that explain why he committed to such a path. He was willing to give up worldly comforts, suffer, and eventually die because he was translating no ordinary book; it was the very word of God. He wrote: "All day on the translations: employed a good while at night in considering a difficult passage; and being much enlightened respecting it, I went to bed full of astonishment at the wonders of God's word: never before did I see anything of the beauty of the language, and the importance of the thoughts, as I do now."[1]

Scan a book on contemporary issues in missions, and it most likely will deal with topics such as globalization, urbanization, migration patterns, and religious pluralism. No doubt these are critical issues that affect the work of missionaries around the world. At the same time, though, scholars tend not to dwell on what should be of overwhelming and overriding significance to the work of world mission today: the word of God.

This section attempts to chart a different course by placing the word front and center. It takes its cues from the legacies of men and women

---

1. John Sargent, ed. *The Life and Letters of Henry Martyn* (Carlisle, PA: Banner of Truth, 1985), 220.

like Henry Martyn, who loved the word, spent their waking hours meditating on its beauty, and gave their lives to proclaiming it to a lost and dying world. Called to be lifelong learners, contemporary missionaries must first and foremost be students of the word. The word must be their delight (Ps 1:2), and their longing should be to see wonderful things within it (Ps 119:18). The nature of their missionary task is simple and clear: they must proclaim the word.

In light of the centrality of proclaiming the word, the following section now addresses several critical contemporary issues in world mission. From the first moment of entering a new field of service, a missionary's need to use the local language to communicate is abundantly clear. Yet rather than merely profile various existing practices in language acquisition, the first chapter of this section focuses on the missionary as communicator of God's word and then demonstrates how that principle should shape every aspect of language learning. Building on this fundamental orientation toward Bible-centeredness in world mission, the next chapter examines how the missionary can apply the unchanging truths of God's word within varied cultural contexts by carrying out grammatical-historical exegesis.

Given that the majority of the world's unreached peoples are not literates, the following chapter then considers the concept of orality and explains how the Bible's grand narrative shapes how we should communicate its message to oral learners. The final chapter considers the apostle Paul as a model missionary. Paul's missionary strategy emphasized both apostolic and pastoral dimensions as he planted churches and led them to sink their roots deeply into the soil of the word of God.

8

LANGUAGE AND WORLD MISSION

Scott N. Callaham

INTRODUCTION

וַיֹּאמֶר אֱלֹהִים יְהִי אוֹר וַיְהִי אוֹר

And God said, "Let there be light," and there was light.

Genesis 1:3

anguage is ingrained in human experience, both suffusing the continual private musings of individual minds and facilitating countless social interactions between people. Awash in language and dependent on linguistic acts for almost every aspect of life, people tend to view language as a human invention to facilitate communication.[1] Yet the Bible indicates that language did not originate with human beings, but with God.[2] Indeed, while the opening verse of Genesis announces the start of God's creative activity, creation actually begins in the third verse with God's spoken word.[3] Notably,

---

1. Daniel L. Everett, *Language: The Cultural Tool* (New York: Pantheon, 2012), 19 and passim; Christopher S. Butler, *Structure and Function: A Guide to Three Major Structural-Functional Theories*, Studies in Language Companion Series 63–64 (Philadelphia: John Benjamins, 2003), 1:2–4. One should note that the leading school of linguistics stands unreservedly opposed to the concept that language is a human-created tool. According to generative linguistics theory, language is instead a genetically transmitted endowment unique to humans. See Andrew Radford, *Syntax: A Minimalist Introduction* (New York: Cambridge University Press, 1997), 8–11.

2. Unless otherwise noted, the Bible translation quoted in this chapter is the ESV.

3. It is possible to suggest that Gen 1:3 marks the creation of language itself. See Jonathan Yovel, "The Creation of Language and Language without Time: Metaphysics and Metapragmatics in Genesis 1," *Biblical Interpretation* 20 (2012): 205–25, esp. 214–16. Even so, communication among the persons of the Trinity would seem to require the existence of language before creation. See Vern Sheridan Poythress, *In the Beginning Was the Word: Language—A God-Centered*

the verb for "create" in Genesis 1:1 only takes God as its subject in the Old Testament and appears rather infrequently. In contrast, the verb of speaking in Genesis 1:3 is the most commonly used verb in Biblical Hebrew, and it pairs with a vast array of subjects.[4] Thus God employs a wholly "ordinary" means to accomplish an extraordinary task that only he can carry out.

God likewise wields the ordinary tool of language today as he works through the church in the extraordinary task of world mission. Recognition that world mission is God-centered should lead to comprehensive rethinking of contemporary missions practice with regard to language. Specifically, the church must recover a Great Commission–derived conception of the missionary as *communicator of God's word*, then structure its whole approach toward language in mission accordingly.

MISSIONARY AS COMMUNICATOR OF GOD'S WORD

The next several sections progressively develop the case for viewing the central and preeminent task of the missionary as communicator of God's word in obedience to the Great Commission. Each section reviews the elements of this task in sequence, first profiling the role of the missionary as communicator, then noting well that God originates the message of missions, and last grounding missions in the word of God. Implications for missionaries' learning and use of language then follow on this review.

COMMUNICATOR: THE MISSIONARY'S PRIMARY ROLE

הַאֲזִינוּ הַשָּׁמַיִם וַאֲדַבֵּרָה וְתִשְׁמַע הָאָרֶץ אִמְרֵי־פִי

Give ear, O heavens, and I will speak, and let the earth hear the words of my mouth.

Deuteronomy 32:1

Abruptly transplanting into a new cultural setting is a profoundly disorienting experience, and thus it is no wonder that the unsettling term

---

Approach (Wheaton, IL: Crossway, 2009), 17–22. Note the significant ontological deduction summarized in the title of Pierce Taylor Hibbs, "Imaging Communion: An Argument for God's Existence Based on Speech," *WTJ* 77 (2015): 35–51.

4. See *DCH*, s.v. "אמר" and "ברא." A search on Bibleworks 10 with Westminster Hebrew Morphology 4.14 (2010) reveals 5,319 appearances of אמר in the Hebrew Bible as a verbal root.

"culture shock" has arisen to describe it. Arrival in a foreign land instantly strips away the comfort of the familiar, leaving in its place an awkward psychological nakedness. Vanished are many subtle social cues and behavioral norms that foster unspoken mutual understandings between people. Furthermore, the acute pain of social ineptness and isolation only intensifies in the absence of all but the most rudimentary means to communicate. As a result, an adult feels as if transformed into a child, or worse, a fool.[5] Since communicating with people presumably lies at the heart of why missionaries uproot from their home contexts and move to culturally distant lands, utter incompetence in language use can strike a devastating blow to one's sense of identity.

Introductions to intercultural communication typically treat language as but one element among a panoply of factors affecting communication. It is certainly true that a range of diverse nonverbal acts color the connotation of most every spoken communication. Therefore missionaries whose home cultures typically devote primary attention to the direct and concise use of language may especially benefit from careful rethinking of culturally conditioned, sociologically significant, nonverbal signals.[6] Yet without deprecating the need for critical review of one's nonverbal communication practices, at the same time it is vital to understand that language is the wellspring out of which all other communicative streams flow. Indeed, the widely propagated statistic that "93 percent of meaning in conversation is nonverbal" is patently untrue.[7] Instead, cooperative and constructive use of language stands as the normal

---

5. William A. Smalley, "Culture Shock, Language Shock, and the Shock of Self-Discovery," in William A. Smalley, ed., *Readings in Missionary Anthropology II* (South Pasadena, CA: William Carey Library, 1978), 693–700.

6. A. Scott Moreau, Gary R. Corwin, and Gary B. McGee, *Introducing World Missions: A Biblical, Historical, and Practical Survey* (Grand Rapids: Baker Academic, 2004), 265–78.

7. A recent example of an approving citation of this statistic in an otherwise linguistically astute work is Tom Steffen and Lois McKinney Douglas, *Encountering Missionary Life and Work: Preparing for Intercultural Ministry* (Grand Rapids: Baker Academic, 2008), 233. The misunderstood statistic derives from Albert Mehrabian, *Silent Messages* (Belmont, CA: Wadsworth, 1971), 43–44, and has to do with how people resolve a perceived conflict between the literal meaning of spoken words and contrasting nonverbal cues. As for the value of verbal communication, Mehrabian writes that "language is by far the most effective medium for expressing complex and abstract ideas" (134).

expectation behind most human interaction.[8] Therefore a crucial goal of cross-cultural missionaries must be to acquire competence in the language of their host culture with all due diligence and urgency. Of course, learning the use of a language within a new cultural setting is not an end in itself, for missionaries clearly intend to use that language to communicate a message. This all-important message is the factor that most distinguishes missionaries from all other learners and users of language. The immediately following sections first establish God as the source of the missionary message and then profile that message's content.

GOD: THE SOURCE OF THE MISSIONARY'S MESSAGE

ῥήματα ζωῆς αἰωνίου ἔχεις.

You have the words of eternal life.

John 6:68

God is the author and owner of the missionary's message. At first glance this statement appears to be a trite observation requiring little justification. Yet due to the gravity of the implications of this seemingly simple assertion, some development of the idea of God as source of the message of missions is essential.

God's unique choice to create human beings in his image (Gen 1:26) suggests that behind many distinctly human qualities lie intimations of a divine pattern. This divine pattern extends to the use of language, for God's first acts after creating humans are to bless them and to speak to them, expecting the human couple to understand. God speaks not merely to issue commands but also to inform the humans about his activity on their behalf (Gen 1:28–30).[9] Then, after the first humans sin, God seeks out the man with the question, "Where are you?" (Gen 3:9). Later God uses language to inaugurate formal covenants of relationship with people. Theologically these covenants are highly significant, with each

---

8. Paul Grice, *Studies in the Way of Words* (Cambridge, MA: Harvard University Press, 1989), 24–31.

9. Initially it appears that God's acts of blessing and speaking follow a paradigm already set in Gen 1:22, when he commands the swimming and flying creatures. Yet unlike his address to animals, God speaks relationally "to" humans in Gen 1:28.

successive covenant carrying forward the Bible's main story line.[10] Then, when the prophets call God's people to return to covenant faithfulness, they frequently and pointedly employ the phrase, "Thus *says* the Lord."

The cumulative effect of the many divine speech acts in the Bible is not to smother the human element in the biblical story by portraying people merely as those "acted on" by an aloof and all-powerful "actor." Instead, the Bible calls humans to a dynamic, relational response.[11] That relational response, since the very first human communication with God, has depended on language.[12] Specifically, on his own initiative God uses language to communicate with people, and people in turn use language to respond to him. Likewise, the missionary's message first derives from God's initiative, and then the missionary's proclamation of that message calls for a response.

As for the rhetorical packaging of God's missionary message, narrating contemporary accounts of God's work in the world may hold some value for illustrating what can happen as humans respond to God in relationship with him. Likewise, stories of God's activity in one's own life may lend an engaging personal tone to the sum total of what a missionary says. Additionally, shaping one's witness in order to address the perceived needs of listeners is ordinarily a sound persuasion strategy. Furthermore, expounding on the need for evangelism—even when addressing the not-yet converted—helpfully underscores the need for world mission. Even so, while believing response is the desired outcome of the missionary's message, it is not the whole of the message. Indeed, too persistent a focus on human response to God can subtly and harmfully shift the stress of the missionary's message away from God. The core of the missionary message— God's message—is God's revelation of himself through his inspired word.

---

10. Peter J. Gentry and Stephen J. Wellum, *Kingdom through Covenant: A Biblical-Theological Understanding of the Covenants* (Wheaton: Crossway, 2012), 138–39; David Noel Freedman, "Divine Commitment and Human Obligation: The Covenant Theme," *Interpretation* 18 (1964): 419–31, esp. 419–20.

11. John Kessler, *Old Testament Theology: Divine Call and Human Response* (Waco, TX: Baylor University Press, 2013), 69–77.

12. Helpful reflections on the relational embeddedness of language appear in Timothy J. Crutcher, "The Relational-Linguistic Spiral: A Model of Language for Theology," *Heythrop Journal* 43 (2002): 463–79.

THE WORD: THE MESSAGE OF MISSIONS

Ὁ λόγος γὰρ ὁ τοῦ σταυροῦ . . . δύναμις θεοῦ ἐστιν.

For the word of the cross . . . is the power of God.

1 Corinthians 1:18

"The missionary message is the word of God" should also be a relatively noncontroversial assertion, yet it can actually face challenge on multiple fronts. For example, one could suggest that such an affirmation defines the missionary message too narrowly. In this line of thinking, the task of missions is too complex to reduce to a singular orientation or formulation.[13] Thus communicating the word of God is but part of the missionary's overall agenda, either in a generalized sense or as one component among many.[14] Alternately, one could suggest extending the scope of the message such that missionaries communicate God's revelation, conceived more broadly. Thus on one hand the missionary message could take a more preapologetic form and emphasize general revelation. On the other hand, in some situations God's supreme special revelation of himself in Jesus Christ could take center stage.[15] Perhaps one could even venture beyond the confines of revelation altogether in order to promote training on vision casting, leadership principles, or the concept of rapid

---

13. This is the concluding suggestion of V. David Garrison, "A New Epoch in Christian Missions: Global Changes since World War II" (PhD diss., University of Chicago Divinity School, 1988), 311.

14. An example of the minimal role that the word of God may play in the envisioning of the missionary task lies in Garrison's six-point definition of the work of a "nonresidential missionary." Notably, none of the six points necessarily entails personal witness to non-Christians. Further, the word of God is present in the following task description only by implication: "Draw up and help to see implemented a wide range of evangelizing ministry options directed toward that population by persistently advocating the evangelization of the population before the world's host of Christian resources." See V. David Garrison, *The Nonresidential Missionary: A New Strategy and the People It Serves* (Monrovia, CA: MARC, 1990), 13.

15. A well-meaning but truncated statement along these lines is, "The aim of foreign missions is to make Jesus Christ known to the world." See Robert E. Speer, "The Supreme and Determining Aim," in Roger E. Hedlund, ed., *Roots of the Great Debate in Mission: Mission in Historical and Theological Perspective*, rev. ed. (Bangalore: Theological Book Trust, 1981), 15–19, esp. 16. Such a goal is deficient according to Jesus' own words in Scripture, for his Great Commission requires more than imparting knowledge about himself.

reproduction, all with the praiseworthy motive of fostering the work of missions.

Yet the notion that God entrusts the missionary with messages beyond the word of God is fatally flawed; it lacks the warrant of the word of God itself. Instead, the classic Great Commission passages explicitly require making disciples, baptizing, teaching obedience to Jesus' commands, proclaiming repentance and forgiveness of sins, and being Jesus' witnesses: actions that derive their meaning from the Bible.[16] As for the significance of other kinds of revelation for the missionary task, general revelation only takes on apologetic value with reference back to the word of God. Similarly, God's special revelation in Jesus transmits through the ages and is accessible to contemporary people only through the word of God. Finally, while worldly wisdom naturally clamors for a hearing and asserts the right to inject itself into nearly every act of human communication, it is perhaps most radically and disturbingly out of place when proffered as a saccharine substitute for the sweet savor of God's word.

So once again, the touchtone of that which is missionary in the missionary's message is God's revelation of himself in his inspired word. However well-meaning and even helpful other acts of training, exhorting, and encouraging may be, those portions of a missionary's message that venture beyond the basis of the word of God are simply not the message the missionary must share in order to obey the Great Commission.

An opposite critical perspective is that "the word of God" is too general a message. According to this line of thinking, the missionary's message should instead be "the gospel." Thus, like Jesus, the missionary should declare "the gospel of God" (Mark 1:14), "the gospel of the kingdom" (Matt 4:23), or simply "the gospel" (Luke 20:1). This message would be a subset of the word of God, concentrating on those elements that correspond to one's definition of the gospel.

Given the crowded field of alternative gospels promoted by reader-identity politics, liberation theology, the "social gospel," and many other types of issue advocacy, it would be helpful to delineate what the

---

16. These Great Commission passages are Matt 28:18–20; Luke 24:45–49; John 20:21–23; and Acts 1:8. The earliest manuscripts of the Gospel of Mark lack material beyond Mark 16:8 such as vv. 15–18. See Bruce M. Metzger, *A Textual Commentary on the Greek New Testament*, 2nd ed. (Stuttgart: Deutsche Bibelgesellschaft, 1994), 102–7.

missionary's gospel should actually be. A brief synopsis with traditional points of emphasis is that the gospel "announces salvation from sin through the blood of Christ and through personal faith in him."[17] A recent and more expansive definition is "The gospel is the announcement that God's kingdom has come in the life, death, and resurrection of Jesus of Nazareth, the Lord and Messiah, in fulfillment of Israel's Scriptures. The gospel evokes faith, repentance, and discipleship; its accompanying effects include salvation and the gift of the Holy Spirit."[18]

Despite the laudable doctrinal precision achieved through professions such as these, the statements' individual components are incomprehensible when disconnected from their native matrix of meaning. That is to say, concepts such as salvation from sin, the blood of Christ, and God's kingdom require explanation in context. Therefore, in the interest of clarity and economy in communication, one might inquire after the minimum body of interpretive context necessary to understand the gospel. However, the message of the biblical text again and again trends in the opposite direction, ever expanding the volume of biblical content needed to interpret and explain the gospel message. To take but a single and perhaps unexpected example, Jesus states that the account of the anointing of his feet with perfume will accompany the gospel in its proclamation throughout the ages (Matt 26:13; Mark 14:9). More comprehensively, in Luke 24:27 Jesus apparently appropriated the entire Old Testament in order to explain himself to his followers on the Emmaus road. If "all Scripture is God-breathed" and indeed "is useful for teaching, rebuking, correcting and training in righteousness" (2 Tim 3:16 NIV), a clear implication follows. Those who would pass judgment on the usefulness of certain parts of the biblical canon—with respect to the preaching of the gospel or otherwise—set themselves against the witness of that canon.

---

17. James Barr, *Fundamentalism* (Philadelphia: Westminster, 1977), 25. Barr represents this faith statement accurately, though he is hardly sympathetic with it.

18. Michael F. Bird, *Evangelical Theology: A Biblical and Systematic Introduction* (Grand Rapids: Zondervan, 2013), 52. An even more comprehensive statement, cast in the framework of honor/shame terminology and incorporating the doctrine of creation, appears in Jackson Wu, *One Gospel for All Nations: A Practical Approach to Biblical Contextualization* (Pasadena, CA: William Carey Library, 2015), 66.

In the end, the only authoritative frame of reference that places flesh on the bare bones of the gospel message is the Bible.[19] Circumstances will require that missionaries abridge, summarize, and of course contextualize the word of God in particular acts of communication. Even so, it is the whole Bible, and not some arbitrarily selected canon within the canon, that comprises the message from God that the missionary must ultimately proclaim.[20]

MISSIONARY USE OF LANGUAGE

As communicators of God's word, missionaries must be effective learners and users of language to carry out this weighty task. Therefore the immediately following sections trace the linguistic journey of the message from its origin point as special revelation, through the missionary, and onward to the receiving community. A final section then advances recommendations for the reenvisioning of missionary language learning.

THE LANGUAGE OF THE MESSAGE

כִּי־קָרוֹב אֵלֶיךָ הַדָּבָר מְאֹד בְּפִיךָ וּבִלְבָבְךָ לַעֲשֹׂתוֹ

The word is very near to you: in your mouth and in your heart, so that you do it.

Deuteronomy 30:14 (author's translation)

Previous mention of the biblical canon's matrix of meaning alludes to the scandalous particularity of the message of the Bible. Within biblical

---

19. Illustrating the problematic nature of faith not comprehensively grounded in Scripture, Carl Henry asserted, "To speak of God and attribute specific characteristics to him apart from a basis in divine revelation is to play the gardener who, after spraying water into the sky from a hose, then welcomes the 'rainfall' as 'heaven-sent.'" See Carl F. H. Henry, *God, Revelation, and Authority* (Waco, TX: Word Books, 1976–1983), 2:18. For a recent, accessible treatment of the crucial Reformation doctrine of *sola Scriptura* and its range of implications, see Matthew Barrett, "*Sola Scriptura* in the Strange Land of Evangelicalism: The Peculiar but Necessary Responsibility of Defending *Sola Scriptura* against Our Own Kind," *SBJT* 19, no. 4 (2015): 9–38.

20. In the words of Jensen, "Only by having Ecclesiastes and the Gospel of John in the same volume can we know what God is saying to us." See Peter Jensen, *The Revelation of God* (Downers Grove, IL: InterVarsity Press, 2002), 161.

narrative, God works through, communicates with, befriends, and loves particular, named people in specific historical and cultural circumstances. Yet most readers of the Bible throughout history have neither been those specially chosen and named people, nor even shared their predominant linguistic, cultural, and ethnic background, for gentile readers of the Bible have outnumbered Jewish readers since the early years of the church. Therefore, due to their distance from the biblical world, contemporary readers may gravitate toward parts of the Bible that seem to address a broader audience such as passages that convey moral or ethical teachings, especially in the New Testament and perhaps some of the Psalms. Indeed, all who take up the Bible possess a strong and altogether natural drive to seek answers to the question "What does the Bible mean for me today?" Yet due to the context richness of language in general and Scripture in particular, in truth it is impossible to disentangle the universal from the specific without draining the biblical text of a great deal of its meaning and eviscerating its spirit. All biblical teachings are steeped in the stubbornly particular lived scenarios of the human condition.[21]

Among the Bible's significant particularities is its revelation in three languages: Hebrew, Aramaic, and Greek. Reception of Scripture composed in these ancient languages has at times led to a sense that the languages themselves possess a special sacred character. Thus even when Jews transitioned to other mother tongues in the diaspora, Biblical Hebrew remained לְשׁוֹן הַקֹּדֶשׁ, "the holy language."[22]

Yet the existence of Aramaic passages in the Old Testament hints not only that other languages could hold some claim to sacred standing, but

---

21. Psalm 133 epitomizes the startling juxtaposition of the universal and particular. The psalm leads with praising a state of affairs likely idealized among all people in every age: "Behold, how good and pleasant it is when brothers dwell in unity!" Lacking any discernible transition, the scene abruptly cuts to narrow focus on a single individual in Jewish national history: "It is like the precious oil on the head, running down on the beard, on the beard of Aaron, running down on the collar of his robes!"

22. John F. A. Sawyer, *Sacred Languages and Sacred Texts* (New York: Routledge, 1999), 26–31. Even Samaritans viewed Biblical Hebrew as a holy language due to its connection with Scripture. See Abraham Tal, " 'Hebrew Language' and 'Holy Language' between Judea and Samaria," in *Samaria, Samarians, Samaritans: Studies on Bible, History and Linguistics*, ed. József Zsengellér (Boston: de Gruyter, 2011), 187–201. Romanticized thinking about Hebrew as an utterly unique language has persisted to the modern era, even for nonreligious reasons. See Liora R. Halperin, "Modern Hebrew, Esperanto, and the Quest for a Universal Language," *Jewish Social Studies* 19 (2012): 1–33.

also that the biblical text itself was the focus of highest esteem rather than its predominant Hebrew language. Indeed, Aramaic as a spoken and religious language retained enough influence into the era of the early church that Aramaic words and phrases appear in the New Testament. Thus Greek transliteration renders Aramaic reported speech, such as Ταλιθα κουμ ("Little girl, I say to you, arise!") in Mark 5:41, the phrase μαράνα θά ("Maranatha" or "Our Lord, come!") in 1 Corinthians 16:22, and Jesus' shouting of the first phrase of Psalm 22 from the cross: Ηλι ηλι λεμα σαβαχθανι, Matthew 27:46, or Ελωι ελωι λεμα σαβαχθανι, Mark 15:34 ("My God, my God, why have you forsaken me?").[23]

Alongside Hebrew and Aramaic, New Testament Greek has also excited the imaginations of its readers sufficiently to generate the notion that it was an exceptional vessel of divine revelation, or "Holy Ghost Greek."[24] However, despite the pervasive influence of Septuagint translation Greek on the New Testament, Biblical Greek itself is a linguistic artifact of the common speech of its era.[25] The Greek of the Bible, just like Hebrew and Aramaic, was a real living language that experienced the kinds of development that historical linguists detect in all languages.[26] The words of each of the biblical languages carried meaning the way words in all languages carry meaning, and their systems of grammar and syntax served primarily linguistic rather than psychological

---

23. The transliteration σαβαχθανι coheres with the Aramaic שבקתני rather than the Hebrew עזבתני. See Emanuel White, "A Critical Edition of the Targum of Psalms: A Computer Generated Text of Books I and II" (PhD diss., McGill University, 1988), part 2, page 89. This is not necessarily evidence that an official written Aramaic edition of Psalms existed in the New Testament era. See Martin McNamara, *Targum and Testament Revisited: Aramaic Paraphrases of the Hebrew Bible*, 2nd ed. (Grand Rapids: Eerdmans, 2010), 319; Timothy Edwards, *Exegesis in the Targum of Psalms: The Old, the New, and the Rewritten*, Gorgias Dissertations 28: Biblical Studies 1 (Piscataway, NJ: Gorgias, 2007), 221.

24. McKnight critiques the "Holy Ghost Greek" concept in Edgar V. McKnight, "Is the New Testament Written in 'Holy Ghost' Greek?," *The Bible Translator* 16 (1965): 87–93. See, however, the allusive statements of Turner in James Hope Moulton, *A Grammar of New Testament Greek*, 3rd ed., vol. 3, *Syntax*, by Nigel Turner (Edinburgh: T&T Clark, 1963), 9.

25. Francisco Rodríguez Adrados, *A History of the Greek Language: From Its Origins to the Present* (Boston: Brill, 2005), 186.

26. The application of findings from diachronic linguistic typology can illuminate poorly understood elements of grammar and syntax in the biblical languages, such as the Biblical Hebrew verbal system. See John A. Cook, *Time and the Biblical Hebrew Verb: The Expression of Tense, Aspect, and Modality in Biblical Hebrew*, Linguistic Studies in Ancient West Semitic 7 (Winona Lake, IN: Eisenbrauns, 2012).

or theological ends.[27] Eventually, following the authoring of biblical texts, the biblical languages passed out of use as means of everyday communication and became objects of study for the purpose of reading Scripture.

Wherever widespread knowledge of the biblical languages has been rare, translations have arisen to transmit the message of the Bible in the languages of the people. If at least one Bible translation is available in a language a missionary can understand, he or she may ask whether study of the biblical languages is a practical use of limited time.[28]

An important preliminary step toward addressing the concern of biblical language use in ministry is to note carefully the framing of the issue as a matter of practicality. The clear implication is that study of the biblical languages does not intrinsically constitute a practical discipline, at least not in the same way one envisions study of evangelism, counseling, or preaching as practical. Furthermore, the significant time and effort one must invest in order to learn biblical languages also makes them inherently impractical to some.

Yet from precisely the opposite perspective one may ask what could possibly be more practical than knowledge of the biblical languages if the central aim of one's ministry is communication of God's word. If an English speaker wants to become an authority on Tang Dynasty poetry, he or she will learn Classical Chinese, despite the availability of English translations. Likewise, though it is possible to attend Shakespearean plays performed in German, in order to receive the full impact of the wit of Shakespeare, no serious German-speaking student of the bard would forgo learning Elizabethan English.[29]

---

27. Barr incisively critiques the mystification of biblical language features in James Barr, *The Semantics of Biblical Language* (Oxford: Oxford University Press, 1961). Stagg addresses the problem of freighting a grammatical feature (the Greek aorist verb form) with more interpretive weight than it can bear in Frank Stagg, "The Abused Aorist," *JBL* 91 (1972): 222–31.

28. An Association of Theological Schools survey revealed that the most-stated reason seminary graduates had not studied biblical languages had to do with the availability of English resources. Though the journal issue in which the survey appeared is significantly out of date (for example, in its recommendations on the use of technology), anecdotally the present availability of a vast and ever-growing array of Bible translations and Bible study tools in English can indeed deprioritize biblical languages among expected competencies of people in ministry. See following discussion and George M. Landes, "What Is Happening in the Work of Seminary Graduates," *TE* 3 (1967): 458–62, esp. 459.

29. Jörg Hasler, "Shakespeare in German," *Shakespeare Quarterly* 23 (1974): 455–57.

Returning to the fact that many modern language translations of the Bible are available, one might bypass discussing the practicality of original language training and simply state that translations exist. Thus why invest significant resources to train a superabundance of translators? This common question arises from an anemic understanding of both the nature of ministry and the nature of language.

As for the nature of ministry, while Bible translation is indeed a task of inestimable importance, not all ministry depends on Bible translation. Biblical interpretation is likewise a task of inestimable importance, but unlike biblical translation, biblical interpretation does actually provide the basis for all Christian ministry. To confirm this bold claim with a thought experiment, one may ask what basis other than biblical interpretation better upholds ministry and promotes its flourishing. All other potential foundations for ministry fracture at the crucial point of not placing primary confidence on God's special revelation of himself in his word, interpreted rightly in context. The purpose of training in biblical languages is not primarily to equip translators, but interpreters of the word of God.

Turning from the nature of ministry to the nature of language, one must understand that all languages contain inherently untranslatable elements in their expressions. After listing several English New Testament translations that were newly published in his time, A. T. Robertson added: "We shall have many more. They will all have special merit, and they will all fail to bring out all that is in the Greek. One needs to read these translations, the more the better. Each will supplement the others. But, when he has read them all, there will remain a large and rich untranslatable element that the preacher ought to know."[30] Untranslatable elements can include techniques that the biblical languages use to point out the most significant ideas in a passage. For example, in Genesis 46:3-4 God speaks to Jacob in a vision: "Then he said, 'I am God, the God of your father. Do not be afraid to go down to Egypt, for there I will make you into a great nation. I myself will go down with you to Egypt, and I will also bring you up again, and Joseph's hand shall close your eyes.' "

---

30. A. T. Robertson, *The Minister and His Greek New Testament* (New York: George H. Doran, 1923), 18–19.

Despite the literalistic translation philosophy of the ESV, this passage does not—and perhaps cannot—accurately convey the focal points of the original Hebrew. Special focus begins in 46:4 with fronting of "I," which the English reader can perceive in the ESV's "I myself." However, the phrase "I myself" appears to be the only attempt to communicate points of emphasis present in the Hebrew, so if an English reader notices this stylistic choice, he or she may believe that God's address to Jacob focuses on going down to Egypt with him. God's declaration that he will accompany the aged Jacob to Egypt is indeed important in the broader story of Jacob, which begins with "These are the generations of Jacob" in Genesis 37:2. Yet still more important is what follows: God's promise to "bring him up" again. This portion of 46:4 reflects four Hebrew words (וְאָנֹכִי אַעַלְךָ גַם־עָלֹה) that all signal syntactic prominence. First there is the fronting of "I" once more. Next appears a paronomastic infinitive construction, which focuses reader attention on the finite verb for "bring up," including the modal context surrounding the verb. In this case the modal context is God committing himself to Jacob in future action.[31] Last, there is the focus particle גַם, which raises God's promise into even greater relief.[32] So every element of this short clause highlights God bringing Jacob back to his land as the most important element in the passage, which happens to be opposite to the emphasis apparently conveyed in the ESV.

Of course, an English reader has recourse to many other English translations, not to mention commentaries, to aid understanding of the original language text underlying Bible passages. That said, one who is untrained in biblical languages cannot adjudicate between competing claims, which multiply with each resource consulted. In the end one must select a preferred interpretation in an ad hoc manner, perhaps arbitrarily favoring one's favorite English Bible translation or choosing a reading reflected in several translations.

This intuition-based approach to biblical interpretation is all the more problematic on the mission field, where the circle of biblical

---

31. For comprehensive treatment of the infinitive absolute and its relation to the expression of modality, see Scott N. Callaham, *Modality and the Biblical Hebrew Infinitive Absolute*, Abhandlungen für die Kunde des Morgenlandes 71 (Wiesbaden: Harrassowitz, 2010).

32. Christo H. J. van der Merwe, "Another Look at the Biblical Hebrew Focus Particle גַם," *Journal of Semitic Studies* 54 (2009): 313–32, esp. 329–31.

interpretation may come to life in a community of two. For example, a host-nation prebeliever refers to a Bible passage with a clearly different meaning or connotation in his or her language than that reflected in the missionary's preferred English Bible translation. Suddenly the accuracy of one or both translations is at stake, as well as the prebeliever's ability to place confidence in God's word.[33] If the missionary can only appeal to the accuracy of English Bible translations, such an act invests English with a level of authority English neither deserves nor can sustain.[34] The missionary may preach the liberating Reformation doctrine of the "priesthood of all believers" but by example may unintentionally establish an enslaving "priesthood of languages" with English as the presiding high priest.

Yet another attitudinal stance behind contemporary questioning of the value of biblical language study may concede that achieving competence in use of the biblical languages is of some theoretical value, but in the end it may suggest that only specialists can hope to wield the biblical languages as an interpretive tool with confidence. Thus everyone but experts should lean on shortcut resources, a prime example being Hebrew and Greek dictionaries and concordances based on Strong's Numbers. Unfortunately, however, assuming that faithful grammatical-historical interpretation of the Bible is one's goal, relying on Strong's Numbers for exegesis is an inherently unsound practice.

Briefly, Strong's system assigns a unique number to every Hebrew and Greek word attested in Scripture, then associates that number with

---

33. For example, in the most widely used Chinese Bible translation (the 和合本 or Chinese Union Version) both Gen 3:5 and 1 Sam 14:27 contain the expression 眼睛就明亮了, literally having to do with "brightness of the eyes." Noticing this exact verbal parallel, a Chinese reader might ask what the two eye-brightening episodes have in common: eating from the tree of the knowledge of good and evil in Genesis, on one hand, and Jonathan eating honey in 1 Samuel, on the other. Several English translations describe Jonathan's eyes as "bright" in 1 Samuel 14, but lack a corresponding expression for the Genesis passage. Only knowledge of both Chinese and Biblical Hebrew would enable the missionary to work out the translational puzzle that the Chinese Bible presents.

34. Jackson Wu relates an illustration from personal experience concerning a text with great theological significance, Rom 8:1, "There is therefore now no condemnation for those who are in Christ Jesus." In Greek the particle ἄρα requires that Paul's salient point in Rom 8:1 be a logical consequence of what has just come before. There is no such "therefore" word in the Chinese Union Version, inserting an unnecessary interpretive seam into the ongoing thought progression of the epistle. Wu relates that the result of pointing to this mistranslation is that his Chinese friends then ironically attempt to verify his claim about the meaning of ἄρα with the aid of English Bible translations. Jackson Wu, personal communication.

the words that King James Bible translators chose to correspond to them. Therefore Strong's Numbers concordances gloss words according to translational equivalents chosen over four hundred years ago in an earlier stage of development of the English language. This outdated English provides an artificial grid of meaning imposed on Hebrew and Greek words, thus anachronistically influencing the perception of their semantic ranges. Even more problematically, since the user of Strong's Numbers resources presumably lacks training in biblical languages, he or she cannot reliably discern the meaning of neighboring original-language words in order to add contextual coloring to the meaning of Hebrew words' translational equivalents and thus referee between several possible meanings. Furthermore, dictionaries primarily provide definitions for words and cannot venture substantial guidance on points of grammar or syntax. Interacting with as fundamental a concept as the information encoded in finite verbs requires training in the biblical languages, which obviates the need for a tool such as Strong's Numbers in the first place.[35]

If missionaries elect not to pursue biblical language training when life circumstances allow it, perhaps for one or more of the reasons noted above, they should take stock of the consequence of this decision. At the most foundational level of ministry, in their primary area of responsibility, they undermine their effectiveness in communicating the word of God. In other words, if the message of Scripture must first cross an unnecessarily broad social, cultural, and translational gap to reach the missionary, then at some point in the process of discipleship, the missionary's lack of training will limit how closely host-nation believers will be able to approach the Bible.[36] Even worse, if the missionary actively discourages host-nation believers from studying the biblical languages themselves, or even does so only passively by personal example, the missionary risks enshrining not only the aforementioned priesthood of languages, but also a priesthood of missionaries. That is to say, the interpretive choices of the

---

35. Finite verbs in Biblical Hebrew, for example, encode a verbal action concept as well as its tense, aspect, modality, voice, person, gender, and number information. The *binyan* system can then load verbal forms with additional categories of meaning.

36. See the helpful distinction and interaction of missionary culture, biblical culture, and target culture in Margo Lyn Menconi, "Understanding and Relating to the Three Cultures of Cross-Cultural Ministry in Russia," *Missiology* 24 (1996): 519–31, esp. 520–22.

untrained missionary can subtly guide a host-nation church's theology rather than close engagement with the word of God.

THE LANGUAGE OF THE MESSENGER

כִּי אֵין מִלָּה בִּלְשׁוֹנִי הֵן יְהוָה יָדַעְתָּ כֻלָּה

Even before a word is on my tongue, behold, O LORD, you know it altogether.

Psalm 139:4

Language is central to personal identity. Even the basic identity marker of one's personal name is to some degree language-specific and not entirely translatable, such that John is not the same as Juan, Johann, Jan, or Ian, even though all of these names share a common etymology. If someone named John learns Spanish as a second language and takes the name Juan for use in Spanish contexts, this new name carries a different connotation from his original name. Then if John should choose to change his name in all language settings to Juan, this transition reflects a conscious choice to represent his identity differently from when he was formerly John. Though a name is indeed an individual identity marker, it also performs a public function; it designates a certain person within his or her society and network of social relationships. This societal function of a person's name is a helpful reminder that language mediates social interactions at all levels, from the most public to the most private.

Despite the integral role that one's preferred language plays in all aspects of life, undertaking the study of another language for the purpose of cross-cultural communication of the word of God entails laying aside the closely held "right" to use one's native tongue. For example, a missionary from Finland theoretically has every right to share the gospel freely in Japan using only Finnish, but if that missionary's calling is to reach Japanese, Finnish will be of little assistance. Instead the Finnish missionary should commit to the life-altering path of embracing the Japanese language to communicate with others, and in some situations even with God.

Admittedly, there is one standout exception to the general rule that missionaries must leave their own languages behind as they carry out the Great Commission in cross-cultural settings. In a case unparalleled in world history, English indisputably stands at the head of a perceived world hierarchy of languages and carries significantly greater transnational prestige than the other international languages: Spanish, Arabic, Russian, French, and Mandarin Chinese.[37] As the world's adopted common language, English pervades all career fields and areas of academic research.[38] Tellingly, English not only supplies the predominant metalanguage but also the primary data source for research in linguistics: the study of language itself.[39] Furthermore, English has become the global church's lingua franca, performing a unifying role similar to that of Latin during many centuries of Western church history.[40] Thus in the present day, Christians can use English as a "neutral" third language to mediate between cultures whose interrelations are particularly sensitive due to past conflict.[41]

The continually rising profile of English among world languages can pressure speakers of other languages to view gaining some knowledge of English almost as a sine qua non for success in contemporary life.[42] Thus native English speakers possess a coveted skill. A natural implication follows: English-speaking missionaries may find that the trade of teaching

---

37. William A. Smalley, "Missionary Language Learning in a World Hierarchy of Languages," *Missiology* 22 (1994): 481–88, esp. 482.

38. Rainer Enrique Hamel, "The Dominance of English in the International Scientific Periodical Literature and the Future of Language Use in Science," *Association Internationale de Linguistique Appliquée Review* 20 (2007): 53–71. See also the statistics on English usage in biblical studies journals published in non-Anglophone countries in Gerald Bray, *Biblical Interpretation: Past and Present* (Downers Grove, IL: InterVarsity Press, 1996), 465–66.

39. Dik allusively critiques the monolingual nature of much generative linguistics research as an "unfortunate whim of the history of linguistics." See Simon C. Dik, *The Theory of Functional Grammar, Part 1: The Structure of the Clause,* ed. Kees Hengeveld, 2nd rev. ed., Functional Grammar Series 20 (New York: de Gruyter, 1997), 14–15.

40. Christine Mohrmann, "How Latin Came to Be the Language of Early Christendom," *Studies: An Irish Quarterly Review* 40 (1951): 277–88. Mohrmann's address illustrates the status of English as the contemporary international lingua franca; a scholar from a Dutch university addressed an Irish society dedicated to the study of Latin, all the while speaking English.

41. Takamitsu Muraoka, *My Via Dolorosa: Along the Trails of the Japanese Imperialism in Asia* (Bloomington, IN: AuthorHouse, 2016), 21.

42. Park discusses extreme behaviors of parents in South Korea who wish to bestow English competence on their children. See Jin-kyu Park, " 'English Fever' in South Korea: Its History and Symptoms," *English Today: The International Review of the English Language* 25 (2009): 50–57.

their own language is not only lucrative, but also facilitates access to nations that restrict open missionary activity.[43]

The widespread use of English as a cover for missionary work raises ethical concerns. At the most basic level, one may ask whether native English-speaking ability itself bestows the gift of teaching the language effectively.[44] As for those who earn an accredited certification in the field of TESOL (Teaching English to Speakers of Other Languages), professional colleagues may question the exploitation of TESOL for the unrelated purpose of carrying out illegal religious activities.[45] Further, Manka Varghese and Bill Johnston warn that the marked imbalance of power between teacher and student can result in religious coercion.[46]

English-teaching missionaries should indeed heed such criticisms and avoid misrepresenting themselves before host-nation institutions and violating students' freedom of conscience. Even so, complicating all discussion of missionary teaching of English is the fact that no one approaches the issue from a value-neutral perspective.[47] Indeed, in light of occasional charges from the Majority World that the entire TESOL project is an outworking of Western-driven native culture-eroding linguistic imperialism, focusing critique solely on the agendas of missionary English teachers seems unduly selective.[48]

---

43. Bradley Baurain, "Teaching English Feeds a Worldwide Craving," *EMQ* 28 (1992): 164–73.

44. Alastair Pennycook and Sophie Coutand-Marin, "Teaching English as a Missionary Language," *Discourse: Studies in the Cultural Politics of Education* 24 (2003): 337–53, esp. 341–42.

45. Christina Biava, "Teachers or Missionaries? Duality of Purpose for ESOL Professionals" (paper presented at the Annual Meeting of the American Association for Applied Linguistics, Long Beach, CA, March 17, 1995), 1–19, esp. 10. Of course, gaining legal residence for the sake of pursuing illegal religious work inflames a moral dilemma that all missionaries to closed countries must face.

46. Manka M. Varghese and Bill Johnston, "Evangelical Christians and English Language Teaching," *TESOL Quarterly* 41 (2007): 5–31, esp. 6.

47. While professing to value "dialogue," Verghese and Johnston do violence to the spirit of dialogue through brusque assertion that "an American foreign and domestic policy driven increasingly by imperialist goals and guided by an evangelical Christian agenda" should result in reevaluation of missionary TESOL work. See Varghese and Johnston, "Evangelical Christians and English Language Teaching," 6, 28.

48. Sardar M. Anwaruddin, "Hidden Agenda in TESOL Methods," *Journal of English as an International Language* 6 (2011): 47–58. For an extended treatment of English and linguistic imperialism see Robert Phillipson, *Linguistic Imperialism* (New York: Oxford University Press, 1992).

Setting aside such weighty matters to return attention to the individual person, each missionary should carefully evaluate whether teaching English as a platform allows a feasible means of performing his or her primary duty. That is to say, the issue at stake is whether teaching English opens greater opportunities for the unifying task of one's life and work as a missionary: communicating God's word in obedience to the Great Commission.

Teaching English can indeed fulfill biblical exhortations to use words and actions to bring glory to God in the name of Jesus, as advocated in 1 Corinthians 10:31 and Colossians 3:17. Yet it should go without saying that teaching in a God-glorifying way, with integrity and excellence, requires a considerable investment of one's limited time and energy. Time and energy are exceedingly precious on the mission field. Expending these resources through English teaching significantly depletes time and energy that one would otherwise dedicate to other activities. Thus an unfortunate phenomenon that may accompany a decision to use English as one's primary missionary language is the narrowing of the window of opportunity—and likely also the atrophy of motivation—to learn the host people's language.

In the end if a missionary never effectively learns the language of the host-nation community, he or she severely limits the scope of ministry only to the atypical people who can cross to the missionary's side of the language bridge.[49] Out of this narrow slice of the population, some smaller fraction may indeed prove somewhat receptive to the transformative message of the Bible as proclaimed in the foreign tongue of English. Yet even then, the broad sociocultural chasm of language can seriously impair discipleship by cordoning off spirituality from all other aspects of life. Accordingly, one may contemplate how many of those who cross the language bridge to the English-speaking missionary have actually left their hearts behind on the far side.

---

49. General statements such as this do not presume to deny that God may sovereignly use any person and language in any situation to glorify himself. When circumstances demand speaking through translation, missionaries would do well to employ guidance in Pat Gustin, "How Not to Get Lost in Translation," *Journal of Applied Christian Leadership* 4 (2010): 126–30.

THE LANGUAGE OF THE COMMUNITY

προσευχόμενοι ἅμα καὶ περὶ ἡμῶν, ἵνα ὁ θεὸς ἀνοίξῃ ἡμῖν θύραν τοῦ λόγου λαλῆσαι τὸ μυστήριον τοῦ Χριστοῦ, δι' ὃ καὶ δέδεμαι, ἵνα φανερώσω αὐτὸ ὡς δεῖ με λαλῆσαι.

At the same time, pray also for us, that God may open to us a door for the word, to declare the mystery of Christ, on account of which I am in prison—that I may make it clear, which is how I ought to speak.

Colossians 4:3–4

Most Christian converts the world over share the experience of hearing the gospel message and responding in their own languages. Thus crossing the bridge of language and culture is rightly the duty of the missionary far more often than it is the burden of the host-nation prebeliever. Proclaiming "the mighty works of God" (Acts 2:11) in languages other than one's own was even the pattern at Pentecost, when the Holy Spirit-wrought miracle was not of a crowd hearing, but of believers speaking.[50] For the sake of the present study it is relevant to note that the speaking of nonlearned languages at Pentecost constitutes an utterly unique, one-time historical event. There is no credible evidence otherwise, as generations of missionaries know all too well.[51]

During the throes of gradual and painstaking language learning, no doubt many a missionary has ruefully prayed for a latter-day gift of tongues. However, the normal path of dedicated learning may actually serve God's purposes in cross-cultural missions far better than would an instantaneous divine imputation of language ability, because adult second-language learning is a thoroughly character-molding process.[52]

---

50. Paul van Imschoot, "De dono linguarum et glossolalia," *Collationes Gandavenses* 9 (1922): 65–70, esp. 66.

51. Gary B. McGee, "Shortcut to Language Preparation? Radical Evangelicals, Missions, and the Gift of Tongues," *IBMR* 25 (2001): 118–23.

52. George Scholl, "Points to be Emphasized in Preparation for Missionary Work," in *World-Wide Evangelization the Urgent Business of the Church* (New York: Student Volunteer Movement for Foreign Missions, 1902), 73–81. Starting his discourse on Holy Spirit empowerment of missionaries, Scholl frankly states, "Let me first indicate a few things that He will not do for you. He will not in a miraculous way impart to you the gift of tongues. You

Prior to arriving on the mission field, the prospective language learner may already have endured a rapid succession of unsettling missionary rites of passage such as abandoning a successful career; selling, giving away, or throwing away most possessions; explaining to noncomprehending friends and family that he or she will not be free to return for graduations, weddings, funerals, holidays, and summer breaks like other expatriates; and bidding tearful farewells to loved ones who will soon pass away. Then, perhaps only a few hours later, landing in the new field of service turns upside down and inside out the missionary's already profoundly disrupted life.

In those first few moments on the field, unable even to utter the simplest thought or request, one may despair of merely surviving in one's new context, let alone communicating the message of the Bible. Forlorn moments such as this may even threaten to blot out hope that the Holy Spirit will be involved in future language acquisition in any way. Indeed, it would be easy to brand language learning a merely "secular" task one would undertake in precisely the same way as would a non-Christian. That said, a disciple of Jesus must reject the dictates of spiritually tone-deaf conventional wisdom and jettison all compartmentalizing and desacralizing tendencies such as these. Instead, if anyone should be prepared to welcome the Spirit into every aspect of life, it is the missionary from whom God has stripped away prideful self-dependency by placement on the mission field. Shaken as perhaps never before, the new missionary can begin rebuilding his or her life on the only foundation fit for weathering the many challenges in missionary work: complete dependence on God and his word.[53]

Desperate dependence on God opens an opportunity for the Holy Spirit to renovate the missionary's character through language learning.

---

will have to learn the language of the people to whom you go as you learned Greek and Latin and Hebrew in college and seminary" (79).

53. Insistence on the need to depend on God and embrace the equipping of the Spirit in language learning by no means implies that existing approaches to language learning are necessarily incompatible with the recasting of missionary language acquisition envisioned in this chapter. Note the full-spectrum dependence on God manifested in the life of missionary language-learning theorist Tom Brewster, recounted in Daniel Roy Brewster, "Only Paralyzed from the Neck Down: A Biography of the Life and Ministry of E. Thomas Brewster" (DMiss diss., Fuller Theological Seminary, 1995).

Specifically, the Spirit instills motivation, promotes endurance, and undergirds performance in missionary learning of language. As for motivation, the Spirit kindles the strongest of motivations in the missionary heart: an ultimately unexplainable, fierce, irrational love for a host nation's people. Love surrenders the right to a comfortable lifestyle in a familiar cultural setting. Love infuses missionary prayers like Paul's petitions for his fellow Jews: "Brothers, my heart's desire and prayer to God for them is that they may be saved" (Rom 10:1). Love tempers the sting of rejection, derision, contempt, and even betrayal if through such agonizing experiences some may yet encounter Christ. With special regard to language learning, love commits a missionary to stoop below the level of barest intelligibility in the host culture. Actions such as these begin expressing the missionary's sacrificial love for a people well before coherent verbal articulation of love is possible.

In addition to stoking the flame of motivation, the Spirit also supplies endurance in language learning. Endurance is crucial since language acquisition is an inherently lengthy process, and ideally one that advances throughout life.[54] Through the constantly effacing and error-laden process of learning a new language in daily living, missionaries incarnate love for a host nation's people and tangibly cast their lot with them.[55] Missionaries thrust down even deeper roots within a host culture when a defining characteristic of their presence is dependence. Humble dependence on native speakers significantly fosters missionary endurance and increases effectiveness in learning their language. True humility and dependence manifest the work of the Spirit on the missionary soul.[56]

---

54. Kirby asserts that the missionary's transformation from self-confident ministry professional in his or her native context to humble learner in the host culture is radical enough to merit the religiously nuanced label "conversion." See Jon P. Kirby, "Language and Culture Learning IS Conversion . . . IS Ministry," *Missiology* 23 (1995): 131–43, esp. 137. Yet "converted" missionaries should bear in mind the paradox lying at the heart of their unique role; they are *learners* carrying a message to *teach*. Interreligious dialogue, contra Kirby, has by no means replaced evangelism in the missionary task.

55. See discussion of missionary presence within a host culture in John Howard Yoder, *Theology of Mission: A Believers Church Perspective*, ed. Gayle Gerber Koontz and Andy Alexis-Baker (Downers Grove, IL: InterVarsity Press, 2014), 315–17.

56. Tim A. Dearborn, "Spiritual Disciplines Born of the Travail of Language Learning," *EMQ* 27 (1991): 26–29.

Last, the Holy Spirit provides performance in missionary language learning. That is to say, during divinely appointed times of sharing, teaching, or preaching God's word, missionaries may experience a leap ahead in their language ability for the occasion. The Spirit sharpens attention, calms nerves, eases recall of learned vocabulary, facilitates contextualized inference of the meaning of unfamiliar terms, and enables interpretation of varied speaker accents. In brief, the Holy Spirit imparts bold confidence in the face of critical self-awareness of weaknesses in language use. This action of the Spirit is thematically in line with the dramatic empowerment of Old Testament prophets to proclaim the word of the Lord.[57] Interestingly, in the New Testament Luke records that the "filling" of the Spirit leads immediately to spoken acts, including praise (Luke 1:41), prophecy (Luke 1:67), testimony (Acts 4:8), and confrontation (Acts 13:9).[58] When the Holy Spirit actively augments language ability for the sake of communicating the word of God, a vulnerable sense of the fear of God intermingles with the assurance of his presence.

REENVISIONING MISSIONARY LANGUAGE LEARNING

τοσαῦτα εἰ τύχοι γένη φωνῶν εἰσιν ἐν κόσμῳ καὶ οὐδὲν ἄφωνον· ἐὰν οὖν μὴ εἰδῶ τὴν δύναμιν τῆς φωνῆς, ἔσομαι τῷ λαλοῦντι βάρβαρος καὶ ὁ λαλῶν ἐν ἐμοὶ βάρβαρος.

There are doubtless many different languages in the world, and none is without meaning, but if I do not know the meaning of the language, I will be a foreigner to the speaker and the speaker a foreigner to me.

1 Corinthians 14:10–11

As sketched above, the missional trajectory of the word of God begins in special revelation. Then the missionary receives the message of the Bible

---

57. Paul van Imschoot, *Théologie de l'Ancien Testament* (Tournai: Desclée, 1954–1956), 1:184–87.

58. Thomas R. Schreiner, *New Testament Theology: Magnifying God in Christ* (Grand Rapids: Baker Academic, 2008), 442–48. Paul's filling with the Spirit in Acts 9:17 leads to several "immediate" acts, culminating in proclamation about Jesus in the synagogues of Damascus (Acts 9:20).

and proclaims it to the receiving community. Normally this communicative process requires that missionaries be proficient learners and users
of language: ideally the three biblical languages on one hand and the host
culture's language on the other. Willingness to submit to language learning first expresses self-denying love for the word of God, and second for
the people whom God calls missionaries to serve. If the missionary task
is indeed to communicate the word of God, as advocated and stressed
repeatedly in this chapter, then programs of missionary language learning should direct missionaries purposely toward this end.

Yet, surprisingly, commonly employed missionary language-learning
systems do not appear overtly designed to support spiritual goals. On one
hand, the Barefoot Language Learning method incorporates a degree of
religious consciousness as it lays out five categories of people with whom
to seek language interaction: kin groups, neighborhood groups, providing groups such as traders, recreational groups, and finally "believing
groups."[59] On the other hand, this spiritual awareness fades from view
by the end of the program, when a successful learner will "be prepared
to make a contribution to the local community by helping to solve its
problems, answer its questions, and clarify its issues."[60] A newer method
called the Growing Participator Approach (GPA) maintains a number
of goals throughout six discrete phases of a learner's development in
language use. Goals not specifically pertaining to language include "To
become richly integrated into communities of practice, the smaller net-
works of relationships within the larger language community," and "To
know the world as much as possible as it is experienced by host people, in
able [sic] to fully share life with them through language."[61]

Generously speaking, it is possible that "making a contribution to
the local community," "becoming richly integrated into communities of

---

59. Donald N. Larson, *Guidelines for Barefoot Language Learning: An Approach through
Involvement and Independence* (Fresno, CA: Link Care, 1984), 162. To the "believing" group
a learner would try to pose questions such as these: "What can you tell me about people
of your own faith? What do you do together when you meet? How do you talk with one
another? What do you talk about?" (167).

60. Larson, *Guidelines for Barefoot Language Learning*, 326.

61. Thor Andrew Sawin, "Second Language Learnerhood among Cross-Cultural Field
Workers" (PhD diss., University of South Carolina, 2013), 183. As Sawin notes (163), the
Growing Participator Approach is an unpublished system distributed without cost or
licensing, so this chapter cites GPA materials through Sawin's dissertation.

practice," and "sharing life" may be missionary code phrases leveraged to avoid offense within the linguistics guild or to sidestep the surveillance of governments that prohibit missionary activity. Though camouflaging a missionary's language learning intentions may be necessary in the face of hostile government policies, these opaque goal statements remain problematic.[62] Their chief flaw is that missionaries could actually envision them as worthy aims, thus assuming that the purpose of learning a language is missionary-centered—to "share life"—rather than God-centered.[63]

Instead, the need for God-centeredness in missionary language learning should be quite clear by this point. Certainly a missionary must also be able to function socially within a society—to be able to explain why he or she lives so far from home, to arrange with one's neighbors for children to play together, to buy food, and so forth—but these necessary acts themselves do not constitute Great Commission obedience. With the clear goal of communicating the word of God continually in mind, the design of missionary language-learning programs should take into account the following factors at a minimum: language or languages to learn, degree of competency to achieve, and optimal methods to employ.

As for which language or languages one should learn, it is often reasonable to default to the native language of the people whom God calls the missionary to serve. One of the many beautiful aspects of the word of God is its translatability, which is to say that a "word fitly spoken" (Prov 25:11) in one's native tongue speaks directly to the soul.[64] This "heart language"

---

62. Teaching foreigners Chinese was a capital offense in the early 1800s. Therefore language teachers for Robert Morrison would bring shoes to meet with him in order to bolster the ruse that he employed them as cobblers. See J. Barton Starr, "The Legacy of Robert Morrison," *IBMR* 22 (1988): 73–76, esp. 73. Pressing on through adversity, Morrison was the first Protestant to publish the New Testament in Chinese. See Thor Strandenaes, *Principles of Chinese Bible Translation: As Expressed in Five Selected Versions of the New Testament and Exemplified by Mt 5:1–12 and Col 1*, Coniectanea Biblica: New Testament Series 19 (Stockholm: Almqvist and Wiksell, 1987), 14.

63. The frequently voiced cliché that discipleship is essentially equivalent to "reproducing ourselves" manifests a similarly human-centered misunderstanding of the Great Commission task. See for example John C. Maxwell, "Spiritual Reproduction," https://www.sermoncentral.com/content/a-John_Maxwell_07_23_07?ac=true (accessed May 19, 2017).

64. Since the earliest days of the Christian movement, the long-term survival of churches in mission fields has hinged on the availability of Scripture in the vernacular. See discussion of the historical case of the Carthaginian church (68–69) and the present phenomenon of the church in Africa (182–209) in Lamin Sanneh, *Translating the Message:*

dynamic is at play even during stages of language learning in which errors in pronunciation, vocabulary, and sentence structure ring most gratingly in the ear. Thankfully, the Holy Spirit can enable a missionary's love to cover a multitude of linguistic "sins," provided that the missionary continues to press on in intentional development of language ability.

Yet there are also scenarios in which learning a certain people group's language cannot be a missionary's initial or only priority. For example, it may first be necessary to learn a national language in order to live in a certain country. This national language may also hold the status of a regional lingua franca. Examples of such languages include Spanish for most of Central and South America, French for West Africa, Bahasa for several nations in Southeast Asia, and Mandarin Chinese for large parts of East Asia. A missionary's language learning goals for this first "survival" language may be modest in order to facilitate moving on to more in-depth study of a certain people group's language. However, missionaries should remember that languages held in common between diverse ethno-linguistic groups also hold value in ministry, such as when speakers of different languages can use their common one to share the gospel or worship together. Also, a certain people group's language may be infused with a fixed ideology that stands sufficiently distant from the Bible to require borrowing more religiously malleable terms from the common language. Of course, some people groups may resent any use of a lingua franca due to its linkage with a painful colonial past or present. For these and other reasons, it is wise to hold in tension the question of whether to use a "national" or "vernacular" language in the course of missionary work, and often best to consider developing competence in using both.[65]

Several constraints influence the level of language competence missionaries can achieve through their initial period of residence on the field. These factors include perceived language difficulty, missionary language-learning aptitude, and length and quality of time dedicated to language learning. As for the difficulty of certain languages, those that

---

The Missionary Impact on Culture, American Society of Missiology Series 13 (Maryknoll, NY: Orbis, 1990).

65. Carol V. McKinney, "Which Language: Trade or Minority?," *Missiology* 18 (1990): 279–90; Jacob A. Loewen, "Language: Vernacular, Trade, or National?," in Smalley, *Readings in Missionary Anthropology II*, 663–72.

are closest in vocabulary, grammar, and syntax to a missionary's native language will normally require less time in dedicated study than languages that are poles apart in these respects. For example, in order to develop a certain level of proficiency under similar conditions, native speakers of English who learn Chinese may require three to four times the instructional period required for learning Spanish.[66] As for an individual missionary's language-learning aptitude, a key variable factor is motivation.[67] Just as is true with instruction in the biblical languages, training programs can fuel the motivation of learners of modern languages by clearly and consistently connecting language learning with spiritual objectives.[68]

The topic of spiritual objectives for missionary language learning leads to consideration of the optimal learning methods to employ. At the outset of this discussion it is important to note the rule of "any," which is simply that *anyone* can use *any* method to learn *any* language. Certainly there are more and less effective methods for advancing toward given language-learning goals. Yet the diversity of variables affecting language learning suggests that missionary-sending organizations resist the urge to require a single approach that may not fit the learning preferences and personalities of all missionaries, their circumstances, and their learning goals equally well. Sharply dichotomous thinking about language-learning approaches is unhelpful, such as "Normal language acquisition is a social activity, not an academic activity."[69] Unfortunately, folk language-learning theory developed on the subjective basis of missionary experience or opinion—underlying statements such as "Textbooks can ruin an American's acquisition of a foreign language" and "Children learn to

---

66. Betty Lou Leaver, Madeline Ehrman, and Boris Shekhtman, *Achieving Success in Second Language Acquisition* (New York: Cambridge University Press, 2005), 25–26.

67. Ruth Mehr, "The Role of Motivation in Language Learning," *Dialog on Language Instruction* 21 (2010): 1–10; Kimberly A. Noels, Luc G. Pelletier, Richard Clément, and Robert J. Vallerand, "Why Are You Learning a Second Language? Motivational Orientations and Self-Determination Theory," *Language Learning* 50 (2000): 57–85, esp. 57–58, 75–79.

68. Waltke states that the most important task of a Biblical Hebrew teacher is not specifically language oriented, but rather it is to nurture students' theological motivation. See Bruce K. Waltke, "How I Changed My Mind about Teaching Biblical Hebrew (or Retained It)," *Crux* 29, no. 4 (1993): 10–15, esp. 10.

69. E. Thomas Brewster and Elizabeth S. Brewster, "Language Learning *Is* Communication—*Is* Ministry!," *IBMR* 6 (1982): 160–64.

speak by first listening; adults should, too"—can detrimentally influence language-learning policy for mission organizations.[70] The present
ascendancy of the GPA method in missionary language-learning circles is
worrisome for this reason among others; many of the fundamental theories and methodologies of GPA are controversial and unsupported by the
majority findings of research in the fields of theoretical linguistics and
second-language acquisition.[71] Furthermore, GPA eschews use of "exter-
nal representations" of language that involve reading and writing due to
its exclusive development of listening and speaking skills.[72]

Focusing solely on oral and aural aspects of language learning may
appear to fit some missionaries' learning needs. Perhaps a certain people
group either has no written language, or few use whatever writing
system that does exist. Orally based cultures function differently from
literacy-based cultures, so an important part of missionary enculturation
can include attempting to understand an oral people's language and culture more intimately within an emic, native frame of reference. Furthermore, the personalities and learning preferences of some missionaries
may cohere well with a listening, speaking, and activity-based approach.

However, in the end, missionary neglect of literacy may not actually
be wise in either of these situations. In the case of an oral culture, missionaries should consider not only their own short-term need to speak
a language, but also the long-term health of the church within the culture using that language. Eventually, following development of an ever-
more-comprehensive series of crafted Bible stories, missionaries must
consciously work toward enabling unmediated access to the word of God
by a national church.[73] Treating host culture Christians as equals requires
encouraging their leaders to acquire the greatest degree of equipping

---

70. David Harrill Roberts, "Deschooling Language Study in East Africa: The Zambia
Plan" (paper presented at the Delaware Symposium on Language Study, Newark, DE, October 1979), 6, 9.

71. Sawin, "Second Language Learnerhood among Cross-Cultural Field Workers,"
165–74.

72. Sawin, "Second Language Learnerhood among Cross-Cultural Field Workers,"
153–54.

73. Distribution of audio recordings of the entire Bible on small, inexpensive, dedicated
solar-powered devices or by file transfer between smartphones represents a historically
unprecedented opportunity to reach oral and oral-preference peoples with the word of God.

possible, including the ability to read the Bible in their own language.[74] Furthermore, aside from scenarios such as early missionary contact with peoples who speak unwritten languages, literacy is necessary for full participation in host cultures. As for consideration of missionary learning preferences, it is simply pedagogically unsound to require introverts, deductive thinkers, and visual learners to surrender their most effective learning techniques and submit to a system that appeals exclusively to the strengths of extroverts, inductive thinkers, and auditory-kinesthetic learners.

Admittedly, explicit training in reading and writing may scarcely be necessary in the case of languages such as Italian with highly regular grapheme-phoneme correspondence. That is to say, learning to read and write in alphabetical languages with few or no irregularly spelled words should be relatively easy for most learners. Yet even in the case of languages such as Chinese that employ a nonalphabetical means of recording sound and meaning in writing, literacy is no less crucial to the missionary task.[75] Regarding the sociocultural use of language, missionaries should be able to function as literate adults and thus understand the meaning of posted signs, read nonpicture menus, and be able to converse with others through handwritten notes or text messages. In sum, attaining literacy in the language of the people should be an integral aspect of language learning for those who work in literate societies.

Of course, the supreme goal of literacy in a people's language is to be able to read and communicate God's word. In the terminology of second-language acquisition, this goal requires learning *language for specific purposes* (LSP). On one hand, effective LSP training can serve as an overlay atop any general missionary language-learning program and thus freely employ altogether different learning strategies, such as explicitly

---

74. Promotion of literacy for the sake of universal reading of the Bible has until recently featured prominently in the agenda of missions work, and it has led to the transformation of societies. See Robert D. Woodberry, "The Missionary Roots of Liberal Democracy," *American Political Science Review* 106 (2012): 244–74, esp. 249.

75. Contrary to popular belief and the assumptions of some learning strategies, the relationship between the sounds of speech and Chinese writing is not entirely arbitrary. Compound characters commonly contain both semantic and phonetic elements, with the phonetic element cuing pronunciation. See Yi-Ping Chen, "Word Recognition and Reading in Chinese" (DPhil diss., University of Oxford, 1993), 26–30.

focusing on literary use of religious language.[76] Thus through LSP training, for example, a missionary studying Chinese might learn that the traditional biblical terminology for "sin" employs the same word that non-Christian Chinese use to express "crime" and then adjust his or her discussion of sin to avoid misunderstanding.[77]

On the other hand, ideally missionary language-learning programs should not treat acquiring biblically and theologically oriented language as if such a goal were somehow ancillary to the main objectives of language acquisition. Instead, from the very beginning of their presence on the field, missionaries should intentionally train to be "bilingual" in the common language of the people and the spiritually shaped language of the church. Missionary language learning should be worshipful and thus a joyous end in itself rather than only a perfunctory means to an end. Study of Scripture, singing worship songs, and prayer in the target language all dramatically foster transitioning from viewing one's second language as a code to embracing it as a true language: a voice as fit as any other to exclaim the worship of "ransomed people . . . from every tribe and language and people and nation" (Rev 5:9) in the presence of God for eternity.[78]

LANGUAGE AND WORLD MISSION

Particularly for monolingual Christians, the task of language learning for the sake of world mission can appear daunting at the outset. Mentors should guide new missionaries to understand that language learning is not a training program to endure but a lifelong process to embrace in fulfillment of a divine calling. The author of life and language, the redeemer of humans and their tongues, is the "Alpha and the Omega" (Rev 1:8; 21:6; 22:13), who is worthy of all adoration and praise. May the church return

---

76. Claus Gnutzmann, "Language for Specific Purposes vs. General Language," in *Handbook of Foreign Language Communication and Learning*, ed. Karlfried Knapp and Barbara Seidlhofer (New York: de Gruyter, 2009), 517–44, esp. 518–19.

77. This Christianized sense of 罪 uniformly translates the verb of "sinning," ἁμαρτάνω, in Rom 3:23 in colloquial modern translations such as the Worldwide Chinese Bible New Testament (环球圣经译本) of 2015, the Chinese New Living Translation (新普及译本) of 2013, and the Mandarin Version (普通话本) of 2004.

78. Ideally songs and prayers should be indigenous rather than translated from another language in order to acquire not just the vocabulary but also the heart of a people in worship. See Lindy Scott, "Singing into the Wind: Uses and Abuses of 'Christian' Songs in Our Foreign Language Classes," *Journal of Christianity and Foreign Languages* 5 (2005): 75–81, esp. 77.

to God-centeredness in world mission. May God's redeemed people learn
languages for the sake of his glory, such that "the earth will be filled
with the knowledge of the glory of the LORD as the waters cover the sea"
(Hab 2:14). May all peoples come to love and worship forever the one
who has exalted above all things his name and his word (Ps 138:2). אָמֵן
and ἀμήν!

9

GRAMMATICAL-HISTORICAL EXEGESIS AND WORLD MISSION

Will Brooks

INTRODUCTION

Displaying a puzzled expression, a student raises a hand and asks, "How do we know what the answer is?" In my classes on biblical interpretation, I often employ interpretive exercises such as sentence diagramming and discourse analysis. These exercises lead to lengthy discussions about which grammatical relationships are evident in the text and which are not. The students always have a wide variety of opinions and reasons for their interpretive decisions, and inevitably these discussions lead to the question posed above: How can we know with any degree of certainty which judgment is correct?

This question is difficult to answer, which has led many in modern times to embrace a high degree of flexibility in determining the meaning of texts. Yet, convinced that the most reliable indications of textual meaning indeed derive from the author, I always answer students' questions by pointing them back to the text. Though in the case of biblical interpretation we certainly do not have direct access to the original authors, we do have access to authors' thoughts preserved in writing through the ages. Using clues from grammar, historical background, and literary context, we move as close as possible toward an understanding of intended meaning.

In this chapter, I want to address how biblical interpretation is done in cross-cultural contexts. What challenges do we face when we seek to determine the original author's intention and apply that intended meaning to contemporary contexts, especially settings where multiple cultural perspectives coexist? Or what about when interpreters—missionaries for example—have a vastly different cultural perspective from that of their audience? How do these cultural considerations affect the interpretative process? In this chapter I argue that in spite of these challenges, the grammatical-historical method of interpretation is the method best suited for cross-cultural interpretation. I first respond to a few challenges, and then I explain what the process of interpretation can look like in cross-cultural situations.

Before proceeding, though, two terms require definition. The first is "hermeneutics." Though many today use the term to mean analyzing a text or idea within a contemporary context that itself supplies meaning, I use the term in the traditional sense, which is "that science which delineates principles or methods for interpreting an individual author's meaning."[1] Exegesis, then, is the implementation of those principles, and interpretation is an attempt to understand authorial intent.[2]

A second term is "culture." Paul Hiebert defines culture as "the more or less integrated systems of ideas, beliefs, and values and their associated patterns of behavior and products shared by a people who organize and regulate what they think, feel, and do."[3] In a related sense, then, *cross-cultural* thinking pertains to aspects of culture that may be similar or can be shared from culture to culture. Though often used somewhat interchangeably with "cross-cultural," the term "intercultural" has in view the interaction that takes place when people from distinct cultures communicate across the cultural divide.

OBJECTIONS TO THE GRAMMATICAL-HISTORICAL METHOD AS A CROSS-CULTURAL HERMENEUTIC

---

1. Grant R. Osborne, *The Hermeneutical Spiral: A Comprehensive Introduction to Biblical Hermeneutics*, rev. ed. (Downers Grove, IL: IVP Academic, 2006), 21. See also Walter C. Kaiser Jr. and Moisés Silva, *Introduction to Biblical Hermeneutics: The Search for Meaning*, rev. ed. (Grand Rapids: Zondervan, 2007), 17.

2. Robert L. Thomas, "Current Hermeneutical Trends: Toward Explanation or Obfuscation?," *JETS* 39 (1996): 241–56, esp. 247–48.

3. Paul Hiebert, *Anthropological Insights for Missionaries* (Grand Rapids: Baker, 1985), 30.

With those initial definitions in view, let us consider some possible objections against using grammatical-historical exegesis as a cross-cultural hermeneutic. To begin, several of those who have proposed alternative methods for cross-cultural hermeneutics have essentially conflated the grammatical-historical method and the historical-critical method.[4] Thus one could ask, "Isn't grammatical-historical exegesis the same thing as the historical-critical method of interpretation?" The primary difference between these two methods is the skeptical stance toward the biblical documents inherent in the historical-critical method. More specifically, a fundamental presupposition of the historical-critical method is an anti-supernatural bias toward events recorded in Scripture. Thus knowingly or even unwittingly, scholars who use this approach reject the inerrancy and historical reliability of the Bible.[5]

The grammatical-historical method, on the other hand, does not assume a critical or skeptical stance toward the historical reliability of Scripture. Instead, the philosophical presuppositions of the grammatical-historical method include commitment to the inspiration, inerrancy, and authority of the Bible; thus this method is used in order to discern the original author's intent.[6] Walter Kaiser further explains that the grammatical-historical method reaches beyond the study of grammar and history to include syntax and theology as well: "If the term were not so awkward and clumsy, the truth of the matter is that the method should be called grammatical-contextual-historical-syntactical-theological-cultural exegesis, for each of

---

4. Archie C. C. Lee, "Cross-Textual Hermeneutics," in *Dictionary of Third World Theologies*, ed. Virginia Fabella and R. S. Sugirtharajah (Maryknoll, NY: Orbis, 2000), 60–62; Larry Caldwell, "Third Horizon Ethnohermeneutics: Re-Evaluating New Testament Hermeneutical Models for Intercultural Bible Interpreters Today," *Asia Journal of Theology* 1 (1987): 313–43, esp. 315; and Caldwell, "Teaching Biblical Interpretation in Intercultural Contexts: A Plea for Teaching Biblical Interpretation Using Only the Bible," in *Controversies in Missions: Theology, People, and Practice of Mission in the 21st Century*, ed. Rochelle Cathcart Scheuermann and Ed Smither, EMS Series 24 (Pasadena, CA: William Carey Library, 2016), 269–81, esp. 273–74; Enoch Wan, "Ethnohermeneutics: Its Necessity and Difficulty for All Christians of All Times," ETS Microform, ETS-4772 (1995): 1.

5. For a basic description of the skeptical orientation of the historical-critical method, see Robert L. Plummer, *40 Questions about Interpreting the Bible*, 40 Questions Series, ed. Benjamin L. Merkle (Grand Rapids: Kregel, 2010), 92–93.

6. Bruce K. Waltke and Charles Yu, *An Old Testament Theology: An Exegetical, Canonical, and Thematic Approach* (Grand Rapids: Zondervan, 2007), 86–92.

these concerns, and more, must participate in the exegetical venture."[7] In summary, the most reliable means to recover what the original authors of Scripture meant is to interpret the language they used within its historical and literary context.[8] Analysis of the author's grammar and syntax enables the interpreter to understand what the author meant through his choice of words and information structure, and research on the historical setting helps the interpreter to grasp what prompted the author to write specific passages.

A second question that some might ask is, "Isn't grammatical-historical exegesis a Western method of interpretation?" Larry Caldwell is one scholar who advances this argument.[9] He notes that both the historical-critical and grammatical-historical approaches are approaches to hermeneutics that developed out of Western philosophical presuppositions. Caldwell is indeed correct in stating that the historical-critical method and its antisupernaturalism are outgrowths of Western philosophical presuppositions deriving especially from the Enlightenment.

In contrast, though the grammatical-historical method also largely matured in the context of Western culture, it is not a method that demands uniquely Western thought processes or presuppositions. Instead, at its core, the grammatical-historical method attempts to determine an author's meaning through the study of language usage within the author's cultural and historical setting. Such an approach should be used in every culture to equip believers in "rightly handling the word of truth" (2 Tim 2:15). David Sills makes this point when he writes, "In order to avoid the errors of imaginative minds, believers with the Bible in their language must be taught how to interpret God's Word. The historical-grammatical method for understanding the original intent of the author is the most

---

7. Walter C. Kaiser Jr., *Toward an Exegetical Theology: Biblical Exegesis for Preaching & Teaching* (Grand Rapids: Baker, 1981), 90.

8. Robert H. Stein, "The Benefits of an Author-Oriented Approach to Hermeneutics," *JETS* 44 (2001): 451–66, esp. 463. That is not to say, though, that Stein or any other particular proponent of this approach views this task as accomplishable through word study alone. As Stein writes about what the "authors meant by their words," he has in view the grammar, syntax, and literary context of those words as well.

9. Larry W. Caldwell, "Receptor-Oriented Hermeneutics: Reclaiming the Hermeneutical Methodologies of the New Testament for Bible Interpreters in the Twenty-First Century" (PhD diss., Fuller Theological Seminary, 1990), 345; Caldwell, "A Response to the Responses of Tappeiner and Whelchel to Ethnohermeneutics," *JAM* 2 (2000): 135–45, esp. 139–40.

faithful method of interpretation, even when there is no knowledge of biblical languages."[10] Kaiser agrees and critiques those who argue that each culture should use its own indigenous and idiosyncratic hermeneutic methodologies when studying Scripture. He states, "It is simply not true that there are as many approaches to the text of Scripture as there are cultures and societies."[11] The church has developed the grammatical-historical method over the course of its history to determine the intention of the original author as effectively as possible.

Indeed, the quest for the author's meaning through the study of word usage is not an approach exemplified solely in recent church history. Although many church fathers favored allegory, in the fourth century the Antioch school of interpretation emphasized an expressly nonallegorical, literal approach. Interpreters such as Theodore of Mopsuestia and John Chrysostom used a grammatical-historical approach in search of authors' meaning.[12] Chrysostom and others argued that those who allegorized the text were no longer servants of the Word but were manipulating the words and images of Scripture for their own theological purposes.[13]

Unfortunately, as the boundaries of the church expanded to Western Europe through missionary efforts, the Antioch school's focus on literal exegesis was largely forgotten. Hughes Oliphant Old explains the dynamic of this period:

> The speed with which the missionary work was being done and the political and cultural motives for which many accepted baptism meant that great masses of only partially converted people had been received into the Church. Basic Christian doctrines were poorly understood, the Christian life was poorly practiced, and the ways of paganism were not entirely left behind.[14]

---

10. M. David Sills, *Reaching and Teaching: A Call to Great Commission Obedience* (Chicago: Moody, 2010), 53.

11. Kaiser, *Toward an Exegetical Theology*, 121.

12. Sidney Greidanus, *Preaching Christ from the Old Testament: A Contemporary Hermeneutical Method* (Grand Rapids: Eerdmans, 1999), 91–96; Dennis E. Johnson, *Him We Proclaim: Preaching Christ from All the Scriptures* (Phillipsburg, NJ: P&R, 2007), 105–6; Plummer, *40 Questions about Interpreting the Bible*, 89.

13. Johnson, *Him We Proclaim*, 106.

14. Hughes Oliphant Old, *The Reading and Preaching of the Scriptures in the Worship of the Christian Church* (Grand Rapids: Eerdmans, 1999), 3:189.

Believers in these areas found it increasingly difficult to read and interpret Scripture, and as a result interpreters used their own imaginations in expounding on the details in biblical texts.[15] These indigenous interpretive approaches led believers further and further away from the original authors' meaning.

A renewed emphasis on understanding the literal meaning of Scripture arose during the Reformation. Dennis Johnson explains that the Reformers

> recognized that distortions in the church's piety and practice (indulgences, veneration of saints and images, etc.) typically arose from errors in doctrine, that errors in doctrine arose from errors of biblical interpretation, and that specific errors of biblical interpretation were attributable to a hermeneutic method that gave too large a place to ecclesiastical tradition (with its political dimension) in determining what God's Word teaches.[16]

For the Reformers, emphasis on the literal meaning of Scripture was not merely an outgrowth of their cultural perspective. In fact, during the Reformers' time, the culturally preferred means of interpretation was still allegory, and the result was rampant theological confusion and heresy. In contrast, the Reformers emphasized the literal meaning of Scripture in response to the cultural misinterpretation of their day. The Reformers' call to return to the study of the grammar and historical setting of biblical authors set the stage for modern biblical interpretation.

A third question that is sometimes posited is, "Isn't it arrogant to speak of a cross-cultural process of interpretation?" In other words, "Doesn't that just mean that a few Westerners decide the rules that people in every other culture need to follow?" This question is similar to the previous one, and furthermore it calls into question the judgment of interpreters who are trained in the West yet do interpretation in the Majority World. Given that the Western church has essentially dominated the last five hundred years of church history, it is certainly possible that Westerners could continue to control the interpretive conversation through inertia alone.

---

15. Johnson, *Him We Proclaim*, 109–10.
16. Johnson, *Him We Proclaim*, 110.

Augustine, in his book *On Christian Teaching*, states, "The most expert investigator of the divine scriptures will be the person who, first, has read them all and has a good knowledge—a reading knowledge, at least, if not yet a complete understanding—of those pronounced canonical."[17] Augustine's context and the theological discussions of his day were far different from ours. So he does not always use the same terms that we do, and he does not frame his conversations within the same kinds of questions we ask. In fact, in his writings he often discusses the allegorical meaning of Scripture. When he does mention various meanings of Scripture, though, he is often talking about metaphors and typology that were intended by the original author. In his book *The Literal Meaning of Genesis*, he explains how his perspective on this issue developed over time: "In my book on Genesis *Against the Manicheans* I frequently explained the text in the figurative meaning. I now believe that the literal meaning must be sought."[18] Along the same lines, Augustine urges that when interpreters are confronted with multiple possible meanings of a text, "let us choose that one which appears as certainly the meaning intended by the author."[19] In that sense, his advice is helpful in answering the question that my students often pose: "How do we determine which interpretation is the correct one?" We evaluate each interpretation based on how well it plausibly explains the author's intention. And how do we know the intention of the original author? We know it by studying what he wrote.

The reason that the grammatical-historical method is helpful as a cross-cultural hermeneutic is not because Westerners developed it and thus the Western church should now tell the rest of the world the correct way to read Scripture. The grammatical-historical method is helpful as a cross-cultural hermeneutic because it gives interpreters the tools to analyze and understand the words, grammar, context, and theology of the original authors. Moreover, many non-Westerners have contributed to the development of this approach and see it as the approach that is most beneficial for evangelicals of all cultures. One contemporary example is

---

17. Saint Augustine, *On Christian Teaching*, Oxford World's Classics, trans. R. P. H. Green (Oxford: Oxford University Press, 1997), 35.

18. Saint Augustine, *The Literal Meaning of Genesis*, trans. John Hammond Taylor, Ancient Christian Writers Series, ed. Johannes Quasten, et al. (New York: Paulist, 1982), 2:35.

19. Augustine, *Literal Meaning of Genesis*, 1:45.

Daniel Espiritu, who teaches philosophy in the Philippines. He responds to those who claim that each culture can determine its own rules of interpretation by stating that evangelicals "cannot engage in an 'endless play' with the biblical texts." He then argues, "The evangelical insistence on doing rigorous exegesis to get at the probable intended meaning of biblical texts, replacing allegorizing, spiritualizing, and moralizing, is not so much the out-growth of western worldview as it is the inevitable offshoot of evangelical presuppositions and worldview."[20]

A final question that some might ask is, "How does a literal process of interpretation relate to peoples and cultures who are oral learners?" Given that 70 percent of the world's peoples are oral learners, this question is a critical one.[21] A simple answer to this complex problem is that even though these peoples cannot read the written word of God, they can learn to engage with it in ways that achieve similar results. They must be taught the principles of biblical interpretation in such a way that they are able to understand the original authors' intent and to apply it to their cultural context.

Missionaries may lead people in such contexts through a process that introduces the teachings of Scripture orally. Often the first step is to communicate the stories of the Bible by using a Chronological Bible Storying approach.[22] Translators can also produce audio recordings of parts of the Bible as they finish translating it. Once the translation is complete, these

---

20. Daniel L. Espiritu, "Ethnohermeneutics or Oikohermeneutics? Questioning the Necessity of Caldwell's Hermeneutics," *JAM 3* (2001): 267–81, esp. 278.

21. Sills, *Reaching and Teaching*, 173; Grant Lovejoy et al., eds., *Making Disciples of Oral Learners* (Bangalore, India: International Orality Network, 2005), 3.

22. Oral communication of the message of the Bible is especially urgent among those whose mother tongue is one of the 3,312 of the world's 7,099 living languages that lack any portion of translated Scripture. See Wycliffe Global Alliance, "Scripture & Language Statistics 2017," www.wycliffe.net/statistics (accessed January 24, 2018). For a description of the Chronological Bible Storying approach, see Lovejoy et al., *Making Disciples of Oral Learners*, 12–16, 74–75; Sills, *Reaching and Teaching*, 183–87. It is worth noting that Chronological Bible Storying and oral copies of the Scriptures, while helpful starting points in many cultures, should never be considered an endpoint. These performed speech acts fill the gap while missionaries work to set languages in writing, train leaders in literacy, and translate the Scriptures. Long-term goals for these situations ought to include the people themselves translating biblical studies resources and producing their own theological writings. Incidentally, it is also helpful to note that simply because narrative is most familiar to oral learners, missionaries should not focus only on narrative passages of Scripture. As the people become acquainted with the message of Scripture, missionaries should seek to teach and communicate all of the genres of revelation.

recordings are essentially an oral Bible, through which nonliterate, oral learners can have access to the complete word of God. Although those who are oral learners will not be able to conduct any sort of written grammatical or syntactical analysis, they can learn to identify the main points of the stories as more and more of the Bible appears in their language.

A helpful approach in these situations is to train believers to ask certain questions, often in group settings, that help them better to grasp the author's meaning.[23] By using such questions as, "Who are the main characters in the story?" "What images or symbols are meaningful in this story?" "Is there a specific sin described in this story?" and "What does this story teach us about God's character?" the believers better discern the contours of the story. In a sense, these oral learners will then be using many of the same processes that literates use to analyze a text, despite lacking access to a written text themselves.

AUTHOR-ORIENTED CROSS-CULTURAL MODEL[24]

Now that we have answered some basic questions about the grammatical-historical method and its use as a cross-cultural hermeneutic, it is appropriate to show how this method can be used in a real-life setting. This is a two-part process: determining meaning in literary context and then applying the meaning to the contemporary setting.

DETERMINING MEANING IN LITERARY CONTEXT

The first step in this method is the determination of the original author's meaning in literary context. Thus it is necessary to determine the type of

---

23. Many oral societies are also group-based cultures, in that they prefer to make decisions as a group. In those cases, since they already discuss and make decisions as a group, it may be helpful for them at times to study Scripture as a group. This proposal, though, certainly does not mean that they will never study Scripture in an individual setting. I am simply stating that this approach may be beneficial to them due to their culturally preferred learning style.

24. I first developed this process in William P. Brooks, "Critiquing Ethnohermeneutics Theories: A Call to an Author-Oriented Approach to Cross-Cultural Biblical Interpretation" (PhD diss., Southern Baptist Theological Seminary, 2011), and then summarized it in "Hermeneutic Principles for Developing a Global Theology," *Southern Baptist Journal of Missions and Evangelism* 1 (2012): 46–60. I recently referenced it in bullet-point format in "Hermeneutics for Healthy Churches," *EMQ* (January 2017).

literature under consideration. Each genre of Scripture has its own specific rules that govern the writing and reading of that type of literature.[25] Once the interpreter identifies the genre and the specific rules governing that type of literature, the next step of study should focus on three areas: linguistics, culture and history, and theology and missiology.

Linguistics

At the most basic level, understanding written texts would not be possible without knowledge of semantics, which is to say, the range of meaning manifested in individual words, and the interpreter must determine for those individual words the meaning intended by the original author.[26] In view of the need to prepare expository sermons, Stephen and David Olford encourage interpreters to concentrate especially on "significant" words, "unknown" words (words with unclear meaning), and "difficult" words (words with known semantic ranges, but that manifest challenging use in context).[27] Regarding the contextual coloring of word meaning, Moisés Silva explains, "The context does not merely help us understand meaning; it virtually *makes* meaning!"[28] The interpreter should continually bear in mind that semantics is but the first level of linguistic analysis.

Beyond grasping the meaning of individual words, the next level of linguistic study of a written text has to do with grammar. Grammar comprises the laws that govern how words in a language interact with one another.[29] Examples of these interactions include how adverbs express manner, place, time, or degree of action with modified verbs; how adjectives depict the attributes of nouns; and whether participles act in a primarily adverbial, verbal, adjectival, or substantival way in a given clause.

Then, on the level of the clause and the sentence, one must grasp an author's use of syntax.[30] Syntax refers to laws regulating the structuring of

---

25. Robert H. Stein, *A Basic Guide to Interpreting the Bible: Playing by the Rules* (Grand Rapids: Baker, 1994), 75.

26. Stein, *Basic Guide to Interpreting the Bible*, 101.

27. Stephen F. Olford and David L. Olford, *Anointed Expository Preaching* (Nashville: B&H, 1998), 120–23.

28. Moisés Silva, *Biblical Words and Their Meaning: An Introduction to Lexical Semantics* (Grand Rapids: Zondervan, 1983), 139.

29. Osborne, *Hermeneutical Spiral*, 57.

30. Osborne, *Hermeneutical Spiral*, 113.

sentences, including word order. Just as every language has its own rules of grammar, each language also possesses unique means of expressing concepts that elude simple definition such as focus (emphasis or prominence) and modality (expressions of potential rather than certainty). Due to differences between languages in matters of grammar and syntax, ultimately some linguistic signals a biblical author intends to send to readers are not possible to render fully in a given translation language.

Last, it is necessary to conduct discourse-level literary analysis, which requires understanding the communicative function of language at levels higher than the sentence. In general terms this implies gaining a context-sensitive understanding of the progression of blocks of ideas such as in paragraphs, which some authors stress as absolutely essential for biblical exposition.[31] Spanning linguistic concerns from semantics to literary analysis, Hershael York explains,

> To truly comprehend the sense of words, you must have sufficient context to insure that you have the intended meaning of those words in their context. When it comes to understanding literature, especially the Scriptures, context is everything. Divorced from context, the words of the Bible can be—and unfortunately often are—twisted and perverted to justify all kinds of evil. Ripping verses out of their context and assigning them a meaning that the author did not intend is doing violence to the Scripture and is an affront to the Word of God.[32]

Kaiser further explains that interpreters must consider the immediate, sectional, book, and canonical context of any passage.[33]

Many helpful works explain how to carry out the technical tasks of grammatical and syntactical analysis in biblical languages and how to apply the results in ministry.[34] At this point it is not necessary to reproduce

---

31. Kaiser, *Toward an Exegetical Theology*, 96; Hershael W. York and Bert Decker, *Preaching with Bold Assurance: A Solid and Enduring Approach to Engaging Exposition* (Nashville: B&H, 2003), 67.

32. York and Decker, *Preaching with Bold Assurance*, 53.

33. Kaiser, *Toward an Exegetical Theology*, 70–71.

34. Resources to aid linguistic analysis for the sake of ministry include, for Biblical Hebrew: Bruce K. Waltke and Michael P. O'Connor, *An Introduction to Biblical Hebrew Syntax* (Winona Lake, IN: Eisenbrauns, 1990); Douglas Stuart, *Old Testament Exegesis: A Handbook*

the insights of those works, but instead to consider how linguistic analysis should be conducted in cross-cultural situations. Ideally every interpreter would have access to training in the original languages so that study of the biblical text can be carried out with the many benefits that come from such knowledge. Unfortunately, in many parts of the world such training is not presently available, and even in some places with access to biblical language training, the purchase price of the Hebrew Bible and the Greek New Testament may be difficult to bear.[35] In many missional settings there is the concurrent challenge of encouraging biblical language study among oral learners.[36] Is it possible for a missionary to encourage study of Biblical Hebrew and Greek in such situations?[37]

While it is preferred to study the Bible in its original languages, it is certainly possible to study it through translation as well. Grant Osborne, though writing for a Western audience, recognizes that many interpreters will not have the opportunity to study the original languages: "Naturally, the person who does not know the original languages will have a perceptibly greater difficulty in dealing with grammar and syntax. . . . However, the task is not completely hopeless for those who have never

---

for Students and Pastors, 4th ed. (Louisville: Westminster John Knox, 2009); and Paul D. Wegner, Using Old Testament Hebrew in Preaching: A Guide for Students and Pastors (Grand Rapids: Kregel, 2009); for Biblical Greek: Daniel B. Wallace, Greek Grammar beyond the Basics: An Exegetical Syntax of the New Testament (Grand Rapids: Zondervan, 1996); Gordon D. Fee, New Testament Exegesis: A Handbook for Students and Pastors, 3rd ed. (Louisville: Westminster John Knox, 2002); David Alan Black, Using New Testament Greek in Ministry: A Practical Guide for Students and Pastors (Grand Rapids: Baker, 1993).

35. This discovery was an important point in the development of Caldwell's thinking on cross-cultural hermeneutics. He explains that when he first started teaching in the Philippines, he taught his students the original languages and made copies of biblical language texts for them to use. One of his brightest students, though, later commented that she was unable to use her copies because rats had eaten them. As a result, Caldwell now encourages students to use indigenous hermeneutic systems. See Larry W. Caldwell, "Towards the New Discipline of Ethnohermeneutics: Questioning the Relevancy of Western Hermeneutical Methods in the Asian Context," JAM 1 (1999): 21–43, esp. 25–29. Caldwell's questioning of biblical-language instruction on the mission field borders on satire. See Larry W. Caldwell, "How Asian Is Asian Theological Education?," in Tending the Seedbeds: Educational Perspectives on Theological Education in Asia, ed. Allan Harkness (Quezon City: Asia Theological Association, 2010), 23–45, esp. 34–36.

36. Sills, Reaching and Teaching, 173; Lovejoy et al., Making Disciples of Oral Learners, 3.

37. Employing communicative teaching methods can indeed facilitate study of the biblical languages for oral learners. See Jennifer Noonan and Paul Overland, "Teaching Biblical Hebrew to Oral-Preference Learners," HHE 19 (2017): 121–34.

studied the languages."[38] Interpreters in these contexts should recognize that they are depending on a translation and study the grammar and syntax of their translation with the aid of reputable commentaries if available.

Thomas Schreiner's method of "tracing the argument" will be helpful to those in contexts where opportunities for Hebrew and Greek study are not currently available.[39] Primarily designed for the study of the Pauline Epistles, the method analyzes the flow of Paul's arguments by examining the coordinate and subordinate statements in his letters. At its most basic level, this type of analysis examines two statements (or perhaps two paragraphs) and asks, "What is the relationship between these two propositions?" Such analysis, perhaps difficult at first, can become a useful tool for examining the basic structure and organization of the text in many genres of biblical literature, even if only through translation.[40]

Culture and History

Following on linguistic study, the second stage of grammatical-historical interpretation has to do with analysis of the cultural and historical setting of the text. Since God's word was given at a specific time in history to a specific people in a specific place, the interpreter must learn as much as possible about the original cultural and historical setting. Kaiser explains, "God's revelation in Scripture made a discriminating use of those cultural materials that were available to the writers in their day."[41] Some of the truths of God's word are intimately connected with certain

---

38. Osborne, *Hermeneutical Spiral*, 58.

39. Thomas R. Schreiner, *Interpreting the Pauline Epistles*, ed. Scot McKnight, Guides to New Testament Exegesis (Grand Rapids: Baker, 1990), 97–126. Admittedly, Schreiner states that diagramming passages in the biblical languages is a necessary prerequisite to "tracing the argument," for he writes with reference to settings in which original-language training is available. However, Schreiner's model is a helpful tool for understanding the overall flow of the passage even in settings where it is not possible to ground interpretation in the biblical languages.

40. It could be said that such a tool might not be helpful when analyzing wisdom literature, such as the book of Proverbs. In some cases, though, the author grouped proverbs thematically, intending for them to be read together to communicate a larger truth. Two examples of display of thematic coherence are Prov 9:13–18 and the collections of sayings for "my son" or "sons" in the introductory chapters of Proverbs. In other cases, seemingly random proverbial statements may be connected with series-type coordinate relationships.

41. Kaiser, *Toward an Exegetical Theology*, 115.

cultural symbols, such as John's use of "lamb of God" in John 1:29 and 36, or phrases such as "Your hair is like a flock of goats" (Song 4:1) in Song of Songs. Unless remaining grounded in the ancient Jewish cultural milieu, these metaphors and similes lose their meaning.

In the same way, an interpreter cannot readily understand some passages without studying the unfolding historical situations depicted in the passage. The connection between history and text can be especially illuminating in the case of narrative passages. For example, an interpreter should seek to understand the exilic and postexilic predicament of the Jews that provides the historical setting for the book of Nehemiah.

While a number of tools exist to guide interpreters in the West through such cultural and historical analysis,[42] many of those tools are currently only available in European languages such as English. In non-European language settings, a dearth of such resources certainly complicates the task of interpretation, but this difficulty does not grant the interpreter the freedom to read contemporary cultural settings into the text. Seeking original authors' meaning remains the goal of interpretation.

Interpreters can take several steps to ameliorate a lack of exegetical resources. First, interpreters can immerse themselves in Scripture. They can learn about the cultural settings of Scripture by reading large portions of Scripture on a daily basis. Sometimes a historical detail listed in Isaiah may be helpful in understanding a text in Nehemiah, or a cultural custom from Exodus may be helpful when interpreting a passage from John. Interpreters can create their own exegetical reference work by compiling a notebook of historical and cultural insights.

A second step that interpreters in such situations can take is to seek out and learn from those who have more knowledge about the biblical culture than they do. In some cases this may be a pastor in another city or village, and it may even be someone of a different ethnic group. In pioneer

---

42. For a general introduction to the New Testament, see D. A. Carson and Douglas J. Moo, *An Introduction to the New Testament*, 2nd ed. (Grand Rapids: Zondervan, 2005). For information about the New Testament from a historical and cultural perspective, see Everett Ferguson, *Backgrounds of Early Christianity*, 3rd ed. (Grand Rapids: Eerdmans, 2003); John E. Stambaugh and David L. Balch, *The New Testament in Its Social Environment*, ed. Wayne A. Meeks, Library of Early Christianity (Philadelphia: Westminster, 1986); Gary M. Burge, Lynn H. Cohick, and Gene L. Green, *The New Testament in Antiquity: A Survey of the New Testament within Its Cultural Contexts* (Grand Rapids: Zondervan, 2009).

areas, the missionary may need to take the lead in this respect and train local believers to understand unique aspects of biblical cultures.

In orally based cultures, the process of learning about the cultural and historical settings of the biblical texts happens before, during, and after the Chronological Bible Storying process. Before narrating the story, the storyteller can begin by explaining its cultural and historical background. After the story ends, the storyteller can lead a discussion time, during which some of the group discussion questions can address the differences between the local culture and the culture within the story.

Hearers also learn about biblical cultures through the chronological arrangement of the stories, because the storyteller begins with the story of creation. Since the stories have a logical, chronological sequence, listeners can reflect on the events and truths of older stories in order to understand newer ones. For example, before listening to the story of John the Baptist's interaction with Jesus (John 1:29, 36), hearers would have already experienced the stories of Abraham and the lamb that became a substitute for Isaac (Gen 22) and the exodus from Egypt, before which the Israelites smeared lambs' blood over their doorposts (Exod 12). Thus when they hear John the Baptist refer to Jesus as "the lamb of God," they will be able to reflect on the preceding stories and apply Old Testament Jewish background to the New Testament.

Theology and Missiology

A third component of determining the intended meaning within a biblical text is the study of the text's theology. York explains how the study of a text's theological emphases affects the determination of the author's meaning: "Every passage of the Bible has something to say about God, his attributes, his character, his will, or his acts in history." He then goes on to explain that these theological truths are not always equally clear: "Sometimes the theological truths are overt, sometimes they are more subtle. The Book of Romans, for example, is clearly theological in most of its content. The Book of Esther, on the other hand, does not even mention the name of God, yet it reveals God's hand even when his face is hidden."[43] Thus each biblical text has a theological agenda. For example, Bryan

---

43. York and Decker, *Preaching with Bold Assurance*, 75.

Chapell suggests for the sake of preaching that interpreters ponder what specific sin the biblical theology of each Scripture passage may confront.[44] This approach is but one way to connect Scripture passages to broader theological issues.

Kaiser and Silva write that in order to do theological study of any text, the interpreter can examine six kinds of evidence that reveal a biblical author's theological thinking.[45] First, one should notice any parts of the text that relate to the unifying story of the Bible. Next, one should identify any terms that take on special theological significance through frequent usage in Scripture. Such terms include "seed," "son," "branch," and "messenger." Third, one should watch for quotations of earlier texts. Fourth, one should also be sensitive to allusions to earlier biblical events, persons, expressions, or terms. Fifth, one should consider how the theological emphases of the text relate to the book in which the passage appears and to the whole of Scripture. Finally, one should notice how the text contributes to the progress of revelation through Scripture. Through examining each of the six kinds of evidence profiled above, the interpreter thinks critically about the text by analyzing how a certain text relates to other biblical texts. The interpreter grows in understanding by asking difficult questions about what the text teaches about God, humanity, salvation, and so on, and how those teachings relate to the rest of biblical revelation. Seeking unity in the diversity of biblical revelation can be a challenging process, but it is one that is worthy of the interpreter's attention. Such theological analysis is the capstone of the exegetical process.[46]

An often-neglected theological emphasis within biblical texts concerns missiology. In stark contrast to this demonstrable neglect is Christopher Wright's assertion that each passage of Scripture has something to say about God's work in redemption.[47] Wright states, "It is God's mission in relation to the nations, arguably more than any other single theme,

---

44. Bryan Chapell, *Christ-Centered Preaching: Redeeming the Expository Sermon*, 2nd ed. (Grand Rapids: Baker, 2005), 48–51.

45. Kaiser and Silva, *Introduction to Biblical Hermeneutics*, 81.

46. Schreiner, *Interpreting the Pauline Epistles*, 135.

47. Christopher J. H. Wright, *The Mission of God: Unlocking the Bible's Grand Narrative* (Downers Grove, IL: InterVarsity Press, 2006), 31–32.

that provides the key that unlocks the biblical grand narrative."[48] Kaiser posits a canonical center for Old and New Testament theology that similarly attempts to make sense of how theology and missiology work together. He explains that center as "God's word of blessing (to use the word especially prominent in the pre-Abrahamic materials) or promise (to use the New Testament word which summarizes the contents of the Old Testament) to be Israel's God and to do something for Israel and through them something for all the nations on the face of the earth."[49] Thus, if Wright and Kaiser are correct, every biblical passage ultimately has something to say about who God is for his people and what he is doing to redeem humanity. People in any culture and setting can conduct this kind of theological and missiological analysis by asking questions related to God's character, human sinfulness, and God's mission. These questions can be modeled for oral learners as the storyteller leads the group in a discussion following the story and poses these questions.[50]

After carrying out grammatical-historical interpretation with the aid of linguistics, culture and history, and finally theology and missiology, the interpreter should attempt to summarize and restate the biblical author's meaning with a single sentence. Focus on the author's intended meaning places interpretation outside the highly subjective realm of the interpreter's transient feelings and situation in life to the greatest extent possible. Distilling meaning to a single sentence helps to ensure that the interpreter exerts significant effort to comprehend the main idea of biblical text. This main idea then cries out for application in the contemporary context.

APPLYING THE MEANING
TO THE CONTEMPORARY SETTING

Whereas determination of the biblical author's meaning is the more "objective" aspect of interpretation, application of that meaning to the contemporary context is decidedly more subjective. It is subjective because the way that meaning applies to the contemporary situation varies from

---

48. Wright, *Mission of God*, 255.

49. Kaiser, *Toward an Exegetical Theology*, 139.

50. Sills, *Reaching and Teaching*, 185–86; Lovejoy et al., *Making Disciples of Oral Learners*, 52.

context to context under the guidance of the Holy Spirit. Hand in hand with the process of determining authors' meaning, interpreters need to think critically about their own cultural perspective, research the target culture's context, discern the implication of the biblical text within a new cultural context, carry out critical contextualization, and communicate biblical truth in a culturally appropriate way.[51]

Think Critically about One's Own Cultural Perspective

At the end of the previous section, the interpreter sought to explain a biblical text's meaning in a single sentence. Then the interpreter could begin to think about application: how the unchanging meaning of the original author relates to the target culture. Yet before considering the target culture's perspective, one should first think critically about one's own reception of the biblical message. Without focused critical thinking about this "hidden" cultural influence, interpreters will naturally view the biblical text through the lens of their own cultural biases and then impose those preconceptions on the message of the Bible, and furthermore treat their cultural perspectives as normative for all cultures.

Caldwell helpfully notes this danger, explaining that the burden rests on the interpreter to overcome these cultural differences so that effective communication of biblical content can take place. He then laments, "In most cases, however, it is the receptor who receives the burden of modifying his or her worldview in order to understand the interpreter's message. Thus, what often happens is that the receptor has to enter into the culture of the interpreter and think more like the interpreter instead of the other way around."[52] When the interpreter (in this case, the missionary) fails to think critically about his or her own worldview and cultural presuppositions, this places an inappropriate burden on hearers to assume a foreign culture's vantage point in order to understand the Bible. Instead of developing culturally appropriate applications, the interpreter—blind to

---

51. Since the application process is more complicated when a missionary applies the truth of a passage to a certain target culture (since biblical culture, missionary culture, and target culture comprise three cultures involved in the process of application) than when a native interprets it for the native's own people (thus involving only two cultures), for the sake of comprehensiveness I focus on the missionary's perspective in this section.

52. Larry W. Caldwell, "Cross-Cultural Bible Interpretation: A View from the Field," *Phronesis* 39 (1996): 13–35, esp. 21–24.

his or her own cultural biases—will develop applications that are better suited to a foreign cultural setting.

The tradition of ancestor worship in East Asian cultures showcases the problem of cultural bias.[53] Westerners tend to be individualistic in outlook, and a Western missionary might reject practices related to ancestor worship on the basis of Romans 10:9 and the understanding that eternal destiny is related to the decision of an individual. East Asians, on the other hand, tend to be group oriented and place emphasis on filial piety. They might participate in these practices and argue they are obeying the command to "Honor your father and your mother" in Exodus 20:12. The point here is not to allow the difficulty of theologically evaluating different points of view to pass without comment, but simply to show how each cultural perspective leads the interpreter to place emphasis on a different passage of Scripture when thinking toward application.[54] Interpreters from every culture should listen to the insights of those from other cultural backgrounds, as doing so helps them to see their own cultural blind spots.

Missionaries, rarely challenged to examine their own cultural perspectives when at home, must examine their own worldviews when entering into and learning about another culture.[55] As interpreters of Scripture, missionaries should reflect on their own cultural perspectives in order to steer away from interpreting Scripture according to their own cultural norms and instead derive meaning from grammatical-historical interpretation.

Research the Target Culture's Context

While traditional Western hermeneutical models have often envisioned a two-horizon process that includes the biblical culture and the interpreter's

---

53. Ancestor veneration grows out of Confucian ideals and is often focused on providing for the welfare and happiness of the dead. Not all of the practices, though, are related to affecting the eternal state of the deceased. Some practices are intended to help people remember their ancestors' positive attributes.

54. At the moment I am neither asserting that the Westerner is correct to appeal to Rom 10:9 nor that the East Asian is correct to look to Exod 20:12. My point is that based on cultural viewpoints, they can both too hastily seize on biblical texts without careful consideration of how the Bible may actually best apply to the situation. Yet armed with critical study of the rituals involved and recognition of their own cultural biases, these believers can indeed apply biblical truth to any cultural practice under consideration.

55. Craig Storti, *The Art of Crossing Cultures*, 2nd ed. (Boston: Intercultural, 2001), 111–14.

culture, Caldwell notes that this model is only truly applicable in monocul-
tural interpretation.[56] When communicating the truths of God's word to
people of different cultures, interpreters must include three horizons in
their model of interpretation. These three horizons include the biblical
culture, the interpreter's culture, and also the target culture.[57] The interpreter's task increases in difficulty when engaged in intercultural work
because of this additional third horizon of the target culture.

Studying the target culture is a complicated process that requires
the investment of years of one's life in culture and language learning.
A fundamental task for the missionary is the identification of the people's worldview. Hiebert defines worldview as the "fundamental cognitive, affective, and evaluative presuppositions a group of people make
about the nature of things, and which they use to order their lives."[58] In a
formal sense, worldview identification is a time-consuming process that
involves the study of the history of a people and their contemporary situation through ethno-semantic analysis; sentence-completion exercises;
sign, ritual, and myth analysis; values identification; aesthetics evaluation; participant observation; and informant interviews.[59]

Deep understanding of worldview provides a number of benefits to
the missionary task. Stephen Grunlan and Marvin Mayers explain, "Cultural anthropology can enable a missionary to understand his prospective
new culture, to enter the culture with minimum culture shock and max-
imum adjustment, to insure that his message is being understood, and to
implant a biblical indigenous church and not transplant the church of his
own culture."[60] Furthermore, worldview identification is a helpful tool
for applying the meaning of the biblical text to the contemporary context.

---

56. Caldwell, "Receptor-Oriented Hermeneutics," 270.

57. The first to propose this three-culture model of interpretation at length was Eugene
Nida, *Message and Mission* (New York: Harper and Row, 1960), 33–58.

58. Paul G. Hiebert, *Transforming Worldviews: An Anthropological Understanding of How
People Change* (Grand Rapids: Baker, 2008), 15.

59. Hiebert, *Transforming Worldviews*, 91–103; Carol V. McKinney, *Globe-Trotting in Sandals: A Field Guide in Cultural Research* (Dallas: SIL International, 2000); James P. Spradley, *The
Ethnographic Interview* (Fort Worth, TX: Harcourt Brace Jovanovich, 1979); Spradley, *Participant Observation* (Fort Worth: Harcourt Brace Jovanovich, 1980); John W. Creswell, *Qualitative
Inquiry and Research Design: Choosing among Five Traditions* (Thousand Oaks, CA: Sage, 1998).

60. Stephen A. Grunlan and Marvin K. Mayers, *Cultural Anthropology: A Christian Perspective* (Grand Rapids: Zondervan, 1979), 32.

Once the missionary develops a grasp of the worldview of the target culture, it is possible to identify the broad categories of thought and pre-suppositions about the nature of reality that relate to truths expressed in specific biblical texts. The missionary can then narrow further study to the cultural norms and practices that the text addresses. During cultural analysis, the missionary should not vocalize judgment on the sinfulness of certain cultural practices.[61] If people detect that the missionary has a critical attitude toward the norms and practices of their culture, they will no longer share freely about these practices. Instead, the missionary should ask questions of cultural informants that elucidate the distinction between the cultural form and the meaning behind that form.

Another element of the culture that the missionary needs to study at this point is the preferred hermeneutical methodologies of the target culture.[62] Familiarity with traditional hermeneutical methodologies enables the missionary to understand how the people will naturally assume that they should approach the interpretation of Scripture. The missionary with this type of awareness can better prepare to confront and correct those tendencies that contradict the intent of the original author. Along similar lines, missionaries should recognize that people of different cultural settings often approach the biblical text with unique questions and focus on different aspects of the subject matter of the text.[63] The missionary who has studied the worldview of the target cul-

---

61. Paul G. Hiebert, "Critical Contextualization," *IBMR* 11 (1987): 104–12, esp. 109; Hiebert, *Anthropological Reflections on Missiological Issues* (Grand Rapids: Baker, 1994), 88–89.

62. I agree with Caldwell concerning the need to study indigenously preferred herme-neutical methodologies but disagree on the purpose for such study. Caldwell argues that missionaries should study those methodologies in order to use them. In contrast I argue that the missionary should study them for the purpose of awareness, for the missionary may need to confront patterns of interpretation that subvert authorial intent. For Caldwell's argument, see Caldwell, "Towards the New Discipline of Ethnohermeneutics," 31–32. For my critique of Caldwell's position, see Brooks, "Critiquing Ethnohermeneutics Theories," 102–20.

63. Kevin Higgins, "Diverse Voices: Hearing Scripture Speak in a Multicultural Envi-ronment" (paper presented at the annual meeting of the Evangelical Missiological Soci-ety, Charlotte, NC, September 2010), 7–10. Higgins reports the results of a study involving believers from "insider movements" in five different cultures. When these men of differ-ent cultures gathered to study Scripture together, they tended to focus on different details of the text despite their desire to pursue the biblical authors' meaning. While I find the insider-movements philosophy to lack biblical justification, Higgins's comments are helpful in highlighting that certain subjects are more interesting or more appealing depending on one's cultural background.

ture will recognize why people in that culture are concerned about certain details of the text rather than others.

Discern the Implication of the Biblical
Text within a New Cultural Context

A third step in the application process returns to the original author's meaning and seeks out its implications, aided by awareness of both the missionary's culture and the target culture. Implications are "those meanings in a text of which the author was unaware but nevertheless legitimately fall within the pattern of meaning he willed."[64] Thus, in view of application, an implication of a text is the author's meaning fleshed out in contemporary terms in new cultural contexts. The interpreter can begin to identify a text's present-day implications by determining what the author meant through what he wrote to his ancient audience. The interpreter should consider what the author hoped his hearers would learn from the story or instruction and what change in belief, value, or practice he championed. Sometimes the author communicates this information in the text through a stated command, and other times the change is implied.

As a student of both the biblical culture and contemporary cultures, the interpreter should be able to determine how transformations of belief, value, or practice in ancient times relate to the contemporary culture. Some of the ways that the text affects contemporary culture are clear because the command in the biblical text is binding on contemporary cultures in the same way that it was on the biblical culture. When the biblical text does not clearly advocate a specific change, though, the interpreter must consider the relationship between those practices of the biblical culture and similar ones in the contemporary culture.

Daniel Doriani explains that biblical instruction is given in seven ways: rules, ideals, doctrines, redemptive acts in narratives, exemplary acts in narratives, biblical images, and songs and prayers.[65] Furthermore, all the instruction in each of these genres capitalizes on one of four themes.

---

64. Stein, *Basic Guide to Interpreting the Bible*, 39.

65. Daniel M. Doriani, *Putting the Truth to Work: The Theory and Practice of Biblical Application* (Phillipsburg, NJ: P&R Publishing, 2001), 82.

The first is duty: what one should do. The second has to do with development of character: how to become a person who does what is right. The third concerns goals: which causes are worthy of one's devotion. A final form of instruction regards discernment: distinguishing truth from error. The interpreter should consider how each text applies to these four themes.[66]

To develop such application, Haddon Robinson proposes an "abstraction ladder."[67] In the case of heavily culturally conditioned implications of a text or commands, the interpreter cannot apply them within contemporary cultures directly. Instead one should "climb the ladder" of abstraction and consider what the command teaches about God and humanity's relationship with him in order to communicate that command to a contemporary audience. Robinson provides as an example the Old Testament law that says, "Don't boil a young goat in its mother's milk" (Exod 23:19; 34:26; Deut 14:21). Robinson suggests that if this confusing command had something to do with a now-unknown pagan worship practice, then the original effect of the command was to prohibit participating in such culture-bound customs. Thus the interpreter should abstract the command in terms of what it teaches about God's character and contemporary expectations of his people. Robinson states that the principle of this passage is, "You should not associate yourself with idolatrous worship, even in ways that do not seem to have direct association with physically going to the idol."[68]

Another helpful example is Romans 10:9, where Paul writes, "If you confess with your mouth that Jesus is Lord and believe in your heart that God raised him from the dead, you will be saved." Paul's command is clear that to be saved one must believe that Jesus was raised from the dead and must confess that Jesus is Lord. Paul says nothing in this passage, though, about the fact that belief in Jesus utterly excludes commitment to other religious systems or objects of worship.[69] While such a point was indeed

---

66. Doriani, *Putting the Truth to Work*, 98.

67. Haddon Robinson, "The Heresy of Application," *Leadership* (1997), http://www.christianitytoday.com/le/1997/fall.

68. Robinson, "Heresy of Application," section 3.

69. Paul does argue that other religious systems are false in other parts of the letter, such as Rom 1:18–3:31, where Paul's major argument is that all people are sinful and that no

an implication of Paul's teaching in this text, it is unstated. For the first-century believer, this exclusivity meant turning away from the imperial cult and the Greco-Roman system of deities. For believers today, the implication of this passage to abandon and turn away from all competing religious claims will look different across varying contexts. For the Hindu in India, it will mean forsaking all other gods. For the atheist in China, it will mean turning away from money and self. For the animist in Zimbabwe, it will mean turning away from sorcery, witchcraft, and the desire for power. For the Muslim in Iran, it will mean forsaking the Qur'an as God's word and Muhammad as God's prophet.

Determining the implication of the biblical text facilitates the text speaking into contemporary situations. Although the author was unaware of the details of future possible situations when he wrote, legitimate implications fall within the thought pattern the author recorded through the words he chose. Since the process of determining implication is difficult and is inherently subjective in nature, less mature interpreters will benefit from seeking the observations and insights of more experienced believers.

Carry Out Critical Contextualization

In order to provide a check against the natural tendency of allowing one's own cultural context to determine understanding of biblical texts, Paul Hiebert proposed a corrective he called "critical contextualization." Hiebert's proposal is less a specific hermeneutical method than it is a system for evaluating cultural traditions and practices in light of biblical revelation. Nonetheless, Hiebert's second and third steps in his critical-contextualization process are helpful at this point in discussion of applying the biblical message.

After an examination of the culture, the missionary studies the relevant Scripture passages with believers in the community.[70] At this point, the missionary takes the lead in explaining how the relevant texts relate to the cognitive, affective, and evaluative dimensions of the people's

---

system of religion can make us righteous before God. It is only by faith in Jesus Christ alone that people are saved.

70. Hiebert, "Critical Contextualization," 109–10; Hiebert, *Anthropological Reflections on Missiological Issues*, 88–89.

worldview. The next step involves developing a critical response, and it involves all of the people together evaluating one or more cultural beliefs and practices in light of the biblical text.[71] Specifically, the people question how the gospel affects those beliefs and customs.

When the people evaluate their own cultures, they can respond in several ways. One response is to leave the questioned cultural practice in place. They may judge some cultural practices to be essentially amoral; thus believers can continue to participate in those practices after choosing to follow Christ. Examples of relatively amoral cultural considerations include whether people in a specific culture prefer lamb or chicken, whether they wear suits or shorts, or whether they drive cars or ride bikes. None of the options is sinful, and in these cases, most Christians will continue to function according to preexisting cultural tendencies.

Alternately, believers may choose to reject a certain cultural practice or belief. The believers might conclude that biblical teaching directly opposes their custom and therefore that they should reject the cultural practice. An example of the principle of rejection in mission history was William Carey's encounter with the practice of sati in India, in which a widow was burned alive on her deceased husband's funeral pyre.[72] Carey confronted this practice as unbiblical and encouraged everyone, believers and unbelievers, to abandon it. Eventually the government outlawed the practice.

Yet believers may also choose to modify a traditional custom.[73] Sills explains that modification may be best in cases in which sinful and nonsinful influences define cultural norms. In some regions of the Andes, a community will come together to build a newly married couple a home, but because of incessant drinking, these times end in drunkenness and fighting. Sills writes, "A missionary encountering such a practice might immediately forbid the entire practice in an attempt to put an end to the debauchery. The problem is that the people will see a foreign religion that does not understand their people and is forcing its rules on them.

---

71. Hiebert, "Critical Contextualization," 110. The following discussion summarizes Hiebert's work found here.

72. Timothy George, *Faithful Witness: The Life and Mission of William Carey* (Birmingham: Christian History Institute, 1998), 151–52.

73. Hiebert, "Critical Contextualization," 110.

The natural response is to reject the foreigner's religion."[74] A far better approach is for the missionary to study the Scriptures with the people, with the end result that they work together to modify the practice and eliminate its sinful aspects.

Hiebert's proposal begins with cultural analysis and identification of certain cultural practices to examine. The principles of his plan, however, also work well when the text comes first, as in the case of a specific preaching or teaching setting. In that case, the meaning of the original author narrows the range of possible cultural practices in view. Involving native believers in both the discussion of the meanings behind cultural forms and the development of new practices remains helpful.

The benefit of critical contextualization is that it avoids syncretism by confronting aspects of culture that violate biblical commands.[75] When believers modify sinful practices by creating functional substitutes, they avoid the possibility of syncretistic "surface accommodation." Surface accommodation takes place when converts overlay Christian terminology and practices on existing belief systems.[76] Their outward actions and phrases have changed, but their worldview remains unaltered. Likewise, involving all believers in the critical-contextualization process creates a hermeneutical community in which believers work together to reshape their worldview in light of their newfound faith in Christ.

Paul Hiebert and Enoch Wan both note the importance of the hermeneutical community. As believers work through critical contextualization to apply the gospel to their specific context, they also have a responsibility to learn from and dialogue with other Christians from other cultures and previous times in history. One is better equipped to apply Scripture within a certain cultural context after learning how believers in various settings throughout church history have both correctly and incorrectly applied Scripture. Hiebert explains how the hermeneutical community functions: "Just as believers in a local church must test their interpretation of Scriptures with their community of believers, so the churches in different cultural and historical contexts must test their theologies with the

---

74. Sills, *Reaching and Teaching*, 208.

75. Hiebert, "Critical Contextualization," 110–11.

76. Gailyn Van Rheenen, *Communicating Christ in Animistic Contexts* (Pasadena, CA: William Carey Library, 1991), 63.

international community of churches and the church down through the ages."[77] Those within this international community help one another to determine those areas where their interpretations are more influenced by culture than by the Scriptures. Such dialogue and interaction, which Wan describes as true ethnohermeneutics, is an ongoing process as the universal church seeks to apply the eternal word in a changing world.[78]

Communicate Biblical Truth in a Culturally Appropriate Way

The final part of the application process is the communication of biblical truth in a culturally appropriate way. Each culture develops its own preferred communication patterns and learning styles. Through analysis of cultures, the missionary should seek to identify these cultural norms and employ them for communication of the biblical message.

In his theory of communication, Charles Kraft explains that communication must be receptor oriented.[79] For effective communication of a message, a communicator must take into account how the recipient will understand the words and symbols used in the message. Kraft explains, "Communicators present messages via cultural forms (symbols) that stimulate within the receptors' heads meanings that each receptor shapes into the message that he or she ultimately hears."[80] This receptor orientation does not require that the missionary change the biblical content, but it does necessitate that the communication of the message of the Bible be understandable.

The missionary should ask the question, "How is truth communicated in this culture?" Western cultures often communicate truth with lists, outlines, and reasoned arguments. In other cultures, though, the relationship between the messenger and the recipient plays a role in how the message is heard.[81] Especially in cultures such as these, missionaries

---

77. Hiebert, *Anthropological Reflections on Missiological Issues*, 103.

78. Wan, "Ethnohermeneutics."

79. Charles H. Kraft, *Christianity in Culture: A Study in Biblical Theologizing in Cross-Cultural Perspective*, rev. ed. (Maryknoll, NY: Orbis, 2005), 115–18.

80. Kraft, *Christianity in Culture*, 116.

81. M. David Sills, "The Great Commission and Intercultural Communication," in *The Challenge of the Great Commission: Essays on God's Mandate for the Local Church*, ed. Chuck Lawless and Thom S. Rainer (Crestwood, KY: Pinnacle, 2005), 79–92, esp. 89.

must consider the impact of nonverbal communication and whether their actions are building or undermining the trust of the people.[82]

Chapell explains that illustrations are a key component in helping recipients to process the biblical truths. He writes, "For a person to process information it is not enough that the information simply be presented. The information must be integrated into the matrix of preexisting stimuli, memory features, and operative procedures that characterize the 'receiver.' "[83] Illustrating the key truths of the passage in cultural terms brings the gospel to life and makes it understandable.[84] The Bible presents several models for using illustrations to communicate in culturally relevant terms. Old Testament prophets occasionally acted out their messages (Isa 20:3–4; Ezek 4:1–4; Zech 11:4–17). Jesus used parables to illustrate the truths he was teaching. Likewise, Paul used cultural statements and beliefs to connect with his audiences (Acts 17:23; Titus 1:12).

The missionary needs to exercise caution at this point to ensure understanding of the meaning behind the cultural forms employed to illustrate biblical truth. Again, it is imperative that the missionary avoid laying the foundation for syncretistic tendencies, such that the interpreter will subsume the biblical story under a familiar cultural one. The missionary needs to solicit the help of cultural informants who can aid in understanding the insider's perspective of myths, stories, and practices before communicating the truths of the gospel. The missionary also must be clear in distinguishing between cultural belief and biblical truth when they oppose each other.

CONCLUSION

This chapter has shown that the author-oriented approach of biblical interpretation is the approach that is best suited to the evangelical worldview, for the grammatical-historical method is the best method for determining biblical authors' meaning. Grammatical-historical interpretation also facilitates application of that meaning to the contemporary context.

---

82. Grunlan and Mayers, *Cultural Anthropology*, 59; Sills, "Great Commission and Intercultural Communication," 86.

83. Bryan Chapell, *Using Illustrations to Preach with Power*, rev. ed. (Wheaton, IL: Crossway, 2001), 52.

84. Chapell, *Using Illustrations to Preach with Power*, 59.

Although the process of interpretation and application can be difficult in places where there are few resources or there are only oral learners, it is by no means impossible. Grammatical-historical interpretation enables believers in any culture to apply the authoritative teaching of the Bible in ways that are suitable to their specific contexts.

10

BIBLICAL THEOLOGY FOR ORAL CULTURES IN WORLD MISSION

Jackson W.

INTRODUCTION

What difference does biblical theology make among oral peoples? By "oral peoples," I refer to those for whom orality is their only or preferred means of communication. Therefore, this question not only concerns nonliterate tribes but also countless educated Westerners who hardly read except by necessity. The latter prioritize movies, television, music, and social media over books and newspapers. In fact, marketers, neurologists, social scientists, and even game designers in recent years have increasingly highlighted the power of stories and visual media to influence the human mind.

At the intersection of biblical theology and orality, we find story or "narrative." Broadly defined, a narrative is any genre that conveys a story. It represents a sequence of interrelated events or states forming a plot that conveys at least some meaningful ideas.[1] Narrative is the most common genre in the Bible. Typically, these narratives present an account of God and his people within some historical and cultural context. For simplicity, I will interchange "narrative" and "story" throughout this chapter.

In recent decades, narrative has played a prominent role in biblical studies. Proponents of narrative theology seek to counterbalance the

---

1. Monika Fludernik, *An Introduction to Narratology* (New York: Routledge, 2009), 159–61; David Rudrum, "From Narrative Representation to Narrative Use," *Narrative* 13 (May 2005): 195–204; Mark Allan Powell, *What Is Narrative Criticism?* (Minneapolis: Fortress, 1991), 23.

traditional emphasis on systematic or dogmatic theology.[2] Narrative criticism has emerged as an approach to interpreting Scripture in a way that treats the Bible like other forms of literature.[3] Richard Hays suggests, "The framework of Paul's thought is constituted neither by a system of doctrines nor by his personal religious experience but by a 'sacred story,' a narrative structure.' "[4] Hays's work has highlighted the importance of intertextuality and catalyzed rethinking of interpretative methodology. Among biblical scholars, major debates concern the influence of narrative on biblical theology. For example, volumes are written about role and shape of narrative within Paul's letters.[5] Much of N. T. Wright's Pauline theology stems from the conviction that Paul draws from an implicit metanarrative or worldview story that permeates the span of Scripture.[6]

Narrative (or story) is a fundamental aspect of our worldview.[7] One reason, as Paul Ricoeur argues, is that history has a "narrative character" about it.[8] Thus our view of the world is entwined with story, each influencing the other. As we attempt to discern meaning from our experience, our perspective will have a story-like quality. Inasmuch as biblical writers speak of God's work in history, so biblical theology takes on a narrative shape.[9]

---

2. Gabriel Fackre, "Narrative Theology: An Overview," *Interpretation* 48 (1983): 340–52.

3. See Powell, *What Is Narrative Criticism?*

4. Richard B. Hays, *The Faith of Jesus Christ: The Narrative Substructure of Galatians 3:1–4:11*, 2nd ed. (Grand Rapids: Eerdmans, 2002), 6.

5. See for example Bruce W. Longenecker, ed., *Narrative Dynamics in Paul: A Critical Assessment* (Louisville: Westminster John Knox, 2002).

6. N. T. Wright, *Paul and the Faithfulness of God* (Minneapolis: Fortress, 2013), 456–537. A recent response to Wright's proposal is found in Joel R. White, "N. T. Wright's Narrative Approach," in *God and the Faithfulness of Paul*, ed. Christoph Heilig, Michael Bird, and J. Thomas Hewitt (Minneapolis: Fortress, 2017), 181–206.

7. See N. T. Wright, *The New Testament and the People of God*, Christian Origins and the Question of God 1 (Atlanta: Augsburg Fortress, 1992), 38–44.

8. Paul Ricoeur, *Time and Narrative*, trans. Kathleen McLaughlin and David Pellauer (Chicago: University of Chicago Press, 1990), 1:91. See also Kevin J. Vanhoozer, *Biblical Narrative in the Philosophy of Paul Ricoeur: A Study in Hermeneutics and Theology* (Cambridge: Cambridge University Press, 2007), 90–96; Stephen Crites, "The Narrative Quality of Experience," *Journal of the American Academy of Religion* 39 (1971): 291–311.

9. The point is sharpened when we account for ways the Bible's canonical form influences interpretation. Wright adds, "Indeed, until the narrative element has been recognized it is open to doubt whether one has yet fully understood what 'worldview' (in the sense I and others use the term) is all about. . . . Paul's worldview had a strongly implicit and frequently explicit narrative. Or rather, like most mature narratives, Paul's worldview had a

The Bible's historical character equips the church in practical ways. Biblical theology is better suited than other forms of theology to make disciples because it engages people at a worldview level. The story of the Bible claims authority over the various personal and social narratives that influence us daily. For N. T. Wright,

> The goal of Paul's theologizing was not to delineate belief systems but to bring about a transformation in the mindset of the believers in the communities of Christ followers he founded. Paul, in other words, wanted to effect what Richard Hays calls a "conversion of the imagination" in the minds of his hearers/readers that would, in turn, revolutionize their social interactions.[10]

Naturally, many authors note the importance of narrative for shaping Christian ethics.[11]

Therefore, this chapter explores how the church might apply biblical theology within oral cultures (and subcultures). Specifically, I will consider ways a biblical "grand narrative" can practically influence the church's ministry across a variety of contexts. Not everyone agrees the Bible has an overarching narrative (rather than simply being a set of collected stories). Nor do all agree about how to discern such a story. Accordingly, the first section suggests such a process. The second section then outlines a broad framework for understanding the grand biblical narrative. Finally, the third section demonstrates the significance of these findings for ministering among oral peoples.

---

set of underlying stories whose tendency to interlock and overlap is not a weakness, but rather a sign that, as with a good novel or play, the subplots and secondary narratives not only illustrate but also materially effect key moments and key transitions in the main plot." N. T. Wright, *Paul and the Faithfulness of God*, Christian Origins and the Question of God 4 (Minneapolis: Fortress, 2013), 456, 461.

10. Summary by Joel White in "N. T. Wright's Narrative Approach," 184. White cites Richard B. Hays, "The Conversion of the Imagination: Scripture and Eschatology in 1 Corinthians," *NTS* 45 (1999): 391–412.

11. See Graham Ward, "Narratives and Ethics: The Structures of Believing and the Practices of Hope," *Literature and Theology: An International Journal of Religion, Theory and Culture* 20 (2006): 438–61; John Navone, "Narrative Theology and Its Uses: A Survey," *Irish Theological Quarterly* 52 (1986): 212–30; N. T. Wright, *Scripture and the Authority of God: How to Read the Bible Today* (New York: HarperOne, 2013); Stanley Hauerwas and L. Gregory Jones, eds., *Why Narrative?: Readings in Narrative Theology* (Eugene, OR: Wipf & Stock, 1997). Crites even argues, "Ethical authority . . . is always a function of a common narrative coherence of life." See Crites, "Narrative Quality of Experience," 310.

ONE STORY TO RULE THEM ALL?

Many scholars acknowledge that the Bible has some sort of overarching story. To varying degrees, theologians throughout history have taken a narrative approach to the Bible.[12] However, contemporary writers have made a rigorous effort to identify more precisely the content of the biblical metanarrative, the authoritative "controlling story" of Scripture.[13]

Much debate focuses on Paul's letters, which do not explicitly use a narrative genre.[14] Even where writers disagree about details, one finds common ground. For example, Morna Hooker states,

> If . . . "narrative approach" means simply the recognition that behind Paul's theological arguments there is a fundamental belief in God's purpose for the world, and that this is inevitably expressed in the form of narrative, then that recognition can, indeed, act as "a necessary exegetical control." . . . Since Paul's theology is concerned with God's activity through history, it is clear that his interpreters should not ignore the role of "narrative."[15]

Similarly, David Horrell says Paul's theology

> has a narrative character; it is not simply a galaxy of symbols and beliefs, arranged in an overarching sky, but rather a story with some sense of temporal extension and direction. Paul's texts are not, of course, narrative in form. . . . Nonetheless, it can be shown

---

12. Craig Bartholomew and Michael Goheen list examples such as Irenaeus, John Calvin, Herman Ridderbos, and James Barr. See Craig Bartholomew and Michael Goheen, "Story and Biblical Theology," in *Out of Egypt: Biblical Theology and Biblical Interpretation*, ed. Craig Bartholomew et al., Scripture and Hermeneutics Series 5 (Grand Rapids: Zondervan, 2006), 144–71.

13. Wright, *New Testament and the People of God*, 42.

14. For scholarly perspectives on the matter, see Longenecker, *Narrative Dynamics in Paul*. Numerous people contend Paul relies on an underlying narrative, such as Richard Hays, *Echoes of Scripture in the Letters of Paul* (New Haven, CT: Yale University Press, 1989); W. A. Beardslee, "Narrative Form in the NT and Process Theology," *Encounter* 36 (1975): 301–15; Ben Witherington, *Paul's Narrative Thought World: The Tapestry of Tragedy and Triumph* (Louisville: Westminster John Knox, 1994); N. T. Wright, "Israel's Scriptures in Paul's Narrative Theology," *Theology* 115 (2012): 323–29.

15. Morna Hooker, " 'Heirs of Abraham': The Gentiles' Role in Israel's Story," in Longenecker, *Narrative Dynamics in Paul*, 85–96, esp. 96. The italics are original and refer to Bruce Longenecker's phrase in his "Sharing in Their Spiritual Blessings? The Stories of Israel in Galatians and Romans," in Longenecker, *Narrative Dynamics in Paul*, 58–84, esp. 83.

that a narrative underpins Paul's "theologizing": the story of God's saving act in Jesus Christ.[16]

Francis Watson is quite critical of efforts to reconstruct a scriptural metanarrative beneath Paul's theology, yet even he says Paul's "gospel must be correlated with 'the story of God and creation' and 'the story of Israel.' "[17]

If an overarching story exists, what method might we use to identify the framework for a grand biblical narrative? What passages mark the deeper structure underlying the Bible's story?[18] We first consider the nature of narrative before examining the biblical text.

FINDING THE
BIBLICAL FRAMEWORK

Inherent in any historical narration is what Paul Ricoeur calls "emplotment." According to Ricoeur, "Emplotment brings together factors as heterogeneous as agents, goals, means, interactions, circumstances, unexpected results."[19] Its purpose is "to draw an intelligible story *from* a variety of events or incidents or, reciprocally, in order to make these events or incidents *into* a story."[20] In this way, writers and storytellers use rhetorical strategies to present narratives, which presuppose some historical reality.[21] Accordingly, structure is both *inherent* within and *imposed* on a story.

---

16. David G. Horrell, *Solidarity and Difference: A Contemporary Reading of Paul's Ethics*, 2nd ed. (New York: T&T Clark, 2016), 93.

17. Francis Watson, "Is There a Story in These Texts?," in Longenecker, *Narrative Dynamics in Paul*, 231–39, esp. 234.

18. Brueggemann states, "The Old Testament is not a metanarrative but offers the materials out of which a metanarrative may be construed," in Walter Brueggemann, *Theology of the Old Testament: Testimony, Dispute, Advocacy* (Minneapolis: Fortress, 1997), 559. However, regarding the Old Testament as metanarrative could be justified either from a canonical perspective (and so interpreting the text as we now have it) or from the view of the divine author, whose mission in history is told across multiple subnarratives.

19. Ricoeur, *Time and Narrative*, 1:65.

20. Ricoeur, "Toward a Narrative Theology: Its Necessity, Its Resources, Its Difficulties," in *Figuring the Sacred: Religion, Narrative, and Imagination*, ed. Mark Wallace (Minneapolis: Fortress, 1995), 236–48, esp. 239, italics original. For characteristics of emplotments, see Anna Borisenkova, "Narrative Reconfiguration of Social Events: Paul Ricoeur's Contribution to Rethinking the Social," *Ricoeur Studies* 1 (2010): 87–98, esp. 94.

21. I say "some reality" since narratives, whether fiction or nonfiction, suppose a time-and-space world governed by certain norms, whether cultural or physical. In stories such

This observation leads scholars to distinguish two key aspects of narrative—chronological sequence and creative sequence.[22] The former is the linear "story line" or logical ordering of events.[23] It is a story's "deep structure" or the "large-scale narrative content."[24] The "creative sequence" refers to "a series of motifs . . . whose order is determined by the choices of the author from an indeterminate number of possibilities."[25] One creatively emplots events in order to establish or emphasize key ideas and themes.[26]

Identifying these two sequences enables us to discern the Bible's grand narrative. Wright claims that a writer's "implicit worldview" is found by noting the chronological (or "referential") sequence.[27] However, Joel White suggests a more rigorous approach "to draw out evidence of a common metanarrative behind" a variety of texts. He says,

---

as *Star Wars* and *Harry Potter*, "reality" includes characters who have extraordinary powers (compared to our own).

22. Writers sometimes use different terminology. Wendland distinguishes narrative and plot. See Ernst Wendland, " 'You Will Do Even More than I Say': On the Rhetorical Function of Stylistic Form in the Letter to Philemon," in *Philemon in Perspective: Interpreting a Pauline Letter*, ed. D. Francois Tolmie (Berlin: de Gruyter, 2010), 79–111, esp. 84. Petersen separates "referential sequence" from "poetic sequence." See Norman Petersen, *Rediscovering Paul: Philemon and the Sociology of Paul's Narrative World*, 2nd ed. (Eugene, OR; Wipf & Stock, 2008), 48–52, 65–81. Via and Polak appropriate terms from Russian formalist narratology: *fabula* for "narrative" or "chronological sequence," and *syuzhet* for "plot" or "creative sequence." Dan O. Via, *The Ethics of Mark's Gospel: In the Middle of Time* (Eugene, OR: Wipf & Stock, 2005), 41; Frank Polak, "Oral Substratum, Language Usage, and Thematic Flow in the Abraham-Jacob Narrative," in *Contextualizing Israel's Sacred Writing: Ancient Literacy, Orality, and Literary Production*, ed. Brian Schmidt (Atlanta: SBL Press, 2015), 217–38, esp. 218.

23. See Chris Baldick, "Fabula," in *The Oxford Dictionary of Literary Terms*, 2nd ed. (Oxford: Oxford University Press, 2001), 93; Viktor Shklovsky, *Theory of Prose*, trans. Benjamin Sher (Normal, IL; Dalkey Archive, 1998), 170.

24. Via, *Ethics of Mark's Gospel*, 41; Polak, "Oral Substratum," 218.

25. Via, *Ethics of Mark's Gospel*, 41.

26. Ricoeur helpfully summarizes, "Any narrative combines, in varying proportions, two dimensions: a chronological dimension and a non-chronological dimension. The first may be called the 'episodic dimension' of the narrative. . . . But the activity of narrating does not consist simply in adding episodes to one another; it also constructs meaningful totalities out of scattered events. . . . The art of narrating, as well as the corresponding art of following a story, therefore require that we are able *to extract a configuration from a succession.* This 'configurational' operation . . . constitutes the second dimension of narrative activity." See Paul Ricoeur, *Hermeneutics and the Human Sciences*, ed. and trans. John B. Thompson (Cambridge: Cambridge University Press, 1981), 278.

27. N. T. Wright, *Paul and the Faithfulness of God*, 463. He draws from Norman Petersen, *Rediscovering Paul*, who is frequently cited by contributors in Longenecker, *Narrative Dynamics in Paul*.

If these texts have similar poetic [creative] sequences that refer, whether explicitly or implicitly, to the same aspects of the OT narrative, that would seem to constitute evidence of a "grand story," about which they are in agreement. If on the other hand, their poetic sequences differ from one another greatly, with major strands of OT tradition popping up in wildly different places for very different text-pragmatic reasons, then it would seem more likely that they are using the OT narrative for essentially illustrative purposes.[28]

This approach helpfully provides objective boundaries for seeking an underlying story spanning the biblical canon.

What is needed now is a compilation of ancient texts that summarize the biblical grand narrative. Many scholars have suggested passages that seem to serve as summaries within the Bible itself. Hood and Emerson's study likely provides the most comprehensive synthesis of such lists to date.[29] They include summaries of Israel's story as found in the Old Testament, early Jewish writings, the New Testament, and early Christian works. We can complement their research by surveying the work of others.[30]

An exhaustive list will not be duplicated here. Instead, I will highlight a small sample of significant biblical passages.

- Old Testament
  - Deuteronomy 26:5–9
  - Joshua 23–24
  - 1 Samuel 12
  - 1 Kings 8 (also 2 Chr 5:2–6:11)
  - 2 Kings 17
  - Nehemiah 9

---

28. White, "N. T. Wright's Narrative Approach," 191. He notes Barclay's basic agreement in John Barclay, " 'Paul's Story' in Paul's Story: Theology as Testimony," in Longenecker, *Narrative Dynamics in Paul*, 133–56, esp. 155.

29. Jason B. Hood and Matthew Y. Emerson, "Summaries of Israel's Story: Reviewing a Compositional Category," *CBR* 11 (2013): 328–48.

30. Two noteworthy essays not cited by Hood and Emerson include Richard Bauckham, "Reading Scripture as a Coherent Story," in *The Art of Reading Scripture*, ed. Ellen F. Davis and Richard B. Hays (Grand Rapids: Eerdmans, 2003), 38–53, esp. 41; Paul House, "Examining the Narratives of the Old Testament," *WTJ* 67 (2005): 229–45, esp. 231. While these authors largely overlap with one another, Bauckham and House each add texts to Hood and Emerson's list.

- • Psalms 78; 105–6; 135–36
  - • Ezekiel 16; 20; 23
  - • Daniel 9
- • New Testament
  - • Matthew 1:1–17
  - • Acts 7; 13
  - • Romans 9–11
  - • Hebrews 11

In these and other texts, we find substantial alignment between the chronological and creative sequences. The following outline traces the major stages within the grand narrative. Naturally, overlap increases as one moves forward historically through the canon since later texts recapitulate previous texts. The New Testament rehearses this broad narrative and culminates with Christ.

Grand Narrative

- • Creation

- • Abraham

- • Israel
  - • Exodus[31]
  - • Canaan[32]
  - • Monarchy[33]
  - • Exile[34]
  - • Restoration[35]

- • Christ

---

31. "Exodus" refers to a range of events, including Israel's deliverance from Egypt, receiving the law at Sinai, and wandering in the wilderness.

32. "Canaan" encompasses the events from Joshua's leading Israel to settle in the promised land through the period of the judges. Various accounts intertwine the exodus with the settlement of Canaan.

33. Especially noteworthy are God's covenant with David, the building of the temple, and increased idolatry in Israel.

34. "Exile" includes the deportations of the northern and southern tribes.

35. "Restoration" perhaps could be conjoined with "exile." Various promises related to restoration from exile include Spirit (law within hearts), land, David, temple (see Jer 31; 33; Ezek 36–37).

Readers should recall that we are primarily concerned with the *sequence* of the many presentations. The precise content varies in certain texts; however, one consistently finds major areas of agreement, such as the reemphasis on God's promises to Abraham, the exodus, and so forth. The main transition points largely refer to the same aspects of the Old Testament narrative.

Two final comments clarify the above picture. First, ancient writers reiterate a common subplot whereby God shows kindness to Israel, who then rebels against God their king. Nevertheless, he shows steadfast love for his people despite their sin. Second, we see clues in the New Testament concerning how this narrative will be completed (although naturally, we cannot expect to find summaries about events that had not yet happened at the time of the New Testament writers). Specifically, we could postulate two final stages, which I will call "church" and "consummation." The former refers to the ingathering of God's people from the nations. The latter designation is meant to be general; it merely refers to all that is brought to completion with the final return of Christ (such as new creation and reconciliation).

A SUPPORTIVE SUBSTRUCTURE?

We have identified the macrolevel of the narrative; we now consider whether the Bible has a supportive substructure. In other words, if the above explanation is correct, we expect to find various strands of confirmation. An exhaustive treatment would require a lengthy essay or book. For now, I will simply note five types of rhetorical, theological, and historical evidence.

A story plot is bound together in part by various small-scale patterns, such as repeated wording.[36] These connections are most evident in the first two types of confirmation: *intertextuality* and *theological themes*.

INTERTEXTUALITY

Biblical writers frequently quote or allude to other passages of Scripture to establish or support an idea. Later Old Testament books use earlier

---

36. Polak describes these small-scale patterns as "microtext," the third level of narrative, which is interconnected with the "macrotext" (chronological sequence) and "plot" (creative sequence). See Polak, "Oral Substratum," 218.

texts, such as when Isaiah employs the exodus narrative.[37] Also, countless scholars have explored Paul's strategic use of the Old Testament.[38] People debate whether certain Pauline passages allude to the Old Testament; however, there is general agreement concerning his explicit quotations.[39] Not surprisingly, Paul routinely highlights passages related to the Old Testament events listed in the above outline. Thus, Paul famously appeals to Abraham in Romans and Galatians. His quotations draw extensively from prophetic texts concerning the exile (see, e.g., Rom 9–11).

Even where Paul and others do not explicitly quote the Old Testament, its influence is evident. Accordingly, the exodus unmistakably shapes the structure and argument of many Pauline texts (see 1 Cor 10:1–11; Rom 5–8).[40] Similarly, the Old Testament frames the four Gospels such that Jesus is variously presented as another Moses and Adam. In fact, some contend that Jesus' life effectively embodies or reenacts Israel's story.[41] In short, the interweaving of biblical texts reinforces the key emphases noted above.

THEOLOGICAL THEMES

Many theological motifs recur throughout the Bible. These themes depend on the major movements inherent in the biblical metanarrative.

---

37. See Bernhard W. Anderson, "Exodus Typology in Second Isaiah," in *Israel's Prophetic Heritage: Essays in Honor of James Muilenburg*, ed. Bernhard W. Anderson and Walter Harrelson (New York: Harper & Brothers, 1962), 177–95. Note a further stage of biblical reuse of these Isaianic writings in Rikki E. Watts, *Isaiah's New Exodus in Mark*, WUNT 88 (Tübingen: Mohr Siebeck, 1997).

38. See Hays, *Echoes of Scripture in the Letters of Paul*; and Stanley E. Porter and Christopher Stanley, eds., *As It Is Written: Studying Paul's Use of Scripture* (Atlanta: SBL Press, 2008).

39. A representative list can be found in E. Earle Ellis, *Paul's Use of the Old Testament* (Grand Rapids: Baker, 1981), 151–53. Regarding the task of identifying quotations, allusions, and echoes, see Stanley E. Porter, "Allusions and Echoes," in Porter and Stanley, *As It Is Written*, 29–40; Stanley E. Porter, "The Use of the Old Testament in the New Testament: A Brief Comment on Method and Terminology," in *Early Christian Interpretation of the Scriptures of Israel*, ed. C. A. Evans and J. A. Sanders (Sheffield, UK: Sheffield Academic, 1997), 79–96.

40. See Daniel Lynwood Smith, "The Use of 'New Exodus' in New Testament Scholarship: Preparing a Way through the Wilderness," *CBR* 14 (2016): 207–43. On Rom 5–8, see N. T. Wright, "The New Inheritance according to Paul," *Bible Review* 14, no. 3 (1998): 16, 47; N. T. Wright, "New Exodus, New Inheritance: The Narrative Substructure of Romans 3–8," in *Romans and the People of God: Essays in Honor of Gordon D. Fee on the Occasion of His 65th Birthday*, ed. Sven K. Soderlund and N. T. Wright (Grand Rapids: Eerdmans, 1999), 26–35.

41. See Richard B. Hays, *Echoes of Scripture in the Gospels* (Waco, TX; Baylor University Press, 2016).

For instance, the temple or sanctuary is a reoccurring image that spans from Genesis to Revelation. It is also a significant thematic device in John's Gospel. Redemption, particularly common in Pauline literature, is rooted in the exodus. Furthermore, the titles "Christ" and "Son of God" recall God's covenant with David.[42]

CANONICAL STRUCTURE

If the metanarrative outlined above is accurate, we would not be surprised to find suggestive clues built into the structure of the canon. In fact, as Jason Hood and Matthew Emerson write, "The canonical shape of the Psalter, Chronicles, and other canonical indicators reveals an interest in summaries of Israel's story."[43] The shape of the canon can indicate the theology of early compilers and perhaps ways we should interpret the Old Testament.[44] For example, Hendrik Koorevaar argues, "The subject of exile and return is present very strongly, both in *all seams within* the canon, and also *at the beginning* and *at the end* of the canon."[45] Subsections within the larger canon story arc feature significant figures and events, such as Adam-Moses (Genesis–Deuteronomy) and Joshua-Jehoiachin (Joshua–Kings) as well as Adam-Cyrus (both within Chronicles and spanning Genesis–Chronicles).[46]

---

42. See 2 Sam 7:13–14; John 1:49; Rom 1:1–4, among other texts.

43. Hood and Emerson, "Summaries of Israel's Story," 344. See also Jason B. Hood, *The Messiah, His Brothers, and the Nations: Matthew 1.1–17* (New York: Bloomsbury, 2011), 39, 42, 48–56.

44. See Stephen G. Dempster, *Dominion and Dynasty: A Theology of the Hebrew Bible*, NSBT 15 (Downers Grove, IL: InterVarsity Press, 2006); Matthew Y. Emerson, *Christ and the New Creation: A Canonical Approach to the Theology of the New Testament* (Eugene, OR: Wipf & Stock, 2013).

45. Hendrik Koorevaar, "The Exile and Return Model: A Proposal for the Original Macrostructure of the Hebrew Canon," *JETS* 57 (2014): 501–12, esp. 510. In contrast, see Greg Goswell, "The Order of the Books of the Hebrew Bible," *JETS* 51 (2008): 673–88; Goswell, "Two Testaments in Parallel: The Influence of the Old Testament on the Structuring of the New Testament Canon," *JETS* 56 (2013): 459–74.

46. Koorevaar, "Exile and Return Model," 507–8. Since Chronicles concludes the Hebrew canon, its internal reference to Adam-Cyrus reflects the macrostructure of the entire Old Testament canon. Another potentially fruitful approach includes John Goldingay, "Middle Narratives as an Aspect of Biblical Theology," in *Biblical Theology: Past, Present, and Future*, ed. Carey Walsh and Mark Elliot (Eugene, OR: Cascade, 2016), 203–13. Goldingay appeals to "middle narratives," which refer to units of narrative text that conjoin many small stories but subdivide the metanarrative. In this way, middle narratives aid memory and organize the grand story. He identifies the first middle narrative as Genesis to Kings, which focuses

EXPLICIT GOSPEL STATEMENTS

From a New Testament perspective, the above metanarrative, if correct, should influence how the biblical writers discuss the gospel. In recent years, many have debated the precise scope of the gospel. For the present purpose, we simply consider passages that explicitly use the verb or noun for "gospel," whether in Hebrew or Greek.[47] Three major themes consistently emerge in explicit "gospel" passages: creation, covenant, and kingdom.[48] Interestingly, these three themes also appear in Wright's proposal concerning Paul's implicit metanarrative.

> We must ask: what are Paul's sub-plots, and how do they relate to the main, overarching plot itself? . . . The first sub-plot, I suggest, is the story of the human creatures through whom the creator intended to bring order to his world. Their failure, and the creator's determination to put that failure right and so get the original plan back on track, demands a second sub-plot, which is the story of Israel as the people called to be the light of the world. This is the level of plot at which the Mosaic law plays out its various roles. . . . Then, because of Israel's own failure, we find the third and final sub-plot, which is the story of Jesus, Israel's crucified and risen Messiah. His work, at the centre of Paul's narrative world, resolves the other sub-plots, and provides a glimpse, as we have just seen, of the resolution for the main plot itself, the creator's purpose for the whole cosmos.[49]

That many scholars affirm the importance of these three plot movements at least suggests that we currently are on the right track. Not surprisingly, creation, covenant, and kingdom shape the contours of the grand narrative sketched above.

---

on "four key figures, Abraham (who can stand for the ancestors in general), Moses, Joshua, and David" (205).

47. That is to say, the verbal root בשׂר and εὐαγγέλιον/εὐαγγελίζω. While a biblical understanding of the gospel cannot be limited to such passages, any correct view of the gospel must at least cohere with explicit references to the gospel.

48. Jackson Wu, *One Gospel for All Nations: A Practical Approach to Biblical Contextualization* (Pasadena, CA: William Carey Library, 2015), 40–46.

49. Wright, *Paul and the Faithfulness of God*, 484–85.

CULTURAL PRACTICES

Finally, we expect that ancient Israel's cultural practices and traditions are often centered on the main points of scriptural metanarrative. After all, social rituals and festivals are tools to reenact and reinforce foundational cultural narratives. In the Old Testament, such practices include keeping the weekly Sabbath, circumcision, and celebrating the Passover. Similarly, the church in the New Testament commemorates Christ's death and resurrection through the Lord's Supper and baptism.

A FEW IMPLICATIONS
AND QUESTIONS

Before turning to a few applications, we should consider a few implications of the biblical grand narrative highlighted above. It is commonplace for people to summarize the biblical metanarrative in four parts: creation, fall, redemption, consummation. In what it affirms, this outline is not mistaken. Practically, however, this sketch of the grand narrative hardly resembles the overarching story suggested by the Bible itself. Such summaries largely skip over the vast majority of the Old Testament, perhaps referencing Israel in passing.[50] Effectively, they "skip from Genesis 3 to Romans 3."[51] This conventional rendering of the grand narrative seems to be a contemporary adaption from systematic theology.[52]

---

50. For examples, see Mark Dever, "God's Plan of Salvation," in *ESV Study Bible* (Wheaton: Crossway, 2008) 2501-3; "The Story," https://thestoryfilm.com (accessed January 23, 2018), which is explained further in George Robinson, "The Gospel as Story and Evangelism as Story Telling," in *Theology and Practice of Mission: God, the Church, and the Nations*, ed. Bruce Ashford (Nashville: Broadman & Holman, 2011), 76-91; Greg Gilbert, *What Is the Gospel?* (Wheaton: Crossway, 2010); Matt Chandler, *The Explicit Gospel* (Wheaton: Crossway, 2012); J. B. Snodgrass, "Mission to Hindus," in *Theology and Practice of Mission: God, the Church, and the Nations*, ed. Bruce Ashford (Nashville: Broadman & Holman, 2011), 238-51. Israel's story is summarized with two pages in Trevin Wax, *Counterfeit Gospels: Rediscovering the Good News in a World of False Hope* (Nashville: Broadman & Holman, 2011).

51. Scot McKnight uses this phrase frequently, including in Ben Witherington, "Dialogue with Scot McKnight on 'King Jesus': Part One," The Bible and Culture (blog), September 10, 2011, patheos.com/blogs/bibleandculture/2011/09/10/dialogue-with-scot-mcknight-on-king-jesus-part-one-2/.

52. Bouteneff notes, "Reading the Pentateuch (or even the whole Bible) as a linear account of 'creation-fall-redemption,' [is] a reading difficult to trace before the eighteenth-century notion of *Heilsgeschichte* but one that captured much modern theological and popular imagination." Peter Bouteneff, *Beginnings: Ancient Christian Readings of the Biblical Creation Narratives* (Grand Rapids: Baker, 2008), 8.

Someone might object that Christians today ought to give more emphasis to the New Testament as the culmination of the Old Testament. I offer a few replies. First, even if one thinks truncated gospel summaries are strategically helpful for evangelism, that fact does not warrant representing them as the Bible's grand narrative, as though they reflect the story outline seen throughout the Bible (as well as in Second Temple Judaism and the early church).

Second, the New Testament writers demonstrably rely on a grand narrative derived from the whole of the Old Testament. Therefore, if people want to convey New Testament teaching in a way representative of the biblical authors' meaning, then they must account for the larger narrative that spans all the Old Testament (and not simply Gen 1–3).

Third, we risk creating a de facto "canon within a canon" by reinforcing an alternative grand narrative that outlines key systematic doctrines that rely on a narrow set of texts. Anyone who respects Paul's understanding of the gospel must account for passages such as Galatians 3:8, where Paul *equates* the Abrahamic covenant with the gospel. Paul states, "the Scripture, foreseeing that God would justify the Gentiles by faith, preached the gospel beforehand to Abraham, saying, 'In you shall all the nations be blessed.' " According to typical explanations of the gospel, Galatians 3:8 is incomprehensible, since the Abrahamic covenant is normally regarded as *background* to the gospel, not the gospel itself.

Fourth, we are left to ponder what subtle assumptions are imported into biblical teaching when we reframe the grand narrative in this way. By not allowing the Bible's own metanarrative to shape our gospel explanations, might one unwittingly minimize major aspects of God's revelation? Do people prioritize efficiency above all else? Might one settle for what is merely true while compromising the essence of biblical teaching?[53]

ISRAEL'S STORY AMONG GENTILES

In theory, most Christians agree the Bible should shape the church's teaching and practice. Even if some practices are specific to their original context, many can at least agree that patterns of behavior should be followed. Since ancient writers consistently use the narrative framework

---

53. For further explanation, see Wu, *One Gospel for All Nations*, 17–28.

outlined above, we naturally infer it should also serve as a model for contemporary ministry. In this section, I will answer two concerns and in the process suggest a few points of application.

First, whenever people hear me stress the importance of teaching Israel's story as a major part of the biblical grand narrative, they often raise similar objections.[54] In some form, I am asked this question: "The people in the Bible were already familiar with Israel's history, so why do I need to reiterate it for contemporary gentiles who are not familiar with this Jewish background?"

From an evangelical perspective, this question seems to cast God's wisdom in doubt since it contests the contemporary relevance of God's self-revelation in history. That is to say, since God in the Old Testament reveals himself in particular cultures, times, and places, Christians need not prioritize the Old Testament's teaching. This line of thinking could quickly veer into functional Marcionism in its consigning the Old Testament to irrelevance.

In contrast, evangelicals confess that the Old Testament is God's revelation. It records how God enters human history and into the concrete circumstances of life. This is precisely what makes the Old Testament relevant to every age and culture. Otherwise, one begins to present abstractly, as though God were distant from the world or were merely a philosophical idea.

Instead, the church should follow the biblical pattern in teaching Israel's story simply because it is the inherent story of the Bible. By adjusting or ignoring it, we subtly begin to turn away from the biblical text and allow (sub)cultural influences to frame our presentation. However, the church has no other overarching story than the one found in the Bible.

Other reasons encourage us to emphasize Israel's role in the biblical metanarrative. Doing so equips readers to interpret the Bible properly in context. Not only does Israel's history give us exegetical boundaries, but the Bible's natural organization simplifies the task of interpretation. One is not forced to speculate how to harmonize doctrines that emerge when philosophical suppositions are forced onto the text. The inherent

---

54. I do not subsume Israel within the broad category "redemption," per conventional summaries.

structure and content of the Bible—which includes Israel's story—help people internalize and understand its message. Paul's letters demonstrate how he prioritized teaching Israel's story even among gentiles. In addition to Romans and Galatians, passages such as 1 Corinthians 10:1–10 show that Paul presumes that his readers have significant knowledge of the Old Testament.

CRAFTING THE BIBLICAL STORY

We now turn to a second question. How do we apply these insights? First, missionaries who work in oral contexts would be wise to reconsider their approach to storytelling. On the one hand, the biblical grand narrative should influence how people craft evangelistic stories. For example, tools such as C2C (Creation to Christ) are designed to introduce the overarching story of the Bible. However, it largely skips from the garden of Eden to Christ. Also, it seems to use biblical stories to support underlying soteriological doctrines rather than vice versa.[55]

In addition, some missionaries need to reevaluate the story sets used to evangelize and teach. Some of the most popular strategies include Chronological Bible Teaching (CBT), Chronological Bible Storying (CBS), and Simply the Story (STS).[56] Depending on the tool, complete story sets often consist of thirty to sixty stories. These sets aim to cover the entire Bible and can require a year or more of study.

How do these story sets compare to the overall narrative seen in the Bible?[57] Consider a forty-two-story set used by Story Runners, which claims to "provide a panoramic overview, from Creation to the Return

---

55. For additional critiques of C2C, see Jackson Wu, "Critiquing Creation to Christ (C2C)," Jackson Wu, April 11, 2013, www.patheos.com/blogs/jacksonwu/2013/04/11/critiquing-creation-to-christ-c2c/; Wu, "Taking the Context Out of the Bible?," April 9, 2013, http://www.patheos.com/blogs/jacksonwu/2013/04/09/taking-the-context-out-of-the-bible-contextualization-among-oral-peoples-series/.

56. For a historical survey of similar methodologies, see Tom Steffen, "Chronological Communication of the Gospel Goes from Country to City" (paper presented at the Evangelical Missiological Society, Southwest Region meeting, March 18, 2011). Also see James Slack, James O. Terry, and Grant Lovejoy, *Tell the Story: A Primer on Chronological Bible Storying* (Rockville, VA: International Centre for Excellence in Leadership, 2003).

57. For a sample of various story sets, see "Story Sets" online: orality.imb.org/resources/?t=13 (accessed January 23, 2018).

of Christ, of God's plan to redeem a people for himself."[58] It only uses nine to ten Old Testament stories.[59] Of these, the first four parts span the period from creation to the flood (Gen 1–9). However, part two ("The Spirit World") in fact does not come directly from the biblical narrative but rather is summary developed from systematic theology regarding the origin of angels and demons. Lessons five through seven briefly survey parts of Abraham's and David's lives. Within these forty-two stories, Israel's story does little to shape the overall narrative; at best, Old Testament passages are treated simply as bridges or predictions that could be removed with little loss to the narrative cohesion of the whole.

By contrast, missionaries and teachers should use the biblical grand narrative shown above to select passages that give proper weight to each major stage in the biblical story. Furthermore, biblical stories can be taught in a layered approach such that first-level accounts (such as creation, Abraham, Exodus, David, etc., conceptualized with the squares below) are emphasized first and frequently. Subsequently, one then could teach second- and third-level stories (represented by circles and diamonds respectively). They support the overarching narrative while reinforcing the first-level stories (squares).

On the graph on page 286, "plot sequence" refers to the order of events or persons within the biblical story. "Presentation sequence" refers to the order teachers use when sharing the grand narrative. When teaching stories within the Bible's grand narrative framework, trainers will first teach first-level stories (squares), followed by second-level stories (circles), then third-level stories (diamonds), and so forth. This layering sequence ensures that listeners have a firm understanding of the Bible's inherent narrative structure, not simply those texts that affirm one's preferred systematic theology. As we progress through successive plot stages, we have greater and greater freedom in selecting which stories and themes we focus on.

Our observations suggest a second application that is implicit within the chronological Bible storying methods mentioned above. When evangelizing or training disciples, churches and missionaries are wise to begin

---

58. For a complete list of stories, see storyrunners.org.

59. Stories 9 and 10 recall Isaiah's prophecies concerning Christ.

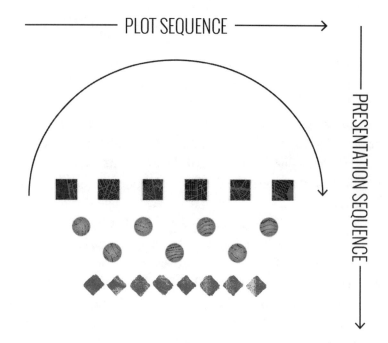

with the Bible's metanarrative since it provides the contextual framework for the rest of Scripture and all Christian doctrine. People tend to remember best what they learn first and thus what gets reinforced. Accordingly, truncated or reductionistic accounts potentially undermine learners' long-term ability to interpret the Bible and contextualize its teaching because they invariably filter all they hear or read through the key points first introduced to them when believing the gospel.

Some might complain that starting with the grand narrative, with its emphasis on Israel's story, casts one adrift from the so-called primary topic of salvation, that is, how an individual is saved through the forgiveness of sin. However, evangelicals have long affirmed that genuine conversion involves more than intellectual assent to doctrine. Being Christ's disciples entails a change of heart and mind. In effect, the gospel reorients a person's worldview, which requires that people understand the context and significance of the gospel message.

By understanding the message of Christ in light of the grand biblical story, a person better grasps the character of God, Christ's work, his mission for the church, and the cost of following Christ. The inherent coherence of the biblical narrative is able to produce a consistent framework for seeing the world, others, and oneself.

We should also recall that the vast majority of gentiles who welcomed Paul's preaching were already familiar with the Jewish story in the Old Testament. "Full gentiles" (nonproselytes), however, were much slower to accept the gospel. Therefore, modern Christians have little biblical warrant to expect modern gentiles, who are unfamiliar with the Old Testament, to respond quickly to the gospel without understanding its broader context.[60]

Our observations remind the church of the need for patience and a big-picture perspective. Since modern gentiles, especially those from non-Christianized cultures, need time to grasp the gospel's implicit grand narrative, missionaries and Evangelists should adjust their expectations and approaches. For instance, they could make more use of "seeker studies," wherein a small group or individual spends a number of meetings simply becoming familiar with the biblical story. These surveys provide the mental categories and perspective to make sense of the gospel and its demands.

THE BIBLICAL STORY
RESHAPES MISSION STRATEGY

We have seen that an accurate view of the Bible's metanarrative should prompt many missionaries, pastors, and teachers to rethink how they instruct their congregations or students. All preaching implicitly conveys some perspective concerning the Bible's grand story. Whatever leaders say about their theology, hearers can discern this story, often unconsciously, through the teacher's selection of topics and texts. The subjects that are most emphasized typically become the de facto framework that shapes one's view of the biblical narrative. Even when teachers draw from the Old Testament, they might consider whether those lessons reflect the function of those Old Testament texts in the Old Testament itself. If the Old Testament passages become mere illustrations for other

---

60. For elaboration, see Jackson Wu, "The Influence of Culture on the Evolution of Mission Methods: Using CPMs as a Case Study," *Global Missiology* 1, no. 12 (October 2014): 1–11.

points, then such texts in fact are relegated to a lower stratum of significance within the grand biblical story.

Furthermore, the observations in this chapter should cause the church and mission organizations to evaluate and develop training materials with the grand narrative in mind. Although numerous books and resources advance true theological propositions, they might not sufficiently emphasize or highlight the major pillars of the biblical story. Consequently, these materials reinforce ideas that are not primary within the narrative.

By "not primary," I do not imply "not important." Rather, the Bible's grand narrative, like any story, has a layered structure of events and explanation. If training materials largely underscore important and true doctrines yet do not reinforce the foundational narrative—including fundamental aspects of Israel's history—then people might unconsciously learn a collection of themes without understanding how the Bible itself links them through its narrative.

Why are people unwilling to share the gospel or nervous when talking about theology? Among countless reasons, one issue is this: many people cannot see how various texts and teachings fit together into a coherent whole. Apart from the Bible's intrinsic narrative structure, one is left to formulate theological systems in a piecemeal fashion. By grasping the grand story, believers can have greater confidence when reading the Bible and discussing it with others. As we have seen, the overarching story is a fundamental starting point for understanding the Christian message. However, people cannot use the grand story if they don't know it.

The discussion in this chapter carries special application for oral contexts. People often contrast the words "oral" and "literate" as though "oral contexts" refer mainly to illiterate tribes. As noted earlier, equating oral contexts with illiteracy is a mistake. With respect to the Christian teaching, many people functionally are oral learners. In practice, they only *hear* the Bible taught. They do not regularly read it, much less reflect rigorously on its content and meaning.

For oral-dependent learners, whether literate or illiterate, biblical interpretation is uniquely challenging. Imagine interpreting the Bible when one cannot (or does not) *read* the Bible. Such a person does not use a written text as a reference. One must then interpret and theologize *via memory*. Accordingly, the structure of the biblical story plays an essential role in organizing information in the mind. When an alien theological framework is imposed on a narrative, listeners experience greater difficulty connecting ideas that reflect the logic of the original authors. However, the Bible's metanarrative has its own boundaries, hierarchies, and patterns. In this way, listeners discern how to relate and prioritize the information they hear.

Other implications no doubt follow from the observations in this chapter concerning the biblical grand narrative. For example, how might these insights influence the process of biblical translation? Might missionaries make different decisions about what books and stories first get translated? Might people need to show greater consistency in how they translate certain terms to ensure readers discern the intertextual connections? Our study also highlights still other potentially fruitful areas of research. For instance, how might studies in memory, oral tradition, and canon formation contribute to more fruitful ministry among oral peoples?

CONCLUSION

This chapter has explored two primary issues. First, to what degree does the Bible itself possess a grand narrative? We used a method suggested by many biblical and literary scholars and drew from numerous ancient summaries of the Bible. The chapter identifies a broad but distinct narrative that improves on popular notions about the Bible's grand story.

Second, what implications and applications follow from knowing the overarching story of Scripture? Although the biblical metanarrative should influence many areas of ministry, it carries special significance in oral contexts in which story plays an indispensable role. In the process, our observations reinforce the importance of biblical theology in shaping church practice, especially Christian missions.

11

PAUL AS MODEL FOR THE PRACTICE OF WORLD MISSION

Will Brooks

INTRODUCTION

Missiologists have often debated the goals and purposes of mission work. Since Scripture points to the apostle Paul as the missionary par excellence, it makes sense to look to him to understand the essential characteristics of the church's missionary task better. The question we can ask is, "Within what framework did Paul conceive of the missionary task?" A subsequent question, then, is, "How did that framework inform Paul's overall missionary goals and strategy?" One of the clearest descriptions that Paul gives of his own mission ambitions and goals is in Romans 15:14–21. In this chapter I will examine Romans 15:8–21 and Paul's biblical-theological understanding of mission. After using Paul's description of his own ministry to understand the essential goals of missionary service better, I will examine Paul's overall mission strategy and show that his mission work combined both apostolic and pastoral dimensions.

PAUL'S UNDERSTANDING OF MISSION

In his letter to the Romans, Paul places significant emphasis on the necessity of Jew and gentile unity in Christ. In the final section of the letter, Romans 14:1–15:13, Paul affirms this theme, and in Romans 15:8–13 Paul gives the ground for this call to unity. Why is it that Jews and gentiles should seek to live in harmony? Why is it that Jew-gentile unity will lead to more fervent worship? What is fascinating is that in his reasoning, Paul uses a biblical-theological argument to make his point that throughout history God has been at work to call both Jews and gentiles to himself. He states that the Old Testament promises to the patriarchs and the New Testament witness to Christ both confirm that God's heart is for all the nations of the earth to worship him.

Paul's main point in this paragraph, which is found in Romans 15:8, is that Christ's life and work have served to confirm the truthfulness of God. More precisely, Paul states that Christ became a servant to the circumcised. Such a statement accords with the biblical data in terms of the primary recipients of Christ's earthly ministry. Though Scripture attests repeatedly to God's desire that all the world's peoples worship him, Jesus' earthly ministry was spent primarily among the people of Israel.

In fact, one could make the same statement concerning mission in the Old Testament. At one extreme, some scholars argue that mission does not exist in the Old Testament,[1] and at the other extreme, some argue that God's intention was for Israel to be a missionary community that sent people to the ends of the earth.[2] The truth, however, lies somewhere in the middle. While God's desire has always been for all people to worship him, in the Old Testament he focuses on a single people in order that he might raise up the one who will bless all people. In that sense, mission in the Old Testament is a case of particularity for the purpose of universality.[3] The outwardly focused work of going to the nations with the good news of God will, in God's great plan, wait until the postresurrection period.

It is with this biblical-theological perspective that Paul gives two parallel purposes to Christ's earthly ministry in Romans 15:8b–9a. The syntax of these two verses is complex, but these two infinitives, βεβαιῶσαι, "to confirm," and δοξάσαι, "to glorify," introduce purpose infinitive clauses that stand in series via δέ, in this case translated as "and."[4] Douglas Moo

---

1. David Bosch, *Transforming Mission: Paradigm Shifts in the Theology of Mission* (Maryknoll, NY: Orbis Books, 1991), 16–20.

2. Walter C. Kaiser Jr., *Mission in the Old Testament: Israel as a Light to the Nations*, 2nd ed. (Grand Rapids: Baker Academic, 2012), 7–10, 20–28, 36–38.

3. Johannes Verkuyl, "Biblical Foundation for the Worldwide Missions Mandate," in *Perspectives on the World Christian Movement*, ed. Ralph D. Winter and Steven C. Hawthorne (Pasadena, CA: William Carey Library, 1999), 27–33, esp. 28.

4. See Daniel B. Wallace, *Greek Grammar beyond the Basics: An Exegetical Syntax of the New Testament* (Grand Rapids: Zondervan, 1996), 590–92.

clarifies that these two infinitives explain the *benefit* that both Jews and gentiles receive from Christ.[5] Christ's earthly ministry confirms and fulfills the promises made to the Jewish patriarchs, and it also initiates and enables the ingathering of gentiles.

To help his readers understand that these two parallel purposes are not at odds with each other, but that they flow naturally out of the character of God, Paul supports his point with four Old Testament citations, from Psalm 18:49 (also 2 Sam 22:50); Deuteronomy 32:43; Psalm 117:1; and Isaiah 11:10. These four references relate to Romans 15:9 in that they use "praise," "sing," "rejoice," "extol," and "hope," which all are variations of "glorify" in 15:9.[6] Moreover, a movement or amplification takes place as the reader moves from the first quotation to the last.[7] In the first, David praises God among the gentiles, but in the second citation, the gentiles themselves are called on to worship. In the third, the gentiles independently praise God, and in the final citation, their hope is firmly fixed on the Messiah, who is reigning over them.

Paul's argument, then, is that gentile worship is not a new idea, but from the beginning of history, God's plan was for all the peoples he created to worship him. To this end, Paul's argument is a biblical-theological one, in that his argument ties together the overarching story of God's redemptive plan. He uses these four citations to show that in terms of redemptive history, Scripture confirms that God has always been at work to this end: that the nations might know and worship him.

We might ask, then, how the emphasis in Romans 15:8–13 on God's overarching plan affected Paul's own mission efforts. In the following section of the letter (Rom 15:14–21), Paul explains that his desire in devoting so much time to the issue of Jewish and gentile unity is not solely or primarily so that there would be peace in the Roman church. Ultimately, his ambition is that all the nations of the earth will be brought into the worship of the risen Lord Jesus. Thomas Schreiner in explaining Romans

---

5. Douglas Moo, *The Epistle to the Romans*, NICNT (Grand Rapids: Eerdmans, 1996), 876–77.

6. Thomas R. Schreiner, *Romans*, ed. Moisés Silva, BECNT (Grand Rapids: Baker Academic, 1998), 757.

7. William Hendriksen, *Romans*, New Testament Commentary (Grand Rapids: Baker, 1981), 477.

15:8–13 states, "By no means, then, is Paul's goal merely to establish socio-logical peace between Jews and Gentiles. The goal of his mission is to bring Jews and Gentiles together in fervent worship and praise of God."[8]

While it may be best to see Romans 15:8–13 and 15:14–21 as comprising different sections of the letter, a clear thematic connection exists, since Jew and gentile unity relates to Paul's missionary goals. In that sense, Paul's biblical-theological basis for mission provides him with a God-centered perspective for his mission efforts.

TRINITARIAN FRAMEWORK

With this connection in mind, we can turn our attention to Romans 15:14–21 and Paul's mission framework. In this text, Paul orients the goals of his mission work in Trinitarian form. First, the Father is the initiator of Paul's mission efforts. In 15:15, Paul uses the aorist passive participial phrase τὴν δοθεῖσάν μοι ὑπὸ τοῦ θεοῦ, "given to me by God," to emphasize that he did not choose this calling himself. It is God who initiated, called, and sent him.

Moreover, Paul explains that it is because of τὴν χάριν, "the grace," that God has given him. In this context, the use of "grace" refers to the apostle-ship and calling that God has given Paul and which Paul did not deserve. The use of grace also harks back to Paul's own salvation and the gospel that he preaches in his mission work (Rom 15:16). Paul has right standing before God and is an ambassador of the gospel of God only through grace.

Paul also explains how the second person of the Trinity relates to his mission. He explains in 15:16 that he is a servant or minister of Christ Jesus to the gentiles. It is for Christ and on Christ's behalf that he per-forms his mission. Christ is the agent for whom Paul goes to the ends of the earth and for whom he establishes churches. Christ is also the object of Paul's mission. As he goes on in 15:16 to explain his "priestly" role to the gentiles, it is clear that the focus of this service is preparing an offering of gentile worshipers. The object of their worship is Christ. In that sense, the Son is both the agent and object of mission.[9]

Paul also makes clear that all he does in mission is aimed at glorifying Christ. In 15:17 he states that he has reason to be proud of the work he

---

8. Schreiner, *Romans*, 752.

9. Moo, *Romans*, 894.

has accomplished for God, but he qualifies that statement with ἐν Χριστῷ, "in Christ." Every aspect of Paul's mission has been done in Christ and for Christ. This interpretation is confirmed when Paul in 15:18 speaks of what "Christ has accomplished through me." Paul's mission is thoroughly Christ-centered in that he is an emissary for Christ, glorifying Christ as Christ works through him, all the while fulfilling the gospel of Christ through the preaching of Christ (15:19–20). To speak of Paul's mission without mention of Christ is inconceivable.

In keeping with this Trinitarian framework, Paul also explains that the Spirit is the one who empowers his mission efforts. In 15:18b–19a Paul employs a series of datives to show the means by which his mission is accomplished.[10] Those means include "by word and deed, by the power of signs and wonders, by the power of the Spirit of God." Paul's emphasis here is on the final term, "Spirit of God," as the primary means through which he accomplishes all that he does.

It is also important to note the purpose of signs and wonders, which is one of the means that the Spirit empowers. In the Acts narrative, the miracles that Paul performs serve to provide opportunities for communication of the gospel (Acts 13:11–12; 14:10–18; 17:18–31).[11] In the context of Romans 15:18–19, this understanding of Paul is confirmed in that the series of datives modifies the phrase "bring the Gentiles to obedience." All that Paul does in the power of the Sprit—signs, wonders, word, and deed—have as their goal the conversion of the gentiles.

Along the same lines, Paul makes clear that it is only through the sanctifying work of the Spirit that the gentiles are made into an acceptable offering. He explains in 15:16 that his aim is that the gentiles will be "acceptable," which he qualifies with the phrase "sanctified by the Holy Spirit." Since Jews saw gentiles as unclean, Paul's use of "sanctified" here is intentional as he once again seeks to break down barriers standing in the way of Jew and gentile unity.[12] What is important for us to note, at this point, is that Paul emphasizes that it is the Holy Spirit who performs this sanctifying work. Here lies a penetrating insight into Paul's understanding of mission.

---

10. Schreiner, *Romans*, 768; Moo, *Romans*, 893.

11. Hendriksen notes that Acts is the best commentary on Paul's work, and yet commentators often do not refer to Acts for this purpose. See Hendriksen, *Romans*, 487.

12. Leon Morris, *The Epistle to the Romans*, Pillar (Grand Rapids: Eerdmans, 1988), 511–12.

Through Paul's preaching of the gospel, the Spirit takes sinful, unclean people and turns them into an acceptable offering of those who worship the risen Lord.[13]

RESULTANT GOALS

With Paul's Trinitarian framework in mind, we can see the goals of his mission, which flow out of that framework.

Purpose

First, we see the *purpose* of his mission is to present gentiles as an offering to God. Schreiner explains that ἡ προσφορά, "the offering," and τῶν ἐθνῶν, "the gentiles," are in apposition, so in other words, the offering *is* the gentiles.[14] Leon Morris explains the unusual phrase this way, "It is his way of saying that he preaches the gospel to the gentiles so that they come to offer themselves to God."[15] Another confirmation of this interpretation is Paul's statement in 15:18, where he speaks of what Christ has accomplished through him, which he explains as bringing "the Gentiles to obedience." By "gentile obedience" he means the obedience of faith, which he uses in Romans 1:5 and 16:26 to speak of gentile conversion.

This idea that the gentiles themselves, or perhaps more precisely their worship, are the offering Paul presents to God corresponds with John Piper's famous statement, "Missions exists because worship doesn't."[16] Paul's mission exists because the gentiles, who had no knowledge of God, now through Christ have access to him. Paul's purpose, then, is to call out a harvest of gentile worshipers who trust in the Son, have been sanctified by the Spirit, and are presented as an offering to the Father.

We are likewise reminded here of the previous verses and the biblical-theological nature of Paul's argument for gentile inclusion. He recognizes the eschatological significance of this period of church history and recognizes that just as God promised throughout the Old Testament, now is the time for all the nations of the earth to be called into the worship of

---

13. Moo, *Romans*, 891.

14. Schreiner, *Romans*, 767.

15. Morris, *Epistle to the Romans*, 511–12.

16. John Piper, *Let the Nations Be Glad!: The Supremacy of God in Missions*, 3rd ed. (Grand Rapids: Baker Academic, 2010), 15.

God. As Andreas Köstenberger explains, "He formulated his proclamation in light of the antecedent theology of the OT and on the basis of the apostolic gospel as called for by his ministry context."[17] In the same way Paul looks back at the Old Testament promises in Romans 15:10–12, some scholars see an allusion in Romans 15:16 to Isaiah 66:20, which speaks of the nations as an offering to God.

In terms of biblical-theological significance we certainly see Paul citing and alluding to the Old Testament promises of gentile inclusion. He does so to argue that every nation united in worship of God has always been part of God's salvation-historical plan. In a biblical-theological sense, we can also look forward in salvation history and see, in Revelation 7:9–10, the fulfillment of God's plan.

Location

In addition to seeing the *purpose* of Paul's mission here, we also see the *location* of Paul's mission. Paul explains in Romans 15:20 that his ambition is to preach in places where Christ has not yet been named. Since Paul's missionary purpose is to call out gentile worshipers, his desire is to go to the parts of the gentile world that have never heard the gospel.

In following the biblical-theological significance of Paul's discussion, an important datum is the Psalm 117 citation in Romans 15:11. In that citation, the psalmist twice commands that "all" the nations worship the Lord. Paul uses πάντα τὰ ἔθνη, "all the nations," and πάντες οἱ λαοί, "all the peoples," to emphasize the scope of that command. As a result, Paul expresses a sense of urgency to take the gospel to the ends of the earth.

Result

Paul also makes mention of the *result* of his work. After mentioning what Christ has accomplished through him and the means by which he has done so, in Romans 15:19b Paul makes the statement, "from Jerusalem and all the way around to Illyricum I have fulfilled the ministry of the gospel of Christ." While scholars debate whether Paul actually preached

---

17. Andreas J. Köstenberger, "Diversity and Unity in the New Testament," in *Biblical Theology: Retrospect & Prospect*, ed. Scott J. Hafemann (Downers Grove, IL: InterVarsity Press, 2002), 144–65, esp. 146.

in Illyricum,[18] Paul's idea is that within these general geographic borders he has finished the work God has given him to do.

A second issue has to do with what Paul means by "fulfilled." He certainly does not mean that he has preached the gospel in every single location or to every single person. Paul understood his task to be one of planting strategic churches, from which the gospel would flow out to the surrounding areas.[19] Michael Bird puts it this way, "Evidently, Paul considered his work in the East complete—complete in the sense that he has established clusters of churches in many major urban areas, churches capable of reproducing his own evangelical efforts in that location and beyond it."[20]

In a biblical-theological sense, a connection exists between Paul's completion of the work of planting churches in these areas and the citation of Isaiah 11:10, which references the Messiah ruling over the gentiles. How does Christ rule over the nations? He does so in the church, through which believers are discipled into obedience and through which they are taught everything that Christ has commanded. It is for this reason that Paul can say his work is fulfilled once a healthy, thriving, theologically sound church is planted.

Confirmation

Finally, Paul explains the *confirmation* of his work. In keeping with his biblical-theological theme, Paul returns to the Old Testament (Isa 52:15) to support his motivation for planting churches where Christ has not been named. The Old Testament confirms Paul's calling and desire to take the gospel to the ends of the earth. He understands his mission work to be a fulfillment of the Abrahamic promise that through the Messiah, God will bless all the nations of the earth. Furthermore, Paul sees his work,

---

18. For a view that says it is plausible, see Eckhard J. Schnabel, "Paul the Missionary," in *Paul's Missionary Methods: In His Time and Ours*, ed. Robert L. Plummer and John Mark Terry (Downers Grove, IL: InterVarsity Press, 2012), 29–43, esp. 41. For a view that says Jerusalem and Illyricum are not necessarily inclusive and Paul's preaching need only extend near those boundaries, see Schreiner, *Romans*, 769.

19. Moo, *Epistle to the Romans*, 896; Schreiner, *Romans*, 770.

20. Michael F. Bird, "Paul's Religious and Historical Milieu," in Plummer and Terry, *Paul's Missionary Methods*, 17–28, esp. 20.

and the work of missionaries who will come after him, as a fulfillment of Isaiah's eschatological vision.

PAUL'S STRATEGY FOR MISSION

With this Trinitarian framework and these biblical-theological goals in mind, we can turn to Paul's strategy. By examining the narrative of Acts and the teaching in Paul's letters, we see that Paul's mission work combines both apostolic and pastoral dimensions. We can summarize Paul's strategy with these statements: *Under the leadership of the Holy Spirit, Paul sought to honor Christ by shining the light of the gospel in the darkest parts of his world with a contextualized message that led to planting churches in strategic locations. He then sought to promote perseverance by laying a strong biblical and theological foundation, raising up a diverse group of leaders, and maintaining contact with the churches he planted.* Let us look at each of these items in turn.

UNDER THE LEADERSHIP OF THE HOLY SPIRIT

When dealing with Paul's Trinitarian framework, we already considered how the Holy Spirit was the primary means through which Paul accomplished his work. It is the Holy Spirit who sanctified the offering of gentiles and brought them into a right relationship with Christ through Paul's preaching. In this section it is worth examining the specific ways in which the Holy Spirit led Paul in his mission efforts.

Luke records in Acts 13:1–4 that the Holy Spirit spoke to the church at Antioch, directing Saul and Barnabas to leave and begin "the work to which I have called them" (Acts 13:2). Again, in Acts 13:4, Luke records that they were "sent out by the Holy Spirit." Darrell Bock notes this Trinitarian perspective in that the Father has been mentioned throughout the Acts narrative, the Son calls Saul (Acts 9:4–6), and the Spirit now commissions him.[21]

During his first missionary journey, Paul is "filled with the Holy Spirit" as he responds to opposition and subsequently performs a miracle in blinding a magician (Acts 13:5–12). Like many other miracles in Acts,

---

21. Darrell L. Bock, *Acts*, ed. Robert W. Yarbrough and Robert H. Stein, BECNT (Grand Rapids: Baker Academic, 2008), 440.

the result is that someone who witnessed the miracle trusts in Christ (Acts 13:12; see also 14:3, 10; 16:18, 26; 19:11; 28:4, 8–9). Later in that journey, in Pisidian Antioch, Luke explains that many believed Paul's gospel and the word spread throughout the region. The result of Paul's labors in this area is that "the disciples were filled with joy and with the Holy Spirit" (Acts 13:52; see also 19:6). The Holy Spirit not only directs Paul in his travels, but also empowers his preaching and dwells in those who believe the gospel he preaches.

The Holy Spirit not only directs Paul to go to certain locations, but also forbids him to enter certain regions. In Acts 16:6–10, Luke records that they are forbidden by the Holy Spirit to enter Asia. As a result, they then attempt to go to Bithynia, but the Holy Spirit "did not allow them" to enter that region either (Acts 16:7). During the night the Holy Spirit gives Paul a vision of a Macedonian man, to which Paul concludes, "God had called us to preach the gospel to them" (Acts 16:10). Along the same lines, during his time in Corinth, God gives Paul a vision directing him to stay in that city and continue preaching the word there (Acts 18:9–10).

Paul speaks of being "constrained by the Spirit" (Acts 20:22) and that the Spirit promises suffering and hardship for him (Acts 20:23; 21:11). He makes plans and is "resolved in the Spirit" (Acts 19:21) to go to certain places, but he also makes plans tentatively, saying, "I will return to you if God wills" (Acts 18:21). He also explains that it is the Spirit who selected the elders of the churches (Acts 20:28). It is not an overstatement to say that the Spirit initiates, directs, and empowers all of Paul's missions efforts.

PAUL SOUGHT TO HONOR CHRIST

Paul spent a year and a half in Corinth, and yet after he left, the church struggled with numerous sins and even began to question Paul's apostolic ministry. In response, Paul wrote several letters not only reminding them of the gospel but also defending his own ministry among them. At several points in 1 and 2 Corinthians, Paul clarifies the aim of his mission work.

In 2 Corinthians 4:16–5:10, Paul reflects on the suffering of this earthly life and the fact that God is preparing believers for an "eternal weight of glory" (2 Cor 4:17). He writes that believers must not focus on the seen but on the unseen (2 Cor 4:18). Then in 2 Corinthians 5:9 he explains that his goal in all he does is to please God. The underlying narrative is that, unlike his opponents, Paul's aim is not to please people, nor is his goal about seeing earthly results. He labors in such a way that he honors Christ in all that he does.

In 2 Corinthians 5:10, Paul explains the reason for this aim. He recognizes that when this earthly life is over, everyone "must appear before the judgment seat of Christ." In 1 Corinthians 3 Paul makes a similar point. He explains that he sees himself as God's fellow worker (1 Cor 3:9), and he recognizes that one day all he has done will come to light. He writes, "each one's work will become manifest, for the Day will disclose it" (1 Cor 3:13).

With this eternal mindset in view, Paul considers the ethical implications of how he goes about his work. In 1 Corinthians 3, he explains that he laid the foundation of the church with care. He knew that if he laid a foundation other than Jesus Christ, that foundation would be burned up on the day of judgment. Along the same lines, in 2 Corinthians 4, Paul explains that his goal to honor Christ affects how he approaches the preaching of the gospel. He writes that he has "renounced disgraceful, underhanded ways" (2 Cor 4:2). He refuses to manipulate people for his own personal gain or reputation.

Unlike so many in his day and ours, Paul is not a "peddler" (2 Cor 2:17) of God's word, out for personal financial gain or the praise of people through the veneer of earthly success. In contrast, he sees himself as "commissioned by God" and speaking "in the sight of God" (2 Cor 2:17). Likewise, he seeks to persuade people (2 Cor 5:11), but he does so in the knowledge of the fear of the Lord.

BY SHINING THE LIGHT OF THE GOSPEL
IN THE DARKEST PARTS OF HIS WORLD

In ways that honor God, Paul seeks to shine the light of the gospel in places of great darkness.[22] In our study of Romans 15:14–21, we have already seen that in terms of location, Paul's goal was to preach the gospel in the places of least access, the places where Christ had not yet been named. In many

---

22. For a more complete argument on how Paul's demonology affected his missiology, see my article "Pauline Spiritual Warfare: How Paul's Understanding of Satan Influenced His Philosophy of Missions," *Great Commission Research Journal* 3 (2011): 97–113.

other parts of the New Testament, we see how Paul's understanding of Satan and the forces of darkness affects his work in these areas.

When Paul explains his own calling, he often uses warfare imagery. During his speech before King Agrippa in Acts 26:18, Paul explains that the goal of his preaching is "that they may turn from darkness to light and from the power of Satan to God." In Colossians 1:13 he speaks of redemption in the same terms. Paul knows that Christ has called him to preach the gospel so that the darkened eyes of the gentiles may see the light of the glory of God in Christ Jesus (2 Cor 4:4). Paul knows that to proclaim Jesus to a world in spiritual darkness is to proclaim illuminating truth. He knows that Satan was a powerful spiritual being who has turned against God and is now wreaking havoc in the world, and he knows that his calling as a missionary is a calling to confront the domain of the enemy.

Paul often uses the same terminology to speak of unbelievers. He describes unbelievers as members of the "domain of darkness" (Col 1:13), followers of "the prince of the power of the air" (Eph 2:2), and captured by the devil "to do his will" (2 Tim 2:26). In 2 Corinthians 4:4 Paul states that Satan has "blinded the minds of the unbelievers," leaving them unable to comprehend the beauty of Christ revealed in the gospel. It is not due to a fault in the gospel that some are perishing, but it is due to the blinding work of Satan. While unbelievers may be able to comprehend that the gospel is primarily concerned with Christ, the blinding work of Satan has left them unable to perceive the glory and majesty of a bloodied Savior slain for sinners.[23]

Despite the dangers Paul faces from his opponents, he is incredibly gracious and compassionate in the midst of their threats. Paul's grace toward them no doubt extends from Paul's understanding of the very character of God, but his grace is also motivated by the fact that he knows his opponents are fallen men under the spell of the enemy. When the people of Lystra misunderstand a miracle and attempt to offer sacrifices to Paul and Barnabas, Paul does not conclude that the people are insane

---

23. Thomas R. Schreiner, *Paul, Apostle of God's Glory in Christ: A Pauline Theology* (Downers Grove, IL: InterVarsity Press, 2001), 137–38; Sydney H. T. Page, *Powers of Evil: A Biblical Study of Satan & Demons* (Grand Rapids: Baker, 1995), 184; Murray J. Harris, *The Second Epistle to the Corinthians*, NIGTC (Grand Rapids: Eerdmans, 2005), 327.

and undeserving of the gospel, but he tears his clothes and pleads with the people to turn from idolatry to Christ (Acts 14:8–18).

Later in Lystra, when these same crowds stone Paul until they think he is dead, Paul does not respond with anger, nor does he determine ministry to these people to be a waste of time (Acts 14:19). Instead, he recognizes that they are opposed to the work of the gospel precisely because as unbelievers they are members of Satan's kingdom. Paul reenters the city and then continues to preach the gospel in the surrounding areas (Acts 14:20–21).

Ultimately, Paul's missionary endeavors display a willingness to suffer so that those belonging to the kingdom of Satan might hear the gospel and believe in it. He finds strength during times of imprisonment because being in prison enables him to share the gospel with prisoners and prison guards (Acts 16:25–31; Phil 1:12). He speaks of suffering as a means of displaying Christ's worth (Col 1:24; 2 Cor 12:9–10) and as necessary for those committed to Christ (Acts 14:22). In fact, eleven different times Luke writes about Paul suffering at the hands of those with whom he seeks to communicate. Paul loves the lost, those captured by Satan, to such an extent that he is willing to endure anything to give them an opportunity to hear the gospel.

WITH A CONTEXTUALIZED MESSAGE

Paul sees himself as a steward of the mysteries of God (1 Cor 4:1–2), and he desires to honor God by communicating those truths in a trustworthy way. As Eckhard Schnabel explains, "The central process of missionary work is the oral proclamation of the good news of Jesus, the crucified and risen Messiah and Savior of the world."[24] The people Paul encounters on his missionary journeys, though, often have different cultural and religious backgrounds from him. As a result, Paul adjusts his approach to preaching the gospel. The content of his sermons and letters differs based on the needs and cultural background of his audience.

In Acts, when Paul enters a new city, he goes to the synagogue first. Theologically, he goes there because he believes the Jews have salvation-historical

---

24. Eckhard J. Schnabel, *Early Christian Mission: Paul and the Early Church* (Downers Grove, IL: InterVarsity Press, 2004), 1480.

priority (Rom 1:16; 2:9),[25] and perhaps more practically, he knows Godfearers will be there who will be both open to the gospel and familiar with the Old Testament (see Acts 13:48; 14:1; 17:12; 18:4, 7). When he preaches in those contexts, he explains that Jesus is the Messiah promised in the Old Testament. He states that the Old Testament foresaw the need for the Messiah to suffer and to rise from the dead (Acts 13:17–41; 17:3; 28:23). Acts 17:2–3 provides a good summary of Paul's approach among Jews: "He reasoned with them from the Scriptures, explaining and proving that it was necessary for the Christ to suffer and to rise from the dead."

By way of contrast, when Paul preaches to a gentile audience, he knows that they have little to no knowledge of the one true God. Instead of using the Old Testament to show that Jesus is the Messiah, he explains the existence of the living God and states that God is the creator of all (Acts 14:15–17; 17:24–31). In response to the idol worship in Lystra, Paul says, "We bring you good news, that you should turn from these vain things to a living God, who made the heaven and the earth and the sea and all that is in them" (Acts 14:15). Paul's speech in Athens reveals that though he starts with creation, his goal of proclaiming Christ stays the same (Acts 17:22–28). In that context, Paul speaks of God's existence, autonomy, and sovereignty over all creation. He then transitions and speaks about the man whom God raised from the dead and appointed as the righteous judge of humankind (Acts 17:29–31).

Another interesting comparison is Paul's use of different terminology with different audiences. In Acts 16:31, when speaking with the Philippian jailer, Paul says, "Believe in the Lord Jesus." Just a few verses later, though, when preaching at the synagogue in Thessalonica, Paul refers to Jesus not as Lord but as Christ (Acts 17:3). And then in Acts 20:21, when summarizing his work in Ephesus among both Jews and gentiles, Paul speaks of "faith in our Lord Jesus Christ."

Though the speeches in Acts differ depending on the audience, they also have similarities. Certainly one of the common themes is Paul's biblical-theological approach to gospel communication. In each of his speeches, his argument ties together the overarching story of God's redemptive plan. At Pisidian Antioch, Paul recounts how God worked in Israelite history,

---

25. Schnabel, *Early Christian Mission*, 1481.

which culminated in the coming of Christ (Acts 13:17–41). He explains how the Davidic covenant and the promises to the forefathers were all fulfilled in Christ (Acts 13:22–23, 32–34). Among gentiles, Paul starts with creation (Acts 14:15–17; 17:24–28), recounts God's provision for humankind, and moves toward explaining that Jesus is Lord and judge of all humanity (Acts 17:29–31).

While the process of contextualization certainly includes how the gospel is communicated, that process continues through conversion and beyond. Postconversion, believers must think through how the gospel changes and informs their cultural norms. They must reevaluate their worldview in light of biblical truth. In Paul's letters, we see him modeling that process. One of the reasons the church in Corinth struggles with sexual sin is that prostitution is rampant in that city. Paul, then, in 1 Corinthians must help them to think about sexuality from a biblical perspective.

The same is true of the church at Colossae. Like many of the gentiles whom Paul led to Christ, Colossian believers came from an animistic background. When they became believers, these animistic tendencies did not simply disappear, which is why a false teacher was able to influence them with teaching that had some of the same tendencies.[26] Moo explains that these believers "were preoccupied with spiritual beings, probably because they viewed them as powerful figures capable of having a significant influence on their lives."[27] Paul, then, wrote that letter to help them think through the critical issues of their context in a Christ-centered way.

Paul's statement in 1 Corinthians 9:19–23 explains his approach to contextualization as he writes, "I have become all things to all people, that by all means I might save some" (1 Cor 9:22). Paul is willing to give up his rights for the sake of proclaiming the gospel, and he does so not so that the gospel will be more acceptable, but that it will become more understandable. He gives up his rights to think about the gospel according to his own cultural background so that he can help people in other cultural contexts understand the gospel and apply it to their lives. This process

---

26. Clinton Arnold, *The Colossian Syncretism: The Interface between Christianity and Folk Belief at Colossae* (Grand Rapids: Baker, 1996).

27. Douglas J. Moo, *The Letters to the Colossians and to Philemon*, Pillar (Grand Rapids: Eerdmans, 2008), 59.

starts with the way he communicates the gospel to them and continues as he teaches them to think about their cultural norms and practices in gospel-centered ways.

THAT LED TO CHURCHES
PLANTED IN STRATEGIC LOCATIONS

Paul's ambition is to preach the gospel in the darkest parts of his world, the parts where Christ has not yet been named. His ambition, though, is not to preach the gospel only, but to preach the gospel in a way that results in churches being planted in those locations. In Romans 15:19b he explains that his work is "fulfilled" once a church has been established in some location. In a biblical-theological sense, these churches fulfill the Old Testament promises that Christ will rule over the nations, since Christ is the head of the church.

Paul sees himself as a "master builder" who through the preaching of the gospel lays the foundation of a church, and that foundation is Jesus Christ (1 Cor 3:10–11). Ultimately, though, neither the results of his efforts nor the church itself belong to Paul, but to God (1 Cor 3:7, 9). Schnabel explains this concept: "The effectiveness of missionary work and of church ministry does not depend on persons or programs, it does not depend on rhetorical techniques or methods of accommodation, but only on God's activity." He continues, "The churches that are established as the fruit of missionary work belong neither to Paul nor to other teachers: the church is 'God's field, God's building.' "[28]

On a practical level, Paul understands that God does not intend for believers to be isolated individuals, but he recognizes that they need the fellowship of other believers. Paul's evangelistic actions are set within "an ecclesiological intention."[29] For this reason he does not leave converts alone, but he gathers them into congregations of believers. Moreover, Paul's planting of churches is a fulfillment of the Great

---

28. Schnabel, *Early Christian Mission*, 948–49.

29. Paul Bowers, "Fulfilling the Gospel: The Scope of the Pauline Mission," *JETS* 30 (1987): 185–98, esp. 188; Christopher R. Little, *Mission in the Way of Paul: Biblical Mission for the Church in the Twenty-First Century*, Studies in Biblical Literature 80, ed. Hemchand Gossai (New York: Peter Lang, 2005), 58; Eckhard J. Schnabel, *Paul the Missionary: Realities, Strategies and Methods* (Downers Grove, IL: InterVarsity Press, 2008), 231–32.

Commission.[30] Paul understands that the thrust of Jesus' command is the making of disciples, and he also knows that disciples can only be made in the context of a local church.[31] As a result, Paul's missionary strategy is centered on the planting of churches.

What is not always clear is why Paul chooses to visit certain locations. In some cases, the cities he visits hold regional influence. For example, in Cyprus, Luke mentions Salamis and Paphos. Salamis was the most influential city in Cyprus from the eleventh century BC until 15 BC, when an earthquake struck Paphos, and it was rebuilt as the capital city.[32] Thus Salamis and Paphos were cities of strategic importance. On the other hand, it is unclear why Paul would visit a location of less importance such as Lystra, especially when Luke references that the people were speaking Lycaonian (14:11).

Paul at least attempts to plant churches in all of the regions of the Roman Empire, though he is prevented from entering Bithynia (Acts 16:7). That he makes plans, strategizes what fields he should enter next, and prays for the Holy Spirit's direction is clear from Acts and his letters. That he mentions in Romans 15:24 his plans to go to Spain and his need for financial assistance displays that his preparation and calculation often took place years in advance.

While Paul does not give reasons for the locations that he chooses, Luke makes it clear that Paul would preach to anyone, anywhere. He often goes to the synagogue (Acts 13:5, 14; 14:1; 17:2, 10, 17; 18:4, 19; 19:8) and in Rome, while on house arrest, he calls the rulers of the synagogue to himself (28:17). He does not just interact with Jews there, though. Luke records that Paul also communicates with Godfearers while at the synagogue (Acts 13:48; 14:1; 17:12; 18:4, 7). In addition to synagogues, Paul also preaches in the "whole island" (Acts 13:6), the "marketplace" (Acts 17:17), in the "hall of Tyrannus" (Acts 19:9), and "in public and from house to house" (Acts 20:20). He evangelizes the upper class (Acts 13:7; 17:12),

---

30. Schnabel, *Paul the Missionary*, 232. It is likely that Paul never read Matthew's Gospel, since most evangelical scholars conclude that Matthew wrote about the time of Paul's death. I am assuming, however, that Paul was familiar with the oral tradition behind Matthew's Gospel and thus familiar with the Great Commission.

31. Chuck Lawless, *Discipled Warriors: Growing Healthy Churches That Are Equipped for Spiritual Warfare* (Grand Rapids: Kregel, 2002), 43–48.

32. Schnabel, *Early Christian Mission*, 1079–80; Bock, *Acts*, 442.

those in need of miraculous healing (Acts 14:8), and even whole families (Acts 16:31; 18:8).

Though Paul never directly mentions his hope that the gospel will flow out from the churches he plants into the surrounding areas, evidence does exist that it happened. Paul spent three years in Ephesus, during which it appears he met Epaphras and led him to Christ. Epaphras was from Colossae, and after sitting under Paul's teaching, he returned to Colossae and started the church there. In his letter to the Colossian church Paul refers to Epaphras as a "beloved fellow servant" through whom these believers learned the gospel (Col 1:7).

HE SOUGHT TO PROMOTE PERSEVERANCE

Some scholars understand Paul's ministry as characterized by planting churches as quickly as possible and then abandoning them to fend for themselves.[33] Gunther Bornkamm espouses this mentality when he writes, "It is perfectly astonishing to see how short a time he took in traversing fields where he worked, and how quickly he left scarcely founded churches and traveled farther, instead of taking time to care for them and train them."[34] A closer study of the New Testament documents, however, reveals that Paul is deeply concerned, not just for the *existence* of churches, but also for the *health* of those churches.[35] In fact, with the exception of Ephesus and Corinth, Paul never leaves a city on his own initiative but is always forced to leave.[36]

Paul does not consider his mission a success if converts make an initial decision to follow Christ and later abandon him.[37] Paul often emphasizes perseverance as a mark of genuine faith and necessary for salvation (Rom 8:13; 1 Cor 6:9–11; Gal 5:21; 6:8–9; Col 1:21–23). In 1 Corinthians 15:1–2,

---

33. Michael Green, *Evangelism in the Early Church* (Grand Rapids: Eerdmans, 1970), 169; John Knox, "Romans 15:14–33 and Paul's Conception of His Apostolic Mission," *JBL* 83 (1964): 1–11, esp. 6–7.

34. Gunther Bornkamm, *Paul*, trans. D. M. G. Stalker (Minneapolis: Fortress, 1971), 54–55.

35. I like how Merkle words this dynamic in saying that Paul sought not only to *push* back the darkness but also to *keep* back the darkness. Benjamin L. Merkle, "The Need for Theological Education in Missions: Lessons Learned from the Church's Greatest Missionary," *SBJT* 9, no. 4 (2005): 50–61, esp. 58.

36. Schnabel, *Paul the Missionary*, 197; Bowers, "Fulfilling the Gospel," 193.

37. Schreiner, *Paul, Apostle of God's Glory in Christ*, 39, 66–67, 271–305.

Paul writes, "Now I would remind you, brothers, of the gospel I preached to you, which you received, in which you stand, and by which you are being saved, if you hold fast to the word I preached to you—unless you believed in vain." The Corinthian believers' continuing faithfulness to Christ is evidence that their faith is a genuine faith.

Philippians 2:16 shows that Paul sees a connection between the usefulness of his work and the perseverance of the churches he plants. He uses the phrase "holding fast to the word of life" to describe the perseverance he envisions, and then adds, "so that in the day of Christ I may be proud that I did not run in vain or labor in vain." Paul's work is only of value if believers stay faithful to Christ long after Paul has left the city.

In 1 Thessalonians 2:17–3:10, Paul explains his longing for the Thessalonian believers to continue in the faith. He states that his concern for them is rooted in his early departure from their city (1 Thess 2:17) and in his inability to return to further instruct and encourage them (1 Thess 2:18; 3:2). Paul is aware that since his departure from the city the believers have faced some persecution, and his concern is that some have turned away amid the trial (1 Thess 3:3). He writes, "For this reason, when I could bear it no longer, I sent to learn about your faith" (1 Thess 3:5). Paul's use of the first-person singular in this verse signifies the depth of his concern for this congregation of believers.[38] Their continued allegiance to Christ is his concern.

In the last part of 1 Thessalonians 3:5, Paul explains that he sent Timothy to learn about their faith because he fears "that somehow the tempter had tempted you and our labor would be in vain." Paul's fear is rooted in his knowledge of satanic activity.[39] He knows that Satan is behind the persecution and that he will use the trial to tempt the believers to turn away from the faith. If they are to make such a decision, Paul will consider his work in the city to have been done in vain.[40] Gene Green explains that Paul's labor

---

38. Gene L. Green, *The Letters to the Thessalonians*, ed. D. A. Carson, Pillar (Grand Rapids: Eerdmans, 2002), 164.

39. Green, *Letters to the Thessalonians*, 165.

40. Schreiner, *Paul, Apostle of God's Glory in Christ*, 39.

was in danger because this young church, bereft of leadership and struggling without full Christian instruction, faced Satan-inspired persecution that was designed to lead them to give up and abandon their allegiance with the living God. . . . Paul entertained the fear that his labors to establish a church in that city might have been futile. The question was whether they had abandoned their new loyalty or whether they had continued firm and stable.[41]

Schreiner notes that understanding Paul's missionary efforts and his concern for the churches he planted is necessary for the correct interpretation of his letters. He writes that the letters "serve as pastoral words to churches [Paul] established to ensure that they would stand in the faith. Paul did not conceive of his mission as successful if his converts initially believed in his gospel and then lapsed. His work was in vain unless his converts persisted in the faith."[42] Paul writes to the churches because he knows that their faith will be tested, and he knows that his work will be nullified if converts turn away from the faith. He writes to nurture, encourage, exhort, correct, and rebuke with the goal that believers will endure to the end.

Paul not only writes letters to encourage perseverance, but he instructs believers before his departure from a city that persecution is a fundamental part of the Christian life. In his first letter to the Thessalonian believers, Paul reminds them of his instruction concerning persecution when he writes, "For when we were with you, we kept telling you beforehand that we were to suffer affliction, just as it has come to pass" (1 Thess 3:4). Likewise, in Acts when Paul and Barnabas are able to make their first return visit to Lystra, Iconium, and Antioch, they tell the believers that "through many tribulations we must enter the kingdom of God" (Acts 14:22). Paul knows that perseverance through times of trial is necessary for salvation, so he teaches the believers to expect it and be prepared for it.

We should also note that Paul's teaching on this issue reflects Jesus' own teaching in the parable of the sower (Matt 13:3–9; Mark 4:3–9; Luke 8:4–8). Critical to the interpretation of that parable is Jesus' explanation

---

41. Green, *Letters to the Thessalonians*, 165.

42. Schreiner, *Paul, Apostle of God's Glory in Christ*, 39.

of the parable to the disciples (Matt 13:18–23; Mark 4:14–20; Luke 8:9–15). Jesus explains that the seed sown on the first three soils does not produce fruit because the devil snatches the seed away, the recipients fall away during a time of testing, and the recipients love the pleasures of the world too much. The latter two results indicate a lack of depth and maturity in faith, which is why these recipients do not persevere or overcome. Notice, too, Luke's description of the final seed, the one that bears fruit: "They are those who, hearing the word, hold it fast in an honest and good heart, and bear fruit with patience" (Luke 8:15). The phrases "hold it fast" and "bear fruit *with patience*" (emphasis mine) indicate endurance amid many trials. It is possible that the fruit envisioned here is the faithful, long-suffering, persevering faith that endures to the end.

BY LAYING A STRONG BIBLICAL
AND THEOLOGICAL FOUNDATION

How does Paul promote perseverance in the churches he planted? The first way he promotes perseverance is by laying a strong biblical and theological foundation. Paul is committed to the theological development of his churches because he knows that churches without a strong theological foundation will not endure to the end. As a result, when Paul is with a church, he takes every opportunity to teach them and train them for ministry, and, in fact, when he is not forced out of a city, Paul stays for several years and teaches the believers daily.

In Acts, Luke shows that Paul is a gifted teacher who uses his gift to build up the church. Consider Paul's long-standing relationship with the church in Antioch. In Acts 11:19–26, the church in Jerusalem sends Barnabas to investigate the situation in Antioch that resulted in the planting of a church in that city. Barnabas is glad when he sees that the existence of the church is a work of God's grace, but he also knows that the church needs strong theological teaching that will build up the congregation, so he calls Saul to come assist him.[43] Barnabas and Saul teach the church for an entire year.

On two later occasions Paul and Barnabas spend time teaching in Antioch. After completing their first missionary journey, they return to

---

43. Bock, *Acts*, 415–16.

Antioch and give a report of their work to the sponsoring congregation (Acts 14:27).[44] Luke writes that the missionaries then stay with the
church "no little time" (Acts 14:28). Darrell Bock comments that these
verses show "a sense of ongoing pastoral care."[45] Although new elders
have been installed and the missionaries have moved on to other fields,
Paul and Barnabas still have a desire to teach this congregation. Then,
after the Jerusalem council, Paul and Barnabas again return to Antioch
and resume teaching and preaching in the church (Acts 15:35). Although
there are many unreached areas where they have yet to plant a
church, the missionaries still have a strong desire to build up the church
at Antioch. They stay there for "some days" (Acts 15:36) as they continue
to teach the word of the Lord.

Paul spends three years in Ephesus, teaching on a daily basis (Acts
19:9) in homes and in public (Acts 20:20). Paul describes the content of
his teaching as "anything that was profitable" (Acts 20:20), which he later
describes as "the whole counsel of God" (Acts 20:27). His work could be
summarized as teaching to any listener the gospel and all it entails for
life and godliness.[46] Paul also spends time teaching a congregation of
believers in Troas (Acts 20:7–12). Since Paul was leaving the next day, he
continued to teach until midnight. After Eutychus falls asleep, tumbles
out of a third-story window, and dies, Paul raises him from the dead and
then continues to speak with the congregation until daybreak. Bock comments on the connection this long evening has with Paul's commitment to
develop his churches:

> In sum, this unit gives us a sense of Paul the pastor. Here he seeks
> to instruct his people as he departs. One of the highest priorities
> for Paul in ministry is that his people will be equipped theologi-
> cally and spiritually to persevere after he is gone. In a sense this
> is the Pauline legacy, to ensure that he leaves behind not a mon-
> ument to himself, but Christians who are a monument to God in
> their faithfulness. It is also clear that what makes this ministry

---

44. John B. Polhill, *Acts*, NAC 26 (Nashville: Broadman & Holman, 1992), 320.
45. Bock, *Acts*, 484.
46. Polhill, *Acts*, 424; Bock, *Acts*, 627–28.

possible is the commitment of time that people give to hearing the Word.[47]

Paul takes advantage of every minute he has with these believers.[48] He knows that his departure is imminent, and he seeks to use the few hours he has to nurture the congregation toward faithfulness. His teaching is the means by which Paul is able to strengthen these believers theologically and spiritually.

RAISING UP A DIVERSE GROUP OF LEADERS

The second method that Paul uses to promote perseverance is the intentional development of a diverse group of leaders.[49] Acts and the Pauline Epistles mention a hundred different people associated with Paul, and at least thirty-eight are considered coworkers.[50] Many of those were people who were won to Christ and discipled as a direct result of Paul's church-planting efforts.[51] Moreover, the backgrounds of those partners are quite diverse.

Titus is a good example of a leader whom Paul develops. Titus is a gentile who was most likely converted during Paul's time in Syria. Paul disciples him, and Galatians 2:1–3 shows them traveling together and doing ministry together.[52] Later, Titus travels on Paul's behalf to Corinth, Crete, and Dalmatia: all places where Paul conducted mission work.[53] A similar explanation could be given for the actions of Priscilla and Aquila, who

---

47. Bock, *Acts*, 622.

48. Polhill, *Acts*, 418.

49. For a more complete discussion of the diversity of Paul's coworkers, see my article, "A Biblical Understanding of the Diversity of Paul's Missionary Coworkers," in *Reflecting God's Glory Together: Diversity in Evangelical Mission*, ed. A. Scott Moreau and Beth Snodderly, EMS 19 (Pasadena, CA: William Carey Library, 2011), 209–25.

50. E. Earle Ellis, "Paul and His Coworkers," *NTS* 17 (1970–1971): 437–39; Eckhard J. Schnabel, *Paul the Missionary*, 248; D. Michael Martin, *1, 2 Thessalonians*, NAC 33 (Nashville: Broadman & Holman, 1995), 48.

51. Schnabel, *Paul the Missionary*, 255.

52. Regarding this point, I would argue that Gal 2:1–3 relates to Acts 11:30 and Paul's famine visit to Jerusalem. For an explanation of this view, see Richard N. Longenecker, *Galatians*, WBC 41 (Nashville: Thomas Nelson, 1990), 46; Schnabel, *Early Christian Mission*, 1430–31.

53. William D. Mounce, *Pastoral Epistles*, WBC 46 (Nashville: Thomas Nelson, 2000), 590.

lead a house church (1 Cor 16:19) and become Paul's traveling companions (Acts 18:18; Rom 16:3).

Tychicus and Epaphras are two other coworkers whom Paul most likely led to Christ, discipled, and then worked alongside. Tychicus is Paul's companion on his third journey (Acts 20:4), and later Paul sends him to deliver letters in Ephesus, Colossae, and to Philemon. In Ephesians 6:22, Paul writes that Tychicus will "encourage your hearts," which indicates that his role is more significant than merely delivering a letter. Epaphras was most likely converted during Paul's time in Ephesus, and then he takes Paul's teaching, returns to his hometown of Colossae, and starts the church there (Col 1:7).

It is clear that Paul spends considerable time teaching the believers in the churches he plants. At the same time, he also spends time doing ministry with them. When he meets Timothy, he wants Timothy to accompany him, and Paul uses this time to mentor Timothy and to model for him how to plant new churches and strengthen existing ones (Acts 16:1–5). In the same way, Paul refers to Euodia and Syntyche as struggling "side by side with me in the gospel" (Phil 4:3), an indication of their evangelistic labors in Philippi. He mentors Archippus and encourages him to embrace his calling (Col 4:17). Paul mentors these less mature believers by involving them in his mission efforts.

MAINTAINING CONTACT WITH
THE CHURCHES PAUL PLANTED

The final method that Paul uses to promote perseverance in the churches he plants is maintaining contact with them. He does so by revisiting, writing letters, and sending coworkers to them. Paul makes it a habit of returning to churches planted on previous missionary journeys in order to strengthen and encourage the believers. For example, at the end of their first missionary journey Paul and Barnabas do not return directly to Antioch, but instead visit existing congregations to strengthen and encourage them (Acts 14:22–23).

Thus, before beginning his second missionary journey, Paul once again visits those churches to strengthen them further (Acts 15:41). In fact, revisiting the churches is the impetus for the second missionary journey (Acts 15:36). Acts 16:5 gives a summary statement of Paul's work with existing churches: "So the churches were strengthened in the faith, and they increased in numbers daily." John Polhill explains the importance of the statement:

> It underlines the importance of Paul's concern to fortify and nurture the churches of his prior missionary efforts. He was not only concerned with planting the seed but also to see them grow and bear fruit. This led him to undertake the rigorous trip to southern Galatia through rugged terrain and mountain passes. He accomplished what he sought: the churches were strengthened. They flourished. They were more prepared than ever to carry on when he left.[54]

At the start of the third missionary journey Paul once again returns to strengthen the churches he previously planted (Acts 18:22–23). Then, after spending several years in Ephesus, Paul speaks of his desire to revisit existing congregations (Acts 19:21). Within this framework, it is easy to understand why Paul later writes of his "anxiety for all the churches" (2 Cor 11:28). Paul's love and concern for the churches motivates him to visit them often to strengthen their theological foundation.

Perhaps no other ministry demonstrates Paul's concern for the churches like his letter-writing ministry does.[55] Bird makes this point when he writes, "Although the letters 1–2 Timothy and Titus are usually called the 'Pastoral Epistles,' this is somewhat a misnomer, since *all* of Paul's letters are pastoral in one sense or another. In the letters, we see Paul the pastor at work exhorting, encouraging and admonishing his converts and co-workers. The letters provide pastoral care when he is absent."[56] Paul's letters demonstrate his deep concern that the churches get their theology right.

Paul needs to confront erroneous teaching in almost every letter he writes.[57] In Galatians, the believers add to belief in Christ alone for

---

54. Polhill, *Acts*, 344.

55. Bowers, "Fulfilling the Gospel," 190.

56. Michael F. Bird, *Introducing Paul: The Man, His Mission and His Message* (Downers Grove, IL: InterVarsity Press, 2008), 24.

57. The information in this paragraph on the various heresies is taken from Andreas J. Köstenberger, L. Scott Kellum, and Charles L. Quarles, *The Cradle, The Cross, and The Crown:*

salvation by requiring circumcision and the observance of other elements of the Mosaic law. In Thessalonians, the believers are focused on eschatological issues and not on living in accordance with the gospel. In Corinthians, the church has fallen into disunity by celebrating various Christian leaders (1 Cor 1:12). They are not living in accordance with the gospel by permitting sexual immorality (1 Cor 5:1–13) and by engaging in lawsuits among members (1 Cor 6:1–11). In Ephesians and Colossians, believers are giving too much attention to spiritual powers. Paul's concern is that these churches will drift away from the biblical gospel and his work will be in vain.

Paul's letters display a deep and long-lasting commitment to the theological development of the churches he planted. Benjamin Merkle summarizes Paul's letter writing ministry: "[Paul's] goal was not merely to plant churches and let them loose, regardless of the consequences. Rather, Paul wisely maintained a healthy on-going relationship with his churches so that the work of the gospel continued to flourish."[58] Paul writes to correct false doctrine and to encourage faithfulness until the end. His churches often need guidance in thinking through both basic and more complex theological issues. At times they even need guidance in determining appropriately contextualized practices. In these times of need, Paul is ready and willing to come alongside the churches and to assist them in thinking through these issues.

In addition to revisiting and writing, Paul also maintains contact by sending coworkers to assist the churches. Paul's sending of coworkers to existing churches reveals his concern for the theology of those churches.[59] When difficulties arise in his churches, Paul cannot always return to assist them. If he cannot return, though, he sends a coworker (often with a letter) to help the church work through their issues. In this way, Paul uses his vast network of coworkers to continue the ministry of theological development in his churches.

An Introduction to the New Testament (Nashville: Broadman & Holman, 2009), 419, 444, 480, 588, 610.

58. Merkle, "Need for Theological Education in Missions," 55.

59. Bowers, "Fulfilling the Gospel," 190.

CONCLUSION

Paul viewed his mission from a Trinitarian perspective. He understood that the Father is the initiator of mission, the Son is the agent and object of mission, and the Spirit is the one who empowers mission. It is this Trinitarian perspective that drove Paul to the parts of the world that had no access to the gospel in order to call people to know and worship the risen Lord Jesus.

Moreover, Paul's strategy combined both apostolic and pastoral dimensions. Paul was not solely concerned with the planting of churches in new locations, but he was equally concerned that those churches stayed healthy, had strong leadership, and were able to persevere in the faith.

In sum, Paul understood his mission work within the framework of the grand narrative of Scripture. In a biblical-theological sense, he understood that now is the time for the fulfillment of the promises to the patriarchs. Now is the time for the gospel to go to the ends of the earth. As a result, the church today should follow Paul's example of urgent and passionate cross-cultural evangelism, of making sure that all the ἔθνη (peoples) have an opportunity to hear and respond to the gospel.

AFTERWORD

What about you?

_____

In this book we have addressed the theology of world mission, the strategy of world mission, and current issues in world mission from the perspective that the church of Jesus Christ must found every aspect of the missionary task on Scripture. Now the Holy Spirit–inspired word of God is calling you, our reader, to join the church in obeying the Great Commission. How will you respond?

BIBLIOGRAPHY

Adrados, Francisco Rodríguez. *A History of the Greek Language: From Its Origins to the Present*. Boston: Brill, 2005.

Aland, Barbara, et al., eds. *The Greek New Testament*. 4th rev. ed. Stuttgart: Deutsche Bibelgesellschaft, 1983.

Allison, Dale C., Jr. *The New Moses: A Matthean Typology*. Eugene, OR: Wipf & Stock, 2013.

Altstadt, Robert A., and Enoch Wan. "The Salvation of the Unevangelized: What the Literature Suggests." *Global Missiology* 2, no. 2 (2005): 1–21.

An, Hannah S. "The Prophet like Moses (Deut. 18:15–18) and the Woman at the Well (John 4:7–30) in Light of the Dead Sea Scrolls." *The Expository Times* 127 (2016): 469–78.

Anderson, Bernhard W. "Exodus Typology in Second Isaiah." Pages 177–95 in *Israel's Prophetic Heritage: Essays in Honor of James Muilenburg*. Edited by Bernhard W. Anderson and Walter Harrelson. New York: Harper & Brothers, 1962.

Anderson, Courtney. *To the Golden Shore: The Life of Adoniram Judson*. Valley Forge, PA: Judson University Press, 1987.

Andrews, Stephen J. "Some Knowledge of Hebrew Possible to All: The Value of Biblical Hebrew for the Church." *Midwestern Journal of Theology* 17 (2018): 28–51.

Anwaruddin, Sardar M. "Hidden Agenda in TESOL Methods." *Journal of English as an International Language* 6 (2011): 47–58.

Aquinas, Thomas. *The "Summa Theologica" of Thomas Aquinas*. Translated by Fathers of the English Dominican Province. 22 vols. London: R. & T. Washbourne, 1912–1925.

Arnold, Clinton. *The Colossian Syncretism: The Interface between Christianity and Folk Belief at Colossae*. Grand Rapids: Baker, 1996.

Augustine. *On Christian Teaching*. Oxford World's Classics. Translated by R. P. H. Green. Oxford: Oxford University Press, 1997.

———. *The Literal Meaning of Genesis*. Translated by John Hammond Taylor. Ancient Christian Writers. Edited by Johannes Quasten et al. New York: Paulist, 1982.

Baab, Otto J. *The Theology of the Old Testament: The Faith behind the Facts of Hebrew Life and Writings*. New York: Abingdon, 1949.

Baldick, Chris. "Fabula." Page 93 in *The Oxford Dictionary of Literary Terms*. 2nd ed. Oxford: Oxford University Press, 2001.

Barclay, John. " 'Paul's Story' in Paul's Story: Theology as Testimony." Pages 133–56 in *Narrative Dynamics in Paul: A Critical Assessment*. Edited by Bruce Longenecker. Louisville: Westminster John Knox, 2002.

Barker, Kenneth L., and Waylon Bailey. *Micah, Nahum, Habakkuk, Zephaniah*. NAC 20. Nashville: Broadman & Holman, 1998.

Barr, James. *Fundamentalism*. Philadelphia: Westminster, 1977.

———. *The Semantics of Biblical Language*. Oxford: Oxford University Press, 1961.

Barrett, Matthew. "*Sola Scriptura* in the Strange Land of Evangelicalism: The Peculiar but Necessary Responsibility of Defending *Sola Scriptura* against Our Own Kind." *SBJT* 19, no. 4 (2015): 9–38.

Bartholomew, Craig G. *Introducing Biblical Hermeneutics: A Comprehensive Framework for Hearing God in Scripture*. Grand Rapids: Baker, 2015.

Bartholomew, Craig G., and Michael Goheen. *The Drama of Scripture: Finding Our Place in the Biblical Story*. 2nd ed. Grand Rapids: Baker, 2014.

———. "Story and Biblical Theology." Pages 144–71 in *Out of Egypt: Biblical Theology and Biblical Interpretation*. Scripture and Hermeneutics Series 5. Edited by Craig Bartholomew et al. Grand Rapids: Zondervan, 2006.

Bauckham, Richard. *Gospel of Glory: Major Themes in Johannine Theology*. Grand Rapids: Baker, 2015.

———. "Reading Scripture as a Coherent Story." Pages 38–53 in *The Art of Reading Scripture*. Edited by Ellen F. Davis and Richard B. Hays. Grand Rapids: Eerdmans, 2003.

———. *The Testimony of the Beloved Disciple: Narrative, History, and Theology in the Gospel of John*. Grand Rapids: Baker, 2007.

Bauer, Georg Lorenz. *Theologie des alten Testaments: Oder Abriß der religiösen Begriffer der alten Hebräer; von den ältesten Zeiten bis auf den Anfang der christlichen Epoche.* Leipzig: Weygand, 1796.

Baurain, Bradley. "Teaching English Feeds a Worldwide Craving." *EMQ* 28 (1992): 164–73.

Bavinck, Herman. *Reformed Dogmatics.* Vol. 2, *God and Creation.* Translated by John Vriend. Grand Rapids: Baker, 2006.

———. *Reformed Dogmatics.* Vol. 3, *Sin and Salvation in Christ.* Translated by John Vriend. Grand Rapids: Baker, 2006.

Beale, G. K. *A New Testament Biblical Theology: The Unfolding of the Old Testament in the New.* Grand Rapids: Baker, 2011.

———. *The Temple and the Church's Mission: A Biblical Theology of the Dwelling Place of God.* Downers Grove, IL: InterVarsity Press, 2004.

———. "The Use of Hosea 11:1 in Matthew 2:15: One More Time." *JETS* 55 (2012): 697–715.

Beardslee, W. A. "Narrative Form in the NT and Process Theology." *Encounter* 36 (1975): 301–15.

Beasley-Murray, G. R. *Baptism in the New Testament.* Grand Rapids: Eerdmans, 1973.

Beekman, John, and John Callow. *Translating the Word of God: With Scripture and Topical Indexes.* Grand Rapids: Zondervan, 1974.

Beentjes, Pancratius C. "Oracles against the Nations: A Central Issue in the 'Latter Prophets.'" *Bijdragen: Tijdschrift voor filosofie en theologie* 50 (1989): 203–9.

Best, Ernest. *Following Jesus: Discipleship in the Gospel of Mark.* Journal for the Study of the New Testament Supplement Series 4. Sheffield: JSOT, 1981.

Biava, Christina. "Teachers or Missionaries? Duality of Purpose for ESOL Professionals." Paper presented at the Annual Meeting of the American Association for Applied Linguistics. Long Beach, CA, March 17, 1995.

Bird, Michael F. *An Anomalous Jew: Paul among Jews, Greeks, and Romans.* Grand Rapids: Eerdmans, 2016.

———. *Crossing Over Sea and Land: Jewish Missionary Activity in the Second Temple Period.* Peabody, MA: Hendrickson, 2010.

——. *Evangelical Theology: A Biblical and Systematic Introduction.* Grand Rapids: Zondervan, 2013.

——. *Introducing Paul: The Man, His Mission and His Message.* Downers Grove, IL: InterVarsity Press, 2008.

——. "The Letter to the Romans." Pages 177–204 in *All Things to All Cultures: Paul among Jews, Greeks, and Romans.* Edited by Mark Harding and Alanna Nobbs. Grand Rapids: Eerdmans, 2013.

——. "Paul's Religious and Historical Milieu." Pages 17–28 in *Paul's Missionary Methods: In His Time and Ours.* Edited by Robert L. Plummer and John Mark Terry. Downers Grove, IL: InterVarsity Press, 2012.

Bird, Michael F., and Preston M. Sprinkle, eds. *The Faith of Jesus Christ: Exegetical, Biblical, and Theological Studies.* Peabody, MA: Hendrickson, 2009.

Black, David Alan. *Using New Testament Greek in Ministry: A Practical Guide for Students and Pastors.* Grand Rapids: Baker, 1993.

Black, Stephanie L. *Sentence Conjunctions in the Gospel of Matthew: καί, δέ, τότε, γάρ, οὖν and Asyndeton in Narrative Discourse.* The Library of New Testament Studies 216. Sheffield, UK: Sheffield Academic, 2002.

Blendinger, C., D. Müller, and W. Bauder. "Disciple, Follow, Imitate, After." Pages 1:480–94 in *NIDNTT.*

Blomberg, Craig L. *Matthew.* NAC. Nashville: Broadman, 1992.

——. "Matthew." Pages 1–110 in *Commentary on the New Testament Use of the Old Testament.* Edited by G. K. Beale and D. A. Carson. Grand Rapids: Baker, 2007.

Bock, Darrell L. *Acts.* BECNT. Edited by Robert W. Yarbrough and Robert H. Stein. Grand Rapids: Baker Academic, 2008.

——. *Luke: 1:1–9:50.* BECNT. Grand Rapids: Baker Academic, 1994.

Bockmuehl, Klaus. *Books: God's Tools in the History of Salvation.* Vancouver: Regent College, 1986.

Boer, Martinus C. de. *Galatians.* New Testament Library. Louisville: Westminster John Knox, 2011.

Borisenkova, Anna. "Narrative Reconfiguration of Social Events: Paul Ricoeur's Contribution to Rethinking the Social." *Ricoeur Studies* 1 (2010): 87–98.

Bornkamm, Gunther. *Paul.* Translated by D. M. G. Stalker. Minneapolis: Fortress, 1971.

Bosch, David J. "Theological Education in Missionary Perspective." *Missiology* 10 (1982): 13–33.

———. *Transforming Mission: Paradigm Shifts in Theology of Mission*. Maryknoll, NY: Orbis, 1991.

———. *Transforming Mission: Paradigm Shifts in Theology of Mission*. 20th anniversary ed. Maryknoll, NY: Orbis, 2011.

Bouteneff, Peter. *Beginnings: Ancient Christian Readings of the Biblical Creation Narratives*. Grand Rapids: Baker, 2008.

Bowers, Paul. "Fulfilling the Gospel: The Scope of the Pauline Mission." *JETS* 30 (1987): 185–98.

Bray, Gerald. *Biblical Interpretation: Past and Present*. Downers Grove, IL: InterVarsity Press, 1996.

Brewster, Daniel Roy. "Only Paralyzed from the Neck Down: A Biography of the Life and Ministry of E. Thomas Brewster." DMiss diss., Fuller Theological Seminary, 1995.

Brewster, E. Thomas, and Elizabeth S. Brewster. "Language Learning *Is* Communication—*Is* Ministry!" *IBMR* 6 (1982): 160–64.

Brooks, William P. "A Biblical Understanding of the Diversity of Paul's Missionary Coworkers." Pages 209–25 in *Reflecting God's Glory Together: Diversity in Evangelical Mission*. Edited by A. Scott Moreau and Beth Snodderly. EMS 19. Pasadena, CA: William Carey Library, 2011.

———. "Critiquing Ethnohermeneutics Theories: A Call to an Author-Oriented Approach to Cross-Cultural Biblical Interpretation." PhD diss., The Southern Baptist Theological Seminary, 2011.

———. "From Healthy Church to Healthy Church: Why Sending and Planting Models Are Insufficient." Paper presented at the annual meeting of the Evangelical Missiological Society, Southeast Region. April 2016.

———. "Hermeneutic Principles for Developing a Global Theology." *Southern Baptist Journal of Missions and Evangelism* 1 (2012): 46–60.

———. "Hermeneutics for Healthy Churches." *EMQ* (January 2017). https://www.emqonline.com/node/3605.

———. "Pauline Spiritual Warfare: How Paul's Understanding of Satan Influenced His Philosophy of Missions." *Great Commission Research Journal* 3 (2011): 97–113.

Brown, Jeannine K. "Creation's Renewal in the Gospel of John." *Catholic Biblical Quarterly* 72 (2010): 275–90.

Brueggemann, Walter. *Theology of the Old Testament: Testimony, Dispute, Advocacy*. Minneapolis: Fortress, 1997.

Burge, Gary M., Lynn H. Cohick, and Gene L. Green. *The New Testament in Antiquity: A Survey of the New Testament within Its Cultural Contexts*. Grand Rapids: Zondervan, 2009.

Butler, Christopher S. *Structure and Function: A Guide to Three Major Structural-Functional Theories*. 2 vols. Studies in Language Companion Series 63–64. Philadelphia: John Benjamins, 2003.

Cable, Paul S. "*Imitatio Christianorum*: The Function of Believers as Examples in Philippians." *TynBul* 67 (2016): 105–25.

Caird, G. B. *New Testament Theology*. Edited by L. D. Hurst. Oxford: Clarendon, 1994.

Caldwell, Larry W. "Cross-Cultural Bible Interpretation: A View from the Field." *Phronesis* 39 (1996): 13–35.

———. "How Asian Is Asian Theological Education?" Pages 23–45 in *Tending the Seedbeds: Educational Perspectives on Theological Education in Asia*. Edited by Allan Harkness. Quezon City: Asia Theological Association, 2010.

———. "Receptor-Oriented Hermeneutics: Reclaiming the Hermeneutical Methodologies of the New Testament for Bible Interpreters in the Twenty-First Century." PhD diss., Fuller Theological Seminary, 1990.

———. "A Response to the Responses of Tappeiner and Whelchel to Ethnohermeneutics." *JAM* 2 (2000): 135–45.

———. "Teaching Biblical Interpretation in Intercultural Contexts: A Plea for Teaching Biblical Interpretation Using Only the Bible." Pages 269–81 in *Controversies in Missions: Theology, People, and Practice of Mission in the 21st Century*. Edited by Rochelle Cathcart Scheuermann and Ed Smither. EMS 24. Pasadena, CA: William Carey Library, 2016.

———. "Third Horizon Ethnohermeneutics: Re-evaluating New Testament Hermeneutical Models for Intercultural Bible Interpreters Today." *Asia Journal of Theology* 1 (1987): 313–43.

———. "Towards the New Discipline of Ethnohermeneutics: Questioning the Relevancy of Western Hermeneutical Methods in the Asian Context." *JAM* 1 (1999): 21–43.

Callaham, Scott N. "Biblical Hebrew in Chinese: Fostering the Rethinking of Teaching Method through Language Defamiliarization." *HHE* 19 (2017): 103–19.

———. "But Ruth Clung to Her: Textual Constraints on Ambiguity in Ruth 1:14." *TynBul* 63 (2012): 179–97.

———. *Modality and the Biblical Hebrew Infinitive Absolute.* Abhandlungen für die Kunde des Morgenlandes 71. Wiesbaden: Harrassowitz, 2010.

Campbell, Constantine R. *Paul and Union with Christ: An Exegetical and Theological Study.* Grand Rapids: Zondervan, 2012.

Campbell, Douglas A. "Faith and Participation in Paul." Pages 37–61 in *"In Christ" in Paul.* Edited by Michael J. Thate, Kevin J. Vanhoozer, and Constantine R. Campbell. Tübingen: Mohr Siebeck, 2014.

Carbajosa, Ignacio. *Faith, The Fount of Exegesis: The Interpretation of Scripture in Light of the History of Research on the Old Testament.* Translated by Paul Stevenson. San Francisco: Ignatius, 2013.

Carson, D. A., and Douglas J. Moo. *An Introduction to the New Testament.* 2nd ed. Grand Rapids: Zondervan, 2005.

Carson, D. A., Peter T. O'Brien, and Mark A. Seifrid, eds. *Justification and Variegated Nomism.* 2 vols. Grand Rapids: Baker, 2001–2004.

Carson, D. A., and H. G. M. Williamson, eds. *It is Written: Scripture Citing Scripture—Essays in Honour of Barnabas Linsars, SSF.* New York: Cambridge University Press, 1988.

Chalmers, Aaron. "The Importance of the Noahic Covenant to Biblical Theology." *TynBul* 60 (2009): 207–16.

Chandler, Matt. *The Explicit Gospel.* Wheaton, IL: Crossway, 2012.

Chapell, Bryan. *Christ-Centered Preaching: Redeeming the Expository Sermon.* 2nd ed. Grand Rapids: Baker, 2005.

———. *Using Illustrations to Preach with Power.* Rev. ed. Wheaton, IL: Crossway, 2001.

Charry, Ellen T. *By the Renewing of Your Minds: The Pastoral Function of Christian Doctrine.* New York: Oxford University Press, 1997.

Chen, Yi-Ping. "Word Recognition and Reading in Chinese." DPhil diss., University of Oxford, 1993.

Cherbonnier, Edmond La Beaume. "The Theology of the Word of God." *Journal of Religion* 33 (1953): 16–30.

Childs, Brevard S. "Old Testament Theology." Pages 293–300 in *Old Testament Interpretation Past, Present, and Future: Essays in Honour of Gene M. Tucker*. Edited by James Luther Mays, David L. Petersen, and Kent Harold Richards. Edinburgh: T&T Clark, 1995.

——. *Old Testament Theology in a Canonical Context*. Philadelphia: Fortress, 1985.

Ciampa, Roy E. *The Presence and Function of Scripture in Galatians 1–2*. WUNT 2. Tübingen: Mohr Siebeck, 1998.

Cockerill, Gareth Lee. *The Epistle to the Hebrews*. NICNT. Grand Rapids: Eerdmans, 2012.

Coker, David W. "Jesus as the Prophet like Moses in the Fourth Gospel." ThM thesis, Southeastern Baptist Theological Seminary, 2012.

Collins, John J. *The Scepter and the Star: The Messiahs of the Dead Sea Scrolls and Other Ancient Literature*. New York: Doubleday, 1995.

Cook, John A. *Time and the Biblical Hebrew Verb: The Expression of Tense, Aspect, and Modality in Biblical Hebrew*. Linguistic Studies in Ancient West Semitic 7. Winona Lake, IN: Eisenbrauns, 2012.

Creation to Christ. http://t4tonline.org/wp-content/uploads/2011/05/creation-to-christ-oral-version-english.pdf. Accessed January 4, 2018.

Creswell, John W. *Qualitative Inquiry and Research Design: Choosing among Five Traditions*. Thousand Oaks, CA: Sage, 1998.

Crites, Stephen. "The Narrative Quality of Experience." *Journal of the American Academy of Religion* 39 (1971): 291–311.

Crowe, Brandon D. *The Last Adam: A Theology of the Obedient Life of Jesus in the Gospels*. Grand Rapids: Baker, 2017.

Crutcher, Timothy J. "The Relational-Linguistic Spiral: A Model of Language for Theology." *Heythrop Journal* 43 (2002): 463–79.

Dallimore, Arnold. *George Whitefield: The Life and Times of the Great Evangelist of the 18th Century Revival*. 2 vols. Carlisle, PA: Banner of Truth, 1970–1980.

Das, A. Andrew. *Galatians*. Concordia Commentary. St. Louis: Concordia, 2014.

Davidson, Andrew Bruce. *The Theology of the Old Testament*. Edited by S. D. F. Salmond. New York: Charles Scribner's Sons, 1914.

Davies, John A. *A Royal Priesthood: Literary and Intertextual Perspectives on an Image of Israel in Exodus 19.6*. JSOTSup 395. London: T&T Clark, 2004.

Davies, W. D., and Dale C. Allison. *The Gospel according to Matthew*. 3 vols. The International Critical Commentary. Edinburgh: T&T Clark, 1989–1997.

Dayton, Edward R., and David A. Fraser. *Planning Strategies for World Evangelization*. Grand Rapids: Eerdmans, 1980.

Dearborn, Tim A. "Spiritual Disciplines Born of the Travail of Language Learning." *EMQ* 27 (1991): 26–29.

Dempster, Stephen G. *Dominion and Dynasty: A Theology of the Hebrew Bible*. NSBT 15. Downers Grove, IL: InterVarsity Press, 2006.

deSilva, David A. *Introducing the Apocrypha: Message, Context, and Significance*. Grand Rapids: Baker Academic, 2002.

Dever, Mark. "God's Plan of Salvation." Pages 2501–3 in *ESV Study Bible*. Wheaton, IL: Crossway, 2008.

Dik, Simon C. *The Theory of Functional Grammar, Part 1: The Structure of the Clause*. 2nd rev. ed. Functional Grammar Series 20. Edited by Kees Hengeveld. New York: de Gruyter, 1997.

Dockery, David. "Baptism." Pages 55–58 in *Dictionary of Jesus and the Gospels*. Edited by Joel B. Green, Scot McKnight, and I. Howard Marshall. Downers Grove, IL: InterVarsity Press, 1992.

Dodd, C. H. *According to the Scriptures: The Sub-Structure of New Testament Theology*. London: Nisbet, 1952.

Doriani, Daniel M. *Putting the Truth to Work: The Theory and Practice of Biblical Application*. Phillipsburg, NJ: P&R, 2001.

Dumbrell, William J. *Covenant and Creation: A Theology of the Old Testament Covenants*. Carlisle, UK: Paternoster, 1984.

———. *The Faith of Israel: A Theological Survey of the Old Testament*. Grand Rapids: Baker, 2002.

———. *The Search for Order: Biblical Eschatology in Focus*. Eugene, OR: Wipf & Stock, 1994.

Dunn, James D. G. *Jesus' Call to Discipleship*. Cambridge: Cambridge University Press, 1992.

Editorial Staff, imb.org. "12 Characteristics of a Healthy Church (A Summary of David Platt's Teaching)." August 31, 2016. https://www.imb.org/2016/08/31/2016083112-characteristics-healthy-church/.

Edwards, Timothy. *Exegesis in the Targum of Psalms: The Old, the New, and the Rewritten*. Gorgias Dissertations 28: Biblical Studies 1. Piscataway, NJ: Gorgias, 2007.

Eichrodt, Walther. *Theology of the Old Testament*. 2 vols. Translated by J. A. Baker. Philadelphia: Westminster, 1961–1967.

Eißfeldt, Otto. "Israelitisch-jüdische Religionsgeschichte und alttestamentliche Theologie." *Zeitschrift für die alttestamentliche Wissenschaft* 44 (1926): 1–12.

Eitel, Keith E. "The Enduring Legacy of Adoniram Judson's Missiological Precepts and Practices." Pages 129–48 in *Adoniram Judson: A Bicentennial Appreciation of the Pioneer American Missionary*. Edited by Jason G. Duesing. Nashville: B&H Academic, 2012.

Ellis, E. Earle. "Paul and His Coworkers." *NTS* 17 (1970–1971): 437–9.

——. *Paul's Use of the Old Testament*. Grand Rapids: Baker, 1981.

Emerson, Matthew Y. *Christ and the New Creation: A Canonical Approach to the Theology of the New Testament*. Eugene, OR: Wipf & Stock, 2013.

Enns, Marlene. "Educating to Become Wise: Intercultural Theological Education." Pages 55–72 in *The Old Testament in the Life of God's People: Essays in Honor of Elmer A. Martens*. Edited by Jon Isaak. Winona Lake, IN: Eisenbrauns, 2009.

Esler, Philip F. *Galatians*. London: Routledge, 1998.

Espiritu, Daniel L. "Ethnohermeneutics or Oikohermeneutics? Questioning the Necessity of Caldwell's Hermeneutics." *JAM* 3 (2001): 267–81.

Everett, Daniel L. *Language: The Cultural Tool*. New York: Pantheon, 2012.

Fackre, Gabriel. "Narrative Theology: An Overview." *Interpretation* 48 (1983): 340–52.

Farley, Edward. *Theologia: The Fragmentation and Unity in Theological Education*. Philadelphia: Fortress, 1983.

Fee, Gordon D. *New Testament Exegesis: A Handbook for Students and Pastors*. 3rd ed. Louisville: Westminster John Knox, 2002.

——. *Pauline Christology*. Peabody, MA: Hendrickson, 2007.

Ferguson, Everett. *Backgrounds of Early Christianity*. 3rd ed. Grand Rapids: Eerdmans, 2003.

Fiddes, Paul S. "Baptism and Creation." Pages 47–68 in *Reflections on the Water: Understanding God and the World through the Baptism of Believers*. Regent's Study Guides 4. Edited by Paul S. Fiddes. Macon, GA: Smyth & Helwys, 1996.

Fischer, Georg. *Theologien des Alten Testaments*. Neuer Stuttgarter Kommentar—Altes Testament 31. Stuttgart: Katholisches Bibelwerk, 2012.

Fitzmyer, Joseph A. *Romans: A New Translation with Introduction and Commentary*. Anchor Bible 33. New York: Doubleday, 1993.

Flemming, Dean. *Recovering the Full Mission of God: A Biblical Perspective on Being, Doing, and Telling*. Downers Grove, IL: InterVarsity Press, 2013.

Fludernik, Monika. *An Introduction to Narratology*. New York: Routledge, 2009.

Fowler, Stanley K. *More than a Symbol: The British Baptist Recovery of Baptismal Sacramentalism*. Studies in Baptist History and Thought. Eugene, OR: Wipf & Stock, 2007.

France, R. T. *The Gospel of Matthew*. NICNT. Grand Rapids: Eerdmans, 2007.

Freedman, David Noel. "Divine Commitment and Human Obligation: The Covenant Theme." *Interpretation* 18 (1964): 419–31.

Fretheim, Terence E. *God and World in the Old Testament: A Relational Theology of Creation*. Nashville: Abingdon, 2005.

Gage, Warren Austin. *The Gospel of Genesis: Studies in Protology and Eschatology*. Winona Lake, IN: Carpenter, 1984.

Garland, David E. *Luke*. ZECNT. Grand Rapids: Zondervan, 2012.

Garrett, James Leo. *Systematic Theology: Biblical, Historical, and Evangelical*. 3 vols. Grand Rapids: Eerdmans, 1995.

Garrison, V. David. *Church Planting Movements: How God Is Redeeming a Lost World*. Bangalore: WIGTake Resources, 2004.

———. "A New Epoch in Christian Missions: Global Changes since World War II." PhD diss., University of Chicago Divinity School, 1988.

———. *The Nonresidential Missionary: A New Strategy and the People It Serves*. Monrovia, CA: MARC, 1990.

Gentry, Peter J., and Stephen J. Wellum. *Kingdom through Covenant: A Biblical-Theological Understanding of the Covenants*. Wheaton, IL: Crossway, 2012.

George, Timothy. *Faithful Witness: The Life and Mission of William Carey*. Birmingham: Christian History Institute, 1998.

Gerstenberger, Erhard S. *Theologies in the Old Testament*. Translated by John Bowden. New York: T&T Clark, 2002.

Gilbert, Greg. *What Is the Gospel?* Wheaton, IL: Crossway, 2010.

Gill, David W. *The Opening of the Christian Mind: Taking Every Thought Captive to Christ.* Downers Grove, IL: InterVarsity Press, 1989.

Gnilka, Joachim. *Das Matthäusevangelium.* 2 vols. Herders Theologischer Kommentar zum Neuen Testament. Freiburg: Herder, 1988.

Gnutzmann, Claus. "Language for Specific Purposes vs. General Language." Pages 517–44 in *Handbook of Foreign Language Communication and Learning.* Edited by Karlfried Knapp and Barbara Seidlhofer. New York: de Gruyter, 2009.

Goheen, Michael W. "A History and Introduction to a Missional Reading of the Bible." Pages 3–27 in *Reading the Bible Missionally.* Edited by Michael W. Goheen. Grand Rapids: Eerdmans, 2016.

———. *A Light to the Nations: The Missional Church and the Biblical Story.* Grand Rapids: Baker, 2011.

Goldingay, John. *Approaches to Old Testament Interpretation.* 2nd ed. Leicester, UK: Apollos, 1990.

———. *Do We Need the New Testament? Letting the Old Testament Speak for Itself.* Downers Grove, IL: IVP Academic, 2015.

———. "Middle Narratives as an Aspect of Biblical Theology." Pages 203–13 in *Biblical Theology: Past, Present, and Future.* Edited by Carey Walsh and Mark Elliot. Eugene, OR: Cascade, 2016.

———. *Old Testament Theology.* 3 vols. Downers Grove, IL: InterVarsity Press, 2003–2009.

Goldstein, Jonathan. *1 Maccabees.* Anchor Bible 41. New York: Doubleday, 1976.

Gorman, Michael J. *Becoming the Gospel: Paul, Participation, and Mission.* Grand Rapids: Eerdmans, 2015.

Goswell, Greg. "The Order of the Books of the Hebrew Bible." *JETS* 51 (2008): 673–88.

———. "Two Testaments in Parallel: The Influence of the Old Testament on the Structuring of the New Testament Canon." *JETS* 56 (2013): 459–74.

Green, Gene L. *The Letters to the Thessalonians.* Pillar. Grand Rapids: Eerdmans, 2002.

Green, Joel B. "The Problem of a Beginning: Israel's Scriptures in Luke 1–2." *BBR* 4 (1994): 61–86.

Green, Michael. *Evangelism in the Early Church*. Grand Rapids: Eerdmans, 1970.

Greenman, Jeffrey P. "Mission as the Integrating Center of Theological Education." Pages 193–210 in *The Bible in World Christian Perspective: Studies in Honor of Carl Edwin Armerding*. Edited by David W. Baker and W. Ward Gasque. Vancouver: Regent College, 2009.

Greidanus, Sidney. *Preaching Christ from the Old Testament: A Contemporary Hermeneutical Method*. Grand Rapids: Eerdmans, 1999.

Grice, Paul. *Studies in the Way of Words*. Cambridge, MA: Harvard University Press, 1989.

Grunlan, Stephen A., and Marvin K. Mayers. *Cultural Anthropology: A Christian Perspective*. Grand Rapids: Zondervan, 1979.

Guder, Darrell L. "*Missio Dei*: Integrating Theological Formation for Apostolic Vocation." *Missiology* 37 (2009): 63–74.

Gustin, Pat. "How Not to Get Lost in Translation." *Journal of Applied Christian Leadership* 4 (2010): 126–30.

Hahn, Scott W. "Canon, Cult, and Covenant." Pages 207–35 in *Canon and Biblical Interpretation*. Edited by Craig Bartholomew et al. Grand Rapids: Zondervan, 2006.

———. "Kinship by Covenant: A Biblical Theological Study of Covenant Types and Texts in the Old and New Testaments." PhD diss., Marquette University, 1995.

Halperin, Liora R. "Modern Hebrew, Esperanto, and the Quest for a Universal Language." *Jewish Social Studies* 19 (2012): 1–33.

Hamel, Rainer Enrique. "The Dominance of English in the International Scientific Periodical Literature and the Future of Language Use in Science." *Association Internationale de Linguistique Appliquée Review* 20 (2007): 53–71.

Hamilton, Victor P. *The Book of Genesis, Chapters 1–17*. NICOT. Grand Rapids: Eerdmans, 1990.

Harkness, Allan. "Indoctrination." Pages 630–33 in *Encyclopedia of Christian Education*. 3 vols. Edited by George Thomas Kurian and Mark A. Lamport. Lanham, MD: Rowman & Littlefield, 2015.

Harmon, Matthew S. *She Must and Shall Go Free: Paul's Isaianic Gospel in Galatians*. Beihefte zur Zeitschrift für die neutestamentliche Wissenschaft 168. New York: de Gruyter, 2010.

Harrington, Daniel J. *Invitation to the Apocrypha*. Grand Rapids: Eerdmans, 1999.

Harris, Murray J. *The Second Epistle to the Corinthians*. NIGTC. Grand Rapids: Eerdmans, 2005.

Hasel, Gerhard F. *Old Testament Theology: Basic Issues in the Current Debate*. 4th ed. Grand Rapids: Eerdmans, 1991.

Hasler, Jörg. "Shakespeare in German." *Shakespeare Quarterly* 23 (1974): 455–57.

Hauerwas, Stanley, and Gregory Jones, eds. *Why Narrative?: Readings in Narrative Theology*. Eugene, OR: Wipf & Stock, 1997.

Hay, David M. "Paul's Understanding of Faith as Participation." Pages 45–76 in *Paul and His Theology*. Edited by Stanley E. Porter. Leiden: Brill, 2006.

Hayes, John H., and Frederick C. Prussner. *Old Testament Theology: Its History and Development*. Atlanta: John Knox, 1985.

Hays, Richard B. "The Conversion of the Imagination: Scripture and Eschatology in 1 Corinthians." *NTS* 45 (1999): 391–412.

———. *Echoes of Scripture in the Gospels*. Waco, TX: Baylor University Press, 2016.

———. *Echoes of Scripture in the Letters of Paul*. New Haven, CT: Yale University Press, 1989.

———. *The Faith of Jesus Christ: The Narrative Substructure of Galatians 3:1–4:11*. 2nd ed. Grand Rapids: Eerdmans, 2002.

———. "Galatians." Pages 11:181–348 in *NIB*.

Heinisch, Paul. *Theologie des Alten Testamentes*. Bonn: Peter Hanstein, 1940.

Hendriksen, William. *Romans*. New Testament Commentary. Grand Rapids: Baker, 1981.

Henry, Carl F. H. *God, Revelation, and Authority*. 6 vols. Waco, TX: Word Books, 1976–1983.

Hibbs, Pierce Taylor. "Imaging Communion: An Argument for God's Existence Based on Speech." *WTJ* 77 (2015): 35–51.

Hiebert, Paul. *Anthropological Insights for Missionaries*. Grand Rapids: Baker, 1985.

———. *Anthropological Reflections on Missiological Issues*. Grand Rapids: Baker, 1994.

———. "Critical Contextualization." *IBMR* 11 (1987): 104–12.

———. *Transforming Worldviews: An Anthropological Understanding of How People Change*. Grand Rapids: Baker, 2008.

Higgins, Kevin. "Diverse Voices: Hearing Scripture Speak in a Multicultural Environment." Paper presented at the annual meeting of the Evangelical Missiological Society. Charlotte, NC. September 2010.

Hoefer, Herbert. *Churchless Christianity*. Pasadena, CA: William Carey Library, 2002.

Hood, Jason B. *The Messiah, His Brothers, and the Nations: Matthew 1.1-17*. New York: Bloomsbury, 2011.

Hood, Jason B., and Matthew Y. Emerson. "Summaries of Israel's Story: Reviewing a Compositional Category." *CBR* 11 (2013): 328-48.

Hooker, Morna. " 'Heirs of Abraham': The Gentiles' Role in Israel's Story." Pages 85-96 in *Narrative Dynamics in Paul: A Critical Assessment*. Edited by Bruce Longenecker. Louisville: Westminster John Knox, 2002.

Horrell, David G. *Solidarity and Difference: A Contemporary Reading of Paul's Ethics*. 2nd ed. New York: T&T Clark, 2016.

House, Paul. "Examining the Narratives of the Old Testament." *WTJ* 67 (2005): 229-45.

Huang Yi Zhang. *Jiu yue shen xue: Cong chuang zao dao xin chuang zao*. Hong Kong: Tien Dao, 2003.

Hübner, Hans. *Biblische Theologie des Neuen Testaments*. 3 vols. Göttingen: Vandenhoeck & Ruprecht, 1990-1995.

Hurtado, Larry W. *Destroyer of the Gods: Early Christian Distinctiveness in the Roman World*. Waco, TX: Baylor University Press, 2016.

———. "Jesus' Divine Sonship in Paul's Epistle to the Romans." Pages 217-33 in *Romans and the People of God*. Edited by Sven K. Soderlund and N. T. Wright. Grand Rapids: Eerdmans, 1999.

Hwang, Jerry. "The *Missio Dei* as an Integrative Motif in the Book of Jeremiah." *BBR* 23 (2013): 481-508.

Hybels, Lynne. "Lynne Hybels Answers, 'What Is an Evangelical?' " *Sojourners*. October 7, 2011. https://sojo.net/articles/what-evangelical/lynne-hybels-answers-what-evangelical.

Imschoot, Paul van. "De dono linguarum et glossolalia." *Collationes Gandavenses* 9 (1922): 65-70.

———. "Heilige Geest." Cols. 474-85 in *Bijbelsch Woordenboek*. Edited by Adrianus van den Born et al. Turnhout: Brepols, 1941.

———. *Théologie de l'Ancien Testament*. 2 vols. Tournai: Desclée, 1954–1956.

Irenaeus. *Adversus haereses*.

Jacob, Edmond. *Theology of the Old Testament*. Translated by Arthur W. Heathcote and Philip J. Allcock. London: Hodder and Stoughton, 1958.

Jensen, Peter. *The Revelation of God*. Downers Grove, IL: InterVarsity Press, 2002.

Johnson, Dennis E. *Him We Proclaim: Preaching Christ from All the Scriptures*. Phillipsburg, NJ: P&R, 2007.

Josephus. *Antiquitates judaicae*.

Joüon, Paul. Ruth: *Commentaire philologique et exégétique*. Rome: Pontifical Biblical Institute, 1924.

Kaiser, Otto. *Der Gott des Alten Testaments: Theologie des Alten Testaments*. 3 vols. Göttingen: Vandenhoeck & Ruprecht, 1993–2003.

Kaiser, Walter C., Jr. *Mission in the Old Testament: Israel as a Light to the Nations*. 2nd ed. Grand Rapids: Baker Academic, 2012.

———. *Toward an Exegetical Theology: Biblical Exegesis for Preaching & Teaching*. Grand Rapids: Baker, 1981.

Kaiser, Walter C., Jr., and Moisés Silva. *Introduction to Biblical Hermeneutics: The Search for Meaning*. Rev. ed. Grand Rapids: Zondervan, 2007.

Kautzsch, Emil. *Biblische Theologie des Alten Testaments*. Tübingen: J. C. B. Mohr, 1911.

Keefer, Arthur J. "The Use of the Book of Proverbs in Systematic Theology." *Biblical Theology Bulletin* 46 (2016): 35–44.

Keesmaat, Sylvia C. "Exodus and the Intertextual Transformation of Tradition in Romans 8.14–30." *Journal for the Study of the New Testament* 54 (1994): 29–56.

Keller, Timothy. *Center Church*. Grand Rapids: Zondervan, 2012.

Kessler, John. *Old Testament Theology: Divine Call and Human Response*. Waco, TX: Baylor University Press, 2013.

Kirby, Jon P. "Language and Culture Learning IS Conversion . . . IS Ministry." *Missiology* 23 (1995): 131–43.

Knox, John. "Romans 15:14–33 and Paul's Conception of His Apostolic Mission." *JBL* 83 (1964): 1–11.

Koh Kok Chuan. Personal communication.

Koorevaar, Hendrik. "The Exile and Return Model: A Proposal for the Original Macrostructure of the Hebrew Canon." *JETS* 57 (2014): 501–12.

Köstenberger, Andreas J. "Diversity and Unity in the New Testament." Pages 144–65 in *Biblical Theology: Retrospect & Prospect*. Edited by Scott J. Hafemann. Downers Grove, IL: InterVarsity Press, 2002.

———. *John*. BECNT. Grand Rapids: Baker, 2004.

———. *A Theology of John's Gospel and Letters*. Grand Rapids: Zondervan, 2009.

Köstenberger, Andreas J., L. Scott Kellum, and Charles L. Quarles. *The Cradle, the Cross, and the Crown: An Introduction to the New Testament*. Nashville: Broadman & Holman, 2009.

Kraft, Charles H. *Christianity in Culture: A Study in Biblical Theologizing in Cross-Cultural Perspective*. Rev. ed. Maryknoll, NY: Orbis, 2005.

Landes, George M. "What Is Happening in the Work of Seminary Graduates." *TE* 3 (1967): 458–62.

Larson, Donald N. *Guidelines for Barefoot Language Learning: An Approach through Involvement and Independence*. Fresno, CA: Link Care, 1984.

Lawless, Chuck. *Discipled Warriors: Growing Healthy Churches That Are Equipped for Spiritual Warfare*. Grand Rapids: Kregel, 2002.

Lawson, William H. *Ears to Hear: A Guide for the Interpretation of the Bible*. Penang, Malaysia: Institute for Biblical Interpretation, 1994.

———. *The Lion Roars from Zion: A Guide for the Interpretation of the Book of Amos*. Rev. ed. Penang, Malaysia: Institute for Biblical Interpretation, 2003.

———. *Obedient unto Death: A Guide for the Interpretation of Paul's Epistle to the Philippians*. Rev. ed. Penang, Malaysia: Institute for Biblical Interpretation, 2003.

Leaver, Betty Lou, Madeline Ehrman, and Boris Shekhtman. *Achieving Success in Second Language Acquisition*. New York: Cambridge University Press, 2005.

Lee, Archie C. C. "Cross-Textual Hermeneutics." Pages 60–62 in *Dictionary of Third World Theologies*. Edited by Virginia Fabella and R. S. Sugirtharajah. Maryknoll, NY: Orbis, 2000.

Lee, Chee-Chiew. "Once Again: The Niphal and the Hithpael of ברך in the Abrahamic Blessing for the Nations." *JSOT* 36 (2012): 279–96.

Levison, John R. *Portraits of Adam in Early Judaism: From Sirach to 2 Baruch.* Journal for the Study of the Pseudepigrapha Supplement Series 1. Sheffield: JSOT, 1988.

Lewis, Rebecca. "Promoting Movements to Christ within Natural Communities." *International Journal of Frontier Missiology* 24 (2007): 75–76.

Lind, Millard C. "Refocusing Theological Education to Mission: The Old Testament and Contextualization." *Missiology* 10 (1982): 141–60.

Little, Christopher R. *Mission in the Way of Paul: Biblical Mission for the Church in the Twenty-First Century.* Studies in Biblical Literature 80. Edited by Hemchand Gossai. New York: Peter Lang, 2005.

Loewen, Jacob A. "Language: Vernacular, Trade, or National?" Pages 663–72 in *Readings in Missionary Anthropology II.* Edited by William A. Smalley. South Pasadena, CA: William Carey Library, 1978.

Lonergan, Bernard J. F. *Method in Theology.* London: Darton, Longman & Todd, 1971.

Longenecker, Bruce, ed. *Narrative Dynamics in Paul: A Critical Assessment.* Louisville: Westminster John Knox, 2002.

———. "Sharing in Their Spiritual Blessings? The Stories of Israel in Galatians and Romans." Pages 58–84 in *Narrative Dynamics in Paul: A Critical Assessment.* Edited by Bruce Longenecker. Louisville: Westminster John Knox, 2002.

Longenecker, Richard N. *Epistle to the Romans.* NIGTC. Grand Rapids: Eerdmans, 2016.

———. *Galatians.* WBC 41. Nashville: Thomas Nelson, 1990.

———. *Introducing Romans: Critical Issues in Paul's Most Famous Letter.* Grand Rapids: Eerdmans, 2011.

———, ed. *Patterns of Discipleship in the New Testament.* Grand Rapids: Eerdmans, 1996.

Lovejoy, Grant, et al., eds. *Making Disciples of Oral Learners.* Bangalore, India: International Orality Network, 2005.

Lucas, Ernest C. *Daniel.* Apollos Old Testament Commentary. Downers Grove, IL: InterVarsity Press, 2002.

Luz, Ulrich. *Matthew 1–7.* Hermeneia. Minneapolis: Fortress, 2007.

Macaskill, Grant. *Union with Christ in the New Testament.* Oxford: Oxford University Press, 2014.

Marshall, I. Howard. *New Testament Theology: Many Witnesses, One Gospel.* Downers Grove, IL: InterVarsity Press, 2004.

Martens, Elmer A. *God's Design: A Focus on Old Testament Theology.* 2nd ed. Grand Rapids: Baker Books, 1994.

Martin, D. Michael. *1, 2 Thessalonians.* NAC 33. Nashville: Broadman & Holman, 1995.

Maxwell, John C. "Spiritual Reproduction." https://www.sermoncentral .com/content/a-John_Maxwell_07_23_07?ac=true. Accessed May 19, 2017.

McGavran, Donald A. *The Bridges of God: A Study in the Strategy of Missions.* New York: Friendship Press, 1955.

———. *Understanding Church Growth.* Grand Rapids: Zondervan, 1970.

McGee, Gary B. "Shortcut to Language Preparation? Radical Evangelicals, Missions, and the Gift of Tongues." *IBMR* 25 (2001): 118-23.

McKenzie, John L. *A Theology of the Old Testament.* Garden City, NY: Doubleday, 1974.

McKinney, Carol V. *Globe-Trotting in Sandals: A Field Guide in Cultural Research.* Dallas: SIL International, 2000.

———. "Which Language: Trade or Minority?" *Missiology* 18 (1990): 279-90.

McKnight, Edgar V. "Is the New Testament Written in 'Holy Ghost' Greek?" *The Bible Translator* 16 (1965): 87-93.

McNamara, Martin. *Targum and Testament Revisited: Aramaic Paraphrases of the Hebrew Bible.* 2nd ed. Grand Rapids: Eerdmans, 2010.

Mehr, Ruth. "The Role of Motivation in Language Learning." *Dialog on Language Instruction* 21 (2010): 1-10.

Mehrabian, Albert. *Silent Messages.* Belmont, CA: Wadsworth, 1971.

Menconi, Margo Lyn. "Understanding and Relating to the Three Cultures of Cross-Cultural Ministry in Russia." *Missiology* 24 (1996): 519-31.

Merkle, Benjamin L. "The Need for Theological Education in Missions: Lessons Learned from the Church's Greatest Missionary." *SBJT* 9, no. 4 (2005): 50-61.

———. "Paul's Ecclesiology." Pages 56-73 in *Paul's Missionary Methods: In His Time and Ours.* Edited by Robert L. Plummer and John Mark Terry. Downers Grove, IL: IVP Academic, 2012.

Merwe, van der, Christo H. J. "Another Look at the Biblical Hebrew Focus Particle גם." *Journal of Semitic Studies* 54 (2009): 313–32.

Merwe, van der, Christo H. J., Jacobus A. Naudé, and Jan H. Kroeze. *A Biblical Hebrew Reference Grammar*. 2nd ed. New York: Bloomsbury, 2017.

Metzger, Bruce M. *A Textual Commentary on the Greek New Testament*. 2nd ed. Stuttgart: Deutsche Bibelgesellschaft, 1994.

Middleton, J. Richard. *The Liberating Image: The Imago Dei in Genesis 1*. Grand Rapids: Brazos, 2005.

———. *A New Heaven and a New Earth: Reclaiming Biblical Eschatology*. Grand Rapids: Baker, 2014.

Moberly, R. W. L. *Old Testament Theology: Reading the Hebrew Bible as Christian Scripture*. Grand Rapids: Baker Academic, 2013.

Mohrmann, Christine. "How Latin Came to Be the Language of Early Christendom." *Studies: An Irish Quarterly Review* 40 (1951): 277–88.

Moo, Douglas. *The Epistle to the Romans*. NICNT. Grand Rapids: Eerdmans, 1996.

———. *Galatians*. BECNT. Grand Rapids: Baker, 2013.

———. *The Letters to the Colossians and to Philemon*. Pillar. Grand Rapids: Eerdmans, 2008.

Moore, Russell D. "Theology Bleeds: Why Theological Vision Matters for the Great Commission, and Vice Versa." Pages 103–20 in *The Great Commission Resurgence: Fulfilling God's Mandate in Our Time*. Edited by Chuck Lawless and Adam W. Greenway. Nashville: B&H Academic, 2010.

Moreau, A. Scott, Gary R. Corwin, and Gary B. McGee. *Introducing World Missions: A Biblical, Historical, and Practical Survey*. Grand Rapids: Baker Academic, 2004.

Morris, Leon. *The Epistle to the Romans*. Pillar. Grand Rapids: Eerdmans, 1988.

Moschos, John. *The Spiritual Meadow*. Translated by John Wortley. Cistercian Studies 139. Kalamazoo, MI: Cistercian, 1992.

Moulton, James Hope. *A Grammar of New Testament Greek*. 3rd ed. Vol. 3, *Syntax*. By Nigel Turner. Edinburgh: T&T Clark, 1963.

Mounce, William D. *Pastoral Epistles*. WBC 46. Nashville: Thomas Nelson, 2000.

Müller, Mogens. *The Expression "Son of Man" and the Development of Christology: A History of Interpretation*. Sheffield, UK: Equinox, 2008.

Muraoka, Takamitsu. *My Via Dolorosa: Along the Trails of the Japanese Imperialism in Asia*. Bloomington, IN: AuthorHouse, 2016.

Nanos, Mark D., ed. *The Galatians Debate*. Peabody, MA: Hendrickson, 2002.

Nässelquist, Dan. "Disciple." In *The Lexham Bible Dictionary*. Edited by John D. Barry. Bellingham, WA: Lexham Press, 2012-2015.

Navone, John. "Narrative Theology and Its Uses: A Survey." *Irish Theological Quarterly* 52 (1986): 212-30.

Newbigin, Lesslie. *The Gospel in a Pluralist Society*. Grand Rapids: Eerdmans, 1989.

———. *Trinitarian Theology for Today's Mission*. Eugene, OR: Wipf & Stock, 2006.

Nida, Eugene. *Message and Mission*. New York: Harper & Row, 1960.

Niehaus, Jeffrey J. *Biblical Theology*. Vol. 1, *The Common Grace Covenants*. Wooster, OH: Weaver, 2014.

Niles, D. T. *That They May Have Life*. New York: Harper & Brothers, 1951.

Noelliste, Dieumeme. *Toward A Theology of Theological Education*. Seoul: World Evangelical Fellowship Theological Commission, 1993.

Noels, Kimberly A., Luc G. Pelletier, Richard Clément, and Robert J. Vallerand. "Why Are You Learning a Second Language? Motivational Orientations and Self-Determination Theory." *Language Learning* 50 (2000): 57-85.

Nolland, John. *The Gospel of Matthew*. NIGTC. Grand Rapids: Eerdmans, 2005.

Noonan, Jennifer, and Paul Overland. "Teaching Biblical Hebrew to Oral-Preference Learners." *HHE* 19 (2017): 121-34.

Novenson, Matthew V. *Christ among the Messiahs: Christ Language in Paul and Messiah Language in Ancient Judaism*. New York: Oxford University Press, 2015.

Oakes, Peter. *Galatians*. Paideia: Commentaries on the New Testament. Grand Rapids: Baker, 2015.

Oehler, Gustav Friedrich. *Theologie des Alten Testaments*. 3rd ed. Stuttgart: J. F. Steinkopf, 1891.

Old, Hughes Oliphant. *The Reading and Preaching of the Scriptures in the Worship of the Christian Church*. 3 vols. Grand Rapids: Eerdmans, 1999.

Olford, Stephen F., and David L. Olford. *Anointed Expository Preaching*. Nashville: Broadman & Holman, 1998.

Osborne, Grant R. *The Hermeneutical Spiral: A Comprehensive Introduction to Biblical Hermeneutics*. Rev. ed. Downers Grove, IL: IVP Academic, 2006.

―――. *Matthew*. ZECNT. Grand Rapids: Zondervan, 2010.

Page, Sydney H. T. *Powers of Evil: A Biblical Study of Satan & Demons*. Grand Rapids: Baker, 1995.

Pao, David W. *Acts and the Isaianic New Exodus*. Eugene, OR: Wipf & Stock, 2016.

Pao, David W., and Eckhard J. Schnabel. "Luke." Pages 251–414 in *Commentary on the New Testament Use of the Old Testament*. Edited by D. A. Carson and G. K. Beale. Grand Rapids: Baker, 2007.

Park, Jin-kyu. " 'English Fever' in South Korea: Its History and Symptoms." *English Today: The International Review of the English Language* 25 (2009): 50–57.

Pate, C. Marvin, et al. *The Story of Israel: A Biblical Theology*. Downers Grove, IL: IVP Academic, 2004.

Payne, J. Barton. *The Theology of the Older Testament*. Grand Rapids: Zondervan, 1962.

Pearce, Preston. Personal communication.

Pennycook, Alastair, and Sophie Coutand-Marin. "Teaching English as a Missionary Language." *Discourse: Studies in the Cultural Politics of Education* 24 (2003): 337–53.

Petersen, Norman. *Rediscovering Paul: Philemon and the Sociology of Paul's Narrative World*. 2nd ed. Eugene, OR: Wipf & Stock, 2008.

Phillipson, Robert. *Linguistic Imperialism*. New York: Oxford University Press, 1992.

Piepenbring, C. *Théologie de l'Ancien Testament*. Paris: Librairie Fischbacher, 1886.

Piper, John. *Let the Nations Be Glad!: The Supremacy of God in Missions*. 3rd ed. Grand Rapids: Baker, 2010.

Piper, John, and Justin Taylor, eds. *The Power of Words and the Wonder of God*. Wheaton, IL: Crossway, 2009.

Pitre, Brant. *Jesus the Bridegroom: The Greatest Love Story Ever Told.* New York: Image, 2014.

Plummer, Robert L. *40 Questions about Interpreting the Bible.* 40 Questions Series. Edited by Benjamin L. Merkle. Grand Rapids: Kregel, 2010.

Polak, Frank. "Oral Substratum, Language Usage, and Thematic Flow in the Abraham-Jacob Narrative." Pages 217–38 in *Contextualizing Israel's Sacred Writing: Ancient Literacy, Orality, and Literary Production.* Edited by Brian Schmidt. Atlanta: SBL Press, 2015.

Polhill, John B. *Acts.* NAC 26. Nashville: Broadman & Holman, 1992.

Porter, Stanley E. "Allusions and Echoes." Pages 29–40 in *As It Is Written: Studying Paul's Use of Scripture.* Edited by Stanley Porter and Christopher Stanley. Atlanta: SBL Press, 2008.

———. "Luke: Companion or Disciple of Paul?" Pages 146–68 in *Paul and the Gospels: Christologies, Controversies, and Convergences.* Edited by Michael F. Bird and Joel Willitts. London: T&T Clark, 2011.

———. "The Use of the Old Testament in the New Testament: A Brief Comment on Method and Terminology." Pages 79–96 in *Early Christian Interpretation of the Scriptures of Israel.* Edited by C. A. Evans and J. A. Sanders. Sheffield, UK: Sheffield Academic, 1997.

Porter, Stanley E., and Christopher Stanley, eds. *As It Is Written: Studying Paul's Use of Scripture.* Atlanta: SBL Press, 2008.

Postell, Seth D. *Adam as Israel: Genesis 1–3 as the Introduction to the Torah and Tanakh.* Eugene, OR: Pickwick, 2011.

Powell, Mark Allan. *What Is Narrative Criticism?* Minneapolis: Fortress, 1991.

Poythress, Vern Sheridan. *In the Beginning Was the Word: Language— A God-Centered Approach.* Wheaton, IL: Crossway, 2009.

Preuß, Horst Dietrich. *Old Testament Theology.* Translated by Leo G. Perdue. 2 vols. Louisville: Westminster, 1995–1996.

Quarles, Charles L. *A Theology of Matthew: Jesus Revealed as Deliverer, King, and Incarnate Creator.* Phillipsburg, PA: P&R, 2013.

Raabe, Paul R. "Look to the Holy One of Israel, All You Nations: The Oracles about the Nations Still Speak Today." *Concordia Journal* 30 (2004): 336–49.

Rad, Gerhard von. *Genesis: A Commentary.* Translated by John H. Marks. Old Testament Library. Philadelphia: Westminster, 1961.

———. *Old Testament Theology*. 2 vols. Translated by D. M. G. Stalker. New York: Harper, 1962–1965.

———. "Das theologische Problem des alttestamentlichen Schöpfungs-glaubens." Pages 138–47 in *Werden und Wesen des Alten Testaments*. Edited by Paul Volz, Friedrich Stummer, and Johannes Hempel. Beihefte zur Zeitschrift für die alttestamentliche Wissenschaft 66. Berlin: Töpelmann, 1936.

———. "Typologische Auslegung des Alten Testaments." *Evangelische Theologie* 12 (1952–1953): 17–33.

Radford, Andrew. *Syntax: A Minimalist Introduction*. New York: Cambridge University Press, 1997.

Richard, H. L. "Christ Followers in India Flourishing—but outside the Church: A Review of Herbert E. Hoefer's *Churchless Christianity*." Page 150 in *Understanding Insider Movements: Disciples of Jesus within Diverse Religious Communities*. Edited by Harley Talman and John Jay Travis. Pasadena, CA: William Carey Library, 2016.

Ricoeur, Paul. *Hermeneutics and the Human Sciences*. Edited and translated by John B. Thompson. Cambridge: Cambridge University Press, 1981.

———. *Time and Narrative*. Vol. 1. Translated by Kathleen McLaughlin and David Pellauer. Chicago: University of Chicago Press, 1990.

———. "Toward a Narrative Theology: Its Necessity, Its Resources, Its Difficulties." Pages 236–48 in *Figuring the Sacred: Religion, Narrative, and Imagination*. Edited by Mark Wallace. Minneapolis: Fortress, 1995.

Ridderbos, Herman N. *Paul: An Outline of His Theology*. Translated by John Richard de Witt. Grand Rapids: Eerdmans, 1975.

Roberts, David Harrill. "Deschooling Language Study in East Africa: The Zambia Plan." Paper presented at the Delaware Symposium on Language Study. Newark, DE. October 1979.

Robertson, A. T. *The Minister and His Greek New Testament*. New York: George H. Doran, 1923.

Robinson, George. "The Gospel as Story and Evangelism as Story Telling." Pages 76–91 in *Theology and Practice of Mission: God, the Church, and the Nations*. Edited by Bruce Ashford. Nashville: Broadman & Holman, 2011.

Robinson, Haddon. "The Heresy of Application." *Leadership Journal*. 1997. http://www.christianitytoday.com/pastors/1997/fall/7l4020.html.

Routledge, Robin. *Old Testament Theology: A Thematic Approach*. Downers Grove, IL: InterVarsity Press, 2008.

Rudrum, David. "From Narrative Representation to Narrative Use." *Narrative* 13 (2005): 195–204.

Sailhamer, John H. "Hosea 11:1 and Matthew 2:15." *WTJ* 63 (2001): 87–96.

———. *The Meaning of the Pentateuch: Revelation, Composition, and Interpretation*. Downers Grove, IL: InterVarsity Press, 2009.

———. *The Pentateuch as Narrative: A Biblical-Theological Commentary*. Grand Rapids: Zondervan, 1992.

Sanneh, Lamin. *Translating the Message: The Missionary Impact on Culture*. American Society of Missiology Series 13. Maryknoll, NY: Orbis, 1990.

Sargent, John, ed. *The Life and Letters of Henry Martyn*. Carlisle, PA: Banner of Truth, 1985.

Sawin, Thor Andrew. "Second Language Learnerhood among Cross-Cultural Field Workers." PhD diss., University of South Carolina, 2013.

Sawyer, John F. A. *Sacred Languages and Sacred Texts*. New York: Routledge, 1999.

Schnabel, Eckhard J. *Early Christian Mission: Jesus and the Twelve*. Downers Grove, IL: IVP Academic, 2004.

———. *Early Christian Mission: Paul and the Early Church*. Downers Grove, IL: IVP Academic, 2004.

———. "Paul the Missionary." Pages 29–43 in *Paul's Missionary Methods: In His Time and Ours*. Edited by Robert L. Plummer and John Mark Terry. Downers Grove, IL: IVP Academic, 2012.

———. *Paul the Missionary: Realities, Strategies and Methods*. Downers Grove, IL: IVP Academic, 2008.

Schnelle, Udo. *Theology of the New Testament*. Translated by M. Eugene Boring. Grand Rapids: Baker, 2009.

Scholl, George. "Points to Be Emphasized in Preparation for Missionary Work." Pages 73–81 in *World-Wide Evangelization the Urgent Business of the Church*. New York: Student Volunteer Movement for Foreign Missions, 1902.

Schreiner, Josef. *Theologie des Alten Testaments*. Neuen Echter Bibel—Altes Testament 1. Würzburg: Echter, 1995.

Schreiner, Thomas R. *Galatians*. ZECNT. Grand Rapids: Zondervan, 2010.

———. *Interpreting the Pauline Epistles*. Guides to New Testament Exegesis. Edited by Scot McKnight. Grand Rapids: Baker, 1990.

———. *New Testament Theology: Magnifying God in Christ*. Grand Rapids: Baker, 2008.

———. *Paul, Apostle of God's Glory in Christ: A Pauline Theology*. Downers Grove, IL: IVP Academic, 2001.

———. *Romans*. BECNT. Edited by Moisés Silva. Grand Rapids: Baker Academic, 1998.

Schreiner, Thomas R., and Shawn D. Wright, eds. *Believer's Baptism: Sign of the New Covenant in Christ*. NAC Studies in Bible & Theology. Nashville: Broadman & Holman, 2015.

Scott, James M. *Paul and the Nations: The Old Testament and Jewish Background of Paul's Mission to the Nations with Special Reference to the Destination of Galatians*. Tübingen: Mohr Siebeck, 1995.

Scott, Lindy. "Singing into the Wind: Uses and Abuses of 'Christian' Songs in Our Foreign Language Classes." *Journal of Christianity and Foreign Languages* 5 (2005): 75–81.

Sechrest, Love L. *A Former Jew: Paul and the Dialectics of Race*. New York: Bloomsbury T&T Clark, 2009.

Sellin, Ernst. *Theologie des Alten Testaments*. 2nd ed. Leipzig: Quelle and Meyer, 1936.

Senior, Donald, and Carroll Stuhlmueller. *The Biblical Foundations for Mission*. Maryknoll, NY: Orbis, 1983.

Shaw, Perry. *Transforming Theological Education: A Practical Handbook for Integrative Learning*. Carlisle, UK: Langham Global Library, 2014.

Shklovsky, Viktor. *Theory of Prose*. Translated by Benjamin Sher. Normal, IL: Dalkey Archive, 1998.

Sills, M. David. "The Great Commission and Intercultural Communication." Pages 79–92 in *The Challenge of the Great Commission: Essays on God's Mandate for the Local Church*. Edited by Chuck Lawless and Thom S. Rainer. Crestwood, KY: Pinnacle, 2005.

———. *Reaching and Teaching: A Call to Great Commission Obedience*. Chicago: Moody, 2010.

Silva, Moisés. *Biblical Words and Their Meaning: An Introduction to Lexical Semantics*. Grand Rapids: Zondervan, 1983.

———, ed. "ἔθνος." Pages 2:89–93 in *NIDNTTE*.

Slack, James B., James O. Terry, and Grant Lovejoy. *Tell the Story: A Primer on Chronological Bible Storying*. Rockville, VA: International Center for Excellence in Leadership, 2003.

Smalley, William A. "Culture Shock, Language Shock, and the Shock of Self-Discovery." Pages 693–700 in *Readings in Missionary Anthropology II*. Edited by William A. Smalley. South Pasadena, CA: William Carey Library, 1978.

———. "Missionary Language Learning in a World Hierarchy of Languages." *Missiology* 22 (1994): 481–88.

Smith, Daniel Lynwood. "The Use of 'New Exodus' in New Testament Scholarship: Preparing a Way through the Wilderness." *CBR* 14 (2016): 207–43.

Smith, Gordon T. "Spiritual Formation in the Academy: A Unifying Model." *TE* 33 (1996): 83–91.

Smith, Stephen R. "Gospel Presentations Used in T4T Packages." http:// t4tonline.org/wp-content/uploads/2011/02/3d-Gospel-Presentations -Used-in-T4T-Packages.pdf. Cited 4 January 2018.

Smith, Stephen R., and Ying Kai. *T4T: A Discipleship ReRevolution*. Bangalore: WIGTake Resources, 2011.

Snodgrass, J. B. "Mission to Hindus." Pages 238–51 in *Theology and Practice of Mission: God, the Church, and the Nations*. Edited by Bruce Ashford. Nashville: Broadman & Holman, 2011.

Sommer, Benjamin D. "Dialogical Biblical Theology: A Jewish Approach to Reading Scripture Theologically." Pages 1–53 in *Biblical Theology: Introducing the Conversation*. Edited by Leo G. Perdue, Robert Morgan, and Benjamin D. Sommer. Library of Biblical Theology. Nashville: Abingdon, 2009.

Speer, Robert E. "The Supreme and Determining Aim." Pages 15–19 in *Roots of the Great Debate in Mission: Mission in Historical and Theological Perspective*. Edited by Roger E. Hedlund. Rev. ed. Bangalore, India: Theological Book Trust, 1981.

Spradley, James P. *The Ethnographic Interview*. Fort Worth, TX: Harcourt Brace Jovanovich, 1979.

———. *Participant Observation*. Fort Worth, TX: Harcourt Brace Jovanovich, 1980.

Spykman, Gordon J. *Reformational Theology: A New Paradigm for Doing Dogmatics*. Grand Rapids: Eerdmans, 1992.

Stade, Bernhard. *Biblische theologie des Alten Testaments*. Tübingen: J. C. B. Mohr, 1905–1911.

Stagg, Frank. "The Abused Aorist." *JBL* 91 (1972): 222–31.

Stambaugh, John E., and David L. Balch. *The New Testament in Its Social Environment*. Library of Early Christianity. Edited by Wayne A. Meeks. Philadelphia: Westminster, 1986.

Starr, J. Barton. "The Legacy of Robert Morrison." *IBMR* 22 (1988): 73–76.

Steffen, Tom. "Chronological Communication of the Gospel Goes from Country to City." Paper presented at the Evangelical Missiological Society Southwest Region meeting. March 18, 2011.

Steffen, Tom, and Lois McKinney Douglas. *Encountering Missionary Life and Work: Preparing for Intercultural Ministry*. Grand Rapids: Baker Academic, 2008.

Stein, Robert H. *A Basic Guide to Interpreting the Bible: Playing by the Rules*. Grand Rapids: Baker, 1994.

———. "The Benefits of an Author-Oriented Approach to Hermeneutics." *JETS* 44 (2001): 451–66.

———. *Mark*. BECNT. Grand Rapids: Baker, 2008.

Storti, Craig. *The Art of Crossing Cultures*. 2nd ed. Boston: Intercultural, 2001.

"The Story." https://thestoryfilm.com. Accessed January 23, 2018.

Strandenaes, Thor. *Principles of Chinese Bible Translation: As Expressed in Five Selected Versions of the New Testament and Exemplified by Mt 5:1–12 and Col 1*. Coniectanea Biblica: New Testament Series 19. Stockholm: Almqvist and Wiksell, 1987.

Strauss, Mark L. *Mark*. ZECNT. Grand Rapids: Zondervan, 2014.

Strong, Augustus H. *Systematic Theology: A Compendium Designed for the Use of Theological Students*. Valley Forge, PA: Judson, 1907.

Stuart, Douglas. *Old Testament Exegesis: A Handbook for Students and Pastors*. 4th ed. Louisville: Westminster John Knox, 2009.

Sun, Wendel. "Biblical Theology and Cross-Cultural Theological Education: The Epistle to the Romans as a Model." *Global Missiology* 4, no. 12 (2015): 1–14.

——. *A New People in Christ: Adam, Israel, and Union with Christ in Romans*. Eugene, OR: Pickwick, 2018.

Tal, Abraham. " 'Hebrew Language' and 'Holy Language' between Judea and Samaria." Pages 187–201 in *Samaria, Samarians, Samaritans: Studies on Bible, History and Linguistics*. Edited by József Zsengellér. Boston: de Gruyter, 2011.

Talman, Harley, and John Jay Travis, eds. *Understanding Insider Movements: Disciples of Jesus within Diverse Religious Communities*. Pasadena, CA: William Carey Library, 2016.

Tan, Kang-San. "In Search of Contextualised Training Models for Chinese Christian Diaspora in Britain." *Transformation* 28 (2011): 29–41.

Tan, Sunny Boon-Sang. "Community-Building: A Formative Principle in Theological Education (with Special Reference to the Baptist Theological Seminary, Malaysia)." ThM thesis, Regent College, 1994.

Thielman, Frank. *Theology of the New Testament: A Canonical and Synthetic Approach*. Grand Rapids: Zondervan, 2005.

Thomas, Robert L. "Current Hermeneutical Trends: Toward Explanation or Obfuscation?" *JETS* 39 (1996): 247–48.

Tong, Clement Tsz Ming. "The Protestant Missionaries as Bible Translators: Mission and Rivalry in China, 1807–1839." PhD diss., University of British Columbia, 2016.

Travis, John J., and J. Dudley Woodberry. "When God's Kingdom Grows like Yeast: Frequently Asked Questions about Jesus Movements within Muslim Communities." *Mission Frontiers* 32, no. 4 (2010): 24–30.

Turner, David L. *Matthew*. BECNT. Grand Rapids: Baker, 2008.

Van Rheenen, Gailyn. *Communicating Christ in Animistic Contexts*. Pasadena, CA: William Carey Library, 1991.

VanderKam, James C. *The Dead Sea Scrolls Today*. 2nd ed. Grand Rapids: Eerdmans, 2010.

Vanhoozer, Kevin J. *Biblical Narrative in the Philosophy of Paul Ricoeur: A Study in Hermeneutics and Theology*. Cambridge: Cambridge University Press, 2007.

Varghese, Manka M., and Bill Johnston. "Evangelical Christians and English Language Teaching." *TESOL Quarterly* 41 (2007): 5–31.

Verkuyl, Johannes. "Biblical Foundation for the Worldwide Missions Mandate." Pages 27–33 in *Perspectives on the World Christian Movement*.

3rd ed. Edited by Ralph D. Winter and Steven C. Hawthorne. Pasadena, CA: William Carey Library, 1999.

Via, Dan O. *The Ethics of Mark's Gospel: In the Middle of Time.* Eugene, OR: Wipf & Stock, 2005.

Vogels, Walter. "Restauration de l'Égypte et universalisme en Ez 29,13–16." *Biblica* 53 (1972): 473–94.

Vriezen, Theodorus C. *An Outline of Old Testament Theology.* Translated by S. Neuijen. Newton, MA: Charles T. Branford, 1958.

Wallace, Daniel B. *Greek Grammar beyond the Basics: An Exegetical Syntax of the New Testament.* Grand Rapids: Zondervan, 1996.

Waltke, Bruce K. "How I Changed My Mind about Teaching Biblical Hebrew (or Retained It)." *Crux* 29, no. 4 (1993): 10–15.

Waltke, Bruce K., and Michael P. O'Connor. *An Introduction to Biblical Hebrew Syntax.* Winona Lake, IN: Eisenbrauns, 1990.

Waltke, Bruce K., and Charles Yu. *An Old Testament Theology: An Exegetical, Canonical, and Thematic Approach.* Grand Rapids: Zondervan, 2007.

Walton, John H. *The Lost World of Genesis 1: Ancient Cosmology and the Origins Debate.* Downers Grove, IL: InterVarsity Press, 2010.

Wan, Enoch. "Ethnohermeneutics: Its Necessity and Difficulty for All Christians of All Times." ETS Microform, ETS-4772 (1995).

Ward, Graham. "Narratives and Ethics: The Structures of Believing and the Practices of Hope." *Literature and Theology: An International Journal of Religion, Theory and Culture* 20 (2006): 438–61.

Ware, Bruce A. "Believers' Baptism View." Pages 19–50 in *Baptism: Three Views.* Spectrum Multiview Books. Edited by David F. Wright. Downers Grove, IL: InterVarsity Press, 2009.

Watson, Francis. "Is There a Story in These Texts?" Pages 231–39 in *Narrative Dynamics in Paul: A Critical Assessment.* Edited by Bruce Longenecker. Louisville: Westminster John Knox, 2002.

———. *Paul and the Hermeneutics of Faith.* 2nd ed. London: Bloomsbury T&T Clark, 2016.

Watts, Rikki E. "Consolation or Confrontation: Isaiah 40–55 and the Delay of the New Exodus." *TynBul* 41 (1990): 31–59.

———. "Echoes from the Past: Israel's Ancient Traditions and the Destiny of the Nations in Isaiah 40–55." *JSOT* 28 (2004): 481–508.

——. *Isaiah's New Exodus in Mark*. WUNT 88. Tübingen: Mohr Siebeck, 1997.

Wax, Trevin. *Counterfeit Gospels: Rediscovering the Good News in a World of False Hope*. Nashville: Broadman & Holman, 2011.

Weber, Jeremy. "Outpacing Persecution: Why It's the Best of Times and the Worst of Times for India's Burgeoning Churches." *Christianity Today* 60, no. 9 (2016): 38–47.

Wegner, Paul D. *Using Old Testament Hebrew in Preaching: A Guide for Students and Pastors*. Grand Rapids: Kregel, 2009.

Wendland, Ernst. " 'You Will Do Even More Than I Say': On the Rhetorical Function of Stylistic Form in the Letter to Philemon." Pages 79–111 in *Philemon in Perspective: Interpreting a Pauline Letter*. Edited by D. Francois Tolmie. Berlin: de Gruyter, 2010.

Wenham, Gordon J. "Sanctuary Symbolism in the Garden of Eden Story." Pages 399–404 in *I Studied Inscriptions from before the Flood: Ancient Near Eastern, Literary, and Linguistic Approaches to Genesis 1–11*. Edited by Richard Hess and David Toshio Tsumura. Winona Lake, IN: Eisenbrauns, 1994.

Westermann, Claus. *Elements of Old Testament Theology*. Translated by Douglas W. Scott. Atlanta: John Knox, 1982.

White, Emanuel. "A Critical Edition of the Targum of Psalms: A Computer Generated Text of Books I and II." PhD diss., McGill University, 1988.

White, Joel R. "N. T. Wright's Narrative Approach." Pages 181–206 in *God and the Faithfulness of Paul: A Critical Examination of the Pauline Theology of N. T. Wright*. Edited by Christoph Heilig, J. Thomas Hewitt, and Michael Bird. Minneapolis: Fortress, 2017.

Wilkins, Michael J. "Disciples and Discipleship." Pages 202–12 in *Dictionary of Jesus and the Gospels: A Compendium of Contemporary Biblical Scholarship*. 2nd ed. Edited by Joel B. Green, Jeannine K. Brown, and Nicholas Perrin. Downers Grove, IL: InterVarsity Press, 2013.

Williams, Sam K. *Galatians*. Abingdon New Testament Commentaries. Nashville: Abingdon, 1997.

Williamson, Paul R. *Sealed with an Oath: Covenant in God's Unfolding Purpose*. Downers Grove, IL: InterVarsity Press, 2007.

Witherington, Ben. "Dialogue with Scot McKnight on 'King Jesus': Part One." *The Bible and Culture* (blog). September 10, 2011. http://www

.patheos.com/blogs/bibleandculture/2011/09/10/dialogue-with-scot
-mcknight-on-king-jesus-part-one-2.

———. *Paul's Narrative Thought World: The Tapestry of Tragedy and Triumph.* Louisville: Westminster John Knox, 1994.

Woodberry, Robert D. "The Missionary Roots of Liberal Democracy." *American Political Science Review* 106 (2012): 244–74.

Woolsey, Andrew A. "The Covenant in the Church Fathers." *Haddington House Journal* 5 (2003): 25–52.

Wright, Christopher J. H. *The Mission of God: Unlocking the Bible's Grand Narrative.* Downers Grove, IL: InterVarsity Press, 2006.

———. *The Mission of God's People: A Biblical Theology of the Church's Mission.* Grand Rapids: Zondervan, 2010.

Wright, N. T. "The Book and the Story." *The Bible in TransMission.* September 1, 2001. http://www.biblesociety.org.uk/uploads/content/bible_in _transmission/files/2001_special_edition/BiT_Special_2001_Wright .pdf.

———. *The Climax of the Covenant: Christ and the Law in Pauline Theology.* Minneapolis: Fortress, 1991.

———. "Israel's Scriptures in Paul's Narrative Theology." *Theology* 115 (2012): 323–29.

———. "New Exodus, New Inheritance: The Narrative Substructure of Romans 3–8." Pages 26–35 in *Romans and the People of God: Essays in Honor of Gordon D. Fee on the Occasion of His 65th Birthday.* Edited by Sven K. Soderlund and N. T. Wright. Grand Rapids: Eerdmans, 1999.

———. "The New Inheritance According to Paul." *Bible Review* 14, no. 3 (1998): 16, 47.

———. *The New Testament and the People of God.* Christian Origins and the Question of God 1. Atlanta: Augsburg Fortress, 1992.

———. *Paul and the Faithfulness of God.* Christian Origins and the Question of God 4. Minneapolis: Fortress, 2013.

———. "Reading the New Testament Missionally." Pages 175–93 in *Reading the Bible Missionally.* Edited by Michael W. Goheen. Grand Rapids: Eerdmans, 2016.

———. *The Resurrection of the Son of God.* Christian Origins and the Question of God 3. Minneapolis: Fortress, 2003.

———. "Romans." Pages 10:393–770 in *NIB.*

———. *Scripture and the Authority of God: How to Read the Bible Today*. New York: HarperOne, 2013.

Wu, Jackson. "Critiquing Creation to Christ (C2C)." Jackson Wu (blog). April 11, 2013. http://www.patheos.com/blogs/jacksonwu/2013/04/11/ critiquing-creation-to-christ-c2c.

———. "The Influence of Culture on the Evolution of Mission Methods: Using CPMs as a Case Study." *Global Missiology* 1, no. 12 (2014): 1–11.

———. *One Gospel for All Nations: A Practical Approach to Biblical Contextualization*. Pasadena, CA: William Carey Library, 2015.

———. Personal communication.

———. "Taking the Context Out of the Bible?" Jackson Wu (blog). April 9, 2013. http://www.patheos.com/blogs/jacksonwu/2013/04/09/taking -the-context-out-of-the-bible-contextualization-among-oral-peoples -series.

Wycliffe Global Alliance. "Scripture & Language Statistics 2017." http:// www.wycliffe.net/statistics. Accessed January 24, 2018.

Yoder, John Howard. *Theology of Mission: A Believers Church Perspective*. Edited by Gayle Gerber Koontz and Andy Alexis-Baker. Downers Grove, IL: InterVarsity Press, 2014.

York, Hershael W., and Bert Decker. *Preaching with Bold Assurance: A Solid and Enduring Approach to Engaging Exposition*. Nashville: Broadman & Holman, 2003.

Yovel, Jonathan. "The Creation of Language and Language without Time: Metaphysics and Metapragmatics in Genesis 1." *Biblical Interpretation* 20 (2012): 205–25.

Zimmerli, Walther. *Old Testament Theology in Outline*. Translated by David E. Green. Edinburgh: T&T Clark, 1978.

ABOUT THE AUTHORS

Will Brooks (PhD, The Southern Baptist Theological Seminary) teaches at two seminaries in Asia. He is the author of *Love Lost for the Cause of Christ* (Wipf & Stock, 2018).

Scott N. Callaham (PhD, Southwestern Baptist Theological Seminary), is Lecturer in Biblical Hebrew and Old Testament at Baptist Theological Seminary, Singapore. He has written numerous articles across a broad range of subjects and is the author of *Modality and the Biblical Hebrew Infinitive Absolute* (Harrassowitz, 2010).

John D. Massey (PhD, Southwestern Baptist Theological Seminary) is Associate Professor of Missions and Associate Dean of Masters Programs at the Roy Fish School of Evangelism and Missions. He is the co-editor and co-author of *Making Disciples of All Nations: A History of Southern Baptist Missions* (Kregel, forthcoming) and *Theology and the Global Church* (B&H Academic, forthcoming).

Trey Moss (M.Div., The Southern Baptist Theological Seminary; PhD candidate, The Southern Baptist Theological Seminary), is the Assistant to the Director of Research Doctoral Studies at Southern Seminary. Trey also serves as a pastor at Antioch Church, a multi-ethnic missional community, in Louisville, KY. He is a contributor to *The Letters of Ignatius: Apostolic Fathers Greek Reader Vol. 1* (GlossaHouse, 2015).

Wendel Sun (PhD, University of Chester), is President of International Chinese Theological Seminary, an institution dedicated to training house church leaders in Asia. He is the author of *A New People in Christ: Adam, Israel, and Union with Christ in Romans* (Pickwick, 2018).

Sunny Tan (Th.D., Asia Baptist Graduate Theological Seminary) is Academic Dean and Lecturer of Systematic Theology at Malaysia Baptist Theological Seminary. He pastored a Baptist church for ten years before joining the seminary. His publications include articles in reference works and the booklet *Child Theology for the Churches in Asia: An Invitation* (Child Theology Movement, 2007).

Jarvis J. Williams (PhD, The Southern Baptist Theological Seminary) is Associate Professor of New Testament Interpretation at The Southern Baptist Theological Seminary. He is the author of many journal articles and *Maccabean Martyr Traditions in Paul's Theology of Atonement: Did Martyr Theology Shape Paul's Conception of Jesus's Death?* (Wipf & Stock, 2010), *For Whom Did Christ Die? The Extent of the Atonement in Paul's Theology* (Paternoster, 2012), and *Christ Died For Our Sins: Representation and Substitution in Romans and Their Jewish Martyrological Background* (Pickwick, 2015).

Stephen I. Wright (PhD, University of Durham) is Vice Principal and Academic Director at Spurgeon's College, London, where he teaches New Testament, Hermeneutics, and Homiletics. He previously served in local Anglican ministry in northern England and as Director of the U.K. College of Preachers. He is the author or co-author of several books, including *The Voice of Jesus: Studies in the Interpretation of Six Gospel Parables* (Paternoster, 2000), *Alive to the Word: A Practical Theology of Preaching for the Whole Church* (SCM, 2010), and *Jesus the Storyteller* (Westminster John Knox, 2014).

Jackson W. (PhD, Southeastern Baptist Theological Seminary) has worked as a church planter and now teaches theology and missiology for Chinese pastors. His books include *Saving God's Face* (WCUIP, 2013), *One Gospel for All Nations* (WCL, 2015), and *Reading Romans with Eastern Eyes* (IVP, forthcoming). He serves as the book review editor for the Mission and Culture section of *Themelios*. In addition to his published journal articles, he maintains a blog at jacksonwu.org.

SUBJECT INDEX

A

Abraham 15–16, 38–42, 47, 54, 59–61,
    63, 68–69, 78–85, 87, 90–92,
    95, 97, 140–45, 142n34, 143n37,
    144n38, 253, 279n46, 285, 298
absolute commitment 123
Adam 34–38, 54, 56–61, 63, 74, 78, 80,
    86–88, 92
  Adam, and Eve 35, 72–73, 81–83,
    85, 88
African traditional religions 158
allegory 243
animism 182, 262, 395
apologetics 23, 25, 25n63, 212–13
application, contemporary 23–31,
    255–66
Assyria 12, 18–19

B

Babylon 18
baptism 31, 47, 50, 54, 122, 149–75, 182,
    185n11, 203, 213, 243, 281
  baptism, availability of water
    for 164–65
  baptism, immersion 154–56,
    154n10, 154n11, 165–66
  baptism, infant 153, 161, 165

baptism, nondisciple 153, 155, 161
baptism, opposition to 164–74
baptism, "re-" 165
baptism, theology of 150–61
baptism, timing of 158, 162
baptism, with sand 164
baptismal regeneration 160
baptizers, qualifications of 163
Bible stories 246–47, 253
  Bible stories, crafting 284–87
Bible translation 154, 180, 218–21, 289
Bible, cultural and historical setting
    of 251–53
  Bible, the message of mission
    212–15
biblical authority xi, xii, 3–7, 167, 168,
    215n19, 319
biblical framework 273–77
biblical interpretation (see
    hermeneutics)
biblical text, implications within a new
    cultural context 260–62
  biblical text, transforming
    contemporary culture 260
biblical thought process 191–92
Buddhism 158

C

Caesar 173

calling 79, 86, 98–100, 111, 139, 164, 179, 185, 192, 194–95, 194n21, 223, 237, 294, 298, 302, 314, 319

canon 3, 6, 105, 196, 215, 273n18, 275, 279, 282, 214

canonical structure 279

Carey, William 149

Christ, earthly ministry, purpose of 292–93

Christ, glorification of 294–95

Christology 38, 53, 59

Chronological Bible Storying 284

Chronological Bible Teaching 284

church, as hermeneutical community 264

church, healthy 5, 60, 179, 185, 188, 191, 203, 308

church expansion, effect on biblical interpretation practices 243–44

church planting 306–8

church tradition 153

church unity 53–54, 61, 99–100, 138, 141, 150, 163–64, 167, 291, 293–95, 316

churches, laying a biblical and theological foundation for 311–13

churches, need to strengthen in mission 314

churches, theological development of 316

Churchless Christianity 169–71

circumcision 81–82, 140, 140n22, 281, 316

circumcision, of the heart 94, 97, 159

communicating the gospel to oral peoples 284

communicating the word of God 226, 231, 236

communicating the word of God, cultural considerations 265–66

communication, cross-cultural 209–10, 223, 256

communication, receptor-oriented 265

community formation 196–98

consensus faith 150, 167

contextualization 303–6

contextualization, critical 262–65

covenant 11, 14, 17, 19n45, 25–26, 28–29, 39, 52, 55, 59–60, 67–101, 126, 135n10, 210–11, 280

covenant, new 21, 30, 30n69, 46, 49, 54–55, 57, 59, 62, 65, 68–69, 91, 93–100

creation 11–14, 23–25, 34–35, 35n8, 37, 41, 57, 67, 69–75, 78, 80, 83–89, 91–96, 207–8, 280

creation, new 11, 20–23, 30–31, 38, 44, 51, 54, 58, 69, 78, 84, 96, 99

creation covenant 73–74

Creation to Christ 25n64, 284

critical thinking, self-addressed 256–57

cross-cultural and intercultural, distinction of terms 240

crucifixion 41, 54, 119

cultural bias 256

cultural context, research upon 257–60

cultural practices 281

culture shock 209

culture, definition of 240

D

David 42, 47, 49, 63, 68–69, 89–92,
    95–97, 145, 276n33, 276n35, 279,
    279n46, 285, 293, 305
decontextualization 14, 27
dependence upon God 228–29, 228n53
disciplemaking 152, 175
disciples 131, 135–36, 152, 156–57, 161–
    63, 165, 169
discipleship 5, 105–29, 159, 167, 173–74,
    184–85, 190–91, 314
    discipleship, centrality in mission 126
    discipleship, visibility of 127
discourse analysis 249, 251

E

ecclesiology 53, 149–50, 159, 161–67,
    170, 172, 174
Egypt 14, 16, 18–19, 19n45, 43, 46–47, 49,
    52, 83–85, 87, 219–20, 253, 276n31
election 11, 14–17, 23, 25–28, 78, 185
emplotment 273
endurance 229
eschatology 9, 30
ethnicity 12–13, 24, 24n62, 42, 53, 60,
    163
evangelism 23–24, 25n64, 179, 186–87,
    191, 193, 211, 218, 229n54, 282,
    285, 287, 317
evolution 25
exclusivism 23
exegesis 191
    exegesis, grammatical-
        historical 132, 153, 161, 221,
        239–67,
            exegesis, grammatical-
                historical, author-
                oriented cross-cultural

            model of 247–66
    exegesis, grammatical-
        historical, helpfulness
        of 245–46
    exegesis, grammatical-
        historical, objections
        to 240–47
exegetical resources, lack of 250,
    252–53
exile 18, 26, 43n36, 47–49, 64, 70n8,
    93, 96, 134, 276, 278–79
exodus 94, 253, 276, 276n31
    exodus, new 42, 45–46, 61, 100

F

fairness 15
faith 6, 14, 29, 33, 40–42, 48, 52–53,
    55, 55n78, 79, 82, 85, 87, 92,
    98–99, 112–13, 128–29, 137–38,
    140, 140n24, 140n26, 141–43,
    142n33, 142n34, 143n37, 144n38,
    147–48, 150, 152–53, 156–59, 161,
    164–66, 171, 173–75, 188, 203,
    214, 261n69, 264, 282, 296, 304,
    308–11
    faith, profession of 116, 153, 159,
        165–66, 166n23, 173, 175
family 42, 52n68, 113, 115, 119, 158, 161–
    62, 167, 170, 172–73, 228
forgiveness 94, 96, 117, 121, 121n14, 126,
    137, 213, 286
fulfillment of OT promises 38–42, 50,
    54, 57, 59, 80, 82, 95–96, 98,
    142n34, 144, 214, 298–99, 304, 317

G

Galatians 137–44
gentiles 9–11, 13, 16, 21–22, 29, 40, 42,

42n32, 47, 49, 59–60, 62, 64–65,
78, 83, 85, 87–89, 91–94, 96, 98–
101, 131–48, 287, 293, 298
God, center of mission 208, 232
God, source of the missionary's
message 210–12
God, sovereignty of 21, 27, 45, 86,
92, 100, 136, 158, 167, 226n49
gospel, contextual embeddedness
214–15
gospel, definition of 214, 214n18
gospel, metanarrative influence
upon 280–81
grace 15, 17n37, 44, 75, 79, 82, 124–25,
128–29, 159–62, 164, 166, 180,
202, 294, 302, 311
Great Commission 27–28, 56–57, 59,
61, 61n96, 63–64, 103–5, 121,
126, 131, 144, 147, 151, 153–54,
159, 162–63, 165, 177, 199, 203,
212n15, 213, 307, 319

H

hermeneutics 182–83, 186, 195, 219–21,
239–67, 240, 253
hermeneutics, and oral
learners 246–47, 253, 288–89
hermeneutics, cross-cultural 244
Hinduism 157, 168, 170, 262
historical–critical method 241
history of religion 9, 9n16
history, and OT theology 9n16
Holy Spirit 5, 21–23, 31, 45–46, 50,
52, 54, 56, 62, 65, 67, 94, 97–99,
103–4, 124, 141, 141n29, 142n34,
143, 144n38, 146, 151, 155–60,
164, 166, 170–72, 174–75, 178,
180–81, 214, 227–30, 227n52,

228n53, 230n58, 233, 256,
276n35, 295–96, 299–300, 307,
317, 319

I

idols 21, 93, 134, 142n34, 173, 200n34,
261, 276n33, 303–4
image of God 12–13, 24, 72, 210–11
inclusivism 28n66
India 149, 149n1, 168–71, 262–63
indigenous theologians 184
infinitive absolute 19, 19n44, 220,
220n31
instruction of new believers 310
interfaith dialogue 29
interpretation, contextual 4, 283
interpretation, indigenous
methods of 243, 259–60
interpretation, three horizons
of 222n36, 258
interpretation, Western methods
of 242
intertextuality 6n9, 270, 277–78, 289
Islam 157, 169, 171–72, 262
Israel, covenant with 68–69, 83–89, 91
Israel's story, importance within grand
narrative of Scripture 282–84
Israel's story, teaching to
gentiles 283

J

Jeremiah 20
Jerusalem Council 136
Jesus 5–6, 24, 26–27, 30, 30n69, 33–65,
69, 96–101, 104–29, 131–75, 177,
190, 195–203, 212–14, 212n15,
217, 226, 228, 230n58, 253, 261,
261n69, 266, 273, 278, 280, 292–

94, 301-7, 310-11, 317
Jesus, accompanying 113
Jesus, actions and suffering 118
Jesus, adherence to 108
Jesus, as teacher 118
Jesus, authority of 151
Jesus, imitation of 124
Jesus, learning from 109-17, 124,
    127-28
Jesus, listening to 109
Jesus, response to 108, 117
Jesus, understanding 114, 118
Jew-gentile binary 136-37
John, Gospel of 121-23
Jonah 22
Joshua 276n46
judgment 11, 17-20, 21n51, 23, 28-30,
    75, 78, 301
Judson, Adoniram and Ann 149, 149n1

K

kingdom 22, 22n57, 35, 47-48, 53, 59,
    63, 69, 71, 74, 87-89, 91, 98,
    107-12, 114-16, 123, 128, 135-36,
    142n34, 146-47, 164, 201, 214,
    280, 303, 310
kingship 38, 42, 49, 63-64, 71, 74
knowing God 21, 178, 181, 186

L

land 276n35
language 207-38
    language, community 227-30
    language, creation of 207n3
    language, emic perspective on 235
    language, heart 232
    language, missionary use of 215-37
    language, missionary's native 223-
        26
language, national 233
language, oral and aural aspects
    of 235
language, use in ministry 201-3
Language for Specific Purposes
    (LSP) 236
language learning 210, 227-38
    language learning, as a spiritual
        task 228
    language learning, Barefoot
        Method 231
    language learning, effect of
        language difference on 233-34
    language learning, GPA
        Method 231-32, 235
    language learning, motivation 234
language performance 230
languages, biblical 180, 215-23, 231,
    234, 242, 249-50, 250n35,
    251n39
languages
    Arabic 195n24, 224
    Bahasa 224
    Biblical Aramaic 216-17
    Biblical Greek 103-4, 154, 216-
        17, 221n34, 227n52, 249n34,
        250-51
    Biblical Hebrew 179-80, 179n3,
        180n4, 216-17, 220, 221n33,
        222n35, 227n52, 249n34, 250-
        51
    Chinese 154n11, 155, 180n4,
        221n33, 221n34, 224, 232n62,
        234, 236, 236n75, 237, 237n77
    English 154-55, 180, 218, 218n28,
        219-22, 221n33, 224-26,
        224nn38-40, 224n42, 234, 252

Finnish 223
French 224, 233
Italian 236
Japanese 223
Latin 223, 223n40, 227n52
Russian 224, 274
Spanish 223–24, 233–34
law 21, 43–44, 46, 61n96, 86, 87n46, 89, 92, 94, 96, 106, 125–26, 135, 136n9, 137, 140–42, 261, 276n31, 280, 316
life transformation 178
linguistics 207n1, 224, 224n39, 232, 235, 248–51, 255
literacy 235–36
literary context, as determinant of meaning 247–55
loanwords 154, 154n11
Lord's Supper 49, 281
Luke-Acts 119–21

M

Mark, Gospel of 117–18
mark, of the church 170
mark, of the disciple 163
Matthew, Gospel of 106–17
mediator 17, 17n37, 30, 30n69, 44, 46, 92, 125, 158
Messiah 22, 22n57, 33–34, 39, 41–42, 43n36, 44, 46–53, 57, 63–65, 96–97, 145–46, 214, 280, 293, 298, 303–4
metaphor 155–56, 159, 202n37, 245, 252
mission, ethics of 225, 301
mission, influence upon theological education 194–203
mission field, initial arrival on 228
mission in the OT 292
mission of God 69–72, 75–76, 79–81, 84–86, 90–98, 254
mission of God's people 55, 76–78, 81–83, 86–89, 92, 98–100
mission strategy 178–93
mission strategy, biblical metanarrative influence upon 287–89
missional tasks 194–95
missionary as communicator of God's Word 208–15
missionary, non-residential 212n14
monotheism 9, 16n34, 157
Moses 42–46, 61–63, 97, 279n46
movements 27, 188
movements, Christward 168–69, 169n26
movements, insider 168–74, 259n63
movements, people 24n62

N

narrative substructure, supporting 277–81
narrative, definition 269
new heart 21, 94, 98
NT use of the OT 6, 278, 293
Noah 68, 75–78, 83

O

obedience in relationship 197
oracles against the nations 19–20
oral cultures 271
orality 269
ordinance 161–63

P

participle 10n17, 152, 152n7, 248
Paul 36, 184–85
Paul, and raising up leaders 313–14

Paul, as pastor 312

Paul, maintaining contact with the churches he planted 314–16

Paul, mission, confirmation of 298–99

Paul, mission, honoring Christ 300–301

Paul, mission, letter writing 315

Paul, mission, location of 297

Paul, mission, purpose of 296–97

Paul, mission, relationship with Pauline epistles 310

Paul, mission, result of 297–98

Paul, mission, strategy for 299–316

Paul, mission, trinitarian framework 294–96

Paul, model for the practice of world mission 291–317

Paul, preaching to gentiles 304–5

Paul, preaching to Jews 303–4

Paul, sending of coworkers to existing churches 316

Paul, teaching ministry 311

Paul, understanding of mission 291–99

Paul, use of the OT 278

peace 60, 173, 293–94

Pentecost 227

people groups 131, 157

perseverance 187, 308–11

pluralism 28n66

preaching (see proclamation)

preparation for mission work 190, 196–200

proclamation 48, 57–58, 61–62, 65, 69, 100, 104, 108, 117, 129, 138, 140, 146–47, 156, 159, 162, 164–66, 166n23, 175, 179–82, 186, 189, 192, 195, 200, 203n38, 211, 214, 218, 227, 230, 230n58, 254, 287, 294–304, 306–7, 309, 312

prooftexting 4–5, 4n3, 5n4

purification 160

R

reader identity politics 213

redemption (see restoration)

Reformers 244

repentance 28, 33, 48, 98, 107–8, 121, 121n14, 159, 213–14

reproduction 182, 184–85, 191

reproduction, rapid 212–13

restoration 10, 17, 19n45, 21n51, 21n53, 34–38, 46–50, 55–58, 63–64, 69, 71, 78–79, 82, 86, 93–94, 97, 100, 110, 128–29, 199, 276

resurrection 31, 37–38, 40–41, 46, 48–50, 54, 58, 64, 69, 96, 98, 112, 118, 121, 124, 129, 140, 143–46, 156, 158, 172, 214, 281

revelation 4n1, 4n2, 22, 31, 46, 68, 85, 118, 137, 139, 211–13, 215–17, 215n19, 219, 230, 251, 254, 262, 282–83

Ruth 11, 11n20, 29–30

S

salvation 13, 14n28, 17, 17n38, 19n41, 26–29, 28n66, 40, 42, 43, 45, 47, 49, 52–54, 65, 68–69, 71, 75, 84–85, 88–89, 111, 120, 128–29, 133, 136–37, 147, 151, 153, 159,

161, 175, 195n23, 200, 214, 254,
273, 281n50, 286, 294, 297, 303,
308, 310
Satan 35–36, 302–3, 309–10
scientism 25
Scripture, inerrancy of 241
Scripture, literal meaning of
244–45
Scripture, metanarrative of 270,
272–76, 278, 281–82, 293, 304–5
Scripture, narrative approach
to 272
Scripture, sufficiency of xi, xii
sequence, chronological 274
sequence, creative 274
Sermon on the Mount 43, 61, 109
Servant 22n56, 22–23, 26, 94
service 107–10
sexuality 13, 24
signs and wonders 295
Simply the Story 284
sin 1, 15, 35–37, 43n36, 46, 53, 57–58,
62, 70–71, 75, 77, 79, 89, 94, 96,
156, 159–60, 171, 199, 214, 237,
247, 254, 277, 286, 305
social gospel 213
social sciences 131
son of Abraham 145
son of David 47, 92, 145
Son of God 26, 35, 45, 47, 49–50, 56,
67, 69, 103, 138–39, 139n20, 151,
156, 178, 188, 195n23, 294, 299,
317
Son of Man 36n13, 48, 57, 63, 115,
146–47
sound doctrine 188
speech acts 20, 29
speech acts, divine 211

spiritual warfare 301–3
storytelling 24
Strong's Numbers 221–22
suffering 303
surface accommodation 264
symbolism 159

T
tabernacle 73, 77, 85–88
temple 21, 36, 38, 63–64, 73, 77–78,
87–88, 93, 134–35, 276n33,
276n35, 279
The Prophet 42–46
theological diversity 8–11
theological education 5n6, 177–203
theological education, advancing
mission 184–90
theological education, for
missionaries 25n63, 190–93
theological education, formal 180,
183–84, 189–90
theological education, goals
of 198–203
theological education,
informal 179
theological nature of the missionary
task 179
theological themes, recurring 278–79
theological thinking 195–96
theology and missiology 253–55
theology, biblical 3–7, 4n3, 25n65,
67–101, 184–85, 255, 270–71,
291, 298, 304–5
theology, biblical, Catholic 8n13
theology, biblical, for oral
cultures 269–89
theology, biblical, Jewish 8n13
theology, biblical, Protestant 8

theology, confronting error in 315–16
theology, liberal 167
theology, liberation 213
theology, narrative 269–70
theology, New Testament 33–65, 153
theology, Old Testament 3–31
theology, sacramental 160, 161, 166
theology, systematic 4, 4n1, 4n3,
    24n61, 153
Tobit 134
Torah (see law)
training disciples 285
    training indigenous
        interpreters 250
    training leaders 177, 181, 183, 185,
        188–89
transdenominational
    evangelicalism 150, 154
transfiguration 43–44, 61, 109
trinity 67, 156–60, 175

U
unevangelized, fate of the 28,
    28n66
union with Christ 33–65, 159

W
wisdom 200–201
women 30, 42n32, 47, 116, 120
word of God, direct access to the 235
    word of God, response to 211
world religions 23
worldview 182, 258–59, 271
    worldview, biblical 181, 186, 203
    worldview, transformation of 181,
        195–96, 199, 286
worship 14–17, 27, 35, 60–61, 65, 77,
        88, 134–35, 135n10, 149, 151,

166, 169, 173, 178–79, 186, 233,
    237–38, 237n78, 291–94, 317
worship, and missions 296–97
worship, of ancestors 182, 257,
    257n53
worship, of idols 93, 261, 304

SCRIPTURE INDEX

Old Testament

Genesis

1 ....70, 70n9, 72, 77, 80, 202
1-2 ....36n13, 38, 70, 75
1-3 282
1-9 285
1-11..........................13, 78
1:1.................................20
1:2 ....70, 76, 84
1:3 .....84, 207, 207n3, 208
1:3-31 76
1:4 23
1:9-10...........................84
1:10 23
1:12................................23
1:16............................... 80
1:18................................23
1:21................................23
1:22 ....13, 210n9
1:25 23
1:26 210
1:27............................... 12
1:28 ....38, 41, 72, 76, 199, 210n9
1:28-30 .... 70, 210
1:31................................23
2:4...................................34
2:7....................37, 202n36
2:15 ....73, 86
2:16-17 70

2:17...............................79
3 .... 24, 35, 75, 202, 281
3:5...................35, 221n33
3:9...............................210
3:15 ....36, 71, 75
5:1.................................34
5.....................................74
6-9 78
6:18 73
7:23b 79
8:1-2 76
8-9...................................76
9:1 77
9:1-17 77
9.....................................76
9:7...................................77
9:9-10 76
9:11.................................76
10 16
10:32 ....141n27
12:1-3 .... 41, 59, 78, 140, 145
12 80
12-50 .... 142n34, 143
12:2 90
12:3 ....15n30, 40, 59, 139n20, 140, 141, 142, 143n36, 143n37, 144
12:4 82
12:10-20.......................79

14:5 ....141n27
15 ....79, 80, 80n32
15:5 40
15:6 ....40, 140, 143n37
15:7...............................80
15:12-16.......................84
15:13-16 80
15:18-20 80
16-17 79
17:1-2 82
17:1-14 145
17..............80, 80n32, 82, 140, 145
17:5............................. 40
17:6...................91, 141n27
17:7......................... 80, 91
17:7-8 59
17:8 90
17:20 ....141n27
18:18......139n20, 140, 141, 141n27, 143n37
18:19.............................. 91
20:1-18......................... 79
22...................... 81, 82, 253
22:3................................82
22:16-18 81
22:17..............................90
22:18 ....40, 59, 91, 140
22:18a 141
25:16 ....141n27

25:23 .... 141n27
26:3 59
26:4 .... 140, 141, 141n27,
141n29
28:14 140
37:2 220
46:3–4 219
46:4 220

Exodus

1 85
1:1–7 83
3:6 85
3:12 86
3:15 85
3:16 85
4 43
4:5 85
4:19 43
4:22 86
4:23 .... 45, 84
5:2 18
6:2–8 85
6:7 84
7:2 .... 61n96
7:4–5 18
7:5 84
7:16 86
7:17 84
8:22 84
9:1 86
9:13 86
9:14 18
9:16 18
10:3 86
10:24–26 86
12 253
14–15 84
14:20–22 84
14:20 84
14:21–22 84
14:21 84
15 .... 84n40
15:14 ... 133, 133n4, 141n27

19 99
19:3 .... 43n40
19:4 87
19:5 87
19:5–6 .... 87, 99
19:6 48
19:9 .... 85, 87
19:16–20 85
20:12 .... 257, 257n54
23:18 .... 133, 133n4,
141n27
23:19 261
23:27 .... 133, 133n4
24 43
24:8 96
24:9 43
24:12 125
24:15–16 43
24:16 44
25:8 85
33:16 .... 88, 133, 133n4,
141n27
34 44
34:24 .... 133n4, 141n27
34:26 261

Leviticus

18:5 140
18:24 .... 133n4, 141n27
19:2 126
26:33 .... 133n4

Numbers

14:14–15 .... 141n27
14:14–16 133
14:15 .... 133n4
14:15–16 133
18:7 73
24:1–4 46
24:8 .... 133, 133n4
25 .... 138n17
25:6–15 .... 135n9

Deuteronomy

4:6–8 89
4:38 .... 141n27
6:5 28
7:1 .... 133, 133n4
7:1–7 .... 141n27
7:6 133
7:6–7 .... 133n4
7:8 26
8:3 202
14:21 261
18 .... 42, 44
18:17–18 44
18:18–19 45
21:23 140
26:5–9 275
27:18 26
27:26 140
28:15 26
28:48 135
28:58 140
30 .... 93, 97
30:6 .... 93, 94
30:10 140
30:14 215
32:1 208
32 .... 70n8
32:43 .... 137, 293

Joshua

1 .... 70n9
1:7 .... 61n96
23–24 275

Judges

2:10 89

Ruth

1:1–18 29
1:14 29
1:16 29

1 Samuel

8:5 89

12 275
13:14............................ 90
14 .... 221n33
14:27.................... 221n33

2 Samuel
6:23............................. 90
7 90
7:9............................... 90
7:11............................. 90
7:12–13 145
7:12–14 145
7:12............................. 91
7:13............................. 91
7:13–14 .... 279n42
7:14..................... 90, 91
7:14–15 92
7:18–29 92
7:19..............................92
7:22..............................92
7:23 92
7:24 92
22:50.........................293

1 Kings
8.................................275
19:21......................... 125
20:37..................... 19n44

2 Kings
4:12 125
5:14 .... 154n10
17...............................275

1 Chronicles
22:13 .... 61n96

2 Chronicles
5:2–6:11 275
36...............................64
36:23...........................63

Nehemiah
9.................................276

Psalms
1 .... 70n9, 126
1:2 206
2................................. 145
2:7 49
2:8................................63
8.................................57
17:50 137
18:49 293
19:1..............................69
22................................217
46:4............................ 20
71:17 (LXX) 142, 144
72:17 91
72:19............................85
78...............................275
80:8–11........................52
84:11 xii
93:1 71
97:3 (LXX) 39
98:3............................39
105–106......................275
110 145
117:1...........................293
117 297
119:18 .... xii, 206
133 ....216n21
135–136 275
136:5–9....................... 14
136:15 14
136:19 14
136:20 14
138:2 238
139:4 223

Proverbs
9:13–18 ....251n40

Song of Songs
4:1 252

Isaiah
2:2–3 .... 133, 134
2:3.............................. 133

5:1–7....................52n70
7 47
7:14.....................59n92
8:9............................. 133
9.................................92
9:3............................. 135
10:7 133
10:24–27..................... 135
11................................92
11:9–10 146
11:10 .... 133, 293, 298
11:12 .... 133, 134
12:4 133
14:2 133
14:12 133
14:24–27..................... 135
14:26 133
16:8 133
17:13 133
19 19
19:22 19
19:24–25...................... 19
20:3–4........................266
25:6–10 .... 143n34
25:7 133
27:2–13 ....52n70
30:28 133
32:15 62
33:3 133
33:12 133
34:1–2......................... 133
34:2........................... 134
35:1–10 20
37:26 133
40–66......................... 146
40:3–5..........................62
40:15 133
40:17 133
41:5 133
42:1–4.........................23
42:4........................... 133
42:4–6..........................96
42:5..............................94
42:6...................94, 146

43...............................99
43:5–7 134
43:9............................ 133
43:10 62
43:12 62
43:20–21 99
44:3.....................142n29
45:1 ....64, 133
49:1 133
49:6........62, 133, 136, 146
49:7............................94
49:8.....................94n62
49:22.......................... 133
51:5 133
52:15 ....133, 298
54:3............................ 133
54:7 134
55:1–2..........................96
55...............................95
55:3–5..........................95
55:3b..........................95
55:5............................ 133
56:6–8 ....143n34
57:15............................69
59:20–21 137
60:1–22 ....143n34
60:2–3............... 133, 134
60:11........................... 133
60:12........................... 133
62:2........................... 133
62:10 133
64:1 133
65:17........................... 20
66:18–19 133
66:20..........................297

Jeremiah
1:5 ....20, 139, 139n21
1:7 139
1:10 139
1:14.....................139n21
1:15–16.................139n21
2:21 ....52n70

4........................... 70n8
12:10–17................52n70
13:21........................... 125
14:6–7....................... 134
20:11........................... 125
27–31........................ 139
27:2–11 20
28:16 125
29:13–14 134
30–31 ....142n34
30:4–8....................... 135
31 .... 96, 97, 276n35
31:7–10 134
31:31–34 ....21, 30, 49,
                    91, 94
31:33 97
32:12–15 125
32:37 134
33.....................276n35
33:14–26............... 91, 95

Ezekiel
4:1–4 266
15:1–8 ....52n70
16 276
17:1–21 ....52n70
19:10–14 ....52n70
20 276
23............................. 276
34:27–28 135
36................................97
36–37 ....276n35
36:22............................67
36:26.............. 21, 94, 97
36:27 .... 21, 94
36:35.......................... 20
47:1–12 21
47:12............................ 21

Daniel
7 ....36n13, 57, 63, 146
7:9–10 146
7:13........................... 146

7:13–14 146
7:14.... 57, 59n91, 144, 146,
                147, 147n53
7:15–27 147
7:18 147
7:21–27 147
9....................................276

Hosea
2..................................99
2:23..............................99
10:1–2...................52n70
11:1 .... 43, 43n37, 45

Joel
2:12–14 28
2:28–32 .... 142n34

Amos
1:3–2:5........................ 15
2:1 15
3:2................................28
9:13–15 20

Jonah
4:11.............................. 12

Habakkuk
2:4...............................140
2:14 238

Zechariah
8:20–22..............143n34
8:22–23 21
11:4–17....................266
13:1–2 21
14:9 20
14:16........................... 134

Malachi
1:2–3............................ 14

New Testament

Matthew

1 ....42n32
1:1........ 34, 38, 47, 96, 145
1:1–17......................276
1:2 145
1:5 145
1:6–16 145
1:17 47
1:18–2:15...................145
1:19.......................116n9
1:21...................... 42, 47
1:23 ....59n92
2:2.................................47
2:13–23......................47
2:15 ......43, 43n37, 47, 145
2:20 43
3:11................155, 155n12
3:13–16 47
3:16 154
3:17...............................47
4:1–11...........................47
4:1–7:29 145
4:3.................................47
4:6.................................47
4:17...................... 107, 108
4:18–19 108
4:18–22........ 107, 108, 128
4:19 116
4:23.....................107, 213
4:24–25 107
5:1 .... 43n40, 107,
                109, 110, 112
5:1–12 117
5–7 46
5:3–12......................... 111
5:6..........................116n9
5:10 ....116n9
5:13 111
5:14 111
5:17–6:24 111
5:20 ....116n9
5:44–48 .... 52n68

6:32............... 135, 135n11
6:33.......................116n9
7:15–20...................... 202
7:20...........................116
7:21...............111, 116, 117
7:24 200
7:24–27...................... 111
7:28 .... 110, 111
7:29 109
8:14–17......................109
8:19 109
8:20 .... 147n52
8:21 119
8:23–27 113
9:6...................... 147n52
9:9.............................108
9:9–13........................ 111
9:10 111
9:14 .... 106, 111
9:17.......................157n14
9:18–26.....................113
10:1 ....107, 112
10:1–4.......................... 48
10:1–5.......................109
10:1–42.....................120
10:2 112
10:5 .... 135, 135n11
10:5–6 145
10:5–39 112
10:5–42 113
10:6 59
10:8 112
10:16..........................201
10:32–39 173
10:34–39 98
10:41...........................116
10:42...........................116
11:1 107
11:19 .... 147n52
11:25...........................118
11:28 129
11:28–30.....................108

11:29–30 129
12:1...............................112
12:8 .... 147n52
12:21.........135n11, 136n12
12:32 .... 147n52
12:40 .... 147n52
12:49–50 ....112, 117
12:50...........................116
13:1–8 114
13:1–53 .... 109, 114
13:2 114
13:3–9.........................310
13:8 114
13:10...........................114
13:10–23 113
13:13–15......................114
13:16–17......................114
13:18–23 .... 114, 311
13:23 114
13:24–30 110
13:33 174
13:36 114
13:36–43...............110, 113
13:37.................... 147n52
13:38 110
13:41................... 147n52
13:51................... 114, 118
13:54–58.....................114
14:13–21......................113
14:22–36.....................113
15:2 112
15:16–20 203
15:21–28 145
15:23 113
15:24 .... 59, 113, 145
15:28 113
15:32–39......................113
16:17 118
16:22–23......................114
16:24 .... 114, 117, 119
16:27.................... 147n52
17:1 44

17:5...................... 44, 109
17:14–20 113
18:1...................... 109, 114
18:1–35 ....110, 114
18:2–4 114
18:5–35...........................114
18:6 115
18:10 115
18:10–20.................... 128
18:15............................115
18:21............................115
18:22 128
19:1–12.........................113
19:13–15.......................115
19:16–20:16..................113
19:28 112
20:20–28 115
20:25............. 135n11, 136
21:1–11 113
21:18–22 113
22:16 107
23:1–25:46...................115
24:1 109
24:9............................ 145
24:14 145
25...............................116
25:31 115
25:31–46.................... 110
25:32 145
25:34–36 116
25:37–39......................115
25:40............................115
25:44............................115
25:45............................115
26:6–13........................115
26:13 214
26:17–19.......................113
26:28.............................96
26:47–50 116
26:56................... 112, 116
26:64............................57
26:69..........................109
26:69–75 116
26:71.............................109
27:46 217

27:55–56 116
27:57 123
27:57–60 116
28:1–10......................112
28............. 42n32, 56, 58
28:16 ....112, 144
28:16–20 .. 46, 57, 151, 174
28:18 ..... 57, 109, 144, 147,
              147n53, 151
28:18–19 147
28:18–20 ......xii, 105, 113,
              126, 213n16
28:18b–20 103
28:19 .....59, 108, 121, 126,
          132, 144, 144n40, 145,
          145n41, 147, 160, 184
28:19a 105
28:19–20146, 147, 152, 158
28:20 ...... 59, 117, 177, 184

Mark

1:1................................ 48
1–3 55
1:10 154
1:14............................ 213
1:14–15...................... 48
1:15 ....48, 98
1:18–20...................... 128
1:21–28 48
1:39–45........................ 48
2:18 107
2:22.....................157n14
3:13–19 55
3:14 109
3:14–15 118
4:3–9 310
4:14–20 311
5:41 217
6:7–13............55n80, 120
8:29............................. 48
8:31 48
8:34.............................119
9:30–32...................... 48
9:32.............................118
9:38–39 118

10:32–34 48
12:29–31 128
14:9 214
15:34 217
15:43 123
16:8 ....213n16
16:15–18...............213n16

Luke

1 39
1:6 ....123n15
1:54 39
1:55 39
1:72–73 .... 39, 96
1:74.............................39
2:32..........135n11, 136n12
3....................................35
3:4–6 62
4:3.................................35
4:9.................................35
4:38..............................35
5:37 ....157n14
6:20 119
6:35–36 .... 52n68
8:1–3 120
8:4–8.........................310
9:1–6 120
9:23.............................119
9:23–27 98
9:31 44
9:50 118
9:51–19:28 120
9:59.............................119
10:1 .... 120n13
10:1–12 120
10:17–20 120
10:17 .... 120n13
10:38 119
10:39 119
10:41............................120
14:26 ....119, 172
14:27............................119
14:33 .... 119, 120
19:8 120
19:9 120

20:1 213
20:36 .... 52n68
21:24 .... 135n11, 136
22:20 96
23:47 ....123n15
23:50 123
23:51 123
24:27 214
24:45–49 ....213n16
24:46–49 121

John

1:12 53
1:14 46
1:17 44
1:25–51 121
1:29 .... 252, 253
1:35 106
1:36 .... 252, 253
1:41 230
1:45 44
1:49 ....279n42
1:67 230
2:11 122
3:14–15 44
3:16 53
3:21 122
3:26 122
3:36 53
4:1 122
4:2 122
4:19 44
4:22 26
4:34 56
5:24 .... 53, 56
5:30 56
6:1–5 45
6 45
6:14 44
6:29 56
6:30–40 45
6:47–51 53
6:66 122
6:67 122
6:68 210

6:68–69 122
6:70 122
7 45
7:16 56
7:40 44
8:9–15 311
8:11 202
8:15 311
8:31 122
9:4 56
9:27 122
9:28 .... 106, 122
10:1–18 53
10:27 122
11:42 56
12:35–36 122
12:37–43 123
12:44–50 ....45, 122
12:45 56
12:46 45
12:47–50 45
12:49 56
13:1 123
13:3–11 123
13:20 56
13:35 123
13:36 121
14 52
14–16 123
14:5 121
14:6 53
14:8 121
14:16 67
14:22 121
14:24 56
15–16 52
15:4 52
16:1 122
17 ....56, 123
17:17 xi
17:21–22 150
17:23 53
19:28 ....123, 127
20 38
20:1–21:23 121

20:21 .... 56, 67
20:21–23 ....213n16

Acts

1:4 .... 142n34
1:8 ..... 40, 62, 146, 213n16
2:11 227
2:33 .... 142n34
2:38 159
2:39 .... 142n34
3 40
3:13 40
3:19 160
3:25 40
4:8 230
6:1 121
6:2 121
6:7 121
7 276
8–9 ....138n17
8:26–40 162
8:26–39 202
8:38 154
8:39 154
9:1 121
9:2 ....120, 126
9:4–6 299
9:10 121
9:15 .... 135n11, 136
9:17 .... 230n58
9:18 159
9:19 121
9:20 .... 230n58
9:25 121
9:26 121
9:38 121
10 202
11:19–26 311
11:30 .... 313n52
12:25 .... 198n32
13:1–4 299
13 276
13:2 299
13:4 299
13:5 307

13:5–12 299
13:6 307
13:7.............................307
13:9 230
13:11–12 295
13:12 300
13:14 307
13:17–41 ....304, 305
13:22–23 305
13:32–34 305
13:46–47 136
13:46 .... 135n11
13:47...............62, 135n11
13:48 ....304, 307
13:52 300
14:1...................304, 307
14:3 300
14:8 308
14:8–18 303
14:10............................ 300
14:10–18 295
14:11 307
14:15 304
14:15–17 ....304, 305
14:19 303
14:20–21 303
14:22 .... 303, 310
14:22–23 314
14:27............163n20, 312
14:28 312
15:7 .... 135n11, 136
15:14 .... 135n11
15:23 .... 135n11, 136
15:35 312
15:36 .... 312, 314
15:41............................ 314
16:1–5 314
16:5 314
16:6–10 300
16:7..................300, 307
16:10 300
16:10–17 .... 40n28
16:15 153
16:18 300
16:25–31 303

16:26 300
16:31...........153, 304, 308
16:33 153
17:2.............................307
17:2–3 304
17:3............................. 304
17:10 307
17:11............................ xii
17:12 .... 304, 307
17:17 307
17:18–31 295
17:22–28 304
17:22–31............. 200n34
17:23..........................266
17:24–28 305
17:24–31.................... 304
17:29–31.............304, 305
18:4 ....304, 307
18:6 .... 135n11
18:7 ....304, 307
18:8 308
18:9–10 300
18:18........................ 314
18:19 307
18:21 300
18:22–23 315
19:6 300
19:8 307
19:9 .... 307, 312
19:11 300
19:21 .... 300, 315
20:4 314
20:5–15 .... 40n28
20:7–12....................... 312
20:9 184
20:20 .... 307, 312
20:21 304
20:22.......................... 300
20:23.......................... 300
20:27 312
20:28 300
20:32...................... 202
21:1–18.................. 40n28
21:11 .... 135n11, 300
21:27–28 .... 40n28

22:16 160
22:21 .... 135n11
26:17....................... 133n6
26:18 302
26:23...................... 133n6
26:28........................ 202
28:4............................ 300
28:8–9....................... 300
28:17..............133n6, 307
28:23 304

Romans
1:1–4 .... 49, 279n42
1:5 .... 59, 60, 99, 129, 296
1:14............................ 136
1:16...................136, 304
1:18–32 .... 36n14
1:18–3:31............. 261n69
2.................................97
2:1–3:20 136
2:9............................ 304
2:15 97
3................................. 281
3:9 136
3:23 .... 36n14
3:29.......... 12, 135n11, 136
3:29–30............... 40, 136
4.....................40, 60, 97
4:17–18 40
4:18 40
4:25 40
5.........................34, 36
5–8.............. 278, 278n40
5:12–14 37
5:12–21 .... 36, 54
6:1–4 159
6:1–5 54
6:4 156
7:7–12 .... 36n14
8:1 .... 221n34
8:1–17 54
8........................ 46n50
8:13 308
8:18–21.................. 36n14
8:29.................... 36n14

8:30 37
9–11 .... 137, 276, 278
9:11...............................136
9:24....................... 135n11
9:30 137
9:30–31...........................137
9:30–33..................... 136
9:31–32.......................137
10:1 ....28, 229
10:9 .... 257, 257n54, 261
11:1 ....28, 137
11:25 137
11:25–26 137
11:25–27.......................137
11:26 137
11:27 137
12:1 165
12:1–2 127
12:2 195
14:1–15:13 291
15 97
15:7...............................137
15:8 ....64, 137, 292
15:8–13 .... 291, 293, 294
15:8–21 ....64, 291
15:8b–9a.....................292
15:9 .... 135n11, 137, 293
15:9–13 64
15:10..................... 135n11
15:10–12 297
15:11 ....135n11, 297
15:12.................... 135n11
15:14–21..............64, 291,
293, 294, 301
15:15 294
15:16 ....135n11, 294,
295, 297
15:17 294
15:18.................. 295, 296
15:18–19......................295
15:18b–19a.................295
15:19–20 295
15:19b 297, 306
15:20 297
15:24 307

16:3 314
16:17 124
16:26 ....135n11, 296

1 Corinthians
1:10–17...................... 163
1:12 316
1:17 .... 203n38
1:18 212
1:24 200
3..................................301
3:7 306
3:9 ....301, 306
3:10 183
3:10–11 306
3:13 301
4:1–2 303
4:6.............................. 124
4:13 183
4:16 124
5:1–13 316
6:1–11........................... 316
6:9–11......................... 308
8:1b 197
8:1c 197
9:19–23...................... 305
9:22 305
10:1–10 284
10:1–11........................ 278
10:31...........................226
11:1 124
14:10–11 230
14:31 124
14:35 124
15:1–2 308
15 .... 34, 37, 38, 58
15:22 37
15:45 37
15:46 199
16:19 314
16:22 217

2 Corinthians
2:17.............................301
3..................................62

3:3...............................97
3:6...............................97
3:7–11 .... 62, 97
3:17..............................63
3:18 ....63, 199
4...................................301
4:2...............................301
4:4.......................63, 302
4:16–5:10 300
4:17........................... 300
4:18 300
5:9............................ 300
5:10 301
5:11 301
5:16–21 58
5:17............... 54, 58, 99
5:21..............................58
10:5 195
11:28....................187, 315
12:9–10 303

Galatians
1:1...................... 138, 143
1–2 .... 137, 139n19
1:4 ....140, 143, 144
1:6–8 138
1:6–12 138
1:10 138
1:10–12 138
1:11–24...........................137
1:13–14........... 138n17, 139
1:14............................. 138
1:15–16....................... 139
1:16..............137, 138, 139,
139n20, 140n23
1:16–24 138
2:1–3...... 139, 313, 313n52
2:2.......................140n23
2:3.............. 140, 140n22
2:4............................. 139
2:7 ....138, 140
2:8.......................140n23
2:9...........135n11, 140n23
2:9b...........................140
2:11........................ 138

2:11–14...........138, 138n15
2:11–15........................ 143
2:12 .... 138, 140n23, 143
2:13 138
2:13–14 143
2:14 .... 138, 143
2:16 ....141, 142
2:16–17 .... 142n34
2:16–21 .... 142n34
2:19–20 54
3:1 140
3:1–5...........................141
3:1–14 ....140, 142n34
3:1–16 142
3:1–29......................140
3........................ 40, 41
3:6............41, 141, 143n37
3:6–9 140
3:7–9 142
3:8.......... 41, 78, 104, 132,
        137, 139n20, 140,
        140n23, 141,
        142n34, 143,
        143n37, 144,
        144n38, 282
3:8a........141, 143, 144n38
3:8a–b.................139n20
3:8b.......141, 142, 143, 144
3:8–9...........................141
3:8–14 144
3:9............................. 142
3:10–14 .... 140, 141
3:11–12....................... 142
3:11–14......................140
3:13 41
3:13–14 ....140, 143, 144,
        144n38
3:14 ....41, 135n11, 137,
        139n20, 140n23,
        141, 142n29,
        142n31, 144n38
3:14a 144n38
3:14b 144, 144n38
3:14a–b..................... 144

3:16 ....140, 142,
        142n34, 144
3:16–29.................141n29
3:22......................41, 142
3:27–29 159
3:27–4:7.......................54
3:28...............................141
3:28–29 .... 144n39
3:29.............141, 143, 144
4:1–11..........................45
4................................45
4:3................................45
4:4–5 45
4:5–7 142
4:6–7 45
4:8................................45
4:9–11........................46
5:2–6 .... 142n34
5:21 .... 142n34, 308
6:8–9........................ 308
6:15 .... 142n34
6:15–16 .... 142n34

Ephesians
1 54
1:4–5 27
1:9–10.......................... 60
1:13 202
1:20–23 50
2–3 60
2:2............................... 302
2:10a 199
2:11–21...................... 136
2:11–22........................54
2:15 60
3:10 60
4.................................54
4:4–6 164
4:11–13.......................188
4:11–16......................188
4:14 188
4:20 124
5:1 124
5.................................54
6:22............................ 314

Philippians
1:12............................ 303
2:6–11 50
2:16 309
2:19–24...................... 125
2:25–30...................... 125
3:1–14 125
3:17............................. 124
4:2–3 125
4:3.............................. 314

Colossians
1:7 .... 124, 308, 314
1:13 302
1:21–23 308
1:24 303
2:11–12...................... 159
2:12 156
2:12–15 160
3:17...........................226
4:3–4 227
4:14 .... 40n28
4:17............................ 314

1 Thessalonians
1:4 185
1:6 124
2:14 124
2:17........................... 309
2:17–3:10 309
2:18 309
3:2.............................. 309
3:3.............................. 309
3:4..............................310
3:5....................187, 309
4:1–6 185
4:9.....................197n29
5:1–2...........................185

2 Thessalonians
2:5.............................. 185
3:7.............................. 124
3:9.............................. 124

1 Timothy

1:3 188
1:10 188
2:11 124
2:13–14 24
4:6 188
4:8 200
6:3 188

2 Timothy

1:5 188
1:6 ....194n21
1:13 185
2:2 185
2:15 . 4, 188, 195, 202, 242
2:26 302
3:7 124
3:10 188
3:14 124
3:15 200
3:16 214
4:17 .... 135n11

Titus

1:9 188
1:12 266
2:10 200
3:4–7 124
3:14 124

Hebrews

1:1–4 46
4:12 ....10, 10n17, 202
4:12–13 ....10n17
5:2 174
5:12–14 202
8:1–5 97
8:6–7 98
8:8 .... 30n69
8:8–12 97
8:13 .... 30n69
9:12 98
9:15 30
10:12 98
10:15–18 97
11 .... vii, 276
11–12 vii
11:38 vii
12:1–2 129
12:24 30
13:7 124

James

3:17 200

1 Peter

1:1 64
1:2 64
1:3 64
1:7 64

1:11 64
1:19–21 64
2:5 64
2:9 65
2:9–10 99
2:21–25 .... 64, 100
3:15 202
3:18–22 64
4:1–2 64
4:13 64

2 Peter

3:16 195

Revelation

1:8 237
5:9 237
6:9–11 147
7:9 .... 164, 178
7:9–10 297
7:9–12 27
14:18 .... 135n11
16:19 .... 135n11
19:15 .... 135n11
20:8 .... 135n11
21–22 38
21:6 237
21:24 .... 135n11
22:2 21
22:13 237

APOCRYPHA

Tobit

13–14 134
13:5 134
13:6 134
13:6–11 134
13:11 .... 135n10
14:3–11 134
14:5 134
14:5–7 134

1 Maccabees   134–35

1–2 ....138n17

1:3 .... 135n10
1:21 .... 135n10
1:24 .... 135n10
1:42 .... 134, 135
2:12 .... 134, 135
2:18–19 134
2:40 134
2:44 134
2:68 135
3:10 134
3:25–26 134
3:48 134

3:52 134
4:11 134
4:14 134
4:45 134
4:54 134
4:60 134
5:1 134
5:9–10 134
5:19 134
5:21 134
5:38 134
5:43 134

5:57 134
7:23 134
8:23–32 .... 135n10
9:23 .... 135n10
9:58 .... 135n10
9:68–69 .... 135n10
10:61 .... 135n10
12:6–18 .... 135n10
12:53 134
13:6 134
13:41 135
14:36 134

Sirach

45:23–24 .... 135n9

Testament of Judah

24:2–6 .... 142n29